Social Standing in America

SOCIAL STANDING IN AMERICA

New Dimensions of Class

RICHARD P. COLEMAN
AND
LEE RAINWATER
WITH KENT A. McCLELLAND

Basic Books, Inc., Publishers   NEW YORK

Library of Congress Cataloging in Publication Data

Coleman, Richard Patrick.
  Social standing in America.

  References: p. 342
  Includes index.
    1. Social classes—United States. 2. Social status.
3. Social mobility—United States. I. Rainwater, Lee,
joint author. II. McClelland, Kent A., joint author.
III. Title.
HN90.S6C64   301.44'0973   77-20426
ISBN: 0-465-07928-8

TO THE MEMORY OF

W. Lloyd Warner

Luxury . . . has many facets, according to the period, country or civilization in question. In contrast, the social drama, without beginning or end, with luxury as its prize and its theme, scarcely changes at all, a choice spectacle for sociologist, psychoanalyst, economist and historian. The privileged and the onlookers—the masses who watch them—must of course agree to a certain amount of connivance. Luxury does not only represent rarity and vanity, but also social success, fascination, the dream that one day becomes reality for the poor, and in so doing immediately loses its old glamour. . . . But luxury is reborn from its old ashes and from its very defeats. It is really the reflection of a difference in social levels that nothing can change and that every movement recreates. An eternal "class struggle."

FERNAND BRAUDEL
Capitalism and Material Life 1400-1800

CONTENTS

PART III

ATTAINMENT OF SOCIAL STANDING

PART IV

A CHANGING CLASS SYSTEM?

PREFACE

THE STUDIES on which this book is based have three main goals. First, to determine whether conceptions of social class in America have changed in important ways over the past two decades. Second, to explore ways in which the qualitative and quantitative traditions of investigating social stratification could be merged in one study which might provide a better grounding for understanding stratification issues. Third, to explore patterns of interrelations among different indicators of social stratification, particularly so-called subjective *versus* objective indicators. With respect to the first goal, we used an approach initially developed by Coleman in a study of social class in Kansas City in the early 1950s. It was possible therefore to determine whether there had been major shifts in class imagery since then. Our findings are to be understood as the most recent assessment in the tradition that begins with Warner's *Yankee City* series and the Lynds' *Middletown* books, and continues through Davis, Gardner, and Gardner's *Deep South* and the later community studies by Warner and those influenced by him.

Our efforts to mesh qualitative and quantitative approaches, and to deal simultaneously with subjective and objective status characteristics, are very much exploratory. We have tried in this book to show how qualitative analysis of open-ended material and quantitative analysis of status estimation scales yield similar and compatible views of the status hierarchy.

Finally, we seek to bridge the gap in stratification research between the focus on subjective evaluations of status that has characterized much empirical research on "prestige scales" and the more objective models of socio-economic position that have flowered in recent times in research on status attainment and the socio-economic career.

The methodological separation between these approaches has no counterpart in most stratification theory which moves readily back and forth between a concern with issues of meaning, image, and evaluation on the one hand, and objective characteristics and position on the other.

A principal theme in our exploration has to do with a concern for social standing as a complex compounding of the individual's position in different hierarchies. We are interested in the "social arithmetic" by which individuals evaluate overall positions on the basis of their own and others' varied status characteristics. In exploring the ways in which objective characteristics are translated into status evaluations, we also try to show how Americans calculate their own and other people's social positions based on a balancing of their various attributes. We suggest that in the end Americans' conception of social standing involves most centrally the assessment that people make of the likely contribution of various kinds of social resources to the overall well-being of the possessors of those resources.

The research reported here was carried out at the Joint Center for Urban Studies of MIT and Harvard. We are grateful to the staff of the Joint Center for assistance in all phases of the study. Our research has been supported by the National Institute of Mental Health (Grant no. RO1 MH18635 SP), the Department of Health, Education, and Welfare's Office of Income Security Policy Research and Evaluation (Grant no. 006-P-20-2-74-01), and the Ford Foundation (Grant no. PNDG 740-0511).

We are grateful to the staff of the Survey Research Center of the University of Massachusetts/Boston (formerly of the Joint Center) for their work in helping to design the questionnaires used in our work and in the collection and coding of data. We have made extensive use in our work of the Panel Survey of Income Dynamics carried out by the Survey Research Center of the University of Michigan. We are grateful for the assistance we have received from the staff of that study and in particular, for helpful comments and criticisms of our work by James N. Morgan, Greg Duncan, and Jonathan Dickinson.

We want to thank several individuals for consultation on quantitative methodology and computer assistance: Claude Fischer, Sally Nash, Jonathan Rainwater, and Joseph Schwartz. We wish to thank a number of people for their helpful consultation, comments, and criticisms at various points in the course of this study: Susan Anderson-Khleif, Phillips

Cutright, Otis Dudley Duncan, Herbert Gans, Ira O. Glick, Robert Hamblin, Gerald Handel, Robert Hauser, Robert Hodge, Christopher Jencks, Joseph Kahl, Carol Rainwater, Martin Rein, Allan M. Shinn, Jr., Paul Siegel, Anselm Strauss, and Marc Swartz. Our failure to profit as much from their help as possible is, of course, our own responsibility.

We wish to thank Anne Aubrey, Kathi Matthews, and Steven Stepak for their help in the preparation of the many versions of this manuscript.

The research reported in this book was conceived and planned jointly by Coleman and Rainwater. Rainwater directed the overall project and took primary responsibility for the quantitative analysis. Coleman carried out the qualitative analysis, as reported in Chapters 2 through 12 and 16. Rainwater carried out the initial quantitative analysis of the status estimation scores. Subsequently, Kent McClelland carried out an intensive analysis of the status estimation data collected in our study and in earlier studies. Rainwater analyzed the Panel Study of Income Dynamics data in the development of the income attainment model reported in Chapters 13 and 14 and the analysis relating the status estimation model to the resource model reported in Chapter 15. Diane Barthel analyzed the data on ethnicity and wrote Chapter 6.

Social Standing in America

Resources
and Rewards

PEOPLE show a lively and constant concern for their own well-being. In all societies people extend this concern, with variably diminished intensity, to a solicitude for the well-being of those closest to them, particularly their kindred, and with rapidly diminished intensity to others more distantly related. Because degrees of well-being are so central to the sense of self, people in all times have thought a good deal about what accounts for the amount of well-being they feel. In simple societies in which almost everyone is considered to be in the same boat, this curiosity expresses itself as an interest in how well nature and the gods treat individuals and why they experience such treatment. The conceptions that people develop of how well they are treated and what accounts for that treatment play an important role in the creation of belief systems such as religion, ethnocentrism, magic, primitive science, and philosophy.

As societies develop technologies capable of producing a surplus over the bare subsistence needs of their members, they uniformly develop patterns of differential social arrangements that result in some members of the society having more of the good things of life than others (Lenski, 1966). People observe the fact that some have more of what everyone values than do others, and begin to build theories that seek to account for it. These theories, as Ralf Dahrendorf has observed, can be taken as the starting point for the development of sociology as a social science. If the differences in well-being in society come to be understood as not simply the product of natural forces (nature arranges that superior persons enjoy a superior level of well-being), then the way is open to the development of theories about how it happens that social arrangements produce differences in well-being and how those social arrangements themselves evolve (Dahrendorf, 1968). A great deal of sociology, as well as of economics and political science, is concerned with developing solutions to one or another piece of the puzzle of the distribution of resources for well-being in particular societies. In the course of their development as modern social sciences over the past two hundred years, each of these fields has developed specialized definitions of aspects of this central issue and specialized vocabularies for discussing them. (The degree of specialization and the development of arcane language have proceeded far enough to obscure the fact that this central issue is common to all three disciplines.)

Terms referring to social classes—working class, middle class, upper class, lower class—have become increasingly common in American discourse; references to one or another class are taken for granted in the mass media. Concepts reflecting in one way or another an understanding that American society is stratified into various levels in terms of power, status, and economic resources are important parts of the intellectual technology used by the various institutions of this society—by government, by business, by voluntary organizations, by political groups, and by citizens and community groups of all kinds. The issue of social stratification—who gets what and how—has become central to the discussion of important problems of the day.

The fairness or unfairness of the distribution of rewards in society has come to the fore in most industrial countries in the last decade—so much so that it has become almost a part of the conventional wisdom to question the effects of any particular public policy on the distribution of such rewards. Those who are interested in environmental issues, for example, must confront the effects of particular anti-pollution or no-growth policies on the distribution of life chances. Even more directly, questions of tax reform, of worker productivity, of inflation control, and of energy policy, all obviously involve questions of who gets what and how, who pays the cost when it is necessary to change the way business is conducted, and who gains. Are the costs and gains fairly distributed?

As a backdrop for any concrete discussion of these issues, either in the relatively dispassionate terms of planning for the future or in the glare of the political arena, the conceptions that Americans have of their society's reward structure provide a context for what is said and done and limit the possible solutions.

In the development of empirical sociological approaches to social stratification, a number of problems have aroused researchers' interests.

The same questions puzzle ordinary people. Taken together, the answers to these questions represent the knowledge that sociology has been able to develop concerning who gets what and why.

The principal question must be that of the actual distribution of goods—the *what* of "who gets what." Prior to that, however, is the necessity of specifying the components of well-being. In general, study has centered not on trying to measure directly the well-being of individuals (that seems an exceedingly complex and demanding task), but rather on the resources that can be turned to good use. Sociologists have been interested mainly in the distribution of occupations and secondarily in the distribution of education. Economists have concentrated on the size distribution of income. They have been fortunate in a technical sense because this variable is readily measured and its distribution is relatively easy to describe.

Once the question of distribution has been settled, often in a very rough way (as in the descriptions of societies in terms of very broad categories like manual *versus* white-collar strata), then it is possible to raise the question of what accounts for that distribution. What is the role of established social arrangements in the given distribution? How can one describe the institutional arrangements of society in terms of their ability to confer advantages on some categories of persons rather than on others? And what is the role of personal characteristics? In connection with the last question, intelligence and developed abilities are sometimes studied, as are ambition and hard work.

At the more abstract level of macrosociology, a great deal of interest has centered not so much on the facts of the distribution of resources for well-being, or even on the detailed study of how social arrangements and personal characteristics interact in producing that distribution, but rather on the relationship between the existence of that distribution and questions of social order, stability, and social productivity. Here research and writing have examined the distribution of power in society and the stability of power relations, norms and their effective scope, and especially the amount and nature of unrest and rebelliousness in society. Much of the interest in social stratification and in distribution of resources for well-being seems to have been directed to the last issue and to issues of mobilization and support, either for the existing order or for the establishment of a new order. Studies of social class or social stratification are routinely read not so much for what they tell us about the dynamics of social ranking in society and consequences for the lives of individuals, as for an inkling of which political forces are likely to enjoy future advantages from the way things are now. Much of the impatience shown by social scientists toward a close understanding of stratified lives can be understood in relation to their basic interest in questions of class support and mobilization rather than the distribution of well-being itself. Writers who take this view and whose own predilections are conservative are loathe to spend time looking closely at the "injuries of class," while those whose interests are in radical change want to mobilize support for that change to create a better distribution in the future. For them, the people studied are best understood as instruments for, or obstacles to, change.

There have, however, always been researchers whose interests lie more in the documentation of class. Some regard documentation as a way of showing the justice of the system as it operates; others see it as a way of demonstrating its injustice. But in both cases the emphasis has been on documentation of the quality of individuals' lives at different levels in the stratification system, rather than on testing their prospects as revolutionary or counter-revolutionary soldiers.

There are two broad perspectives, different but complementary, that can be adopted in considering social stratification in any given society. We will refer to the subjects of the two perspectives as *resources* and *rewards*. The distinction is similar to (but not the same as) that proposed by John Goldthorpe between relational and distributive approaches to stratification (1972). A great deal of social stratification research emphasizes one or the other of these perspectives. Sometimes investigators behave as if only the particular perspective they adopt is useful or important in understanding stratification. Thus, on occasion these perspectives have been defined as competitive rather than complementary. Because work from either point of view is demanding, given the complexity of what is being studied, far too little research has been concerned with the interconnections between them.

Resource Dimensions

The first perspective has to do with understanding the position of individuals in relation to the institutional sources of resources for well-being. Here interest centers on the relationship of individuals to the means of production of social goods—that is, on the social relations of production and on the factors that account for the fate of particular individuals in those relations. Following Keith Hope's methodologically suggestive term, we might call the subject of this perspective *resource space*. The researcher's interest lies in the location of individuals or groups in terms of their access to various kinds of resources and in explaining particular patterns of resource advantage. The core of the Marxist conception of class as embodying the individual's relationship to the means of production is located here, although Marx, Engels, and some later writers have always shown great sensitivity to the other principal perspective of stratification rewards. Weber sought to expand this Marxist focus in his tripartite vision of stratification into issues of class, status, and party, but the inclination of many of his readers to imagine these aspects of the individual's position in resource space as representing different social orders has tended to vitiate his insight. In fact, the first part of Weber's definition of class represents very well the concept of the individual's position in resource space: "The typical chance for a supply of goods, external living conditions, and personal life experiences. . . ."

Weber defines class as that typical chance, "insofar as this chance is determined by the amount and kind of power or lack of such to dispose of goods or skills for the sake of income in a given economic order." However, factors of what Weber called status (*Stande*) and power also affect "the typical chance" for access to the components of well-being.

It would seem more profitable to treat all of the aspects of the individual's access to resources simultaneously if we are to understand their implications for well-being. The individual's relationship to the means of production in modern societies, with their extremely elaborate divisions of labor and with the interpenetration of political and economic institutions, is extremely complex. Clearly, the central element in the conception of class that comes to us through Marx and Weber is that of a group of individuals standing in a similar relation to the social institutions that confer resources—resources that the individuals can use to gain rewards for themselves. Thus, Lenski defines a class as "an aggregation of persons in society who stand in a similar position with respect to some form of power, privilege, or prestige." In this definition, individuals do not belong to one class but many. How much overlapping exists in class memberships is an empirical question. Not only is there no necessary correlation between relative standing with respect to the three hierarchies of class, status, and power, but it often turns out that individuals stand in a multi-dimensional relationship to others even within one of the three systems. Thus, the class of managers has certain interests in common, but the class of managers in one industry may have interests that conflict sharply with the class of managers in another industry. Perhaps even more important, persons at different hierarchical levels within any one industry or organization may form alliances based on shared class interests. Two dramatic examples in recent times illustrate such shared interests. The collusion in the construction industry between union craftsmen and the owners of construction firms seems intended to raise the prices of construction services and split the proceeds between them. Similarly, collusion in government between public servants, such as firefighters, police, or schoolteachers, and political executives at higher levels of authority tends to raise salaries within government service. Thⁱ class interest pits government workers at both high and low hierarchical levels against the mass of taxpayers.

The arena of competitive struggle between unequal powers that characterizes class, defined as a group sharing common interests, is perhaps better conceived as an ecology of games than as a simple stratification. Class mobilization and class alliances are perhaps better understood as complex and shifting political struggles than as set piece battles.

The concept of resource space must be understood to have many dimensions, and the individual's location in it is not readily simplified without reference to the net payoff from all of the resources the individual enjoys.

Reward Dimensions

The second perspective that sociologists have used in describing the stratification system of modern societies involves a focus not on the individual's relations to the means of production—to resources—but rather on the rewards that accrue from the exercise of social and economic power. Here the focus is on the values (in Homan's sense) that people derive from their positions in society rather than on the positions per se. We will argue at several points in presenting the research results below that in modern societies people's interest in stratification focuses most centrally on the question of payoff. Their interest is mainly in who gets what and only derivatively in *how* they get it. It is much easier for people to be uni-dimensional about an individual's rewards than about resources. One's resource situation is defined by the individual's multiple relations to concrete social institutions. The rewards individuals receive do derive through concrete institutional matrices, but these rewards share in common their rewardingness. In planning their own lives as well as in judging others' lives, people develop both explicit and implicit standards by which they judge the commensurability of different kinds of rewards. As we well see in the chapters that follow, there does exist a social arithmetic by which individuals are able to assess the net advantages from the particular privileges they themselves enjoy and those they know others to have. The privileges enjoyed include such things as income, security of tenure, esteem, various kinds of fringe benefits, access to valued persons and avoidance of derogated persons, and the enjoyment of various kinds of tastes. The distribution of those rewards is a complicated question in and of itself; the relationship of the total amount of the reward and of the pattern of different kinds of rewards to the pattern of the individual's resources—or position in resource space—is even more complicated.

The Worlds of Work and Leisure

It is tempting to equate this distinction between resources and rewards with a distinction between the individual's work roles and his family, community, and leisure roles—his personal or leisure-time life. Although any empirical measure of resources will certainly have to do mainly with what goes on in connection with the individual's work role, and any empirical measure of rewards will have to do mainly with what he does away from work, the two dimensions are not really the same. A complete description of a person's position in the stratification system would survey at least four possibilities. Not only are there resources and rewards, but there are also resources and rewards in each of the two sectors, one having to do with work roles and one having to do with non-work roles.

Within the world of work, which is understood to refer to the broad range of institutions, both private and governmental, that operate the society, one can be interested in both resources and rewards. Individuals receive some of the rewards from their roles in these institutions in the course of functioning in them. Others they take away from the job and transfer to family members or enjoy in the course of participation in other institutions.

Those rewards that are enjoyed on the job can be very important; they include such factors as the esteem of co-workers, personal enjoyment of the exercise of power, perhaps aesthetic appreciation of one's work environment, or the pleasures of having a key to the executive washroom. A virtually unexplored aspect of social stratification involves the distribution of these on-the-job rewards. An important question for understanding the distribution of life chances in society involves assessing the extent to which resources are consumed on the job—perhaps monopolized by certain classes—instead of being distributed evenly within the organization or being used outside the organization. The recent movement for job enrichment in the United States and in European countries represents one practical expression of a concern with the distribution of on-the-job rewards. On-the-job consumption, masquerading as "capital" or other kinds of expenditure, could have a strong effect on our conceptions of productivity.

Given that, by definition, only the worker can enjoy the on-the-job rewards while the family can participate in the enjoyment of off-the-job rewards, it is easy to see that workers and non-workers in the family have somewhat different positions in the stratification of life chances. (One thinks of politicians who find their jobs deeply gratifying but whose spouses can hardly wait until they return to their business careers, retire, or are defeated in an election. The on-the-job rewards for politicians, ineffable though they may be, are very powerful ones. By all reports they seldom seem to rub off quite so powerfully on their spouses.)

With respect to individuals' roles outside work institutions, our attention goes most directly to rewards rather than to resources. We easily attend to the rewards individuals enjoy in terms of goods, services, life styles, and social participation. But a place must also be made in any thorough exploration of stratification space for the resources individuals have by virtue of their participation in institutions outside of work. Participation in various kinds of voluntary activities, for example, can function simultaneously as a reward and as a source for gaining future rewards. Thus, being a member of the most prestigious country club in a city can be understood from one perspective as a reward gained through the use of resources derived from the individual's political-economic roles. But the membership may also serve as a resource if the individual is able to use contacts there to further the interests of his career, the business of the company in which he participates, or the segment of government with which he is identified. Also, some of the attributes that individuals have may pay off not only by conferring resources at work, but also by conferring resources away from work. The interest of human capital economists in the role of education in increasing "home production" would be an example.

If we are seeking to provide a full accounting of an individual's position in resource space, we would want to pay attention both to those resources that are relevant to the individual's success in work roles and to those resources that contribute to the rewards derived away from work. When we focus on the family or the married couple rather than on the individual, acknowledging the presence of resources in both sectors is even more important. Many studies of class variations in life style, for example, have emphasized the advantages accruing to family members by virtue of the "volunteer" activities of wives.

Subjective and Objective Perspectives

In short, the student of social stratification may choose to focus on power or on the privilege it buys, on resources or on rewards, on getting or on spending.

There is yet another dichotomy in the perspective researchers can bring to bear on stratification space. We can study the objective distribution of one or another kind of resource or reward—the objective distribution of resources in the world of work, for example, or of rewards in the world away from work—or we can study the conceptions that members of society have about various kinds of resources and rewards. Particularly with respect to the investigation of rewards, however, we will quickly discover that rewards often have an existence only because of the social meaning attached to the activity. Different societies have different conceptions of rewards, and within any particular society we cannot know what is and is not rewarding (putting aside for a moment the question of personal taste) unless we understand something of the social logics of the members of the society. Thus, before we go very far in listing the elements of the reward bundle that makes one set of persons better off than another, we encounter a curious circularity. Some elements in the bundle assume the prior existence of the social inequality they themselves index (see the discussion of the "positional economics" by Hirsch [1976] and the closely related ideas developed by Leibenstein [1976]). For example, we know that a person who belongs to the best country club in town is in some sense better off socially than someone who belongs to the Elks. But the only way we know this is by knowing that there is a community ranking of such organizations in terms of how desirable it is to belong to them, that is, in terms of the capacity they are believed to have for conferring on their members greater or lesser rewards.

Thus it is proper that the objective and the subjective very much interpenetrate each other in the study of social stratification (as in the study of any other aspect of human social life). Because people can be expected to act on the basis of their conceptions of how the stratification system operates, both as a guide to their own personal day-to-day behavior and in terms of their political choices, these conceptions are an important object of study, even though they may not accurately describe how the system in fact operates.

When we ask very general questions about social class in American society, people have an opportunity to range quite widely in expressing their conceptions of what resources are and how people come to possess them, and similarly, of what is rewarding and how rewards are distributed.

The chapters of Part I and Part II concentrate on describing the conceptions people have of the stratification system of the United States and how it operates. We believe that this kind of exploration is important, but we do not offer it as a substitute for detailed exploration of objective distributions and the actual interrelationships of resources and rewards. We believe that exploration of images, meanings, and conceptions is important, both because people act on the basis of those images, meanings, and conceptions and—more specifically—because for some purposes (such as working toward an overall measure of social well-being) only an understanding of the logics that people use in calculating and summing up various kinds of rewards, the logics they use in equating tradeoffs, can move us toward a more precise assessment of the distribution of advantage in society.

And, in a curious way, only through an understanding of the meanings people attach to different kinds of rewards can we work back to the best model of the objective distribution of power in the society. Very simply, the only way we know that a given resource represents a component of power is by knowing what it will get us. Power in the end is defined by its ability to generate rewards for the individual. If we do not know what is rewarding, and—given the incredible complexity of what individuals in modern society derive from their social life—unless we can sum up those rewards, we really cannot assess how the various components of power are combined and weighted. Class struggles and individual competitions for advantages are a constant dynamic element in society. But what is this struggle for? The struggle is for an incredible range of rewards. In order to assess how powerful individuals are—that is, to assess the value of the resources possessed by individuals—we have to relate characteristics in the resource space to characteristics in the reward space. In the end we must calibrate the power represented by the characteristics in the resource space by the value of the rewards they can produce.

In Part III we deal with the issue that, more than any other, has been a concern in modern research on social stratification—social inheritance *versus* mobility. Once we describe stratification at a given time in terms of the distribution of resources and rewards, we can confront the issue of the extent to which resources are passed from one generation to the next. The technically most innovative research of the past decade has been concerned with this question, with the "socio-economic life career" or the "status attainment" process, which begins with the resources an individual gains by virtue of birth and ends with the rewards which the adult is able to find. As with other aspects of stratification, this issue may be studied from the perspective of the objective connections among parental resources, the role of education in mediating or mitigating family background, and the resources of the adult, and it can be studied in terms of the conceptions, meanings, and images that people have about the relevance of the past to the present distribution of resources and rewards.

After discussing how people define issues of opportunity and mobility, we consider the distribution of adult men's occupational and income resources during the mid-career years and then explore the role of schooling and family background in accounting for the observed distribution. Finally, we relate the objective resource distribution to status evaluations of those resources according to the model developed in Parts I and II of the book.

PART I

THE DIMENSIONS OF
SOCIAL CLASS

CHAPTER 1

Popular Conceptions of Class Standing

W̶HEN intellectuals use the word *class*, it may mean any one of a number of things. The word has political and economic connotations as well as social. It may, for example, refer to groupings of people according to their market position, to people who stand in the same relationship to the means of production and who share the same life chances as these are defined in economic terms. When politicians and political scientists speak of class, they are apt to be thinking of pressure groups, of minorities (racial or ethnic) and majorities, of broad categories of people who seek the same things from government and whose political attitudes are similar. Sociologists seek to relate these political and economic conceptions of class to social behavior, formal and informal; some define class as groups of people who interact on planes of equality

One of our research concerns has been to find out how the average American uses words like *class* and *social standing*. Our conclusion is ultimately this: to the public, these words mean societal rank, however achieved. Class is the same, functionally, as social standing. Both refer to a person's position in a status hierarchy based on the relative desirability of life situations. Class may refer to a point on this hierarchy; it need not refer to a whole category. It is the image the audience of others has of where an individual belongs, how high up or how low down. Many Americans wish class or social standing referred to "a person's true quality," to "moral goodness"—but they acknowledge this is not the case.* Social standing is a judgment made entirely on the basis of other characteristics, money being the main one. That is the lay conception of social class, which we shall now set forth in greater detail. Overwhelmingly, class in the public view refers to how individuals seem to stand in the distribution of life chances in America today. Prestige, or status, must be understood to be as much (or more) a result of how well one has fared in the competition for things valued in this society, as a cause of it.

We report in Parts 1 and 2 of this book the results of surveys in the Boston and Kansas City metropolitan areas dealing with perceptions of social class and social standing. The principal Boston survey was carried out in 1971, that in Kansas City in 1972.

The research was designed to increase our understanding of several interrelated issues of importance for developing useful new approaches to the study of social stratification in America. We wanted, for example, to discover what factors Americans thought of as important in establishing an individual's social position or class membership; in short, we wanted to determine the particular dimensions of that standing. For this and other issues of class and social standing we used open-ended conversational questions to allow our respondents to express their understanding in their own words.

To 200 of our respondents, we put this question: "What does the phrase *social class* mean to you—for example, what things are involved in the idea of social class and social classes?" With another 200, we opened our interview with an alternative lead: "Frequently we hear or read about the phrase *social class*, or *social classes*—what does this mean to you?" When that was the first question, the next was: "Do you think there is such a thing as social class or social classes in America—and why do you think this?" From the 400 respondents asked these questions, the answer that came back—when stripped down to its basic message—was this: "Class means differences between people in their social standing— and yes, there is such a thing as social class in America." Beyond this, there was considerable variation among respondents, but nothing that was added changed the basic premise that social class refers to differences between people in status reputation, in how they are rated and treated by the community.

Variations between respondents centered on two things: the number of factors used in explaining status differences and respondents' emotional response to the consequences of these differences. The least

* In this chapter and all following, phrases and whole sentences drawn directly from survey respondents are enclosed by quotation marks to differentiate them from generalizations by the authors.

articulate respondents—especially those lower status as well—tended to speak of social class as single-factored, with differences in wealth as the cause. Average respondents named three factors, adding education and occupation to their explanation. The most articulate and sensitive treated social standing as a multi-factored, richly textured phenomenon, bringing behavioral and value variables into their accounting for status differences. As for the variation in emotional response, many people in both cities called social class "unfair" and "wrong" (or worse—one woman even saying, "It's the dirtiest thing I've ever heard of"), while others seemed resigned to it as "inevitable, given the nature of human nature." The middle view was that "it is one of the more regrettable facts of life."

Given an understanding of the most important factors people perceive as contributing to individuals' social standing, we can explore the issue of the relationship between the magnitude of individuals' status characteristics and the social standing that they gain from them. Once we have learned, for example, that the more money one has, the higher one's social standing, we can raise the question of what is the exact relationship between dollars of income and social standing. How much money does it take to be high in social standing, how much to be average in social standing, how little to be low in social standing? For this purpose we made use of a technique, originally developed in psychophysics, called *magnitude estimation*. We had people characterize with magnitude estimates the social standing associated with different levels of income, different levels of educational attainment, and different occupations. These three criteria were chosen for this quantitative treatment because a long history of sociological research suggests their key importance in establishing individual social standing. From our magnitude estimation experiments, we were able to determine what kinds of incomes, educations, and occupations are associated with average social standing, with double the average, with half the average, and so forth. These findings give us a metric with which to discuss the three dimensions of social class that earlier research, as well as our own, has shown to be the most salient for people's conceptions of class.

Magnitude Estimations of Status

Magnitude estimation was introduced to the social sciences by psychophysicists. (An account of this technique's history and how we have adapted it to our present purposes will be found in Appendix B.) Our

concerns in this experiment were of two kinds: methodological, in that
we were seeking to develop a metric and a field method that would
permit ratio measurement of status variables, and substantive, in that we
were seeking to understand the links between the objective facts of
income, schooling, and job with the subjective images and abstractions
of these facts that people carry about in their heads.

In magnitude estimation experiments—as originated by psychophysicists—the investigator asks participants to judge how much bigger
one thing is than another. Two coins may be used, or two triangles or
two boxes. Or the judgment sought may be of comparative loudness,
length, or brightness. The possibilities are endless. Not just two objects
or two sounds are used, but many. One is taken as a standard—the base,
or centerpoint—against which all others are to be judged, to be psycho-
physically measured. Robert L. Hamblin (1971a, 1971b, 1974) and Allen
M. Shinn, Jr. (1969, 1974) initiated adaptations of this technique to measurement of status variables. They experimented with small groups, testing the comparative desirability of levels of income and education.

Here is how we introduced our magnitude estimation experiment to
survey respondents and explained their participation:

> We showed them a page with three circles of markedly different size.
> We told them that our experiment was "something like a game . . .
> using numbers to tell how big or little different things are." We said
> the circle of middle size was "equal to 100," that if a circle looked twice
> as big it would be "equal to 200," and one that looked half as big
> would be "equal to 50," and so on, with one that looked twenty times as
> big being "equal to 2,000." Following these words of explanation, we
> had respondents try magnitude estimates for the biggest and smallest
> circles.

> Then we said: "In any community . . . people differ in their *general
> standing*. By general standing we mean the amount of prestige or respect
> most people would say a person has because of some characteristic.
> We're interested in [what you think is] the general standing of different
> occupations, educational levels, and levels of living. . . . Just as with the
> circles, we'll set up a benchmark at 100 and rate each [occupation and
> so forth] compared to that. Let's imagine a Mr. A. A. Mim—that's short
> for Mr. Absolutely Average Man-in-the-Middle. We'll consider Mr. Mim's
> general standing to be 100. [For each occupation, education, or living
> level that we name] would you give it a number to show how much
> more or less its general standing is than Mr. Mim's 100." Upon naming
> an occupation (or education or living level) we asked respondents first to
> "decide whether most people would see its general standing as less than
> Mr. Mim's or more than Mr. Mim's." This reduced to almost zero the

number of responses of 100—which would be all too easy otherwise. Occupations named were in this format: "salesclerk in a hardware store." Educational levels were spoken of as "an eighth-grade education," income status as "a $13,500-a-year level of living."

The magnitude estimation experiments were conducted only in the Boston surveys, first in 1970, then in 1971. (Changes in format between the two experiments are described in Appendix B. Suffice to say here that in the 1970 study, the base line of 100 was described to respondents as the general standing of a carpenter—or a man named Mr. Carpenter. Creating the more hypothetical Mr. A. A. Mim for the 1971 survey would appear on every count to represent an improvement in the research design.)

We were looking for several things in this experiment with status measurement. One was a continuous scaling of the variables, with no upper limit imposed on their scores. Most status measurement devices— the Warner Index of Status Characteristics (I.S.C.) (1949), the Hollings-head Index of Social Position (I.S.P.) (1958), and the Coleman Index of Urban Status (I.U.S.) (1971) are examples—have used limited-point scales (seven in each of those named) and discrete categories for their scaling of the component dimensions. Scales for education, income, or occupation like these, with only seven points (or ten or five, as is some-times the case) have become anachronistic in the era of high-speed and large-capacity computers. Path-model statistics requires a more sophisti-cated approach; continua as elaborate as possible are what the path modeler wants, not simplified categories. The scaling of status vari-ables that results from magnitude estimation experiments satisfies this requirement.

Another goal was a metric for each variable based directly on public opinion. Some scales with this characteristic already exist for measure-ment of occupational status—for example, the North-Hatt National Opinion Research Center (N.O.R.C.) scale (1947)—but there are none for education or income derived from opinion sampling. Measurement of these two variables has to date been based directly on their "natural" equivalents—$1 of income equals one point of status score (or a multi-ple, say $1,000, equals one point) and the same for years of schooling— or else on categories developed according to the supposition of the meas-urer. An instance of the latter is an education scale on which one point is assigned for up to seven years of education, two points for eighth-grade completion, three points for nine to eleven years, and so forth. Categori-zations like this of education and income—and similarly ad hoc groupings of occupation—may be satisfactory for some research purposes, and they may even correspond more with the realities of status discrimination than a scaling based on public opinion. But we cannot know that until we have developed measures based on the latter.

A third goal was that our scale points mean the same on each measuring instrument—that a score of 130 on occupational status signifies the same distance from average, for instance, as do scores of 130 for educational status and 130 for income status. By using the same method—magnitude estimation—in each scale's construction, we seem to have achieved this equivalence among the three scales in the meaning of their scores.

Both our qualitative and quantitative approaches were designed to give us information about people's perceptions of the whole range of social standing from lowest to highest. In addition, it seemed important to probe in detail the way individuals actually use the dimensions of status that they mentioned in response to the more abstract question, "What classes are there?", when dealing with much more specific questions about social placement.

"The Finer Points" in Social Standing

When Americans describe how they rank people they know and where they place themselves socially, they talk not just of income, or of income plus education plus occupation. They bring many more things to bear—most prominently moral standards, family history, community participation, social skills, speech, and physical appearance—few of which are measurable or ever have been measured in quantitative studies of status factors. These we will call the *finer points* in social standing.

We learned of these finer points when we moved from abstractions about class to personal references in our questioning of respondents. In one of these personal questions, we asked our interviewees to tell us with which status group they identified themselves, and on what grounds. In others we asked them to describe persons of their acquaintance whom they believed to have social standing higher or lower than their own, and to explain how they would determine the social class standing of someone with whom they were not personally acquainted. Without answers to questions such as these, we would have a very superficial view of the meaning of social class in individual lives.

We find, for instance, this distinction: when Americans talk about people of higher rank, they talk mostly about what they envy in others; then, when they are asked to "talk about someone . . . a bit lower in social standing," they reveal what they take most pride in about themselves. Directly or indirectly they tell us which aspects of their own lives and circumstances they find most satisfactory. For example, in comparing themselves with someone lower in status, they may say, "I have two cars and he has only one" or "My husband has a college education, but hers doesn't." At other times, the prideful comparison is left implicit, as when it is said, "He let alcohol get the best of him" or "They had more children than they could bring up properly on the husband's income." Clearly emerging as a point of self-satisfaction is the notion that alcohol has *not* gotten the best of the speaker, nor have too many children been produced for their proper upbringing.

Once it is understood how individuals handle the various dimensions of status in thinking about the placement of themselves and other individuals, the question of how they sort people into similar positions can be raised. This was very much at the focus of our interests. We wanted to know what social classes people perceive, and how an individual's positions on different dimensions of social standing are combined by fellow citizens into a single statement of the individual's status. One way of phrasing this is to say that we were interested in the tradeoffs individuals make between education, income, and occupation in deciding exactly where a person stands—how many years of education are equal in value to X thousands of income dollars? How much lower can the income of a professional be than that of a clerical worker for both still to have the same social standing? In a more qualitative vein, this issue has to do with the portraits people have in mind of individuals and families at different social standing levels. What are popular images of the life and social identity of people at high- or middle- or low-status levels? To get at these issues in the public's own words, we asked open-ended questions about how many classes people believed there were and what their names might be. We also asked for open-ended responses to a set of class names ranging from "the top class" to "people at the very bottom of the ladder."

To probe in a more systematic way the issue of how people combine such factors as income, education, and occupation in assigning social standings to individuals, we elaborated the magnitude estimation techniques used for single dimensions by having respondents characterize families for which we gave them all three characteristics, for example: "The Jones family—Mr. Jones is the owner of a dry-cleaning store; he

finished the sixth grade and earns $22,600 a year." Regression analysis
of the results of people's responses to these profiles allowed us to measure
in a quantitative way the relative importance of the three factors, just
as we can assess it qualitatively from the way people talk about income,
occupation, and education in response to the general questions about
"what class means to you" and the more detailed ones about how individuals are placed in social classes.

It is our conviction that analysis of these several different kinds of
data from both the Boston and Kansas City samples yields highly consistent results.

We will present our findings on the dimensions of social standing
in five basic categories that seem to represent the most important criteria
brought to bear by the respondents. These are money, job (or occupation), schooling, ethnicity, and a final, less sharply defined category that
we will call life style and social identity. Of these five, one—money—
heavily dominates the others in responses to all of the different kinds of
questions. This element, whether it was called dollars, income, or standard of living, was used by the overwhelming number of our respondents
as the basic, organizing dimension for their perception of social standing.
As we will see, however, social standing or class is not solely a matter
of money, but also involves the issue of how income is derived and how
it is used.

What Social Class Is and What It Is Not

As the reader considers the findings reported in the following chapters, it will be useful to keep in mind several general cautionary observations drawn from the analysis of these data.

One thing the phrase *social class* most certainly does *not* mean to
Americans is a set, agreed-upon number of classes whose names and
characteristics are known to all. Indeed, the ranking system is perceived
as an almost infinitely graded hierarchy—a continuum, as it were—
rather than as a series of discrete groups. As many Bostonians and Kansas
Citians suggested, "There is a top class, a bottom class, and a middle,
with many shadings in each." Or, as some simply said, "There are at least
fifteen to thirty classes, but I couldn't possibly name them all or describe
them." Even use of the word *class* for the kind of status categories we
have in the United States was questioned by an upper-status Boston

woman: "Of course, social class exists—it influences all your thinking. . . . Maybe you shouldn't use the word *class* for it, though— it's really a niche that each of us fits into."

Another thing that social class does *not* mean is a caste system. People are adamant about this, especially those at the middle- and upper-income levels. They acknowledge the existence of social classes only if the possibility and frequency of mobility up and down the ladder are admitted at the same time. Thus, time and again our respondents of white-collar and professional status were moved to say:

> "Social classes aren't closed. Whatever class structure does exist, it can be entered or left by changing economic level."

> "I don't think it is a rigid, once-you're-born-into-it-you-can't-get-out-of-it sort of thing. . . . There is a great deal of fluidity. It's not as static as in some civilizations."

> "We don't have a caste system. There are no difficult boundaries in the minds of the individual."

Although class in America means an up-and-down scaling of people in social standing, the possibility always exists for individuals to accomplish a change in their standing—if, that is, they "have it on the ball" or "put out the effort." Indeed, it is not uncommon to find people treating this feature of the status system—often called *social climbing*—as a central fact about it. In this view, class is more than a ladder; it is a competitive arena—the "game," as it were, that Americans play against one another; it is the nation's motivating force for individual achievement; it offers the prizes that challenge people to effort—or, as a Boston woman put it, "That's why people work so hard to earn more money and educate their children. . . . It's all to improve their social class."

All the many things—from "money" to "how people stand compared to each other"—that Bostonians and Kansas Citians associated with the phrase *social class*, sometimes as proof of its existence and at other times as definition of its meaning, must be considered parts and pieces of what we herein designate as *social standing*. It is our contention that most adult Americans comprehend that all of these things are involved, deny it or fail to voice it though they may—and many did so in the interview situation. The very complexity of the term leads the average person to simplify verbal communication. The truth is, social class is a not-easily-disentangled *gestalt* of causes, contributants, correlates, and consequences. Call it status or social standing, the same applies: it is a multi-dimensional, many-layered aspect of American life. It is both categories and continuum.

Even so, the dominance of income is very much to the fore when one looks at how the social classes are numbered and named by our respondents, and at the finding that almost two-thirds of the variance in social status assigned by our respondents to hypothetical families described by income, occupation, and schooling was accounted for by income.

Our conclusions from analysis of the open-ended material dealing with class will come as no surprise to those acquainted with the literature on social class in the community studies tradition. We believe that the range of views offered by our respondents is best captured by setting forth a system of three major classes within each of which two or more substrata are identified. The three major classes we label Upper Americans, Middle Americans, and Lower Americans. In the world of Upper Americans there are three thematic subdivisions: the old rich of aristocratic family name, the new rich—this generation's success elite— and the college-educated professional and managerial class of more moderate success. Middle Americans are thematically divided into people of comfortable living standard and people just getting along. In the class of Lower Americans there are two main subdivisions by public opinion, people who are poor but working and people who live mostly off welfare.

It is to be understood that not every American perceives all these levels. And, as has been described in much previous research, the particular perceptions of cut-off points for these different levels are likely to vary depending on where the individual respondent is in the class hierarchy.

Our three levels of Upper Americans fit quite well with the Warnerian classes of upper-upper, lower-upper, and upper-middle. However, the group we are calling Middle Americans (which Warner in his later work alternately referred to as "the middle majority" or "the common man level") seems to be undergoing considerable change. How much of this change is image and how much is reality our study does not allow us to say definitely. In Chapter 9, on the Middle Americans, we address the issue of the extent to which the older distinctions between a lower-middle class (that was primarily white-collar) and a working or upper-lower class (that was primarily blue-collar) still obtain, and we attempt a tentative resolution. Within the Lower-American group, which Warner called the lower-lower class, there do not seem to be major changes except in the increasing salience of welfare and public assistance in public images of those at the very bottom of the class system.

Determining whether any given man or woman is an Upper American, Middle American, or Lower American is not so simple as it might first seem. The main core of Upper Americans apply different standards, for example, in determining who belongs in their class than Middle or Lower Americans do when judging whether someone is Upper-American or not; the latter tend to think principally in terms of economic status, while the former look into other credentials and qualifications. Thus someone may seem Upper-American to Middle and Lower Americans but may not be at all accepted as "one of us" by most Upper Americans.

The few main classes and one or two substrata delineated by the respondents clearly do not reflect sufficiently the complexities in status positioning that have emerged from our further inquiries into how Americans rank and place one another. Respondent groupings based on relatively impersonal, generalized images about the status structure gave an exaggerated emphasis to standard of living, almost as if it were the sole criterion for individual classification at all but the social extremes. Their simplified images did not account for all the considerations—cultural, ethnic, racial, and behavioral, as well as occupational and educational—that are in fact brought to bear in individual interactions and judgments of social standing. Further, class images were drawn around prototypical class members—families whose status attributes and assets (or handicaps) were "normal," in harmony with one another, all pointing to the same social position. The place of families or individuals whose status characteristics diverged in their patterning from these implicit norms was another matter; their identification with one or the other of two proximate classes in many instances aroused disagreement among their fellow citizens. It is this diversity in the "status baggage" that Americans carry, with so many not fitting into the expected molds, that makes it difficult for the average person to draw class boundary lines in theory or in fact. As one Kansas Citian, frustrated by our questions, announced: "There are all kinds of people in this country. . . . There's just no arbitrary thing that makes it easy to differentiate people into categories."

A Forward Look

In the preceding pages we have set forth, in preliminary fashion, the principal issues with which we deal. Now, in the pages that follow, we will go into detail. In the remaining chapters of Part I we further specify how Americans think about the various dimensions of social standing—money, jobs, schooling, ethnicity, and life style and identity. In Part II we move on to the status hierarchy. There we examine first how respondents break up what they almost universally perceive as a continuum into class groups. Then we examine in detail the kinds of distinctions that persons at each major level draw among themselves—that is, how Upper Americans distinguish not just three but five or more layers of status within their world, and how Middle Americans divide themselves in ways other than purely economic. Similarly, we look at self-images of Lower Americans.

In Part III we move away from the static perspective of describing a structure as captured at one moment in time to a more dynamic perspective, in which we explore the conceptions our respondents had of the status attainment *process*. Then, using different data from a national sample, we look at the actual distribution of the adult resources of job and income that our analysis has told us is so important, and consider the role of family background and schooling in the attainment of those resources for men in the mid-years of their careers. Finally, we show how the distribution of adult resources and the dynamics of the attainment process are combined in the attainment of social class standing as that standing was defined by the respondents in our survey.

In Part IV we consider issues of social standing in the future—first, the conceptions our respondents had of the way the class system is changing and should change, and then some issues related to research needs for better understanding of social class in the future. Finally, we discuss briefly the policy relevance of the social stratification issues raised by our study.

CHAPTER 2

Class as Money

MONEY, far more than anything else, is what Americans associate with the idea of social class. In this association, money is both cause and symbol. For many Americans, other considerations are comparatively inconsequential. One-third of our Boston and Kansas City respondents invoked only this variable in answering the question, "What does social class mean to you?" Their phrasings were various, but the point the same:

> "It's like the amount of income you have. . . . If you make lots of money, that means you are high class, and so on."

> "It means different amounts of dollars, more or less—the different levels people are living at."

> "It means like the poor—or class of people on welfare—and then those who have money. . . . It means that society looks upon you differently."

This single-factor conception of social class was especially strong among respondents of low to average income and blue-collar occupation, particularly the men. A Boston factory worker was typical. He said: "Money, money, money, plain and simple—that's what's involved in social class. . . . You get the money, you can get all the class and prestige you want." A craftsman in Kansas City echoed him: "It's money that makes social class—money controls everything." And a young black man from Boston's South End put it most succinctly: "It's money, man! Some made it, some didn't."

With this standard, our respondents found it indisputable that there *is* social class in America. As a Kansas City woman observed, "Of course there's such a thing as class—financial-wise we have classes of the poor, the middle, the rich, and the very rich." Others testified in similar vein to the existence of social class, pointing to differences in monetary status as both the root of class and its representation. Thus does the focus on money or income broaden to include standard, or level, of living:

> "There are those who can only afford a Chevy and those who can afford a Cadillac and go to fancy parties."

> "There are different living standards. The Kennedys live one way. A college graduate lives another way, a janitor a third."

> "Definitely you can't compare migrant workers to a president of a bank or the Rockefellers. The different distinctions are from money."

When social class is viewed as "all a matter of money," its existence is most dramatically illustrated by the monetary extremes—wealth at one end of the continuum, poverty at the other. Especially vivid as evidence are differences in housing quality—"You have some people living in mansions and others in slums"—and location. As one Kansas City man phrased it, "There's the ghetto—that's one class—and then there's Mission Hills, where the rich are clustered—that's certainly different."

More broadly, variations in housing and the segregation of neighborhoods up and down the scale seem to constitute ever-present visual reminders of differences in the amount of money people have, and hence, of the existence of classes. Many a Kansas Citian of moderate income said, explicitly or implicitly, "Sure, there's such a thing as social class—just look at these houses here and the ones over in Mission Hills and you know the people aren't the same class. The economic situations are too different." Similarly, Bostonians said over and over, "You live around here and you know that's different from the people who live on Beacon Hill." A Boston-area suburbanite further illustrated the importance of housing difference to class perception:

> "Yeah, we have classes! You can see it just traveling from here in Canton to Boston. The differences between homes here [all single-family] and the multi-family dwellings and slums there show you. Drive one mile [west] here and you can even see mansions. Just by that evidence alone you know there are classes."

Another pointed out:

> "Up on Moss Hill [three blocks away] there's a higher class than the one here on Center Street—those people have more money, nicer cars, lots more things."

We had hoped, when we asked a cross-section of Bostonians and Kansas Citians to "tell us about a few people you would think of as in a social class above your own," that the respondents from each status level would detail many fine points of difference between themselves and people immediately above them in rank. Their answers did not, however, do this. What they told us was in a much more general sense what Americans up and down the scale *envy* most about people whom they individually perceive as occupying a much higher position, those who— compared to themselves—seemingly "have life made."

The prime envy is that "they have more money . . . and they're able to live a lot better." This, in essence, is what four out of every five of our respondents acknowledged as the most salient difference between themselves and those above them in social standing. When asked to suggest "all the things that make you think people are in a social class above your own," they replied like this:

"Let's face it, the difference is materialistic. They have more money than I do."

"They make a lot more money and—if you want to weigh it up like that— they live much better."

"These people who are making much more money than you are think they are better, that they're in a higher class."

People who "have more money" are envied for that alone. Ultimately, though, it is what this "more money" buys that is most envied. This is what aroused the most passionately envious characterizations of the people our respondents ranked above themselves. More money is thus said to buy "a nicer," "bigger," "better" house, certainly "more expensive," probably "beautiful," and in some cases "practically a mansion." Further, more money buys a "house that is better located," which might be anywhere from "in nicer, newer, higher middle-class neighborhoods" to "right along the water in Hingham" (a Boston suburb on Massachusetts Bay). More money also buys a car that is "better," "bigger," "more expensive" than one's own—possibly even "two cars" or "three cars," up to "Every time a kid graduates, he gets a new car." It buys "more expensive clothes than mine" and maybe, if there is enough of it, "a half-million dollars' worth of jewelry." Finally, it buys "more free time," "wonderful vacations," "domestic help," and all sorts of costly recreation. (But more money may buy "more headaches" too, since sometimes people who have it don't handle it well; or as one Kansas City man said, "They're better off than I am if you look at what they have, but they're also deeper in debt!")

Less money, by the same token, means lower standing. The dominant explanation for another family's belonging to a lower social class than one's own is that "they have less money . . . and can't live as well as we do." Or, as a Boston man summarized it, "The people lower than me would generally be the ones who have less money and consequently less things. They just can't have as much or do as much as me and my family can. It's that simple."

More explicitly revealing of pride in one's possessions and of fine lines in status distinction were the many graphic descriptions of differences in living standard cited by people in Boston and Kansas City. From these, we learned which accomplishments in material well-being meant most to the people of each successively higher socio-economic level. For example, those just one step up from the worlds of poverty and welfare pridefully established these distinctions between themselves and those less fortunate:

> "They are living in public housing, while I'm living in something I pay for myself."

> "That would be someone without any money or a job—the unemployed."

> "Welfare recipients—they rely on government handouts for a living."

> "They wear old, raggedy clothes."

> "They have practically no income and lots of kids."

In turn, Middle Americans just getting along specified these differences between themselves and those of marginal or Lower-American status:

> "He lives in a lousy house—he has to rent."

> "They have small children but no car."

> "The children have had to work while still in school."

One notch up, Middle Americans of comfortable living standard clarified the difference between themselves and those just getting along with statements such as:

> "They live in a two-family house—not a single-family like ours."

> "The children might not have as many varied outfits."

> "They would have to save to go out to eat on their anniversary."

A Boston man who had achieved a standard of wealth considerably above Middle-American-comfortable said, "People who don't have custom clothes or a Cadillac like I do are judged worse off." Other men and women in both cities who had attained similarly above-average rank suggested of those who hadn't:

> "They live in a less expensive neighborhood, in small houses."

"They don't have two cars."

"They have to entertain in their own homes."

By comparing themselves with people who can afford less in the way of housing, cars, clothes, and recreation, Americans at each socio-economic level find a measure of satisfaction—sometimes considerable —in their own lot in life. And nowhere is this more starkly revealed than among those people who are near but not on the bottom of the ladder, for no matter how badly off they may look to the rest of society, it is a major source of pride to them that at least *their* clothes are *"not* raggedy" and that *they* are *not* dwelling "in the slums like the real lower class."

Assessing the Status of Income Levels

If money is the measure of a person's social standing in America, as so many respondents in our Boston and Kansas City surveys so blithely proclaimed, then we might assume, if we take things very concretely, that a person with an annual income of $20,000 a year is socially valued as having double the status of a person with an annual income of $10,000. Or, to go to the extremes, a person with an annual income of $5,000,000 has 500 times the social status of the $10,000-a-year person and 10,000 times the status of a person with an annual income of just $500. This third person would not be quite so bad off when compared with the person earning $10,000—even so, he or she would still have just 5 percent as much standing, socially speaking. But these differences seem exaggerated statements of how Americans rate one another according to income. Money as the measure of status is probably not very much like that.

Perhaps money has more the character of a ranking variable— which is to say that while a person making $10,000 a year is judged to have more status than a person making $9,000, the status ratio between them does not exactly reflect this dollar-mark comparison. Or, to take another hypothesis, perhaps the way money measures status varies from one point on the income scale to another. Perhaps the person who made $10,000 in 1971—a period when that figure was close to the national average—was then judged as having 11 percent more status than the person making just $9,000, but the person making $90,000 did not have nine times the status of the $10,000-a-year individual; perhaps only six, or four, times. Changing ratios like this are a possibility. How does money measure status?

We sought to answer this question by having respondents in two of our Boston surveys make social standing estimations for different income levels. (See Appendix B for a full description of our method and its rationale.) We asked the respondents in the second of the two surveys (which provides the better data set of the two) to imagine an average man. We called him "Mr. Absolutely Average Man-in-the-Middle" and defined him as average in every way; half the people were better off than he, and half the people were worse off than he in all of the various ways that one might think about social standing. We said that he should be given a social standing equal to 100. Then we asked our respondents to estimate the social standing of people who had different characteristics in relation to our average man, Mr. Mim. If they thought a person with a particular characteristic had twice Mr. Mim's standing, they should give him a score of 200; if he had one-third of Mr. Mim's standing, they should give him a score of 33, and so on. Using this method, our respondents proved able to indicate their sense of the community standing that was attached to different levels of income, to different educational levels, and to different occupations.

From our analysis of the results, we were able to construct the picture of Mr. Mim that was implicit in the mind of our average respondent. Mr. Mim had an income of $9,400, slightly more than twelve years of schooling, and a job as perhaps an accounting clerk in a government department, a television-and-radio repairman, or a fireman. In the analysis that follows, keep in mind Mr. Mim's characteristics in order to have some sense of the status magnitudes represented by the status scores respondents gave us.

From their responses to the income items, we can derive a best estimate for 1971 of the amount of status attached to different income levels and can answer the question of how the objective continuum of income amount is related to the subjective evaluations people make of the status of individuals who have those particular levels of living. From our analysis, for example, we are able to say that although a person with $28,000 of income in 1971 had about three times as much money as Mr. Mim, he had only about twice as much status, while someone with $4,700 of income had both half as much money and half as much status as the average man.

Our best estimates of the relationship between income and status of income are derived from regression analysis of the average responses of our sample. The averaging method we used involved calculating a geometric mean. The mean calculated in this way comes much closer to representing the central tendency of a normal distribution of status scores than would the arithmetic mean. (See Appendix B for an explanation of why the geometric mean is preferred to both the arithmetic mean and the median with this kind of data.)

As noted, we had collected two sets of status estimations in Boston, one from a sample of nearly 600 persons in 1970 and the second from a sample of similar size in 1971. In addition, we were able to compare our two data sets with six data sets collected by three other investigators in studies as early as 1962. This proved to be important in estimating the reasonably constant relationship between income and income status, since the meaning of a dollar changed a great deal from 1962 to 1971; in nominal amounts, incomes increased about 60 percent during that period.

To get some feeling for the raw data, let us look at the geomeans of the responses of the respondents in our 1971 survey:

$1,800 = 22	$ 9,200 = 105	$ 41,300 = 221
2,900 = 28	10,000 = 114	59,700 = 318
3,800 = 42	11,900 = 131	78,200 = 342
4,900 = 57	13,500 = 132	98,500 = 362
5,800 = 68	15,600 = 137	180,000 = 565
6,900 = 78	18,500 = 180	360,000 = 644
8,100 = 98	27,400 = 211	720,000 = 615

The dollar amount on the left is the income stimulus. The number on the right shows how much status, as expressed in geomean, was associated by our respondents with this income; this is the ratio comparison with Mr. Mim's score of 100. Thus, a status score of 22 for $1,800 of income means that respondents believed that persons with such an income had only 22 percent as much income status as Mr. Mim. Similarly, the status score of 565 for an income of $180,000 meant that, on the average, respondents believed that people with that level of income had 5.65 times the income status of Mr. Mim.

We have graphed these average responses to each income item in Figure 2-1. Observe that the status of income goes up very rapidly at first and that the rate of increase in status then declines sharply. To be sure, each higher income level tends to involve more status until we get to the last item, and we are entitled to regard that as an error of measurement (much as we regard the somewhat more frequent reversals in our 1970 data). As income goes from $1,800 to $9,200 the income status judgment, as well as the dollars, has increased five times, but going from $9,200 to

FIGURE 2-1
Income Status and Income Amounts

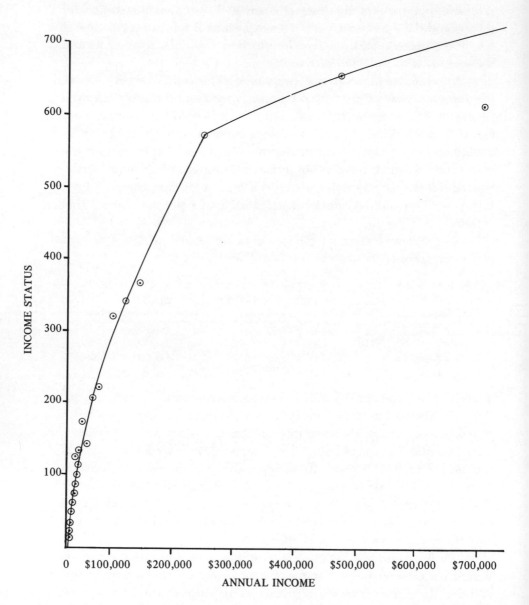

$180,000, we observe that while the dollars increase almost twenty times, the status increase is not quite sixfold.

We can easily see that there is a decreasing rate of increase in the status of income, as income increases. This fits very well the concept of the power law of the subjective magnitude of stimuli. If we draw an analogy between income as a social stimulus and light as a physical stimulus, it seems perfectly reasonable that, as each of these kinds of stimuli becomes greater or more intense, people convert them into subjective perceptions—brightness or social status—but that the rate of conversion from the objective event to its subjective meaning need not be one for one. Using linear regression of the logarithms of both the income amounts and the status means (S_i), we are able to estimate what the rate of conversion might be. If we try to define one coefficient of conversion for the whole range of income, we get the following formula:

$$S_i = \frac{(INC)^{.6}}{2.5}$$

By most standards this expression produces a very close fit, that is, a very high correlation, between income and income status. For our 1971 data this power equation accounted for 93 percent of the variance in status means, and for 1970 it accounted for 96 percent of the variance.

If we take these results for 1971, we can say that as income increases, status increases by less. To be exact, status increases in proportion to the three-fifths power of income. This would mean that when income doubles, income status increases about one and a half times. However, we have seen in our very rough visual exploration of the data that, in fact, through the range up to about $13,000, status seems to increase proportionately with income; so our result of the three-fifths power seems to be an underestimate for those income levels. On the other hand, at higher income levels, status seems to increase by less than the three-fifths power. Thus, even though we have very high correlations, perhaps we ought to look at the data a little more closely. One way to do so is to graph the data in a form that brings out the linearity of the relationship in the power (or log-log) form. This we have done in Figure 2-2. If a single power accounts for the pattern of increases in income status as income increases, then our plotted points should fall very neatly on a straight line. In our case, that straight line would have a slope of three-fifths—that is, income status would increase three (log) units for each five (log) units that income increased. We do not really observe the dots making one straight line; instead they seem to make two different lines, one fitting very nicely the first nine or ten dots lower down and the other

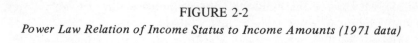

FIGURE 2-2

Power Law Relation of Income Status to Income Amounts (1971 data)

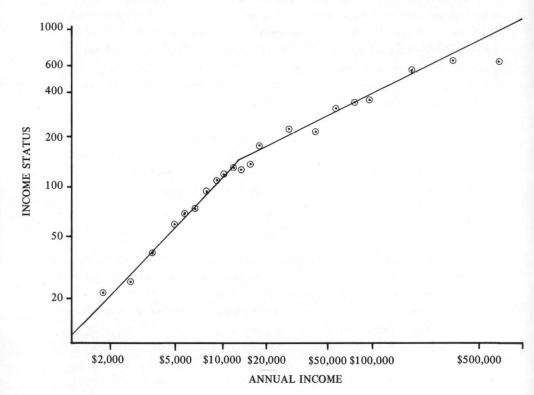

fitting not quite as well the ten or eleven dots higher up. The line that fits the lower half of the income level has a much higher slope than the one that fits the upper half. This represents visually what we have calculated by looking at the numbers—that the fivefold increase of income from $1,800 to $9,200 is matched by roughly a fivefold increase in status, while the income increases in the higher income levels are seldom matched by proportionate increases in status. If we want to use these data to estimate the quantitative relationship between income levels and income status, we need a more complex formula, one that takes into account that up to a certain point the exponent in the power law seems to be about 1.0, and above that level it seems to be about 0.5.

If we had only one data set, we might be reluctant to make such a conclusion. It could be that the departures from a single slope are simply the function of random variations in respondents' answers, of some systematic distortions in our questions, or in the way the fieldwork was carried out. This led us to take a close look at the results of the other studies we had available. We discovered that all of them showed a bend in the data—our 1970 data, Hamblin's two data sets, Shinn's three data sets, and Schmidt's data set. The bends in our two data sets took place around $13,000 to $14,000; for Hamblin they were at $8,800, and for Shinn around $12,000. These were all amounts above the median income at the time the studies were done. They were fairly close to the mean income.

The fact that our 1971 data bent at a little over $13,000 led us to a hypothesis related to another part of the study that was concerned with establishing the incomes people define as representing certain global levels of living (like poverty, just getting along, comfort, prosperity, or being rich). The $13,000-plus amount occurred in the range that our respondents defined in the 1971 survey as a comfortable level of living for an average family. Further, looking at the results from Hamblin's 1962 survey on, it seemed to us that there might be a relationship between given income amounts as they changed over time and the kinds of changes that have taken place in people's standards for a sort of minimum average income. In related research, Rainwater (1974) had analyzed the responses to a Gallup Poll question asked from 1946 through 1969: "What is the average amount of money a family of four needs to get along in this community?" That analysis had shown that the mean response to these Gallup Poll questions in each of the 18 surveys analyzed fit very closely to what would be predicted on the assumption that the response represented a constant proportion of the per capita disposable income that would be available to a family of four. (*Per capita disposable income* is defined as the total personal income in the nation in a given year, minus personal taxes and certain non-tax payments, divided by the population of the country. A standard per capita income for a family of four would be four times that amount.) The average amount considered necessary to get along turned out to be slightly more than half of this family disposable personal income amount (F.D.P.I.), or slightly more than twice the per capita disposable income. For early 1971, when our fieldwork was done, per capita disposable income would have been around $3,500, so that the amount for a family of four would have been around $14,000. If the status of income were somehow related in people's minds to an appreciation of the average amount of money available to families (F.D.P.I.), then perhaps our two-slope relationship would bend at about that amount. Testing that idea out on all eight data sets (collected in five different years over a nine-year period) would enable us to decide how reasonable such an hypothesis was.

So now we wanted to estimate, not the relationship with dollars of income, but with the ratio of dollars of income to the family disposable income amount for particular years. Thus, for each of the data sets we divided the income amount by the family disposable personal income for that year and then analyzed them—visually by plotting them on the same graph and statistically by calculating regressions for each data set. It did seem that the point at which the regression line bent was at about the family disposable personal income amount for each of the data sets. Furthermore, the exponents for the lower and upper segments did not spread too widely. For the lower segment they ranged from 0.84 for the Boston 1970 survey to 1.04 for one of Shinn's data sets. There was somewhat more variability in the upper segment exponents, ranging from 0.38 for one of Shinn's and Schmidt's data sets to 0.54 for our 1970 Boston data.

Given that there are only a few data points in each of these data sets, however, these could all be random variations around one true value. Therefore, having standardized the income stimuli as ratios to disposable personal income, we carried out one regression using the income items from all of the data sets. This regression produced a gratifyingly high coefficient of determination (0.985) and showed the coefficient for amounts up to 100 percent of family disposable personal income to be 0.95, and that for amounts above family disposable income to be 0.48. Neither of these coefficients is significantly different from our convenient simplification of 1.0 for the lower segment and 0.5 for the higher segment. So let us decide for the purposes of the rest of discussion to regard these as the powers that describe the relationship between income amounts and income status. This means that we can say:

$$\text{Income status} = 142.8 \, (\text{Income/F.D.P.I.})$$

if the ratio of income to F.D.P.I. is less than or equal to one. If it is greater we express the relation as follows:

$$\text{Income status} = 142.8 \, (\text{Income /F.D.P.I.})^{.5}$$

The fact that this formulation fits all of the data sets indicates constancy in the period of the 1960s and early 1970s (and in all likelihood before and after). The median of the distribution of income status—a status of 100—is assigned to people whose incomes amount to 70 percent of family disposable personal income. The income status of the person who has exactly the family disposable personal income amount is 143. Up to that amount, income status increases proportionately on a one-to-one basis. Above that amount, income status increases in proportion to the square root of income, so that the person whose income is double the F.D.P.I. amount has a status of 1.4 times that of the person at the F.D.P.I. amount—200 *versus* 143. Let us illustrate this general relationship by projecting income statuses for 1978. We will assume that family disposable personal income is about $24,000 in 1978. If so, then we would expect the following relationship between 1978 dollars and 1978 income status:

Income Column	Percent of F.D.P.I.	Income Status	Perceived Level of Living
$ 4,200	17.5	25	dire poverty
8,400	35.0	50	poverty
12,600	52.5	75	just getting along
16,800	70.0	100	almost comfortable
19,200	80.0	125	comfortable
26,400	110.0	150	nearly prosperous
47,000	196.0	200	solid upper-middle class
294,000	1226.0	500	success elite
1,000,000 plus	4904.0	1,000	super-rich

It seems reasonable that people would have a different attitude toward income increases that can move families toward a national average standard of comfortableness than they would toward income increases that move families up from comfortableness toward higher and higher levels of luxury. Perhaps this is what is involved with our two-slope relationship between income amounts and income status. People are saying that, up to the point at which one has whatever is defined as a comfortable level of living (a level of living in which one has all the necessities, a few luxuries, and some security about enjoying them), every dollar counts. Every dollar gives as much additional well-being and as much additional status as the last one did. Above the amount that represents solid comfort, each additional dollar nets less than a proportionate increase in the status derived from income, so that the status value of dollars begins to decline.

Thus, with respect to the status utility of income, until one reaches the F.D.P.I. level we must modify the economists' general rule of decreasing marginal utility of income. And it is important to note that, at any given time, the family income of some 80 percent of the American population is below that amount. This means that, in all likelihood, for more than three-quarters of the population every additional dollar is as valuable as every other dollar. As long as a person is reaching for the standard mainstream package, there is not much of a sense of the decreasing value of money, even if income is rising relative to that of those around. Only when one breaks through that amount does one move into the world of decreasing marginal utility. This means that, for most Americans, when one has one-third more or one-third less income than someone else, one has one-third more or less status. The average person and a person who has half again the average income are still about 50 percent apart in status. But the person who has 50 percent more income than someone who earns the F.D.P.I. amount is only about 40 percent better off in status terms. Going back to the extreme examples with which we started, the individual who has ten times the average person's income has only a little more than five times the status.

The images that people give us when they talk about class, then, can be expressed in a quantitative relationship that takes into account two powers that convert income at any given time to income status. Our nine years of studies (1962–1971) cannot establish a "law of income status," but they strongly suggest one. As long as the income distribution does not change, it is likely that income status will increase proportionately from the lowest levels to an amount just short of one and a half times the median; above that point status gains will be in proportion to the square root of income, reflecting a fairly rapidly diminishing status utility to income.

This conclusion, of course, is based on a highly simplified picture of how individuals derive the income on which their standard of living is based. We need to work with a more complex model that takes into account the conversion of income into status as it derives not only from men's income but also from women's income and from public transfers. (However, since some 70 percent of the variance in family income of families in the 25-to-54-year age range is attributable to the incomes of men, it seems likely that the law of income status derived here will have a great deal to do with the status individuals and families achieve as a result of their level of living.)

Self-Classification by Income

Responses to our open-ended question, "Which social class do you think you are in?", can be subsumed under a general rule[1]: the class identity people claim for themselves is the highest that can be defended on grounds either of attained and demonstrated level of material well-being or the years of schooling completed and credentials acquired, most especially college degrees.

For most Americans, the level of material well-being they have attained is the dominant consideration in their self-placement on the status ladder. (By level of material well-being we mean the kind of house they live in, the car or cars they drive, the way their homes are furnished, the clothes they wear, and the recreations and vacations they afford.) This impressive emphasis on standard of living is found among the college-educated just about as much as among those without such a credential, with differences in the level of well-being achieved among college graduates leading to self-defined sub-categories of those who are "doing well" *versus* those who are "not doing so well." College graduates among our respondents who were "doing well"—earning from $25,000 up to $35,000 a year, and with houses and total life style to match—explained their identification with the college-educated professional and managerial class largely on the basis of the material well-being their incomes permitted them, and they gave their collegiate backgrounds second rank. They would say such things as, "Look at the neighborhood we live in and the material goods available to us, including recreation," or "Judging by our way of life, living here in Medfield . . . and by everything you see in this house, I'd say we are upper-middle class." In contrast, college graduates who were "not doing so well," with incomes below $20,000 a year and living less affluently, placed major emphasis on their college degrees when claiming identification with a class of the college-educated, and would argue, "I'd be in that class based on education and tastes, but I'm not quite in the same category as the successful college grad."

Just as there is a considerable range in the level of material well-being among college graduates, with consequent differences in self-identification, so too is there a considerable range—indeed, an even wider one—among those who did not graduate from college or attend college at all. One group among the non-graduates that is of special interest is made up of those whose income level and standard of living equal or exceed the average college graduate's. No group in our sampling showed so much pride in their economic status as did those prospering without the advantage of college degrees. Regarding the income and material status they had achieved, they testified, "We own a $30,000 home in suburbia and have two cars"; "I make a lot of money [$20,000 a year] and I know a lot of people who are also making this kind of money—I had to go to three parties this week because of business"; and "We have financial security, have traveled a lot, and belong to organizations that have good recreation." Of the people they knew best, they said: "Our friends are all like us—they're living well and can afford most of the things they desire" and "They range from high-school graduates up to college graduates, a few with master's degrees." As for their social standing, they suggested: "Thinking of our income status, we're somewhere between middle-middle and upper-middle"; "We're above the average class but not in the luxury class"; "We're between the ordinary high-school graduate and the bachelor's degrees"; or "I'm something below medicine and the professions—I'm a department head [in a factory] making over $15,000 a year; I'm in that class." They seemed to create for themselves a special, elite category within the class of Americans who are not college graduates, a category of families who are more than merely comfortable, who are, though not rich, definitely leading a good life.

Men and women of more ordinary economic status (and similarly without college credentials) were no less inclined to base their self-image on their income level and standard of living; but they did so with less pride. And, of course, the further down they ranked in economic status, the more this was the case; correspondingly, there were perceptible changes from one major group to the next in the way they rationalized their self-placement on the social ladder. For example, Bostonians and Kansas Citians in our sample who would probably be judged by their fellow citizens as Middle Americans of comfortable living standard spoke with a certain amount of satisfaction about the kinds of houses they occupied and their other material possessions, even while complaining a bit about not having as good a life as they might like. A Kansas City woman of this status presented this rationale for identifying herself as a Middle American of comfortable living standard:

> "My husband earns $10,000 to $12,000 a year. We own our house—and it's comfortable. But we can't afford to say we'd go someplace on vacation without long-range planning. We won't have too much choice of colleges for our kids. They'll have to go close to home."

And a Boston woman said:

> "We're just average. Our house and those of our friends are worth around $20,000 to $25,000. We have one car and our house is a three-bedroom ranch."

Others echoed them, saying: "We aren't hurting for anything" and "We have had the opportunity to own a house. It's not much more than average, but it's out here in the suburbs, which I like."

Down the ladder a step, at the level of Middle Americans just getting along, the tone of self-description shifted to a theme of, "We work hard and don't have too much to show for it—but at least we're not poor and lower class." Here the pride displayed was not so much in possessions as in having "a steady income," "a job that I can count on going to tomorrow as well as today," and in "not being frustrated like the lower class is . . . with not enough money and more bills than you can pay." The economic problems they admit to are "having to pinch pennies," or as a Boston man said, "I drive my car to the ground because I don't have any extra bucks. . . . I'd like a new car—everyone would!" The class label they seem to prefer for themselves is *working class*; this is especially popular with men, who take a measure of pride in its evocation of hard work and physical effort even while it suggests that on the job "we take orders, not give them." (In contrast, comfortable Middle Americans prefer the class labels *middle class* or *middle-middle*.)

Among the people still further down—those who would be considered by their fellows in Boston and Kansas City as lower working class—we found a mixture of hope that they are not down at the bottom in society's eyes and discernible fear that they are ranked much lower than they would wish. Whites at this level tended to vacillate and hedge their responses: "We're in the lower-middle class, but the real low middle class—there's really no extra money." Those closest in standard of living to the class of Middle Americans just getting along often managed to include themselves in that class by defining it to include "people like me who work hard—I have a job and my self-respect," or by separating themselves from the class of poor beneath, saying, "I don't feel poor and know I'm a long way from being rich." Those furthest removed from Middle-American economic status would say, "I'm whatever class it is that means you ain't got much and ain't going to get too much."

Given most of our respondents' sensitive and attentive assessments of their relative positions in the standard of living hierarchy, and the salience it all too clearly has for their sense of identity and worth, is it any wonder that we find little in the way of diminishing marginal status utility of income until we get well past the level Americans call solidly comfortable? And this represents a style of living that for all but 20 to 25 percent of the nation's families seems always to stand out of reach. Given their images of the freedom and security that go with higher levels of income, it is understandable that our respondents envision a rapidly diminishing marginal utility to income increases over that amount. A man who in 1971 or 1972 earned $100,000 a year made more than ten times the income of Mr. Mim, but the Americans we interviewed did not believe that he was even four times better off socially.

CHAPTER 3

Class as Job

Tᴴᴇʀᴇ is a considerable ambiguity about the role of job or occupation in the American public's attribution of social standing. This ambiguity is embarrassing, considering the central role that "occupation" plays in sociological theory and in empirical research on stratification and a host of other substantive issues. Whether sociologists approach stratification from a functionalist perspective, with emphasis on the division of labor, or from a Marxist perspective, emphasizing social relations to production, there is a tendency to consider people's jobs—conceived as positions in a structure—as solid social facts that condition their life chances in fundamental and unambiguous ways. Yet occupations as named categories seem not to convey unambiguous information to the ordinary citizen or to the social science analyst. Thus, for all the emphasis our Boston and Kansas City respondents gave to job (or occupation) as a factor in deciding social class, their statements about its role were markedly vague and tentative.

Usually, when people suggest that something beyond money determines "what social class you belong to . . . what your social standing is," they name "occupation—the type of work you do." If they go beyond that, they add educational background as a third key factor. Men and women from the managerial and professional strata are most inclined to present such a multi-dimensional view, and they express it this way:

"Class is tied mostly to occupation and what people's jobs are. Also a certain amount of class standing is tied to education. It's a mixture of financial standing and those things."

"Social class means money first and your occupation second. If you make good money, you can live in a better neighborhood."

"I think social class is based on your salary—the husband's salary—and your house. Education and cultural background too. And the kind of job—the profession."

Many blue-collar men and women in both our cities said much the same, adding to "how much money you make" such specifics as, "It's what you do for a living—whether you wear a white shirt or a blue shirt." A Kansas City craftsman summed up this three-factor formula for social class by saying, "It's financial, educational, the type of work and working conditions that [determine] what class of people you fit into."

For most Americans occupation, narrowly defined as the type of work one does, seems to be playing a less important role in determining social standing than formerly. They are of the impression that "whether you were blue-collar or white-collar once made a big difference . . . but occupation doesn't actually matter that much anymore." In this they are in agreement with one influential analyst of twentieth-century changes in labor and class structure, Braverman, who observes that the white-collar workers of early capitalism were:

> a favored stratum, closely associated with the employer and the recipient of special privileges. . . . The few who kept his books, sold his product, negotiated on his behalf with the outside world, and in general were privy to his secrets, hopes and plans, were in fact associates in the exploitation of productive workers, even if they themselves were only employees. . . . Those who aided the capitalist in the circulation of his capital, the realization of his profit, and the management of his labor, gained privileges, security and status from this function. . . . [Elaborations of these functions] have now produced their armies of [clerical] wage-workers whose conditions are generally like those of the armies of labor organized in production. . . . From being privileged positions in which one could to a small extent share in the benefits derived by capital from productive labor, they have become mere cogs in the total machinery designed to multiply capital.[1]

For our Boston and Kansas City respondents the change in blue-collar *versus* white-collar status is partially explained by changes in the relationships between job and income that are presumed to have occurred, so that many occupations formerly below average or at the bottom in both pay and respectability have now moved up to average or above in both respects. Welders, plumbers, "cesspool cleaners," "garbage-truck workers," and "sewer-pipe coverers" were among the occupations cited by our sample as having thus risen in status during the post-World War II years.

An even more important cause of the diminished importance of occupation, say Middle Americans, is "the greater emphasis on material things since World War II . . . [which] is especially rampant in the suburbs." In the suburbs, goes this theory, "nobody really cares what you do for a living, as long as you can afford to be there," or, as another Bostonian put it, "If you make money, no matter what your job may be, you can move to a better area, an upper-middle class neighborhood."

Upper-status Americans make a different assessment of how income, occupation, education, and other factors affect social standing when referring to their own part of the class hierarchy. As to income, they acknowledge that "you have to have a certain amount of it" just to be part of the upper-status world, but beyond that, they insist, "too many other things have to be considered to say that income is most important." Among the other things they point to most prominently are occupation, family history, civic activities, and cultural level. Ultimately, said the Upper Americans in our sample, "your prestige depends on the circle you're with socially," and these other considerations determine that in various ways. At the upper edge of the social ladder, for example, "family name is most important." From there down, income may in fact be most significant in determining the "circle you're with" and its status reputation; but our Upper-American respondents preferred talking about the exceptions to this—for instance, about the "people with tremendous incomes here in Kansas City [or Boston] who don't have much couth" and/or "don't do much for the community," and so "don't have much status." They described themselves as sensitive about occupation, claiming that, at this social level, "there are some occupations that have more prestige than others, income aside" (examples are "certain of the professions—doctors, lawyers, etc." and "officers of well-known companies"). Finally, they asserted that "if a person contributes to his community his prestige goes up." The contributions they had in mind ranged from volunteer work in welfare causes through service on committees and fund-raising for the arts to non-political involvement in suburban or municipal government.

It is not always clear, from the way Americans talk, why a particular occupation is thought to stand high or low, other than the ever-present consideration that some jobs are better paid than others. Indeed, respondents in our survey constantly coupled an occupational characterization with either an amount of money or a qualifier like "successful," "average," or "not doing so well." Thus, we have references to "big businessmen," "successful business people," "college graduates in management doing fairly well," and "doctors and lawyers making lots of dough."

Beyond income, however, there is one dimension that cuts across the way respondents characterize occupations, or more generally, an

individual's relationship to the means of production. That is autonomy—
linked usually with security. At the highest levels of social standing,
advantages of autonomy and/or security are thought to be conferred by
inherited money, which allows the individual either not to work at all
or to work in an inherited business. But there are also more modest
degrees of autonomy conferred by being in business for oneself, even
though one didn't inherit the business, or by being in one or another
kind of professional or managerial occupation in which there are fewer
overseers of one's work.

Advantaged Situations

The salience of autonomy and security in the public's judgment of
jobs came out most strongly in response to our questions about who
would be ranked above or below the respondent in social class. There
it developed that, although having more money or less money was a
principal determinant in who would be ranked above or below, the
nature of an individual's control over his socio-economic situation played
an additional, differentiating role. We found, for example, that someone
with more money who had inherited it, rather than having been its
earner, aroused special envy. This was true up and down the social
ladder; *inheritors at all economic levels were named by their acquaintances as examples of persons standing socially higher.* Some of these
were young men who "are going to take over" grocery businesses and
filling stations started by their fathers; others were men and women whose
ancestors had been "extremely wealthy and community leaders in Kansas
City [or Boston] for several generations." The frequency of these citations
suggests that whatever the position and extent of inheritance, this fact
by itself—that the money has been inherited—supplies special advantage.
Nowhere is this more so than in Upper America; among respondents of
this standing it was especially common to find inheritors cited as
examples of persons superior in status. These were variously individuals
or couples who "have some independent income," who "come from an
old moneyed family," whose "daughters have had debuts," who have had
"streets . . . named after them," and—in a few cases—who "have a
United States President in their ancestry."

Inherited money is widely believed to give a special ease to life, as
if it has taken "all the worry out of daily existence." Having it means
that the most critical of all problems, finding enough money for necessities and pleasures, has been pre-solved; life has already been "made" for
you, you don't have to go through the struggle to "make it" yourself.

This is what seems so eminently enviable about inherited wealth. In addition, people with inherited money are thought to be "more comfortable with money" than those who have had to acquire it on their own. Thus, "old wealthy families" are spoken of as "a different breed altogether from the *nouveau riche*, who have compulsive ways of showing off." For the children of these old wealthy families, the advantages seem to be doubled. Not only has their adulthood been made easier but also their whole existence has been one of ease and advantage. Often this has meant "they were educated abroad" or "at well-known prestigious private schools." It has meant that "culture and the opportunity to travel have always been part of their environment"; that they have had, and still do have, "access to prominent people"; and that probably "they have retained a family membership in exclusive clubs." Indeed, through their whole lives, they have reputationally been "the best people."

Also widely envied, but not so much as inheritance of money, is *ownership* of the means for acquiring it. The forms of ownership included in this concept range from proprietorship of a business or operation of an independent professional practice to investments in real estate or stocks and bonds. Any and all of these forms of ownership or self-employment tend to be impressive to people of Middle-American and Lower-American standing. People who are owners in this sense were cited time and again as standing considerably higher on the social ladder:

> "I have a friend who has a small business—he owns his own home, too. He's well off."

> "I have one friend who would be a bit higher than me. He has stocks and things. He's well-to-do, all right."

> "My sister and her husband have invested in real estate and are doing very well. I don't think they have many of the worries that my husband and I have to contend with."

> "My sister-in-law is better off than we are. Her husband is in business for himself—he's a periodontist."

Such ownership is envied not only for the additional money it provides, but also because it places the owners in a "boss" relationship to other people. To Middle Americans being an owner, an investor, a landlord, or a self-employed professional means that one is among the controllers—not the controlled—in the economy; it means that you can manage time and money not as someone else commands or instructs, but at your own whims. It may even mean that people in this group "don't have to be at work from 9 to 5 like the rest of us, if they don't want to," since their investments, their properties, are unceasingly at work for them, producing revenue even while they themselves are idling or vacationing.

Also widely envied as a source of money are "connections"—involvements of any kind that put a person "in touch with important people" or political positions that "open doors for you." This is something apart from inheritance or ownership, although it is commonly associated with both. It is the know-how, the know-where, and the know-who of having access to money and power, and ultimately it means greater control over one's own destiny.

College-educated professional and managerial class people acknowledge such connections as a prime differentiation between themselves and the higher-ranking old rich and new rich success elite. Thus, as examples of persons in a class above themselves, they point to "a federal judge—he is in a position of much greater power and prestige than I," or "a family we know that has broader contact with people in positions of authority; the people they know are spread geographically all over the world." Men who own moderate-sized businesses speak enviously of those who, through banking or commercial associations, "have so much more finances available than myself." To have more finances available— which can be anything from a loan or line of credit to possible investors in one's enterprise, or access to investment in others'—means that one has a half a claim on more money than in fact is already part of one's income or ownership; it is an indirect form of additional wealth.

Political power—whether corrupt or otherwise—seems to be an avenue to higher social standing; it may provide more money or freedom from needing so much of it in order to feel important. To many an average Bostonian or Kansas Citian the people most undeniably higher in status are "the governor of the state," "the mayor of this city," even a city councilman—as in this citation from a Boston suburbanite: "Sonny X ranks higher than I do. He's a big Boston politician, he's always on TV, people around here are always talking about him; I understand he owns half of Scituate [the suburb where this respondent lived]."

The salience of these aspects of one's position in the economy— one's relationships to the means of production—indicates a strong emphasis on *autonomy* and *security* in getting a living, as well as on how good a living one gets. Inheritance, ownership, independent practice, being a professional, and having connections all represent ways of cushioning oneself against the pressures of having a boss and being a salary or wage worker. Holding income constant, the more in the way of these resources a family has, the higher its social standing. Envy of those with greater autonomy perhaps also accounts for the frequency with which people's ability to get away from the job for a vacation was mentioned as evidence of higher social standing (see Chapter 5).

Less Pleasant Positions

Aspects of a job situation that Americans generally consider unpleasant or demeaning were often used by our Boston and Kansas City respondents to characterize individuals of lower social standing than their own. Thus, whenever an acquaintance (or some hypothetical man or woman) had a job that was considered "less interesting," "dirtier," requiring "harder labor," or not as demanding of intelligence, this was taken as the proof, or token, of lower standing. Judgments of this sort about which occupations implied lower social status were frequently independent of differentials in remuneration. Rather than pay, the factors at issue were: (1) the type of work it is—"you look to see if the person is white collar or not," (2) the kind of education required for entry, (3) the levels of skills developed, (4) the authority exercised, and (5) public impressions about the caliber of people recruited into the job.

By these standards, virtually everyone in Boston and Kansas City looked down on "garbage collectors," "our trash hauler," "a junk peddler who goes down the street," and "the common laborer who doesn't have any education." In turn, anyone who had any kind of job looked down on "the people who can't work" or "are too lazy to work, the welfare moochers." Drawing finer lines, skilled craftsmen placed themselves above "unskilled workers who have to work harder and don't earn the money I do"; men in white-collar jobs ranked themselves above "construction workers" and "longshoremen"; college professors considered themselves higher than "auto salesmen"; and a doctor's wife assumed her husband rated above "the man down the street who owns a garden- and lawn-supply house."

In these status distinctions based on occupations, as with those based on education (to be discussed in the next chapter), we found that feelings of superiority can exist even in the absence of any advantage in standard of living. A white-collar worker can feel superior to "people who work with their hands" even while earning little more or no more than they, and a professional can feel superior to an auto salesman or a nursery proprietor without having a noticeable edge on income. This is another illustration of our proposition that when people talk about persons of lesser social standing, they reveal the things about their own position in life in which they take pride, many of which are not connected with how well off they are financially.

In noteworthy contrast, we found *no* blue-collar workers speaking of a white-collar worker as socially superior simply by virtue of the white-collar employment; only those who were clearly better off materially were credited with higher class standing. Indeed, in most instances where occupational characterizations were attached to people of higher class, this economic difference was stated: "They're in a higher income bracket" or "Anyone in that occupation makes a lot more money than the guys in mine."

It is not easy for Americans to acknowledge as social superiors those who do not have a superior standard of living. Sensing that this is the basic measuring stick, they resist acknowledging that anybody who measures no higher on this standard can be socially of higher rank; they want to be able to take full pride in whatever they have earned in the way of material well-being, and they find it diminishing to defer to someone who has earned no more but may expect deference by virtue of collar color (or degrees).

They do not, however, apply this principle when they turn to look at people of equal monetary standing whose other attributes and credentials—educational, occupational, ethnic, manners, moral, or whatever—they believe to be less worthy of respect than their own. Against such individuals they draw lines and establish small or large points of social superiority for themselves: "I'm white-collar; he's blue" and "I'm in a profession; he's more the worker type."

Estimating Magnitudes for Occupational Status

Occupational status or prestige is by far the most widely investigated status continuum. This area of investigation, however, has been beset by methodological difficulties. These difficulties have included finding categorizations that are both comprehensive and meaningful, correlating real-world jobs with occupational titles, getting good matches of titles from study to study and between studies and census data, coping with a list of census occupational titles that changes and grows from census to census as the underlying job structure changes, and trying to understand what is meant by the fairly consistent rankings of public preferences that have emerged from the survey data.

Occupational prestige as now used in sociological research derives most directly from a National Opinion Research Center (N.O.R.C.) inquiry conducted in 1947 and expanded and updated in the early 1960s. The 1947 N.O.R.C. question was as follows:

> Now, I am going to ask you how you would judge a number of occupations. For example, a *railroad brakeman*—which statement on this card best gives your own personal opinion of the general standing that each job has?

The categories of response were:

- Excellent standing
- Good standing
- Average standing
- Somewhat below average standing
- Poor standing
- I don't know where to place that one.

The percentage results were than translated into an "N.O.R.C. prestige score" by weighting the responses from 5 for excellent to 1 for poor. The resulting score for each occupation could range from 20, if everyone judged an occupation to be poor, through 60, if everyone judged an occupation to be average, to 100, if everyone judged an occupation to be excellent. Various studies using the N.O.R.C. format and others relating N.O.R.C. studies to other occupational prestige studies have indicated a high degree of stability in occupational prestige measured in this or in a similar way (Inkeles and Rossi, 1956; Hodge, Siegel, and Rossi, 1964; Treiman and Rossi, 1966).

The N.O.R.C. scores were updated and expanded to many more occupational titles in the 1960s by Hodge, Siegel, and Rossi. This research team first carefully replicated the original N.O.R.C. survey, then used a somewhat more modern sampling method and a nine-point ladder technique instead of the five-category N.O.R.C. scale to establish prestige scores for the more than 350 occupations on the detailed 1960 census list. The Hodge-Siegel-Rossi score (H.S.R.) represents the most comprehensive listing of N.O.R.C.-type prestige scores now available (Hodge, Siegel, and Rossi, 1964; Siegel, 1971).

The designers of the N.O.R.C. scale felt that the occupational prestige score for an individual would prove to be "a useful and valid index for most purposes" of the individual's total societal position in the stratification system (Hatt, 1950:534). Researchers who attempted to put it to use as a status index, however, encountered certain difficulties. The most obvious one was that although the ninety rated N.O.R.C. occupations covered a large portion of the work force, the scale did not rate the many hundreds of other less well-known occupations that researchers sometimes encountered in the field. Until Duncan (1961) published a "Socio-economic Index" based on the N.O.R.C. scores, the researcher's only recourse was to interpolate a scale score for the unrated occupations based on his own judgments of their similarity to rated occupations, an arbitrary procedure at best. Duncan attempted to solve the problem by generating status scores for all of the occupations in the U.S. Census list of detailed occupational titles. Duncan chose a subset of forty-five of the N.O.R.C.-rated occupations that appeared to be closely matched to the corresponding census titles. He regressed the set of N.O.R.C. scores on income and education data for each of the matched occupations from the 1950 census. He found a moderately substantial multiple correlation ($R^2 = 0.83$) between the N.O.R.C. scores and the socio-economic status scores predicted by his regression equation. The predictor variables of income and education were weighted about equally in their contribution to the socio-economic score.

The N.O.R.C. and Duncan Socio-Economic Status (S.E.S.) scores provide a measure of occupational standing that ranges from around ten at the low end to nearly ninety at the high end. But these numbers do not have any particular reference to the subjective sense of magnitude of status people have for different social resources. We do not know how to compare the social standing of a person in a particular job to that of someone at a particular income or educational level. We can say that a score of sixty is higher than one of fifty, and that the status distance from sixty to fifty is the same as that from forty to fifty, but we are not able to make ratio comparisons—that is, to say that one occupation has 50 percent more standing than another—although it is clear from the way people talk about occupations, and from their discussions of education and income, that they do have such a sense about jobs. That is, they do not confine themselves to an "interval level of measurement" in their thinking about the relative social standing of different occupations. It would be useful, then, to move in the direction of a magnitude estimation approach to occupational standing, even though we have such a thorough and carefully developed system as the N.O.R.C. scores and the Duncan S.E.S. derivative.

We have made a first step in this direction by collecting magnitude estimations for eighty occupational titles in our 1970 Boston survey, and by collecting additional estimations for forty-five of these in our 1971 survey. The geometric means of the respondents' status estimations are given in Table 3–1 (in which we have separated the white- and blue-collar occupations to facilitate comparisons).

We observe that the occupation with the highest social standing, the president of a billion-dollar corporation, has a social standing five times that of the average man. The occupation with the lowest social standing, an unemployed man who does odd jobs sometimes, has a social standing equal to 30 percent of that of the average man. The highest occupational standing is thus higher than the highest schooling rating (see Chapter 4), but lower than that for income.

One notes that there is a great deal of overlap between white-collar and blue-collar occupations, in line with the spontaneous observations of the respondents discussed above. For example, thirteen blue-collar occupations rank above the average man, and ten white-collar occupations rank below the average man. Even more interesting, perhaps, is the mixture of white- and blue-collar occupations right around the average-man status—from fireman and welder at 104 down to radio/television repairman and truckdriver at 94 on the blue-collar side, and the white-collar side from bookkeeper and accounting clerk in a government office at 97 through new car salesman at 100 to bank teller at 104.

In general, there is a fairly tight clustering of the occupations in the range of thirty points above and below our average score of one hundred. More than half the occupations on our list fall into this range. This is equivalent to the status range of 1971 incomes from approximately $7,000 to approximately $13,000.

What, then, of the relationship between our magnitude estimation score and the H.S.R. prestige score? The correlation between the two is high, as we would expect. The coefficient of determination is 0.874 for an exponential relationship of the H.S.R. scores to the logarithm of our magnitude estimation scores. This is the form that would be predicted for the relationship of an interval scale to a ratio scale. Its better fit is readily understandable if one plots the two scores on a graph. The relationship is roughly linear up to an H.S.R. score of about sixty, at which point the magnitude status score goes up much more rapidly than the H.S.R. score, due to the fact that the H.S.R. scores approach a limit while our scores have no limit. The relationship between the H.S.R. and our score is one in which the magnitude estimation score increases by 2.5 percent for each point in the H.S.R. score. We could use this relationship to work out the full range of score equivalents, but it would be biased at the top since even the compound interest formula of the exponential relationship cannot compensate for the H.S.R.

TABLE 3-1

Magnitude Estimates for the Status of Occupations:
Geomeans from 1970 and 1971 Surveys

"Blue-Collar" Occupations	Geomean of Standing Estimations	"White-Collar" Occupations
	583	President of a billion-dollar corporation
	438	Chairman of the board of an aerospace company
	324	Physician*
	289	Senior partner of a Wall Street law firm
	264	College professor*
	252	Owner of a factory that employs 100 persons*
	212	Department head in state government*
	194	Manager of a large factory*
	185	Sales engineer
	178	Chemist*
	165	Civil engineer*
	156	Clothing store owner
	154	Optical technician
	149	Salesman for an electrical manufacturing company
	135	Owner of a drycleaning store*
	134	Accountant*
	132	Insurance salesman*
	131	High school teacher*
Construction foreman	127	
Brickmason	127	
Electrician*	125	
	123	Traveling salesman for a wholesale company*
Airplane mechanic*	119	
Plumber	114	
	113	Assistant manager of an office supply company
	112	Office manager of a moving company
Factory foreman*	111	
Bulldozer operator	110	
Tool and die maker*	108	
Plasterer	108	
Fireman*	104	
	104	Bank teller
Welder	104	
Carpenter	103	
Machinist*	103	
	100	New car salesman*
	100	Manager of a small store in a city*
Glasscutter in a factory	98	
	97	Accounting clerk in a government office
	97	Bookkeeper
Machine repairman in a factory	96	
Radio/TV repairman*	95	
Truckdriver*	94	
Automobile repairman*	90	
Barber*	88	
Printing press operator*	88	
	88	Mailcarrier

TABLE 3-1 (continued)

"Blue-Collar" Occupations	Geomean of Standing Estimations	"White-Collar" Occupations
Railroad freight inspector*	88	
Concrete finisher	88	
Housepainter	82	
	81	Expediter
Machine operator in a truck factory*	80	
Metal grinder	80	
Dockworker*	78	
	78	Ordertaker in a wholesale house
Spraypainter	77	
	76	Stockclerk
Restaurant cook*	74	
Taxicab driver*	74	
Punchpress operator	74	
Gardener for a large institution	73	
Coal miner	72	
Assembly line worker*	69	
Hospital attendant*	69	
Restaurant waiter	68	
	66	Shipping clerk*
	66	Salesclerk in a hardware store
Laborer in a furniture factory	65	
Airport baggage machine operator	63	
Filling station attendant*	63	
Loom operator in a knitting mill*	61	
Janitor*	58	
Laborer in a bottling company	57	
Clothes presser*	55	
	53	Downtown newsdealer
	52	Grocery clerk
Parts checker in a factory	52	
Shoe repairman	50	
Garbageman	47	
Ditchdigger	46	
Shoe shiner	31	
Unemployed man who does odd jobs sometimes	30	

*Occupations tested in both 1970 and 1971. Occupations without asterisk were tested only once.

ceiling. But within the range of ten through ninety, we find the following relationships:

H.S.R. Score	Magnitude Estimation Score
10	47
20	51
30	78
40	100
50	128
60	164
70	210
80	270
90	345

Another way of getting a better understanding of what our respondents have in mind when they attach status estimations to different occupations is to examine, just as Duncan did for N.O.R.C. scores, their relationship to the education and income levels typical of each occupation. Using the data from the 1970 census, we correlated mean income (of men who worked fifty to fifty-two weeks of the year) and median education with our magnitude estimation scores. We found, as Duncan did, that schooling and income have roughly the same weight in the overall multiple correlation with our score.[2]

This simplest version of the relationship is a linear one. We find that such a relationship explains 83 percent of the variance in our scores. The regression coefficients tell us that the status attributed to an occupation increases roughly twelve points for every additional year in median education of the men employed in an occupation, and it increases one point for every $250 of mean income for the occupation. In terms of standardized coefficients we find that the two variables are of roughly equal importance. In effect, a standard deviation increase in either median schooling or median income increases the status of the occupation by half a standard deviation.

As with the relationship to the H.S.R. scores, our regression equation does not do very well at the high end of the scale (nor do alternative exponential or power versions). It seems likely that if we wanted seriously to understand the dynamics of occupational prestige above the level of moderately successful people—say above a score of about 200—it would be necessary to collect additional data, using many more occupational titles for that part of the range, and also to collect better data on the incomes and schooling of such people than is available in the census.

A summary of our scale would suggest a series of levels somewhat along the following lines:

White-collar groups

350 and up	Very high status occupations—presidents and chairmen of boards; the most highly successful lawyers and physicians
250–349	Successful business and professional people—top managers; owners of substantial but not mammoth businesses; professors at universities and high-prestige colleges; reasonably successful doctors, lawyers, and architects
175–249	Moderately successful people—persons in the less prestigeful professions—managers at lower levels; owners of smaller businesses
130–174	Middle managers; small-business owners (retail only); manufacturers' representatives; wholesale salesmen, and some technicians
115–129	The lowest level of managerial, professional, and kindred workers
95–114	Entry-level clerical and salespeople; managers of quite small, mainly blue-collar enterprises
Under 95	Clerks in low-status retail and wholesale establishments

Blue-collar groups

115 and up	Foremen and craftsmen where the craft requires quite special skills
100–114	Typical craftsmen and skilled manual and service workers
85–99	Ordinary working-class jobs
70–84	Less securely rewarded working-class jobs
55–69	Marginal blue-collar and service jobs
Under 55	Very poor jobs

In general, our incursion into the measurement of *occupational* status has left us not much more satisfied with this general approach to the measurement of social resources associated with *jobs* than we were before. Let us look at some of the reasons for this dissatisfaction.

First, we have the problem of titling and defining an occupation for public opinion scaling in experiments such as ours. This problem derives from the nature of occupational categories, which tend to be broad and often misleading. For most employed persons, it may be more accurate to say that they have jobs rather than occupations (Hughes, 1959). Having a job implies working for a particular organization for a particular rate of pay. Occupation is in this respect simply a label for a number of jobs that are somehow the same. Since there are millions of jobs and tens of thousands of different kinds (as listed in the Dictionary of Occupational Titles, for instance), the distillation of this complexity down to several hundred occupational titles means the classifying together of jobs that may differ greatly in duties, skills required, relationship to supervision, and compensation. Moreover, as Hodge and Siegel (1966) point out, the amount of heterogeneity within an occupation may differ considerably from occupation to occupation—bank tellers are more alike than salesmen.

Just as there is a great deal of variability within occupations, variability that our respondents would undoubtedly be sensitive to if we described the full details of different jobs in an occupational category, our own results show us what great variability there is in the gross census categories such as "managers, proprietors, and other officials" or even "operatives" or "laborers." Braverman has observed that the assumption that the gross census categories represent skill levels is quite false. That is, laborers are not unskilled and operatives semi-skilled; an average skill differential between persons in the two categories hardly exists.[3] Our respondents certainly perceive a great deal of variation within these categories. We find that ratings of laborers range from 47 to 74, those of operatives from 52 to 104. If we had sampled more broadly within these categories, we would be in a better position to say how much overlap is perceived. Similarly, for the other blue-collar jobs we find a range for service workers from 31 to 108 and for craftsmen and foremen from 50 to 127. In the white-collar area, too, the range is enormous, from 52 to 149 for sales workers; a narrower range from 66 to 104 exists for clerical workers; and then, of course, the broadest range is for managers, proprietors, and other officials, from 100 to over 500. Professionals range from 131 to 324. The common use of these gross occupational categories thus may conceal as much as it reveals about the influence of occupational resources on particular kinds of social behavior and attitudes.

A principal shortcoming of both our scale and the N.O.R.C. scale is that they systematically under-represent what is probably the real-world social standing accorded to managers and proprietors. This is most apparent for three occupations on our list: the senior partner of a Wall Street law firm, the owner of a factory that employs one hundred persons, and the manager of a large factory. In the real world the typical person with any of these three occupations probably has higher status than a college professor, and both the senior partner of a Wall Street law firm and the owner of a factory employing one hundred persons are likely to have higher social standing than a physician.

It may well be that there are differences in the conceptions that people have of the status dynamics of professionals *versus* business people. They may feel that knowing a person's profession tells more about his social standing than simply knowing that he is a manager in a firm. They may feel that one needs to know more about the factory manager or owner and, in particular, one needs to know how much he is paid—that is, how "successful" he really is. Much the same logic seems to apply to the strikingly low status of the banker in the N.O.R.C. scores. Either a banker does not mean a top official of a bank to respondents or, if it does, respondents are rating the occupation unrealistically low.

Much of the traditional sociological thinking on the subject of occupations shows a heavy bias in terms of an underlying paradigm toward the professions, where assumptions concerning the similarity of work done by different persons who share an occupation may be most valid. These assumptions may also apply fairly well to certain craft occupations. But for most persons in management or business operation, a prestige score based on an occupational title is an abstraction that is likely to prove inaccurate as a characterization of their social position in general and as a statement of how much status is derived from their work. When judging the occupational status of the mass of factory workers and office workers, occupational title may be the last thing one needs to consider for proper assessment. It may be enough, indeed, to know just two things: the physical setting of their work and how much they are paid for it. The essential truth of their occupations as status resource may lie therein, with all else redundant or extra.

Our investigation here convinces us that more detailed characterizations of occupation are needed to capture fully the realities of social standing associated with particular positions in the division of labor. It seems reasonable to believe that survey respondents could make more useful, socially relevant, statistically consistent judgments of a person's job prestige if they knew more about it, including: exactly what the job holder does, what kind of organization he or she does it in, and the job's relationship to the organization hierarchy (owner, manager, employee with tenure, union member, day worker, and so on). In Chapter 13 we will show that to include a consideration of employment experience—weeks worked, hours per week—increases the variance for measures of objective "occupational resources" by about a third. The public undoubtedly would also judge in a more accurate way the social standing of jobs defined to include things like unemployment experience.

In the long run, sociologists will have to look for a more complex way of rating jobs than occupational title. We have probably learned enough by now about public response to these titles; we must turn to learning more about the public view of real jobs.

CHAPTER 4

Class as Education

EDUCATION is often mentioned in the same breath with occupation when the American public expands definitions of social class out from solely financial factors. But its role is clearly not that of sufficient cause; at best it is a secondary or tertiary contributant. Bostonians and Kansas Citians at all status levels ranked education far behind income or standard of living in terms of its influence on the amount of prestige people have in their respective communities. There are two facets to this relatively unimpressive evaluation of education. One is that education is not generally perceived as functionally relevant in itself—or, as a young man in Kansas City explained: "Your education just helps you get where you want to go in occupation and income." Looked at this way, education becomes nothing more than a preparatory phase of life, an early step on the road. As such, it is obviously of less importance than the goal, which is a better occupation and/or a bigger income—ultimately, a higher standard of living.

The second element in education's relatively low ranking is the near-universal conviction that while more education is often required for a better occupation, the desired rewards of a higher standard of living do not automatically follow. In other words, "Just because you traveled the road doesn't mean you got where you wanted at the end." For precisely this reason, education is indicted on two counts by people of all status levels: on the one hand, it is too often a deceptive asset, unable to guarantee the higher status it seems to promise; and on the other, its lack, to those who have dropped out too soon, is frequently a devastating handicap. Many in our sample scoffingly referred to education's exaggerated importance, saying for example, "A man can have a good education and still not have a good-paying job; the income he gets is the important thing"; "Education doesn't give much respect unless you've accomplished something; there are a lot of educated people, including Ph.D.'s, running around here without jobs"; or "I've seen men with no education who have been a success, and some completely educated who are no better than bums."

A change widely noted by upper- and middle-status people in our sample is that there has been a great increase recently in the number of college-educated men and women for whom this credential is not pro-ducing the historically anticipated payoff. They lay blame for this on the fact that everybody is going to college now and "there's over-enrollment in different fields"; people "are graduating and can't find jobs," "they can't use their degrees at the sort of work for which they were trained" so "all that education is going to waste."

For all these reasons educational advantages fall far behind financial advantages as an envied symbol of higher status. For every four Bostonians and Kansas Citians in our sample who mentioned more money as the mark of someone higher in status than themselves, only one listed a superior education. Moreover, in most references to more schooling, the envisioned social advantage is not so much the education itself as the acquired credentials that permit entry into a profession—medicine, law, or dentistry, for example—or make possible a position in business management where a great deal more money can be earned, or earned with more autonomy. Indeed, it was quite uncommon to find a better education looked upon as having status value in itself apart from this desired end-product of a better job with a higher income. When people did stress a better education, it was usually linked to attributes of superior intellect and appreciation of the arts; for example, "Maybe a person with a higher education would rank above me—someone who has traveled, read more, has become cultured."

Envied talents or personality traits were as often associated with higher social standing as a better education. "Greater intelligence" ranked first among the attributes mentioned, "more ambition" second. Also intro-duced with significant frequency were assets of physical appearance ("She's beautiful," or "He's better looking than I am"), and skills in social intercourse ("He has a better personality than mine," and "Every-one she comes in contact with has tremendous regard for her—people of great quality seek her out"). Implicit in the praise of these traits and talents is that while they are enviable in and of themselves, they have also been variously useful in acquiring a better education, establishing good connections, "catching a rich husband," and "making lots more money."

A popular explanation for why people are lower in social standing than one's self is that "they had less education." This was suggested as a point of distinction by people from virtually every social level except the lowest. Many a Bostonian or Kansas Citian whose educational credentials included a graduate or professional degree referred to "someone who didn't finish college" or "only has a B.A." as lower in class than themselves—and sometimes sharpened the point by saying of the latter's occupation, "A graduate school education is not required for *that*." Similarly, men and women with bachelor's degrees spoke deprecatingly of "those who had some college but didn't finish—you wouldn't think of them ordinarily as equal in standing." Those who had attended college but had achieved only an associate of arts degree characterized "people who only have a high school education" as having less social status than themselves. A Boston man who earned a certificate in accounting from two years of study at a local business college said, "I know a construction worker who's only a high school graduate; I think people would place him in a lower standing." High school graduates, in turn, said that "high school dropouts would rank lower." And some of the older dropouts considered themselves a rung above those who didn't even start; thus, a 61-year-old man in Kansas City suggested, "Someone with a lower education, maybe only eighth grade, might be in a lower class than I am."

Lack of education was sometimes portrayed as an undeserved, or insurmountable, handicap—"Not having as much education holds 'em back," or "Without an education he had no opportunity to further himself." More commonly, though, people with educational handicaps were also regarded as handicapped by a lack of intelligence ("Some folks just don't have too many brains"), by a lack of ambition ("A lot of people didn't really try"), or by both. The result has been the same: the less educated person "hasn't really gotten marketable skills to my same level," hence cannot earn as much money and has a lower standard of living— and therefore a lower social class position.

What Bostonians and Kansas Citians also revealed, though less consciously, was this "rule": among people who are economic equals, those with the superior educational credentials will use them to express feelings of social superiority. Thus a college graduate living in an area where not everyone has gone so far in school may say, "There are some people in this neighborhood who only have a high school education— they would have a lower social standing." And those who attended one of the nation's prestigious educational institutions will see this as possibly placing them a class or so above those who were not so fortunate. As one said of a neighbor, "He's college, but not Ivy League, and his children aren't either; they went to public school. . . . I think people would say they're in a lower class than my family." So, too, high school graduates typically harbor feelings of superiority toward those of their neighbors and workmates who "did not complete their schooling like I did."

The Status of Education: An Accelerating Function of Years Finished

Among the three major status resources the division of labor, as publicly conceived, is this: income is the end, occupation the means, and education the preparation. Income is everyone's goal, and the more of it the better. Education is a first step toward its attainment—the launching platform, as it were. Education may be deprecated if, following the preparation, there is no income payoff. Occupation is the bridge between education and income, the conversion process; it is what you do with the first to earn the second. This statement of the public view toward education's role is a bit simplified, but not much.

As preparation for jobs and income, education is not a simple continuum with each year of schooling, one through twenty, being equal to every other one in incremental value. Some years of schooling are identified as *completion years*; degrees, diplomas, or credentials are issued to memorialize their finishing. Other years are considered *dropout years*; leaving school during (or following) these years carries connotations of failure, for it means that a phase of schooling that was begun—be it grade school, high school, or college—was not completed. Sociologists who have scaled education as a status ingredient have usually treated it this way, bunching the dropout years together at one scale point, then honoring each completion year with a point of its own. We anticipated patterning of this sort from the public's magnitude estimates but did not find it. Instead, the social standing of education seems a straightforward accelerating function of years of schooling, or—really—of school-leaving age.

We tested fifteen different levels of schooling in our magnitude estimation experiments, most in both the 1970 and 1971 Boston surveys.

The levels ranged from completion of second grade up to having a Ph.D. degree (defined for respondents as four years of graduate study). We did not seek estimates of the status value of professional degrees—the LL.B., M.D., or D.V.M., for example—since these are too closely associated with specific occupations (lawyer, doctor, or veterinarian), and we would not have been able to disentangle the two in our findings. (That is, how much would the rating honor the degree itself and how much the occupation?)

The earlier status estimation researchers had asked about schooling levels as well as about income and occupation. The distribution of years of education changes slowly enough that we cannot expect to find the kinds of changes in the status significance of a particular educational level, from the earliest study by Hamblin to ours, as we find for income. (With much larger samples and exactly comparable methods there might be significant changes, but they would be very small. We believe it takes at least twenty years for there to be substantively interesting changes in the social standing of schooling levels.) Therefore, we analyzed as one set of data not only our own 1970 and 1971 data but also all of the educational status data available from Hamblin's, Schmitt's, and Shinn's studies.

Using dummy variables to represent the different studies, we were able to test how well one slope coefficient would fit all the data sets. The answer was, very well. For the sixty-odd "data points" (that is, mean status scores for a given schooling level in a given study), the multiple correlation was 0.97. Much of the unexplained variation seemed related to the very low—and, even more—to the very high schooling levels.[1] (We have reason to believe that respondents did not always know the significance of graduate degrees such as M.A. or Ph.D.) We weighted the observations by the frequency of each level of schooling; the correlations increased to 0.98 and 0.99, and the residuals were much better behaved. The results from the three other investigators' studies and ours suggest the following status scores for each schooling level compared to the man-in-the-middle's score of 100:

Fourth grade	= 26	Mr. Mim	= 100
Sixth grade	= 35	One year of college	= 106
Eighth grade	= 48	Two years of college	= 123
Ninth grade	= 57	Three years of college	= 141
Tenth grade	= 67	Four years of college	= 160
Eleventh grade	= 78	M.A. (6 years)	= 205
Twelfth grade	= 92	Ph.D. (8 years)	= 250

There seems to be a very close fit in the data sets up through high school graduation. But there is a good deal of variation about what college and advanced degrees might mean. The figures given above for these levels represent our best judgments, made by comparing the different regression equations and their residuals. Comparing 160 as our best estimate for a college degree with occupations in that range, and with the 1971 income amount equivalent in status (about $17,500), makes the estimate seem reasonable. We are less sure about the advanced degrees.

What these results tell us is that the status of schooling increases at an accelerating rate as years of schooling increase. Like the compounding of interest on a savings account, status seems to increase at a fairly constant 16 percent a year from about the seventh grade through college graduation—schooling status doubles for each additional four and a half years of schooling.

In the power law formulation we find an exponent of 2.67—in contrast to the exponents of 1.0 and 0.5 that characterized different ranges of the power law of income and status. We saw there that the marginal status utility of added income decreased the higher above $14,000 the income level was. Here we find that the higher one's schooling, the *more* each year of schooling means. An additional year seems to be worth about five status points at the grade school level, ten points through high school, and about fifteen points for the college years. We estimate the graduate school years are worth about twenty points each.

Our respondents had told us that in their minds education had primarily instrumental value. We would expect, therefore, to find a close relation between the status of different schooling levels and the financial advantages associated with them.

There are two different approaches we can take to answer the question of how educational status is related to economic status. The first stays within our respondents' own frameworks, asking how they equate schooling status and income status. The other approach asks what the relationship is between the educational status levels, as defined in our own and other researchers' studies, and the actual levels of income associated with those educational levels.

In our 1971 survey we asked our respondents to equate income and education levels in terms of status. That is, we asked them to give us an income level equal in status to the status of particular educational levels. Basically the question was, "How much income does a person with status equal to a person with a high school education have to have?" We also asked the reverse; that is, we asked respondents to tell us how much schooling they would expect of a person whose status level was equivalent to that of a given income amount—essentially, "How much education would a person have who is equal in social standing to a person with $12,000 in income?" In psychophysical research this is called *cross-modality matching* and is often used to try to establish a more reliable form of the power law (Stevens, 1971).

We cannot, of course, hope to establish schooling status levels equal to very high incomes, since—as we observed—the range for schooling status is not nearly so wide as that for income status (schooling status seems to have a ceiling of about 250 or less). Therefore, we find that our results become fairly ragged when we get up to the income range of $20,000 to $30,000. Below that, however, our respondents produced quite regular results.

When our respondents estimated what income level was associated with a given educational level, their responses produced a relationship in which the amount of income goes up in approximate proportion to the square of the age at completing school. The income increase expected to match the four years of additional schooling from grammar school to high school graduation is about 65 percent. The income increase expected for the four years from high school graduation to college graduation is about 50 percent.

When the income-education status relationship is looked at the other way around, we find a somewhat different picture. Schooling is expected to increase in proportion to roughly the cube root of the income level. This implies a relationship of education to income, such that income status increases not in proportion to the square of the age at school completion but rather to its cube. Stevens tells us that this kind of discrepancy is a common one in cross-modality matching because of the tendency of respondents to limit the range of whichever dimension they control—income when they are responding by picking income levels equal in status to schooling levels, and schooling levels when they are picking those as equivalents to specified income levels. Stevens suggested that a best estimate of the "true" power function relationship is an average of the two coefficients. In our case that would mean that income would be expected to increase in proportion to the 2.62 power of age at schooling completion; or, phrased the other way around, age at schooling completion would be expected to increase in proportion to the 0.38 power of income.[2]

This 2.62 power, which relates schooling level to predicted income levels of equal status, is roughly the same as the 2.67 power that we found describes the relation of age at school leaving to educational status.

This would be expected, given that the exponent of income status is 1.0 through the range we are talking about. All of this is to say that—at least in dealing with average responses—the people we interviewed were consistent about the interconnections they saw between age at completion of school, schooling status, dollars of income, and income status. Whether they were asked to rate independently the status of schooling and income levels, or asked directly to match schooling levels and income levels in terms of equal status, their answers produced the same pattern of relationships.

That people are consistent in their perceptions of different social resources, status magnitudes, and interrelations is encouraging, but we also want to know how their perceptions of these relations fit with the actual relationships between educational level and income. There are two kinds of data on the income-education association; both produce the same pattern of relationships. We can ask what the median income of men in their thirties and forties at each educational level is, or we can ask what lifetime income is associated with each educational level. The implicit hypothesis is that the status attached to given schooling levels is a function of the realistic observations people make of how much money those in different educational categories actually earn. Certainly our respondents told us over and over again in the open-ended material that that is what is really important about schooling. When we examine the relation of educational status to average earnings we find that the power exponent is 1.5. That is, the status of an educational level increases in proportion to the 1.5 power of the average income of that educational level. It doesn't make much difference whether one thinks in terms of lifetime income or income in the thirties, forties, or early fifties.

Comparing the relationships between educational levels and the actual *versus* the imagined incomes of people at each level, we can conclude that our respondents believe that education's rate of return is greater than it actually is. Using the power log formulas for the relation of actual and imagined incomes to educational status we find, for example, that whereas in actuality people with an eighth grade education earn about three-quarters the income of those who graduated from high school, the expectation of respondents is that they would earn half as much. Similarly, although in fact college graduates earn about 50 percent more than high school graduates, our respondents seem to expect them to earn about 70 percent more.

This anticipation of a higher payoff for educational attainment is not the same thing as believing that there is a high correlation between schooling and income. Our result only allows us to say that people believe that, on the average, the payoff is higher than it really is. It does not allow us to draw any conclusions about perceptions of how surely one can expect those average payoffs. (Certainly from the qualitative responses it would seem that respondents do not believe the correlation between schooling and income is extraordinarily high, because they commonly observe that there are many people who do not seem to be earning the rewards one would expect to be associated with their educational level, and many others who are earning more than would be expected.)

An alternative hypothesis to seeing status of education as associated with expected income gains would suppose that people use education simply as a proxy for the intelligence of different individuals. Is it really the social status attached to different levels of intelligence that is the underlying reality we tap when we ask about the social standing of persons with different educational levels? However, we do not find the kind of simple function this hypothesis suggests we ought. The best functional form for relating measured intelligence (I.Q.) to educational status is an exponential one, but it produces a coefficient of determination of only 0.834. The unevenness of the relationship between educational status and measured intelligence suggests that educational attainment is more appropriately viewed as having a credential effect rather than the effect of a screen for natural abilities. Although it is certainly true that people believe that those with more education are also usually more intelligent, it is unlikely that this belief itself would account for the educational status assigned to particular schooling levels, since—just as people believe that earnings are not always commensurate with educational achievement—they also believe that earnings are not always commensurate with intelligence. Some people earn less than their intelligence "should" produce because they are not willing to put forth enough effort; others earn more because they are willing to put forth extra effort.

There is one other relation of educational status to economic factors that should be mentioned, although the available data do not allow us to explore it very far. This has to do not so much with gains from education in the form of income as with the cost of achieving different educational levels. Economists have observed that the "social costs" of schooling involve both the private costs that individuals assume—tuition and maintenance costs (if they have them) plus foregone earnings that come as a result of going to school rather than working—and public costs, involving subsidization of schooling. We related our data on the educational status levels to data on the social costs of educational levels provided by Hines and others (1970). The coefficient of determination for a power law equation describing this relationship is very high (0.973), so there is clearly a tight relationship between the social cost of different levels of educational attainment and the status assigned to them. The pattern of this relationship is similar to that of income and income status—each additional increment of social cost produces less than a proportionate increment in the social status attached to the respective schooling levels.

Thus, there is a decreasing marginal status utility to education viewed in terms of its cost. More expensive levels of education do not return the same proportion in the way of status as do the less expensive ones. The exponent for the relation between social cost and educational status is 0.6. This means that if one educational level has double the social cost of another, status gain will be only 50 percent. Where the social cost triples, as it does from high school graduation to college graduation, the status gain is not quite double.

Relating the social cost measure to the relationship we have observed for income, we can say that for most people the social costs of education do not return as much in educational status as they would if the equivalent amount of money were added to their incomes. The perception that this is so is perhaps part of the resentment that our respondents expressed over and over again in response to the pressure for college graduation as a credential.

Phrases like those below, which dominated interview responses to our question "How do you get ahead today in the United States?", are illustrative of this view:

> "To get ahead today, you have to have education beyond high school definitely."

> "Social standing depends on whether you go to college or the equivalent thereof."

> "You have to go to college to be respected."

> "People are afraid that if their children don't go to college, they can't find a decent job."

> "Children have to go to college these days in order to be successful. Before, college was a factor in determining prestige. Now it's more a matter of a necessity."

Here, the emphasis is on college as a required passport to a better life; forgotten is the observation that it is no guarantee.

We have no way of making historical comparisons of the status of different educational levels, but certainly we have every reason to expect that the status associated with particular levels has declined over time

and will decline in the future as the distribution of educational attainments changes. Suppose we assume that the public assigns status to
educational levels in terms of the proportion of the population that has
achieved that particular level. The fewer who have achieved it, the
higher the status; the more who have surpassed it, the lower the status.
Assuming the public fits a roughly normal distribution of educational
statuses to the actual distribution of levels of attainment (log normal,
to be exact) we could assign everyone a score in terms of how far above
or below the average each person is in schooling and see what relationship that score has to educational status. We did this for the distribution
of educational statuses in 1971 for men in their thirties, forties, and early
fifties, calculating a standard score for each individual represented by the
place in the normal distribution that the percentile rank for each educational level would represent. Thus, the score could range from roughly
—2 for persons who had less than five years of schooling to almost +2
for those who had some graduate education. In order to develop the
power law relationship here, we then added 3 to each score, giving us
standard scores that range from about 1 to almost 5. These scores correlate very highly with educational status, and they give us a formula
specifying the relationship between the distribution of educational attainments in 1971 and the status attached to them. This formula says that
educational status increases as a 1.5 power of the standard score derived
from the median percentile of the population achieving each educational
level.

Note that this is the same power we find when we relate the median
income (annual or lifetime) of persons at each educational level to their
schooling status.[3] Thus, it is quite likely that, by projecting educational
status backwards and forwards from 1970, we would get the same results
whether we worked with data on income payoffs to education or on the
distribution of educational attainments at a given time. Using the latter
approach, because the data were more readily available, we have calculated the status of education attached to different educational levels
for the years 1940 and 2000 to compare with our 1971 data. Figure 4–1
shows these results for three levels of attainment—grade school graduation, high school graduation, and college graduation. We observe that in
1940 the person with grade school graduation had the same status that
the person with high school graduation had in 1970. The 1940s high
school graduate had almost the same status as a college graduate in
1971—a status about equivalent to that of a person with three years of
college. The college graduate had very high status indeed in 1940,
roughly equivalent to a person with a master's degree in 1970. We project

FIGURE 4-1

Estimates of Changes in Social Standing
of Grade School, High School, and College Graduation
from 1940 to 2000

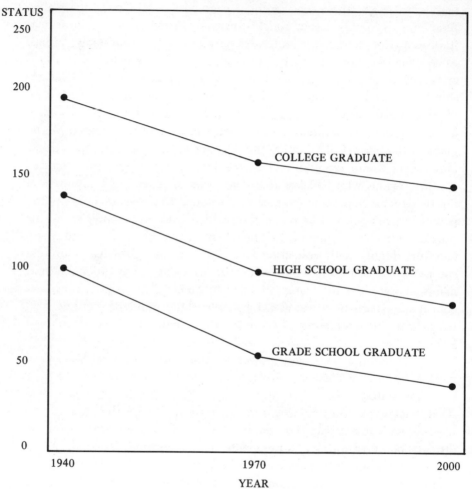

that the 1970 college graduate's status had declined to about 78 percent
of its 1940 level. High school graduate status has declined to 66
percent, and grade school graduate status has declined to 49 percent.

Because the distribution of educational attainments is not projected
to change as much from 1970 to 2000 as it did in the previous thirty years,
the changes in educational status would not be expected to be as great.
By the year 2000 the high school graduate's status will have declined to

85 percent of its 1970 level, the college graduate's to 89 percent, and the grade school graduate's to 76 percent. In the whole sixty-year period, then, the college graduate's status will have declined to 70 percent of its pre-World War II level, the high school graduate's to 56 percent of its pre-war level, and the grade school graduate's to 37 percent of its pre-war level. Thus, in two generations' time, there will have been a very marked devaluation of educational credentials, a devaluation that our respondents spoke about with strong and generally negative feelings in their open-ended comments.

The lower the level of educational attainment, the more rapidly that attainment loses status over this sixty-year period. In our example, grade school loses status at an average rate of 1.6 percent a year, high school at an average rate of 0.9 percent a year, and college at an average rate of 0.6 percent a year.

These projections are based on an assumption that the distribution of educational statuses is tailored to an implicit log normal distribution that does not change. However, if we derived these projections of educational status in past and present from income data, we would reach more or less the same conclusions, since the inequality of the income distribution by education level has not declined markedly in the past, nor is it expected to do so in the future.

Thus we can conclude—as in the case of income status—that as long as the relationship between education and income remains unchanged, with constant inflation of the amount of education required to achieve a given relative place in the income distribution, the inequality of educational status will not change.

This suggests that, overall, the variances of all three of our status variables have probably not changed over the course of the previous half-century, nor—given existing projections of educational, occupational, and income distributions—are they likely to change in the future. This conclusion must obviously remain extremely tentative. If, in the future, comparable data on perceptions about educational, income, and occupational status are collected, it will be possible to test the extent to which their status is unchanging.

Under this assumption, the question of changing inequality of educational attainment appears in quite a different light than under the standard assumption, which looks at the amount of variation in years of schooling. According to this approach, inequality in educational attainment (as measured by the coefficient of variation) declined to 70 percent of its 1940 level by 1970, and by the year 2000 it would be only half of its 1940 level. But on our assumption that people tailor the distribution of educational status in a basically unchanging way to their general im-pressions of the distribution of educational attainment, the degree of inequality of educational status would be essentially unchanged.

It would be interesting to know how much people take into account one another's ages when they judge the status due them on the basis of their schooling. If they evaluate individuals in terms of the educational distribution of their particular age cohorts, then there would be no loss of status as younger generations achieve more education. But if this is not the case, than in the course of the forty years following their cohorts' effective completion of schooling, individuals would experience status losses in the educational area comparable to those diagrammed in Figure 4–1. We have not probed enough into what must be a very com-plex interaction between an individual's status characteristics, age, and historical cohort.

It should be true, however, that if we take age into account as it interacts with income, occupation, and education, schooling status has the most influence on a person's general social standing when that person is young, and that it loses impact as time goes on under the general rule that if it does not pay off in more contemporary characteristics, it is less and less relevant to one's actual social status. It is in this sense that we speak of education as a platform for achieving adult status.

CHAPTER 5

Class as Social Identity and Life Style

INCOME, education, occupation, race, religion, and ethnicity do not exhaust the factors that people associate with the idea of social class. Other matters—family background (the family's social and cultural level in previous generations, not ethnic origin), how people spend their money and where they choose to live, personal appearance, taste, manners, "breeding," and the image created—all are recognized as part of the picture. The ideas about social class we will subsume under this category of social identity and life style are highly varied. By their very nature, identity and life style are complex patterns of many small traits and behaviors. Different people seize on different aspects of these complex *gestalts* to express their understanding that class has to do with how people live and who they and others define them as being, as well as (or as a consequence of) the resources that also differentiate them.

Awareness of these factors of identity and style is found more frequently in the upper echelons of American society, but not there alone. For example, in response to our question, "What is involved in social class?" several blue-collar Bostonians and Kansas Citians invoked the following criteria: "the places you go to," "what you wear and how you dress," "the car you drive," "how much time you have for recreation and what you do," "your environment—your cultural interests," and "belonging to a prominent family." White-collar and professional men and women specified all these factors and more: "It's a matter of books and the reading you do"; "It's the way people discriminate on family heritage"; "It means a person's ability to produce and attain"; "What school you've gone to or your children have gone to"; and "It's upbringing—whether you have couth or are uncouth."

A Boston suburban woman, once a debutante and still a Junior Leaguer, rendered what was probably the most exhaustive delineation of "what social class means":

> "I would suppose social class means where you went to school and how far. Your intelligence. Where you live. The sort of house you live in. Your general background, as far as clubs you belong to, your friends. To some degree the type of profession you're in—in fact, definitely *that*. Where you send your children to school. The hobbies you have. Skiing, for example, is higher than the snowmobile. The clothes you wear . . . all of that. These are the externals. It can't be [just] money, because nobody ever knows that about you for sure."

Class as Snobbery and Cliques

For many, what is central—and critical—about social class are its psychological consequences. Indeed, the verbalizations about class most richly tinged with emotion were those that referred to the snobberies engendered by status-related differences in income, education, family background, occupation, and associations. This is how "class" really hits home, in public and individual awareness of "higher-ups looking down on the lower-downs." Over and over our respondents said: "Social class is mostly snobbery"; "It's people with their noses in the air"; and "It means that some folk think they're better than others." One man in Kansas City pinpointed it: "When you think of social classes, money is involved. . . . The people making a lot of money think they are a lot higher socially than a guy making $7,000 a year." In such behavior patterns and attitudes, people often find their proof of the existence of class:

> "Of course, there's class. Look around you. A man driving a Cadillac feels he can thumb his nose at me because I'm driving an old V.W."

> "You know there's class when you're in a department store and a well-dressed lady gets treated better."

> "A person who earns more dollars doesn't associate with people who earn less. . . . Unless you have dough, don't bother to speak to people who do."

> "Most people look down on the poor like me because you have to live so shabby and can't help yourself."

Plainly, the snubs Americans deal one another constitute an especially painful aspect of what many think is social class.

A closely related aspect of class, often cited as one of its irritants and as proof of its existence, is "cliquishness," or "people trying to be exclusive." Women seem especially conscious of this. A Kansas City cement contractor's wife said:

> "When I think of social class I think of cliques. From childhood on, people seem to have friends in about the same class as they are. If you're poor, you don't hobnob with the well-to-do, and if you're educated, you seem to choose others like you are. If you're in a club or church, there's cliques there, too."

A Boston suburban woman from the white-collar world said:

> "Class is always something you're aware of, especially here in Lynnfield. All the groups are divided, organized according to social status, with people spending half their time worrying about who to keep out."

Further up the ladder, one finds women who have recently arrived in the upper-income world complaining bitterly about the exclusions practiced by those with greater incomes or more illustrious lineage than their own. Thus, a Kansas City woman reported:

> "Is there class? I've seen this: you take the older rich in Kansas City. They belong to certain clubs you wouldn't get into even if you had the money. The membership is handed down from generation to generation."

And a woman in Boston, transplanted from the Midwest, said:

> "New England is one of the most insidious places. If you can't prove your lineage or enough dollars, you can't make it in some of their groups. That North Shore, blue-blood, moneyed cult, full of Mayflower-ancestor worshippers—that's the extreme of trying to keep out people."

All of which is to say that among the many meanings that social class has for Americans, one of the most intensely personal is "some people keeping others out"—out of their cliques, their clubs, even, sometimes, their church groups.

Not everyone in our sample talked of social status groups as artificial or punitively exclusive. Many perceived them as flowing rather naturally, indeed inevitably, from different enthusiasms, different life styles, and different conceptions about one's role in society. A Kansas City carpenter made the point this way:

> "I'm a carpenter and I won't fit with doctors and lawyers or in country club society. We have different interests and want to do different things. We don't always understand each other. People are that way—some people fit together and others don't. I hate to say there are classes, but it's just that people are more comfortable with people of like backgrounds."

And a Boston filling-station operator echoed him:

> "Your own social class is the people on the same plane of living as yourself. It's the people that you have respect for, the people you associate with, work with, and have fun with. . . . People like to be with people like themselves, you know."

Many other men and women in both cities emphasized this aspect of social class—that classes are made up of like-minded people who are comfortable with one another, who "have the same aims or goals, and ideals"; "are in the same circumstances with similar living habits"; "are the same in their thinking—thinking along the same ways"; "have similar ideas, experiences, and environments"; and "come from similar backgrounds . . . live in the same—or same type of—neighborhoods." Most touchingly and optimistically, a Kansas City accountant said, "Social class means the things people have in common: social standing, the common bond!"

But, far from signifying universal brotherhood, social class as a common bond means that the members of a class sense they share an identical, differentiating position on a ladder of social inferiors, equals, and superiors; standing on this ladder is based on who accepts whom. This shared position, as perceived by the Boston and Kansas City public, features intimacy of socializing in which acceptance is informal and implicit:

> "[Class means] the circle of friends you have, the circle you travel in. . . . That's sort of determined by how much money you have to socialize with, to entertain with."

> "It means the people you associate with—usually because of your economic level and theirs, really. . . . It's your friends and close associates."

> "It's who you are, and who you know. . . . It's the class of people you associate with. . . . Some people just do not associate with others."

> "[Social class] refers to just the general social set of peers among whom a person is well accepted."

A shared position also involves formal organizational participation, membership in which confers an official stamp of social acceptance:

> "It's the clubs and organizations a person belongs to . . . [along with] his friends."

> "It means the kind of organization [people] are active in . . . and how one's accepted or not."

Class as Social Identity

Almost as a summation of all these other factors and considerations, we found our respondents saying that social class refers to the status judgments that people pass on one another; that social class is crucially a matter of reputation and images, both of groups and of individuals:

> "[Social class] is how the person is viewed. . . . It depends on how he presents himself. It's mostly economical, but secondarily aesthetic and cultural."

> "It's the prestige society gives you."

> "It means people judge you by the crowds you hang around with."

> "It exists in people's minds more than anything else. I think other people see you in a social class, but it exists mostly in images."

> "It's how you are considered socially—what your family is in the public eye."

> "I'd say it [social class] means how people stand compared to each other."

> "It's all in terms of the opinion of others; as [you are] seen by others."

In this view social class is almost an image of an image, but also something inescapable. As one Bostonian put it: "It's [all] because of standards set up by society. . . . You're put in a class whether you want to be or not."

Class as Life Style

In their efforts to explain their understanding of what social class is all about, our respondents often drew attention to variations in how people used their resources to construct particular life styles. They produced vivid symbols of social differences by drawing attention to differences in leisure-time activities and personal styles which build upon the more basic differences in socio-economic resources. In addition to talking of fairly straightforward differences in level of consumption symbolized by the kinds of housing or automobiles different classes afford, they also drew attention to consumption activities that involve subtler combinations of taste and wherewithal.

Travel and recreation. Of the many uses to which money can be put in creating a particular life style, expensive recreation is the most deeply envied—more so, indeed, than buying nice houses, fancy cars, or other high-priced versions of necessities. When someone is observed spending money for frequent vacations, traveling beyond the borders of the United States, staying at reputedly high-priced resorts, buying second homes, yachts, country club memberships, and season tickets to professional sports or cultural events, this seems to offer especially convincing evidence that "they have a lot more money than I do," possibly even "no money worries at all." Beyond this, it seems to demonstrate that "they really know how to enjoy life."

Among the people we interviewed in Boston and Kansas City, at least one out of three in each social class introduced one form or another of expensive (and envied) recreation as a sign of superior status. The college-educated referred to acquaintances who "own yachts and travel around the world" or "belong to a country club and I don't." Comfortable Americans cited relatives or others who "get away four times as much as I do" or "have season tickets to the Chiefs' games [Kansas City's professional football team]." And Americans who were just getting along, told of "this couple we know who go to Canada a lot in the summer. They're hockey fans, too, and go to every Bruins' home game [in Boston] during the winter." Or "My sister whose husband's a doctor—she's got seven children, but she can leave them with a sitter and go off to Europe or Bermuda without worrying."

Travel, if frequent or wide-ranging, is especially impressive to Americans of average means and/or narrow experience. When they see people who "go skiing every weekend in the winter," "go to Jamaica instead of New York for a weekend," "go to Europe every summer," or "take a world cruise every three or four years," they are awed by the degree of freedom from routine and schedule, as well as from financial worries, that this implies. Being able to "do things on the spur of the moment—just take off whenever they want" truly symbolizes a carefree existence in monetary terms. Traveling abroad, in turn, evokes images of a cosmopolitan, sophisticated outlook. Cultural superiority is symbolized; it seems to say that the traveler is already comfortable in such settings or is in the process of becoming so.

This is not to say that travel is the universal preference among expensive recreations. Nor, for that matter, is having season tickets for athletic or cultural events to everyone's taste. Indeed, very few things that fall into the category of recreation requiring more money evoke unreserved envy. "Exclusive club memberships," for example, arouse antagonism as well as respect, since they perform a socially dichotomizing function: they explicitly separate the "ins" from the "outs," dividing those who can afford to belong and have the connections and credentials from those who have neither credentials nor money, or only the latter. Expensive resorts and restaurants more subtly stratify and dichotomize people according to individual self-conceptions about "where we belong." Speaking of this, a young Kansas City blue-collar worker's wife said, "My husband's boss is in a higher class. . . . He makes a lot more money, and he and his wife go to fancy places where we would not feel comfortable." "Leading an active social life," "going to a lot of parties," and "doing a lot of small group entertaining" also aroused mixed emotions among Middle-American housewives. This was how they imagined the life style of women of superior status to be different from their own; yet—while they admitted it seemed pleasurable enough from the standpoint of being a guest—for the hostess, they said, "It's a lot of effort and work, and I wouldn't want all those obligations."

For many a Bostonian and Kansas Citian of modest means and aspirations, the most envied form of expensive recreation was nothing more lavish than "having a second house where they can go away and just have wonderful vacations in their own place." This suggests pleasure without pretense or undue effort. It symbolizes getting away from it all, self-indulgence, non-involvement, and no concern with pleasing anyone other than one's self. It is the laziest of costly leisures, the simplest of sybaritisms.

Matters of "couth" and "culture." Negative judgment of self-presentation and behavior played an important role in distinguishing people who our respondents characterized as lower than themselves in social standing. Just as lower educational attainment, even when not accompanied by a lower living standard, was often used to make such distinctions, the more personal and behavioral judgment of "less culture" was also often used. In fact, it was nearly as common for our respondents to distinguish themselves from those "lower in class" by referring to differences in manner and motivation, as for them to describe differences in material well-being. The differences in manner and motivation that were invoked amount, in the broadest sense, to differences in behavioral standards; variously these were differences in cultural level, refinement, taste, speech, grooming, manifest intelligence, morals, values, characters, and ambition—all those things. And, further, it can be said that all were mentioned by men and women from every status level as points of distinction between themselves and those of lower station. Thus, people of lower working-class standing were hardly less inclined than the college-educated to say, "Their language isn't as good as mine," or "They don't dress as well," or "Their manners are not what they should be." Differences in emphasis may be noted, though, and these point to the specific behavioral standards that each group takes most pride in as a mark of its superiority to the groups below.

The aspects of manner and motivation to which men and women of Upper-American standing gave most attention were breadth of interest and information, familiarity with the arts, community contribution, and comfort in social interaction with people like themselves. Thus, the Bostonian and Kansas Citians of this level in our sample repeatedly said of persons lower in class standing: "They're less well-informed," "Their interests are less broad," "They're not as well read," "They know nothing about the arts," "He doesn't have as good a command of the English language," "They engage in less socializing—they're less active in the community," and "They have a narrower set of acquaintances with people who get things done."

Middle Americans emphasized character more than culture when judging themselves socially above others. Having "good morals" and "initiative" were the prime virtues they credited themselves with in contrast to those of lower standing. They also placed great store on cleanliness, courtesy, propriety, conformity with mainstream standards in dress and personal appearance, and having well-behaved children. This was especially true of the way Middle Americans just getting along differentiated themselves from people of the classes below. Our respondents at this level had the following sorts of denunciations to make of people "lower in social class" than themselves:

"That would be people with—well, low morals. . . . They gamble and drink and don't take care of their families."

"I'd think they were lower if they didn't keep their houses up, if they weren't very clean about their house and their person."

"They don't show the common courtesies, such as language and respect. They would talk rough."

And they offered specific illustrations:

"We know a couple who is divorced. They take drugs. The wife is on ADC.* They don't care. When people have an 'I don't care' attitude, people look down on them. I know I do."

"A lady I know has seven kids. She just sits around drinking coffee and smoking cigarettes all day. Her husband has a job, but she won't work. . . . Their place is going to pieces."

"A lot has to do with the way a person talks and dresses. I see a woman at the store who shops with an old baby carriage. She's short, wears long dresses, pulls her hair back tight. I'd say she's lower in class than me."

* Aid to Dependent Children.

Similarly scornful judgments of people "below you in class" were made by respondents from the lowest stratum. A Kansas City white woman of this status said, "I know some people whose manners are not what they should be—I wouldn't want to be seen with them." And a black man in Boston echoed her: "I can look at their appearance—if they don't dress well, I don't mix with them."

Judgments from Initial Impressions

Among all our questions about how Americans place each other socially, the one on which answers strayed furthest from a focus on income was, "How would you tell about the social class standing of someone with whom you were not personally acquainted—say someone you read about in the newspaper, saw in the store, or encountered at a public gathering . . . someone who just moved into your neighborhood or came to work where you are employed?" Our respondents interpreted this to mean, "How do you judge people on first meeting?" They answered by saying, in fact or in effect, "By their speech, appearance, dress, manner, actions, and who they associate with." They did not imply that occupation, income, or education were irrelevant to judgments on class; rather, they seemed to be saying that such information was not imperative and that, in any event, the judgment embraces other attributes and assets. Ultimately, as a Kansas City woman suggested, "It's in a feeling you have when you see someone . . . just looking at a person sometimes gives you the clue."

This belief that speech, appearance, manner, and actions are clues to social standing was found at all socio-economic levels to almost equal extent. It was stated as frequently by Middle Americans just getting along as by men and women from the college-educated professional and business classes in our sample, and no less often by people of the very highest status than by people of the very lowest. A Boston woman almost in poverty recited this list of criteria for "telling about someone's social class":

> I would judge by the area they live in, the way they talk, the way they dress, the way they look, the way they act, and the people they socialize with; also by their morals."

A Kansas City blue-collar worker's young wife, just getting along, said:

> "You tell by their dress—the clothes they wear, and how expensive they look. Also by what they said to me, when they tell you about places they've been, where they shop, and what they think is a bargain. . . .

Also by talking to them you see how schooled they are. . . . If I happened
to see them moving in, I'd judge by what they moved into their houses."

A Boston woman, living in comfortable Middle-American suburban style,
said:

"You tell from their manner, dress, apparel. It is from what you see or
hear, from what they seem to be, their manner of speech, and their
clothes—if they're used to buying at Bonwit Teller's, for example. It's
their way of getting along with people. There is a saying here, 'You can
take the woman out of Dorchester [an older, lower-income section of
Boston proper], but not Dorchester out of the woman.' The only bad
thing is that you can see someone in a Cadillac, and that only tells you
what they're aspiring to, not what they are."

Then there was the Boston man of success-elite status who airily
announced that he assessed people's class standing "by their speech,
clothing, possessions, and other non-essentials."

Implicit in the way these individuals eagerly, and in detail,
described how they classify other people at first meeting is the fact that
Americans generally, regardless of class level, are almost continually
judging each other as socially superior, inferior, or equal. Also implicit is
the notion that speech, grooming, and "manner" are contributing factors
to individual status as well as being critical in its communication to the
audience of others.

Speech as a clue and contributor to social class standing includes
diction, accent, vocabulary, grammar, conversational topics, and information imparted. It was the most widely singled out "way that you tell
someone's social class at first meeting." The college-educated would
describe this as a matter of "listening to their diction and speaking
style," "what kind of English they use," "the subjects they choose to
speak about," "what a man says as well as how he says it," and "the
articulation of speech—accents, grammar—and even more subtle, the
manner and attitudes." Middle Americans displayed equal enthusiasm
for speech as a status clue, saying: "A man's vocabulary and usage are
the main thing"; "Speech gives an idea of education"; "I judge by what
they say about themselves"; and "The first thing that impresses me is
people's speech." Some even went so far as to say, "Really, the first time
a person opens his mouth, you can tell."

If speech is indeed so important a sign of class, it is because it is
believed to tell, through both style and content, so many things about
the speaker: level of intelligence, education, values, standards, aspirations, and knowledge. Plainly, the American public would like to believe

that all these things count, along with material well-being, in determining where any given individual ranks in the status structure.

Appearance as an indication of class includes expensiveness of apparel, taste in its choice, grooming, physical form, bearing, stance, neatness, and cleanliness. Upper-status Bostonians and Kansas Citians reported time and again that they relied on all these things, especially apparel and bearing ("how they hold themselves"), plus "manner," to determine whether someone newly met was "one of us." Manner in this context would embrace both style in social relations and manners as a measure of breeding. What upper-status people seem to look for is not so much friendliness per se as general ease in social situations, the projection of self-confidence, grace in interaction with strangers, and the matching of behavior (including speech) to the occasion.

Middle Americans were no less likely to use appearance as a status indicator; those of comfortable living standard displayed a heightened interest in neatness and discretion in dress as a way of dividing the world into categories of acceptable and unacceptable. They made observational judgments like this one, from a woman in Kansas City:

> "I don't really approve of doing it, but I still judge people by their appearance. Yesterday I saw a huge, crude-looking woman walking along the street—and she could have been the nicest person in the world—but the way she looked, with all of her make-up and her clothes, was just terrible."

Men and women just getting along, in turn, seemed especially concerned with cleanliness and specific grooming features, such as "fingernails that aren't dirty," as evidence of personal pride and the desire for acceptance as people of solidly Middle-American status: "If their hands are clean—and especially fingernails clean—you can tell they have some pride in themselves and the way they look."

The way people dress as a clue to social place is undergoing change. It does not, for example, hold the same importance as a short decade ago. It seems a recognized fact at all class levels that one consequence of the changes in social ideals and personal habits that took place during the latter 1960s and early 1970s was that "clothes can fool you now," that apparel has been democratized to a certain extent. Partly this democratization reflects the fact that higher-status people are allowing themselves to appear in public in more relaxed, informal, non-differentiating clothing than was their wont in generations past. And partly it reflects the fact that people from many different status levels use apparel to signify or identify with life styles that are not intimately linked with social class—

that, indeed, are often designed to bridge the gap between high and low or express defiance of conventional standards. Many people in our sample started to say that "how people dress is one way you can tell social class," then reversed themselves, concluding, "No, I guess that's not a good way to tell any more." Addressing this problem, a Boston man said:

> "It's very tough today to [judge social class]. Ten years ago if someone had a neat haircut, shined shoes, clean nails, and so forth, he was in a better class. Today, it doesn't hold true. A guy can be worth a couple of million and have long hair and dungarees and you would never know. There is a more casual environment. A good example was Mrs. Henry Ford's picture on the cover of *Life* where she was wearing a Detroit Lions jersey."

This more casual environment notwithstanding, what people wear still makes a significant difference in the interpretation of their place in society. A Boston suburban housewife of modest income observed, "When I go shopping in Hingham, I see a lot of women that have their own new station wagons, and even in the supermarket they're all dressed up with expensive clothes. They're the ones who live in those big houses along Route 228. They probably have a lot of money in the bank and can go away for a nice long vacation in the summer."

"Who they associate with" suggests reference to the social standing of the people that an individual associates with regularly and comfortably. Bostonians and Kansas Citians in our sample alluded to this clue in multiple ways when listing the things they would take into account in guessing at someone's social class standing. One example was "the social situation in which I met him"; this alone might suffice, if indeed the situation were social, as a clue to "who they associate with." Another was whose parties people attend: "If they were written up for attending a fancy party, you'd know they're wealthy because of where they were." Or, whom they entertain: "You'd judge from the type of visitors they have." Who their neighbors are: "The area of town where they live has a lot to tell you." What clubs they belong to: "If I met the man at the Kan-Citian Club, I would assume that he was upper-middle class or among the very well-to-do." And, of course: "You'd want to know who his friends are." All these things—parties, in-home visits, neighbors, club memberships, friends—seem to suggest to many what social class is ultimately about; it is, in simplest formulation, a matter of who accepts whom as social peer.

In sum, the way people we interviewed responded to our question on "how you tell someone's social class" has affirmed that the social element in class is very important. In paying so much attention to speech, appearance, manner, and associates, and by comparison so little attention to income, occupation, and years of schooling, they have not only indicated that in certain circumstances the former variables must serve as representatives of the latter, but they have also made it clear that these, too, are dimensions of status—"ingredients," as it were, of the individual's place in the status order. Also, what we seem to have learned from the attention Boston and Kansas City people gave to the individual as speaker, physical being, companion, and maintainer of certain standards in upkeep of self and property is this: Americans *want* status to involve these considerations; they want standing to derive from a social evaluation of the whole being, with less attention paid to money than they believe it currently receives and more attention paid to practically everything else.

CHAPTER 6

The Role of Ethnicity*

ETHNIC DIFFERENCES, perhaps even more than differences of class, have provided a ready and colorful pool of traits from which Americans have traditionally drawn to create stereotypic images of various groups on the national scene. Some respondents in Boston and Kansas City identified certain ethnic groups as classes unto themselves; most, however, did not. Instead, they treated these ethnic ties as either status assets or liabilities (assets, that is, for persons white, Anglo-Saxon, and Protestant, and liabilities in varying degree for persons of other color, ancestry, and religion). Respondents who assigned greatest importance to ethnic identification, religious affiliation, and race were most often those who might consider themselves "victims." Thus it was Jews, Irish Catholics, Italian Catholics, and blacks in our sample who were most inclined to bring up these factors, as well as academics and high-income political liberals expressing disapproval of the victimization involved.

When respondents contended that classes in America are formed along racial, religious, and ethnic lines they would put forth their argument in phrases like this: "I think in this country social classes are obviously along income, ethnic, and religious lines," or "Blacks are a distinct class, but they are trying to move up. . . . WASPS, Catholics, poor, middle, rich—they're all classes." When respondents thought of these divisions more as status handicaps—barriers, as it were, to individual advance—than as class groupings, they would acknowledge their importance by saying, "You find people restricted from certain areas, such

---

* This chapter was written by Diane Barthel, who was responsible for analyzing all the responses about ethnicity in our survey.

as clubs, schools, and business positions, because of their race, religion, and heritage." Awareness of these handicaps and the fact that people are thus judged for ancestry or religion (and often thereby excluded from clubs, jobs, and schools) was offered sometimes as a sure sign that "we still have class in the United States."

Some Middle Americans in our sample (although by no means a majority) suggested that members of certain racial and/or ethnic minority groups would generally be looked on as lower in social standing than themselves. They made this suggestion in various ways. Sometimes they cited a specific person of their acquaintance (as a Boston man said, "A black person who works where I do [would be lower]—at present he's at the low end of the pay scale for our particular business"), without necessarily indicating that it was the minority group identification that accounted for the imputed lower standing. In other instances, a whole group would be singled out and certain behavioral patterns characterized, as a Kansas City man remarked of "hillbillies": "The people I know [who are lower] are from the Ozarks. . . . They're sloppy in work and dress and lack education." For the most part this unsympathetic positioning was found among Middle Americans just getting along, especially among those toward the lower edge of that category, both in income and in level of material well-being; of course, for them to be "regular" Americans, and thus not identified as disadvantaged, operates quite clearly as a point of pride.

Higher-status people in our sample displayed, in scattered instances, quite a different kind of pride in themselves relative to racial and ethnic minority groups: a pride in being morally above prejudice. They took the high road of being tolerant of group differences. A Boston woman of the college-educated professional world exemplified this attitude when she said, "Puerto Ricans dress in gaudy colors and are considered by most to be lower class. . . . Most people don't consider that they have a different life style." Thus did she and others like her advocate understanding of the disadvantaged situation of minority groups and hence sympathy with their plight, saying: "You must realize that minority groups have problems—they are caught within their groups because of their appearance, education, and maybe language barriers." Feeling thus, this group of high-status respondents disassociated themselves from the wider public's judgment by announcing, "A lot of people think the Negroes, Puerto Ricans, Jews, and Italians are a lower class than we are, but I don't."

When our Boston and Kansas City respondents commented in various contexts that "the Jews own everything" or "the Irish drink too much," they were repeating stereotypes that seem to have existed throughout our national history. Such labels, while not always so readily pronounced, have served to provide one way for sorting out and dealing with a most diverse population. Yet, and in part because of the often derogatory nature of such stereotypes, ethnic group identification has largely been discouraged. Indeed, it was widely held that all ethnic group members should come together and work to realize a new identification with America because, after all, was not America the melting pot society? But various forms of ethnic conflict, ranging from newspaper campaigns to church-burnings to political movements, have accompanied whatever melting has taken place, and from such confrontations alternative ethnic ideologies have emerged to challenge the dominant assimilationist model.

These alternate ideologies enjoyed a resurgence in the 1960s and early 1970s with assertions of identity and pride among blacks, Chicanos, Orientals, and Indians, and finally among the "white ethnics." The revival of ethnicity quickly became a popular topic both in the mass media and in academic publications.

While no one statement can hope to express what all Americans feel is—and should be—the role of ethnicity in American life, we can explore how our Boston and Kansas City respondents assessed the present extent and significance of ethnicity in general, its importance in determining people's life chances, and their attitudes toward its contribution to the shaping of their own life experiences. From these observations we can then draw some conclusions as to the relative strength and social structural basis of these two major ideologies—that will here be termed the *melting pot* and the *ethnic revival* ideologies—and then speculate both on the significance of their present popularity and their possible future levels and bases of support.

Ethnicity and Class in Boston

Boston has long enjoyed popularity as a favorite research site among historians and sociologists interested in the meshing of class and ethnic structures. The social dominance of the Boston Brahmins, the influx of the Irish and their subsequent rise through politics, the Italian community in the North End, the blacks of Roxbury, and the Jews of Mattapan all demonstrate a social pattern emerging from the interaction of ethnicity with class and status. In Boston Area Surveys of 1969 and 1970 and the Social Standards Survey of 1971, a consistent pattern emerged in terms of religious, ethnic, and racial differences by class. First, considering religion alone, Jews had the largest representation in the middle and upper classes, as compared to Protestants, whose numbers were more evenly spread out among the working, lower-middle, and upper-middle classes, and Catholics, who were heavily concentrated in the working and lower-middle classes. Similarly, in income ranking, Catholics clustered heavily around the middle $8,000 to $14,999 category; Jews were largely in the $15,000 to $24,999 range, with almost 20 percent falling in the $25,000-and-over bracket; and Protestants again showed more of an even curve throughout the middle- and upper-income brackets. As for neighborhood status, 60.8 percent of Catholics in 1969 lived in working-class neighborhoods, while 58.1 percent of Jews lived in what were considered "neat" or "desirable" neighborhoods (as scored by interviewers). Protestants had the largest percentage (17.2) living in the highest-ranking neighborhoods; otherwise they again fell largely between the two other groups with 4.5 percent in the worst-quality neighborhoods, 36.9 percent in working-class neighborhoods, and 41.4 percent in desirable neighborhoods.

These religious differentials can be further broken down according to ethnicity. Clearly, as Lenski and many others have indicated, Protestants must be divided according to race. Blacks in our sample were concentrated in lower-status neighborhoods and had a mean income of approximately $7,000 in 1970. Twenty-four percent had not more than eighth grade education, and very few more had a high school diploma. Significant differences also appeared between the Irish and Italians. While both had a mean income in the $8,000 to $14,999 range in 1970 (with working to lower-middle class ranking as an average), high school education, and residences in working-class neighborhoods, the Irish were less concentrated and more represented in the upper reaches of the classifications, particularly in income and class. In educational level they resembled the white Protestants more than the Italians. While class position produces the widest spread among groups, educational level shows more convergence around the high school diploma, except for the rather surprisingly similar curves of the blacks and Catholics of Canadian origin on the lower side of the scale and the high representation of Jews in the college and higher degrees categories. In sum, while there is some convergence among different groups on each characteristic, a more complicated and less consistent pattern emerges for ethnicity than when we look at religion alone. Ethnicity appears to have some effect in determining income, level of education, neighborhood, and social status in general. While at this point and with these data we cannot untangle what effect is due to ethnicity and what to class, we would simply stress that ethnicity does appear to be tied into the system of social stratification in the Boston area.

Ethnicity and Class in Kansas City

We now turn to quite a different case, for Kansas City's image as the "Heart of America" seems a far cry from the ethnic hodge-podge that is Boston. Here the white Protestants, mostly of northern European origin, clearly dominate in numbers, with smaller populations of northern European Catholics, Italians, Jews, Chicanos, and blacks. The Kansas City Survey picked up rather small numbers of these three last groups, but some tentative conclusions can be drawn.

The most striking finding, in comparison to the discrepancies in Boston, is the similarity of the Catholics to the Protestants on most of the measures of class and status. Both groups have a majority of their members in the $8,000 to $14,999 income bracket; most are high school graduates, have middle-class status, and live in middle-class neighborhoods. Chicanos and blacks, on the other hand, remain clearly separate from the mainstream pattern, being mostly in the lower class and living in lower-class neighborhoods, having less than high school education, and having incomes falling largely in the $2,000 to $5,999 bracket. Indeed, Chicanos and blacks ranked so low they often seemed completely out of the major status system. As for Catholics, recognition was made of a difference between Italians—who were considered among the lowest-ranking ethnic groups—and Catholics from northern European countries, who were accepted for having the same basic cultural background. The structural similarity of the Catholics to the Protestants may indeed have something to do not only with the question of national origin but also with structural conditions, such as comparative group numbers, conditions of emigration, and opportunities and level of competition found in the city at the time of immigration and after.

This similarity in class position, however, is not reflected in friendship choices, for—when asked to name their five closest friends—Kansas City residents overwhelmingly named people of their own religion (Table 6-1). An average of about 65 percent of the Protestants and Catholics indicated that *each* of their five friends was of the same religion. Among blacks and Chicanos, the percentage stayed in the 90 to 100 percent range. These segregated networks are reflected in the low

TABLE 6-1

Ethnicity of Up to Five Friends Named
According to Respondent's Ethnicity: Kansas City, 1972

| Friends' Ethnicity | Respondent (N = 171) | | | | |
| | Minority | | Majority | | |
	Chicano (N = 3)	Black (N = 39)	Catholic (N = 26)	Protestant (N = 103)	Total
Minority					
Chicano	12	0	0	6	18
Black	0	177	1	4	182
Majority					
Catholic	1	0	67	30	98
Protestant	0	7	35	312	354
Total	13	184	103	352	652

$\chi^2 = 1,201.76$; $p < .001$ (d.f. = 9).

rate of intermarriage in Kansas City, with less than 4 percent of marriages involving two people of different faiths. The networks probably stem at least in part from the separate system of parochial schools and colleges attended by many Catholics, in which many of their longer-lasting friendships appear to be formed.

Interestingly, when asked about their friends' ethnicity, a number of people expressed some confusion over what could be considered relevant criteria, and a variety of ethnic labels resulted. Many choose, first of all, to emphasize the fact that their friends were American, and what more could be important? One woman suggested that to raise the question of ethnic background was getting too personal. Others chose to combine the American label with religious preference, as with one man who described his four friends as "American, American, American, and American Catholic." Specific religious denomination was more commonly known in Kansas City than was national background, which may suggest that it is more relevant to know if a person is Methodist or Baptist than German or Scottish. Finally, more exotic labels *did* appear, such as "middle-class suburbanite."

In general, Kansas City residents thought largely of racial and religious differences, while their Boston counterparts were equally at ease in discussing national differences. Yet in both cities we find similar images of what role ethnicity plays, and should play, in the nation in general and in the respondents' own lives in particular. It is to these images and recurrent themes, then, that we must now turn.

Ethnic Ideologies

Ethnic differences in class position and social status should come as no surprise to anyone familiar with the ethnic fabric of American society, for such differences have persisted throughout our history. Several studies have explored to a greater extent the system of ethnic stratification in the United States. In the Boston and Kansas City surveys, however, we were interested in the more subjective side of the question—that is, the common images surrounding ethnicity in America today and the relative support given to the melting pot ideology and its growing rival in the comparatively recent ethnic revival. Boston and Kansas City residents were asked whether they thought there was a melting pot, and then Boston residents were further queried as to whether, indeed, there should be one, or whether group identification should be encouraged; whether there was discrimination against groups other than blacks; and what was their own level of ethnic identification.

First, on the question of what *should* be—the ideal solution to the ethnic question in America—we found rather surprising agreement that the old melting pot idea, with a few modifications, remains the ideal model of ethnic integration into American society. Looking first at selected personal characteristics of the respondents, we found that Catholics, while more likely to be labeled "white ethnics" by the popular press, were more likely than Protestants to state that there should be a melting pot. Those aged thirty to forty-nine favored the melting pot the most strongly, although the majority of those younger and older still favored this idea over separate groups. Also, the second and third generations were more likely to favor continued assimilation, while first- and fourth-generation members tended to favor separate groups. Yet it must be emphasized that even in this latter group, twenty-five respondents favored the melting pot ideal to seven who did not, and that generation is confounded with age, particularly with most of the fourth-generation members being under thirty, and many of them students. As for intermarriage, those who had not intermarried or had married someone of a different ethnicity but same religion were more likely than those who had married someone of a different religion to believe that the melting pot should keep working. Among those who had intermarried religiously, twice as many thought that *both* some melting and some emphasis on ethnic heritage should take place, rather than the ethnic side being stressed altogether.

Several themes predominate in the explanations given, which demonstrates the continued integrative power of this concept. To many, the melting pot *is* America. America itself is taken as symbolizing the coming together of diverse religions, nationalities, and races; therefore it seems only American to melt, and un-American not to:

> "[I prefer the] melting pot—this country always was [one]. That's why it was founded. You know—bring me your poor and tired. There'll always be a minority group that comes in and fights for what it wants and it goes on and on." (Female, age 57, WC, German and Irish ancestry)*

> "It wouldn't be America if everyone stayed by themselves." (Male, 31, WC, English and Swedish)

> "Make separate groups less important. That's the idea of this country. It's why we have one flag instead of forty." (Male, 43, WC, Irish and Dutch)

> "Definitely the melting pot. If people are living in this country they should feel that way." (Female, 27, UM, Scotch and Irish)

> "It is finally going to get all into one. The final answer we can't tell, but this seems to be the purpose of the Constitution. All are equal." (Male, 67, MC, Irish and Polish)

> "I think the melting pot. We're simple Americans, because that's the way God intended it. Everyone will be equal and could afford to run for president." (Male, 35, MC, German)

Given the case being made by the popular press for the benefits America could gain from a reemphasis on ethnicity, what reasons do people find for equating melting with Americanism? For some, it is simply one way of saying that we can become better—stronger, more united, less prejudiced.

> "I think it's going toward the melting pot. I don't think we're as hung up on prejudice. People are learning from their pain. I like to think things are better." (Female, 35, WC, no ethnicity indicated)

> "They call themselves Italian-Americans, Afro-Americans. I can't see this. Unless they become fully Americans they won't reach their full potential." (Female, 61, UM, Irish)

> "They could learn more. If they would contribute more it would be to everyone's benefit." (Female, 30, MC, Italian)

> "I guess we are getting better than we used to be. My sister is married to an Italian." (Female, 37, WC, English and Dutch)

---

* Quotations in this chapter have been identified by source because this is so important a consideration. Status abbreviations have been used as follows: UC means upper-class Upper American, UM signifies upper-middle, MC signifies middle-class Middle American, WC signifies working-class Middle-American, LC signifies Lower-American status. Numbers in subsequent quotations refer, as in the first quotation, to respondent's age.

Kansas City blacks in particular were among those stressing how much better life would be if only different nationalities and races could learn to live together:

"I think we should all be able to live as one. We should share everything to make this a better place to live." (Male, 43, WC, Black)

"It makes it a lot better seeing that two different colors can live together in peace. If they work together it will make a better country." (Male, 42, WC, Black)

"I think it will make a better country when people can look on one another and judge them by their own merits, rather than what side of the tracks they come from." (Female, 63, WC, Black)

As these responses would indicate, one of the reasons why life would be better is that such blending would eliminate much of the basis for ethnic conflict. Groups as such are perceived as being bad for America. A first-generation Portuguese put it bluntly, "If you start dividing the nationalities you'll start dividing the country." Others said:

"We should work to make less emphasis on groups. When people mingle without barriers, they can talk and settle differences instead of having gang wars." (Male, 21, WC, Italian and English)

"We should get together in everything—no harmony in cliques." (Male, 65, WC, French Canadian)

"I think the melting pot should keep working. Maybe then we won't have so much fighting. Each group brings something into the culture as a whole, combining views to make the best possible culture." (Female, 35, MC, Swiss)

"If everyone worked together there'd be more harmony and less chance for crime." (Male, 31, WC, English and Swedish)

Many people emphasized that groups should essentially become melted into the mainstream society and yet maintain certain aspects of their heritage. Such aspects fell more to the cultural side of ethnic identification with much emphasis on foods, holidays, and other customs.

"Diversity is important. If you had it all equal rights at the same time, [it] might be difficult to achieve. People *can* work together and respect their differences." (Male, 28, UM, no ethnic identification)

"I think it's good to retain some aspects of one's ethnic group, like cultural aspects, but all in all, the separate groups should be less important." (Male, 62, UM, no ethnic identification)

"Well, I don't think a black or white answer is possible. I think it would be nice to melt but keep the important ethnic things—holidays, food, etc., but if an ethnic group puts its interests ahead of the country . . . we are lost." (Male, 30, UM, no ethnic identification)

"I'd prefer a melting pot as far as status goes, but it's sort of nice to keep some of the ethnic identification, if a person wants to." (Female, 21, UM, no ethnic identification)

A common sentiment was that groups should "mix" yet retain a sense of their own background and a respect for that of others.

When it comes to perception of what *is*, however, the virtual unanimity of previous answers breaks down. Both in Boston and Kansas City there was an approximately even split between those who thought America's ethnic groups were becoming more alike, and those who thought that ethnic groups continued to remain separate. Again, Catholics more than Protestants were likely to perceive increased assimilation. The first and fourth generations were the most likely to perceive groups as separate, with the second and third generations believing more in the melting pot—possibly because they felt their family or friends experienced it. Those either just entering the social system or far removed from the assimilation process did not feel personally involved. Again, of course, generation is confounded with age, and many students and young people in general in the Boston area seem particularly aware of the current ethnic debate and of the presence and activities of a number of ethnic protest movements.

In terms of the most common images, answers often revealed a battle between those who felt people are "blending," "melting," and "mixing," and those who saw them as sticking together with persons of the same national origin.

"I think people are blending more. I think socially it is going to build this country stronger because they can work together without fear regardless of religious creed or color." (Male, 37, WC, Italian)

"If you leave out people who are noticeably different on sight, you can intermarry very easily and become part of the whole thing—blend in with the rest of society." (Male, 21, MC, Irish)

"The family structure has changed so much because of mobility. Kids move away and marry someone. A Catholic girl marries a Jewish boy and blends in and this keeps going on." (Male, 31, MC, Irish)

As these responses indicate, the melting process is seen as depending heavily on intermarriage, for in Boston and Kansas City alike people thought that any group that could and did intermarry would eventually blend, although those of different races would face considerable difficulty and possibly never melt at all because of it. This, of course, has long been a corollary of the melting pot thesis, with the recurring image of young couples winning out over the Old World prejudices of their parents. And, indeed, a majority of the Boston and Kansas City respondents have at least two ethnic groups in their background. Religious intermarriage is, of course, much rarer, with only 4 percent of respondents in Boston and 3 percent in Kansas City having married someone of a different faith.

People do see the young in particular as leading the way to greater tolerance, through their choosing of friends and spouses with little regard for ethnic background.

> "The younger generation believes in mixing—quite thoroughly. I work in town and see a lot of mixing myself. I guess the more you see of it the more you can accept. The kids associate with different kinds much more today." (Female, 39, WC, Italian)

> "It has always been separate groups, but now it seems to be the melting pot. Nobody in the younger crowd cares what you are." (Male, 65, WC, French Canadian)

> "I don't think younger people today place so much reliance on family background. People are more independent; they make their own friends, don't depend on groups." (Male, 46, UM, French Canadian)

However, an equal number of people thought instead that those of different religions, nationalities, and races were "sticking together"—like it or not:

> "I think it's still ethnic, definitely. I can see this in myself because I'm Irish and my husband is Italian and there was a big argument over that. Ethnic groups seem to stick together in a place." (Female, 20, MC, Irish)

> "Each nationality group tends to stick to its own—the colored, the Italians, the Polish. They seem to stick together." (Male, 50, WC, French Canadian)

> "One's nationality does stick together. I think it's just one's heritage." (Female, 48, MC, Irish)

> "I have to agree that people are sticking with their own kind." (Female, 40, MC, German and Irish)

Such respondents, emphasizing continued group solidarity, often perceive a tension between ethnic-group loyalty and loyalty to the nation, and the possibility of social conflict that results.

> "Ethnic loyalty persists. That little circle is very loyal. They think in common, they share important values. . . . I'm a Yankee and I've seen it." (Female, 48, UM, English)

"This is just exactly some of the problems we're having. Jews here are much more upset about conditions in Russia than the United States; Italians worry about Italy; blacks are on their own group kick; and no one thinks of their problems in terms of America." (Male, 30, UM, Jewish)

"This is kind of a pet peeve. I feel it should be a melting pot; however, there are a large number of ethnic groups that for one reason or another place the loyalty to the ethnic group higher than the loyalty to the country. Because people place so much loyalty and identify themselves with an ethnic group, other people will not think of them as countrymen but as foreigners and outsiders. I think since man is afraid of anything that is not familiar, this leads to social competition, bigotry, and racism." (Male, 26, MC, English and Swedish)

Again, much like those who believe in melting, this group offered several mechanisms that encouraged continued group identification. Some pointed to prejudice as either a natural reaction or the product of early socialization. As one Boston man said, "Society encourages certain prejudices in all of us"; another said, "They still breed prejudice; once in a while someone breaks away, but they really stick together."

Residential segregation was a second and related mechanism, for only in homogeneous ethnic neighborhoods do people believe such differences can manage to continue in force. Bostonians could point to the many neighborhoods in their metropolitan area with a distinctly ethnic flavor. "When you look at Boston you see how the Italians stay in East Boston, the Irish live in South Boston, the Jews in Mattapan, and right down the line. People here are pretty isolated by certain divisions in the city, and when they first came here they felt more comfortable in one group that they were familiar with and they just stayed that way." Similarly, in Kansas City, several talked of "Mexican colonies" and the Italian neighborhoods as evidence for groups' sticking together.

A final basis for ethnic solidarity was seen as coming from the political arena. In Boston, of course, the predominance of the Irish in politics is legendary. More generally, people also emphasized the common practice of voting according to ethnic names and group divisions on specifically racial or ethnic issues. Kansas City residents also mentioned the bargaining that takes place between ethnic groups and politicians. Most respondents in both Kansas City and Boston viewed the impact of ethnicity as an essentially irrational force that disrupts the supposedly more rational political decision-making processes. Thus, although most people still hoped that the melting pot society would someday become reality, when they looked around their neighborhoods and considered the state of the country as a whole, they became divided in their judgments as to whether or not ethnic groups were indeed losing their hold. One basis for such judgments was the assessment of continued discrimination.

Discrimination

Whether they saw Americans as blending or sticking together, most respondents thought that the melting pot was not yet reality for at least some groups still facing discrimination. Respondents were asked if there were any nationality or religious groups, other than the blacks, against which there is still discrimination. The average number of groups named was two to three, although this is hard to estimate, for many people were quite vague in their comments, ranging from "I don't know of any off hand" to "Just about everybody." Many others were quite specific in listing such groups as the Indians, Spanish-speaking Americans, Jews, Italians, and Irish. Yet it was often thought that the only real obstacles to the melting pot's success were the blacks, who could not melt because of their color, and the Jews, "who don't want to."

Here again, age showed a significant relationship, with the youngest respondents being the most likely to name three or four groups and the oldest group (aged fifty and above) more likely to name only one or two.

Specific themes pertained to each group named. Jews were unique for supposedly being envied their success:

"I think people are jealous. The Jews have money. People are always envious of people with money, just because they could pull themselves up." (Female, 37, WC, Italian)

"Oh, yes, Jews are discriminated against. They mostly own everything. That's why there is discrimination. People are jealous." (Male, 36, WC, Italian)

Most Jews themselves emphasized that a particularly subtle form of discrimination operated, more on the interpersonal than on the institutional level.

Aside from the blacks and the Jews, Spanish-speaking peoples were the next-most-often named. They in turn were believed to be persecuted both for their different appearance and because of their language:

"They're the easier-identified, and people fear for their own jobs. It's a real problem." (Male, 20, WC, Polish)

"One thing now is the discrimination against the Spanish-speaking people. We have never set up Spanish-speaking schools so that they are handicapped and disadvantaged today." (Female, 48, UM, Scotch and English)

Indians were not named as often, but when they were they assumed a symbolic value as the group most betrayed by official melting pot ideology:

> "The government put them in shacks on reservations. No education." (Male, 31, WC, English and Swedish)

> "The government robbed them of their land, fooled them, and slaughtered some of them. Then they stuck them on reservations. Now they put up these shacks and expect the people to be happy." (Female, 57, WC, Irish and German)

> "Worse than the blacks, there's discrimination against the American Indian. . . . He lives very far below the poverty level for a human. He's been relegated to the most unusable land in the country. (Male, 43, WC, Irish)

Whenever Italians or Irish were named, it was usually specified that discrimination against them occurs in other geographical areas, particularly the South, although some admit that "Some people still think anyone not born in America is a little strange," or "You still get Boston bluenoses who sneer at Irish and Italians."

Thus we see that, while many people believe that the melting pot is still the most appropriate model for ethnic integration in the United States, they recognize at the same time that some groups have faced—and continue to face—barriers of discrimination in housing, jobs, and social organizations. In terms of their *own* life experiences, however, Boston residents seemed much less ready to credit ethnicity with any determining role.

Level of Ethnic Identification

Most people, it would seem, can trace their ethnicity back for several generations—in Boston, sometimes to the Mayflower. Yet many people, when asked, would rather identify themselves as "all-around Americans" or with no group at all. Catholics more than Protestants, those in the lower class more than those in the middle and upper classes, and those in lower- as compared to higher-status neighborhoods were all likely to show a reluctance to identify with any specific ethnic group.

Lower-status groups tend to emphasize the values of the melting pot and the importance of considering oneself above all an American.

They think of themselves, or claim to think of themselves, as Americans first and wish other people would do them the same courtesy. They suspect that there is something somewhat un-American about calling oneself an Italian or Pole. Or, again, many are so intermarried that "American" is about as specific as they can get.

Indeed, while some people, notably Jews, a few Irish, and the self-labeled New England Yankees, stated their ethnicity with great pride, for many others ethnic identification appeared far more problematic. They preferred instead to emphasize their American-ness as based on either their family's long history in the States or their own mixture of ancestors:

> "Just an old-time all-American boy." (Male, 20, WC, Irish and Indian)

> "My ancestors came from Ireland and Germany, back around the Civil War—that's a long time ago. I'm an American." (Male, 64, MC, German and Irish)

> "Two of my grandparents came from Ireland—early 1900s. The other side was born here. I don't consider myself anything but an average middle-class American." (Female, 34, MC, Irish)

> "American through and through." (Male, 57, WC, Italian)

> "I don't consider myself in any particular group. My grandparents came from France and Italy, but I feel like everyone I'm around." (Male, 50, WC, French and Italian)

> "White middle class. Is that an ethnic group?" (Male, 25, MC, Irish and English)

> "So, in other words, my nationality. I really don't know. I have no prejudice." (Female, 29, WC, Irish and Scotch)

> "I didn't know I was in any." (Female, 42, UM, Swedish and English)

Yet very few cannot recall their ancestry at all. Even those who consider themselves "all-American boys" can trace the ethnic groups in their background.

This fact takes on increasing significance when compared to the overwhelmingly negative responses to the question that followed, which sought to establish the role individuals credited to ethnicity in determining their own life chances. When asked in what ways their lives had been different because of their ethnicity, approximately two-thirds of the respondents said flatly that it had had little effect. Looking first at the social background characteristics, we find that those of the first or second generation were, logically enough, the most likely to say that yes, it had some effect. Once again, however, those with the higher class status were also among the most likely to take the minority viewpoint that their lives had been in some way different.

Part of the explanation is that most Jews with middle- or upper-class standing emphasized their particular family and community life and the socialization of different values that resulted.

"Some of the religious tenets in Judaism, the ethnic emphasis on education and music—these are things that are pretty important to me." (Male, 25, UM, Jewish)

Many middle- and upper-class old-Yankee respondents, on the other hand, called their lives different precisely because they have *not* faced discrimination:

"Certainly different from the black person or anyone who's emigrated. You have some kind of status in having your ancestry dating back. I'm not discriminated against; the family has plenty of money, gets everything socially. The heritage is higher than in any other group." (Female, 24, UM, English)

As for the majority who stated their lives were in no way different, most emphasized ties binding them to others of different backgrounds and the role individuality must play in the choosing of friends and associates.

"I don't think my life is so different from any of my friends who have different backgrounds. We are all trying to get along in the same ways— I mean we all want to have friends, good jobs, a good place to live, food to eat." (Male, 20, WC, Italian)

"No difference at all. It all depends on an individual's make-up." (Male, 64, MC, German and Irish)

Most people also stated they felt no special comfort around their ethnic fellows. While a few emphasized common heritage and a shared sense of ease, most people countered with the variety of their friendships and the fact that they did not need to depend on fellow ethnics for support. Again, the theme of individuality was stressed as weakening the hold of ethnic loyalties.

"I don't think I have any attachment to the Irish. I have too many Italian friends. If I ever went to Ireland, I wouldn't know what to do." (Male, 25, MC, Irish)

"I just enjoy people for themselves. [There are a] lot in the family that I wouldn't want to be with." (Female, 26, WC, Irish)

"Don't have that much of a feeling for them. In fact, I'm not that comfortable among my own—more comfortable with Russians or Swedes. Irish drink too much. Believe me, I know." (Male, 48, WC, Irish)

"No, I feel good among my own, but I call them as I see them individually. You can feel closer to other groups than you can to your own sometimes." (Male, 42, WC, Italian)

When further questioned about their level of ethnic pride, most people returned to this theme of individuality. Ethnic pride was often seen as a crutch, and, as one man said, "I don't need something to fall back on." Others said:

"I'm not ashamed, if that's what you mean, but I don't think it makes any difference. I'm just me. I can't get any pride from being an Italian." (Male, 31, WC, Italian)

"I enjoy being with the group, but I don't eat, drink, and breathe the stuff." (Female, 34, MC, Irish)

Thus, while most people can trace their ancestry, many appear to feel they derive no significant psychological benefits from their ethnicity. They do not admit to feeling particularly comfortable with their fellow ethnics, nor do they admit to a special ethnic pride. Instead, most respondents stressed themes of a common American identity and the role individuality must play in the melting pot society.

By way of summary, then, we can see that certain predominant themes emerge to form an ideology of what is, and what should be, the level of ethnic integration in American society. Ethnic groups are taken as "good" for the individual, insofar as the identities they provide yield a certain sense of belonging and of heritage. They are "good" for the country, insofar as they remain to remind us that we are a "nation of nations"—they are what has made America unique. Yet, they are also considered "bad" for the individual, insofar as they lead to prejudice and limit individual expression, and "bad" for the nation when they stress loyalty to the group and to what it can get from the system rather than stressing working together as Americans. In sum, we find a solid level of support for the melting pot ideology and a distrust for any social movement or philosophy that could lead to an intensification of ethnic group identification.

Conclusion

In 1944 Myrdal described a dilemma facing Americans regarding the question of race.

The "American Dilemma" . . . is the ever-raging conflict between, on the one hand, the valuations preserved on the general plane which we shall call the "American Creed," where the American thinks, talks, and acts under the influence of high national and Christian precepts, and, on the other hand, the valuations on specific planes of individual and group living where personal local interests, economic, social, and sexual jealousies, considerations of community prestige and conformity; group prejudice against particular persons or types of people; and all sorts of miscellaneous wants, impulses, and habits dominate his outlook. [1944; lxxi]

In a similar fashion, Americans are finally coming to face their contradictory attitudes and ideals regarding ethnicity, which have long simmered beneath the surface and occasionally boiled over into overt ethnic conflict. Myrdal himself was typical of the many who believed that the various immigrants then experiencing differing class and status positions would eventually be assimilated into mainstream American society, in contrast to the blacks for whom such differences had become hardened into caste positions that would be exceedingly more difficult to overcome. Yet in the 1970s some Americans, while still strongly believing in the desirability of assimilation, have come to doubt its possible realization. They see neighborhoods of third- or fourth-generation ethnics still sticking together. They hear of or directly experience the continued discrimination faced by blacks, Chicanos, Indians, and sometimes—as it seems—"everyone who didn't come over on the Mayflower." While denying that ethnic background made a difference in their own lives, they often believe that it enters as a factor into politics, educational and occupational success, residential segregation, and status position in general.

Thus the ethnic question has resurfaced in the United States with a peculiar intensity and immediacy. Actually, there are several ethnic questions, most of which—while of key importance for the understanding of ethnic identification—fall outside the scope of our investigation.

We cannot, for example, judge the supposed rising strength of ethnic strongholds or their effectiveness in bringing about social change. The survey method tends to pick up a sense of the wider majority sentiment, in which cells of ethnic sentiment are often either lost or not represented. And, since the broadest question of the role of ethnicity in American life can hardly be resolved simply by a majority vote, our survey should be viewed in conjunction with the many studies that do exist of such ethnic strongholds (compare Nee and Nee, 1973; Light, 1972; Suttles, 1968). Our data would suggest, though, that strong ethnic identification is to be found only among, on the one hand, groups still suffering discrimination from the wider society and, on the other, those with a sufficiently secure class position, who have not intermarried to any great extent, and who can thus enjoy the folkloric aspect of ethnicity while protecting against its more negative aspects.

Similarly, we cannot adequately judge the strength of the relationships between the opinions people voiced in the study and their actual behaviors in day-to-day life. On the most blatant level we find little indication of how much and in what ways people discriminate against those of other ethnicity, religion, or race. Respondents were, for the most part, careful to point out how much *others* discriminate but say of themselves: "I call them as I see them." On the more subtle side, we have no indication of how ethnicity affects minute yet significant patterns of interpersonal interactions. There are, for example, studies on such topics as ethnic differences in how close people stand to each other, how verbal cues can be misunderstood, and how families of different ethnic background differ in room use in their homes. Again, such questions lie more in the line of the ethno-methodologist than the survey researcher, but they should not be dismissed simply because they may be more difficult to tie down.

Finally, we hesitate to attempt an answer to perhaps the most common and popular question: "Is the melting pot working or isn't it?" For how do we judge its success or failure? The question is certainly more complex than a simple listing of ethnic strongholds or figures of ethnic neighborhood segregation or intermarriage would indicate. Coming as a foreign observer, Myrdal himself suggested that the degree of success America had achieved in assimilating many diverse populations would seem nothing short of phenomenal to a European. More recently, Greeley echoed these sentiments in remarking that a similar experiment in the assimilation of diverse nationalities had never been attempted in most European countries, where *foreigner* was traditionally equated with *stranger* and *race* with *nation*, and where citizenship was rarely granted even to long-time foreign residents. Even given this conservative policy (or, possibly, partly because of it), many European countries today face their own ethnic group conflicts, as recent events in France, Belgium, Spain, Ireland, and even supposedly peaceful Switzerland indicate. Such countries have little need for ethnic revivals. America, on the other hand, initially more idealistic in immigration philosophy and policy, now questions the extent to which the philosophy has not become reality for several ethnic populations, and yet this growing realization has not led to an automatic rejection of the melting pot ideology.

Several reasons can be found within the concept itself. In short, what *is* a melting pot, and what can be judged to be its end result? Is it meant to form one undifferentiated type—one distinct "American" personality—based more heavily on one group's input than another's? Or are various ethnic traits permitted to remain if a basic agreement on values and goals can be found? Can such ethnic traits then remain without inevitably acquiring positive or negative status loadings? Such vagaries imbedded in the concept itself have led to recurring debates among historians and other writers as to its meaning and applicability (with some even suggesting that a "salad bowl," in which each element remains distinct yet contributes to the flavor of the whole, is a more appropriate image). Insofar as no one can agree on how much melting must take place, in what areas of life it should occur, or which ethnic traits can remain "to add flavor," we lack a firm standard by which to measure the melting pot's relative failure or success. In our study we do find both significant class differentials among ethnic groups and an emphasis on ethnic heritage, and yet considerable intermarriage and neighborhood integration have indeed taken place, particularly in the suburbs. The question, then, is exactly what remains to form a sufficient basis for ethnic identification?

What we are specifically interested in is how a cross-section of Americans in two quite different metropolitan areas evaluate the extent of ethnic integration, and the images they most commonly employ in discussing ethnicity's role in American life. While the data presented here need to be supported by further work, we have found that for many Boston and Kansas City residents ethnicity is an ambivalent concept, with the good side leading to an appreciation of ethnic folklore and the bad encouraging the perpetuation of ethnic conflict.

The Positive Side: Ethnicity as Folklore

For many Americans, ethnicity adds a certain spice to their otherwise increasingly bland post-industrial existence. It's fun, it adds color, and, as they say, it's good now and then to "remember where we have come from." It gives a sense of heritage and roots to a highly mobile population. Ethnicity in this sense, much like Nisbet's description of *Gemeinschaft*, has definitely acquired a positive connotation:

> *Gemeinschaft* and its various correlates tend to be "good"; that is, one refers to someone as having fallen into bad "associations" or "society," but never fallen into "bad community." All of the cherished, elemental states of mind of society—love, loyalty, honor, friendship, and so on—are emanations of *Gemeinschaft*. [1966:76]

Many respondents spoke of the enjoyable diversity ethnicity provides, of keeping the "important things—like foods and customs." And few would deny that trips to ethnic restaurants or festivals can provide a welcome break from the daily routine, or that celebrating more religious holidays and remembering ethnic customs can also provide a deep sense of personal meaning or of family strength. Our respondents hoped that such ethnic customs and traits would remain even after we are all assimilated to remind us that, indeed, we are somehow special for being a "nation of nations."

> "The melting pot should keep working as long as there is general recognition that the pot exists and that we owe many debts to many cultures."
> (Male, 27, UM, German)

Ethnicity as folklore has another benefit in that it can provide such pleasurable experiences at little cost to the individual. One can, as Michael Novak has suggested, live a Middle-American life in the suburbs with only periodic excursions back to the city's ethnic neighborhoods for groceries and entertainment. One can try out recipes from the old country or perhaps even make it back for a visit. In its folkloric aspect, ethnicity provides a personal fund of traits that can be emphasized or deemphasized at will or as the occasion demands, played up or down for effect or fun without disturbing the individual's basic life pattern and position in society. Any costs that do arise come from the other, darker, side of ethnic identification. The hope is, clearly, that you can have one without the other.

In sum, respondents seem to feel that ethnicity should remain on the "team sports" level of identification—it should give you someone to root for when what is at stake seems little more than a game. It becomes the basis for choice on election day when a choice must be made among candidates for minor office and there is no information to go on beyond name. It becomes the basis for celebrations when an Italian boy "makes good" on the athletic field or a Greek girl becomes an award-winning actress; the feeling that he or she is "one of us" adds to the excitement. (Someone coming from a mixed ethnic background has the privilege of choosing a different side from one contest to the next, depending on which is momentarily the more attractive.) When this choosing-up of sides deepens, then people feel that it is carrying a good thing too far; they believe ethnic identification should be left as a matter for games and sentiment, not elevated to a level where it affects important decisions.

The Negative Side: Ethnicity as Group Conflict

Some people implicitly equated "ethnic" with "conflict," as did one man who said:

"They should melt, but it's a tragedy when the kids don't grow up to speak a foreign language—a cultural loss. They shouldn't keep prejudice; they should cling to the cultural but not ethnic aspects." (Male, 27, UM, English)

For, all in all, respondents feared that the healthy choosing-up of sides would get out of control. While purporting to enjoy diversity themselves, they felt that people in general have little tolerance for diverse ways of life and thus would strike out against what they cannot understand.

"They should try to mingle, instead of having segregation all the time." (Female, 29, WC, English)

"I think the melting pot should keep working so that people will have less differences between them, and maybe under the name American we'll get along better." (Female, 23, MC, English and Irish)

"If everyone were the same in terms of religion and so on, there would be fewer problems." (Female, 38, MC, Jewish)

"I don't think they should lose their identity, but they should mix." (Female, 48, UM, English)

"I don't think it hurts to break down a clannish spirit among peoples." (Female, 61, MC, Irish)

People seemed to feel that the breakdown of a "clannish spirit" should lead to judgments and choices being made on the fairer, more democratic basis of individual merit, and that we will be increasingly free and even encouraged to choose our friends and spouses—along with our governmental representatives—without regard to ethnic background, religion, or race. Boston and Kansas City residents applauded this increasing tolerance that they found in themselves, if not always in their neighbors.

"To me, I think of it as being a melting pot, but everyone I talk to I think is bigoted." (Female, 47, MC, Irish)

"I think everybody should be equal. I think they should respect you for what you are but not look at you as if you were different." (Female, 21, WC, English and Italian)

"[Lack of prejudice] lets people go where they want to go and do what they want without anybody stopping them. . . . People want to be on their own, not to be beholden to their family or whatever." (Male, 56, WC, Black)

Ethnicity is considered as particularly nefarious when used as a tool for political or social change. Boston and Kansas City residents had few kind words for those who vote the straight ethnic line, or for the "radicals" and "trouble-makers" who organize ethnic group protests. Both activities lie outside the ground rules for effecting social change. While many realize that ethnicity has always had some role in electing politicians, deciding educational and occupational opportunities, and determining where people live and with whom they associate, they feel that it definitely should not play such a role in the future.

> "I think that certain racial groups are making ridiculous demands and are hurting themselves instead of raising themselves up and into politics. It's just causing a lot of trouble and could end up in a civil war here in the United States between the blacks and whites." (Female, 40, MC, German and Irish)

> "Groups are still separate. People just naturally stick together. It makes more problems because the radical is trying to beat the other fellow and get all to himself and his groups—all the money the government gives away, power, jobs, and the best of everything for his group when they don't always work to get it." (Male, 73, UM, Irish)

> "I think the politicians are the worst. They appoint people of their own ethnic group to high-paying jobs. When I go to the polls and I don't know them I might say, 'That's a good Irish name,' but I try to judge more by the person." (Female, 47, MC, Irish)

Thus our respondents have little sympathy for the "new ethnicity" —an ideology that emphasizes the failure of American society to bring about equality in the social and economic spheres and an equal share in political control for the various ethnic groups. Rather, they opt for the "old ethnicity," in which one's national heritage was important but definitely second to the fact of one's identity as an American.

From among our samples we can illustrate differences as to the strength with which people adhere to this version of the melting pot ideology, as well as tracing out among whom the ethnic revival shows some signs of support. While the data analyzed here need to be supported by other studies, we have found that the melting pot enjoys its strongest support among the more ethnic populations in both Boston and Kansas City. It is the Boston Irish and Italians and the Kansas City blacks who tend to align most thoroughly with this ideology, to state, "I am an American," and to fear the possible conflict ethnicity implies. Similarly, those of lower-class status, low incomes, less education, and comparatively low-status neighborhoods (all of which are confounded with ethnicity) were more likely to favor blending over sticking together.

One possible explanation for this seeming anomaly is that these people—coinciding in part with what Novak terms the "unmeltable ethnics"—have felt the most pressure to play down their ethnic backgrounds. In Boston, at least, many of these people—immigrants them-selves or only second-generation—felt a need at some time in the past to prove their loyalty to the nation and their "100 percent American-ness" in general. They, more than the established residents and citizens, needed to support the American creed, if only to lessen the prejudice they were likely to incur. Those in more secure positions—both in ethnic and class terms—did not need to fear ethnic affiliation to the same extent, particularly since their own group membership has long ranked high: witness the resounding "I'm a Yankee" of many old-time Bostonians.

Any indication of an ethnic revival, on the other hand, was found only among the student population of Boston and the young, upper middle-class families in both cities. Both groups appeared more aware of the increasing coverage of ethnic stories in the press and more sympa-thetic to the protest movements of blacks, Chicanos, Puerto Ricans, and Indians. Students also had more direct exposure to the issue through the establishment of ethnic studies departments on their campuses and occasionally more active support of ethnic protests.

The fact that most of these students and young professionals were in the upper-middle and upper classes meant that they could feel rela-tively free about discussing the ethnic question without feeling that their acceptability as average Americans might be called into question, some-thing that did seem to bother those in the lower-middle and lower classes. On the contrary, upper middle-class WASPs and Jews, par-ticularly in Boston, were more concerned with proving their uniqueness and the way they differed from the mainstream because of their ethnic heritage.

By way of conclusion, then, we have seen that to ask about ethnic identification is also to ask about what it means to be an American. Clearly, to most of our respondents, the latter identity is still a valid and meaningful form of self-identification, and really the only acceptable one. Ethnic identification can indeed be fun, but only if not taken seriously, for true loyalty must inevitably be given to the nation. Re-spondents fear that any revival of ethnicity would be a daring step backward from our goals of individuality and equal opportunity. They suspect that any attempt at ethnic federalism would only tear apart the fabric of American society, and, in short, they cannot envision any society in which people call themselves anything but Americans first.

Whether the revival of ethnicity adherents can allay these fears remains to be seen. While some may view conflict, particularly rou-tinized conflict, as a sign of a healthy society, to these people it is more a threat to what is and has been achieved than a promise of better things to come. To change their attitudes toward ethnic identification, ethnic leaders would have to change both people's understanding of what it means to be American and their understanding of how group conflict can play a beneficial role in effecting social change.

Until that day, the public will continue to fear the politicization of ethnicity while still appreciating the folkloric color it can provide. People will accept and even welcome some level of ethnic consciousness, as long as it does not interfere with what they conceive of as their more fundamental identity as Americans. In sum, we can say that this complex of attitudes found among Boston and Kansas City residents, and probably held in varying degrees of strength throughout the United States, resembles the classic melting pot ideology of a new and special American character forged from the many national, religious, and racial streams, with each group contributing its own unique flavor to make for the best possible culture.

PART II

CLASSES AND GENERAL SOCIAL STANDING

CHAPTER 7

Images of Classes
and the Continuum

W E HAVE considered in the previous chapters the several dimensions by which Americans characterize their own and their fellow citizens' social position, social status, social standing, and social class, all words by which Americans refer to the same phenomenon. We have seen how income, job, schooling, and less precise characteristics of life style, social identity, and ethnicity—when taken singly—are used to rank and rate people. In this and the succeeding four chapters we shift to an interest in how the various components of social class are combined and weighted to yield general social standing. We want to understand the social arithmetic by which people are placed in classes when those who place them are thinking categorically, and how they are placed on the status continuum when class categories are not salient.

Just because differences in social standing are recognized by Americans as a central fact of life in this country—and that these differences are spoken of as matters of social class—does not mean that there is an agreed-upon number of social classes, with their names known to everyone and their composition understood. On the contrary, it is one of the characteristics of the class structure in the United States that lines of demarcation are not sharp or clearly perceived by the average citizen, and many are not known about at all by people whose lives they do not touch. There is some justification for calling the structure a continuum. Individual movement up and down occurs more in the manner of an escalator than a stepladder—if the latter, it would seem to have an almost infinite number of steps. The major status levels on this ladder are usually spoken of in economic terms—the rich class and the poor class, for example—but definitions and boundary lines for such economic groupings are not clarified in ordinary discourse. Indeed, at first glance, public imagery about social classes is a welter of confusion.

Ultimately, to number and name the American social classes is a task for the social scientist. The status structure is too complex to be comprehended fully by average persons from their inevitably narrow vantage points. This chapter is about our efforts to piece together hundreds of these "narrow" views on the subject and construct from them a single picture that is a summation of public impression about the social class hierarchy. In later chapters we will compare this image-based picture with observations of behavior and use the combination to construct a second picture of the class structure—a picture that, in our view, is more nearly the truth about classes in America than the public image we report here. The image presented here remains part of this later truth but is far from being the whole of it.

We have used three different lines of questioning to tap public imagery about class groups and the status hierarchy. In one, survey respondents were asked in open-end, non-directive fashion to specify their conceptions of the hierarchy, that is, to do their own job of numbering and naming the classes. In another, we named eight classes and asked respondents to imagine what kinds of people belonged to each. In the third line of questioning, we employed the magnitude estimation technique to elicit status placements for hypothetical families.

What Classes Do Americans Talk About?

The lack of any clear public consensus as to the name and number of social classes in the United States emerged most sharply in response to one particular open-ended question: "How many classes would you say there are [in America], and what names would you give to them (or what names have you heard other people use)? What else could you say to describe each of the classes you've mentioned?" Slightly over one-third of the Bostonians and Kansas Citians who were asked this question named three classes, and the rest variously named two, four, five, six, seven, or nine or refused to say. Many who attempted an answer protested the task, as did those who totally refused, on the grounds that—in the words of a Boston man—"You have too many classes for me to count and name. . . . Hell! There may be fifteen or thirty. Anyway, it doesn't matter a damn to me."

Each of these many images—whether of two classes, three classes, five classes, or seven—demonstrates how Americans variously look at the status structure and place themselves in it. For example, whenever a two-class image was offered, one was always a "them" class and the other was "the rest of us," "them" being "the elite," "the moneyed class," "the old rich," or "people in society," and "the rest of us" being "people who have to work for a living," "just ordinary people," and "a plain person like me." This kind of division illustrates how much the rich-and-social people provide a focus for both awe and animus; it tells us that the difference between their way of life and that of "the rest of us" is of special emotional consequence to many in the latter category. (Most of those who gave this sort of response could be characterized as slightly below average in socio-economic standing.)

Images of American society as a three-class structure differ in only one respect from the two-class image: a "rich" class is retained as the top, but a bottom class of "the poor," "people on welfare," or "people in the slums" is separated out from "the rest of us"—who then become a middle class. Such a three-class image was the most common in our survey; it was especially favored by men and women from the blue-collar world, those of both average and somewhat below average income and those of average and somewhat below average educational credentials. For these people, it was a special point of pride that they could distinguish themselves from the poor.

In images of a three-class system, status is almost entirely a matter of money. "It's all in the dough, you know," said a Boston man. The names given to the highest of the three classes illustrate this. It was far more commonly labeled "the rich," "the wealthy," or "the high-income class" (and in one instance, "the plutocrats, millionaires, and billionaires") than either "upper class" or "top class." Similarly, the names applied to the lowest class were more typically "the poor," "the poverty people," or "the lower-income group" than either "lower class" or "bottom class." The middle class was most often referred to as just that, but names such as "middle financial class," "middle income," "medium income," and "average working class" also cropped up with some frequency.

Typical of three-class images are the following, the first from a Boston woman:

"There are three classes: the rich, middle class, and poor. The rich are like the Kennedys, people with money, the blue-bloods. The middle are average Americans, like myself, the average working person. I'm not poor; I'm not on welfare or anything like that. I own my own home. Everything I have is mine, bought and paid for, such as it is. The poor are the unfortunates that haven't been able to make it."

And this, from a Boston man:

"Three classes are the high, medium, and low. The high live in the richer areas of Boston. They've got good positions. They make quite a good deal of money. The medium, or moderate income, are much like myself. I think this neighborhood here is medium income. We don't live in a ghetto. . . . We have a nice house and everything we need, but we're not rich. The low—that's people in the ghetto. Ignorance and apathy play an important role in the lower class."

In characterizations of the highest class, the group's economic supremacy was invariably stressed, especially as manifest in its standard of living: "They've got everything they need and more"; "Both the husband and wife own cars and they have a big house—they can take off for Florida any time they feel like it"; and "They have hardly any money worries—except maybe keeping what they have." Impressions of annual incomes in this highest class of three ran from $25,000 a year or more (this was the lowest cited) through $50,000 to a level vaguely called the "filthy rich."

The level of well-being of the middle-status group was expressed in terms of "They have everything they need, but *not* an abundance" (this description would usually be given in the first person, as, "We have . . ."). And when it came to people in the lowest class, it was believed that "Many are doing without things they actually needed." Impressions of annual earnings in this class ran from "no more than $7,500 a year" through "under $5,000" down to "they just have nothing."

Beyond these financial distinctions, the three groups were compared mostly by their relationship to the world of work. In these terms, the highest class is the world of "big businessmen, top lawyers, and doctors," or else it is "the people who don't have to work" ("the landed gentry," "the people born with a silver spoon in their mouths. . . . they don't have to think of where the money is coming from—it's just there"). The middle status group is "the hardest working group—they have to work for everything they get"; they are the self-proclaimed "forty-hour-a-week working people who are considered the backbone of the country." And the lowest class is considered "unable to qualify for jobs that pay anything substantial, only the low-paying, menial type"; they are "people who don't want to work hard"; "people without jobs—and who can't get work"; or sometimes "people who don't even try to work—they don't care."

These three-class images, featuring so consistently two polar extremes of rich and poor and a broad central area of people whose incomes fall somewhere in between, are obviously over-simplifications of the American social order, and they would lead us to believe that the economic variable provides the only dimension along which people are scaled from high to low. The more complicated descriptions of the class structure volunteered by other Bostonians and Kansas Citians moderate this impression, however, introducing other variables such as education, ethnic identity, and "who your friends are."

Images of the social ladder as having four classes, five classes, six classes—or even, on occasion, eight or nine—exemplify this. They are not simple groupings based solely on financial status, as the three-class images are. Instead, source of income, standard of living, residential location, occupational type, and educational credentials are considered. Further, the respondents who cited any specific number of classes did not show the unanimity in naming and characterizing these classes that we found among those naming just two or three.

To illustrate: the conceptions of a four-class structure that were volunteered suggested no less than four different ways of looking at the status system. In one approach, the perceived class groupings amounted essentially (though not necessarily by the names reported here) to the old rich, the new rich, the middle class, and the lower class; in another, the pattern developed was the rich, the educated upper-middle professional class, the rest of the middle class, and the poor. In a third, the breakdown was the rich, the comfortable suburban middle class, the average working person in the city, and the down-and-out; and in a fourth, the differentiation proposed was the rich, the middle class, the people who are poor but at least work, and the welfare class who won't work or can't work. The same kinds of conceptual differences appeared in the five-class and six-class structures that were presented. All these seeming inconsistencies and variations should be thought of not as confusion but as a rich lode of imagery about the status system; represented therein are the best efforts of usually inarticulate people to express categorically and concretely the underlying continuum of status.

To make sense of this fund of imagery, the essential analytic task is to locate the cuts, or dividing lines, across the status continuum that are explicit or implicit in the names of the classes and the descriptions of their characteristics volunteered by respondents. Thus examined, what this storehouse of verbiage reveals is not only what classes respondents in Boston and Kansas City most readily talked about, but also what status groupings they were most conscious of, even when they did not all use the same words or phrases to describe and name them. All told, thirteen cuts or dividing lines were located by taking this approach to the data, but only six of these emerged with sufficient frequency and strength of supporting argument to be considered centrally significant.

The six cuts, reading from highest down to lowest, are these:

(1) A source-of-income cut, placing those with inherited wealth socially above those with self-earned wealth.

(2) A level-of-income cut, establishing "people who really have it made" financially above those who are "doing well, but aren't really well-to-do."

(3) A cut based on educational credentials and associated occupational accomplishments—"the degrees *versus* the non-degrees"—ranking the former above the latter.

(4) A cut based on publicly perceived income level and associated standard of living—"People who have a comfortable salary and all the necessities plus a few luxuries" *versus* families who are "just getting along."

(5) Another cut based on income and standard of living— "People getting by who have a decent house and the husband has a decent-paying job" *versus* "People who have to work at jobs that don't pay well. . . . Their housing is not slum, but it's undesirable."

(6) A cut based on source of income, this time private earnings *versus* public charity—"The poor who are working and largely self-supporting" *versus* "The welfare class."

Seven major social strata are suggested by these six cuts. Successively, these are:

- the old rich of aristocratic family name,
- the new rich—this generation's success elite,
- the college-educated professional and managerial class,
- Middle Americans of comfortable living standard,
- Middle Americans just getting along,
- a lower working class of people who are poor but not on welfare, and
- the non-working welfare class.

Most Americans could probably be placed rather easily by their fellows (or a social scientist) into one or another of these seven status groups, although a considerable number could not. These classes are thematic images, not all-embracing entities; they represent cores around which status meanings cluster, not categories with absolute and rigid boundary lines.

There are three basic status positions in this structure: the top three groups are Classes *above* the Common Man, the fourth and fifth are Classes *of* the Common Man, and the bottom two are Classes *below* the Common Man. This tripartite division of American society is to a large extent what the respondents who named and described a three-class structure had in mind, even though they tended to describe the highest and lowest classes in rather narrower, polar fashion.

This tripartite perspective also reflects the degree to which men and women of the two Middle-American or Common Man levels regard the lives of people in the upper three categories as enviably different from their own in terms of money, possessions, and level of consumption (and in turn look with distaste on the living standard of the two categories below). The income level we found our respondents associating in the early 1970s with the lowest of the three top categories—the college-educated professional and managerial class—was "$15,000 a year as a minimum." More broadly speaking, such an income was an ideal, or goal of sorts, for Bostonians and Kansas Citians of the Common Man level. On $15,000, they said, you "could lead a good life" (one of our questions asked what income would be required for such); you could "have a second car," you could own a house definitely above average in community status, and you could "have a nice vacation every year." (Further up, an income of $37,500 seemed to mark the dividing line between "people who really have it made" and those who are "doing well, but aren't really well-to-do.")

An income of $7,500 a year—exactly half the $15,000 that marked off the classes *above* the Common Man from those *of* the Common Man—seemed in turn to separate the latter from levels *below* the Common Man; in other words, that is what our respondents thought was needed in the way of annual earnings to "get along" and have "decent housing" instead of feeling poor. For leading a comfortable existence—thus ranking as a Middle American of comfortable living standard—an income of at least $10,000 or $12,000 a year was usually cited by our respondents, with $11,000 the median. Finally, the income most commonly associated with the idea of poverty, and below which a family was commonly ranked as lower class whether they were on welfare or working, was $4,500 a year. We have cited these income-level images not because we would suggest that the seven major strata are essentially income groups, but rather because we wish to convey what incomes were associated with each of these status levels by the people of Boston and Kansas City whom we interviewed. (Further detailing of the standards of living associated with these incomes will be presented in Chapters 8, 9, and 10.)

What Images Do Certain Class Names Call Forth?

While one subsample of Bostonians and Kansas Citians were being asked in open-ended, unstructured fashion to volunteer their impressions of the American social class structure, a more direct approach was used with another subsample of 200 men and women; we channeled this group's vision of the status structure into a mold of our own devisement by presenting them with names for a series of social classes and asking them to tell us what images these various names brought to mind. In this interview, after opening with a general question on class, we asked respondents to tell us what distinctions they would make between two groups, one called *the working class* and the other called *the lower-middle class* (alternating the order of their naming). Then we successively probed images of *the top class, the next-to-top class, the upper-middle class, the middle-middle class, a lower class but not the lowest,* and *the class at the very bottom of the ladder.*

The significance of the response pattern to this experiment is two-fold. First, the status imagery called forth by our eight hypothetical class names differed markedly according to the social standing of respondents; and second, all the major cuts across the status continuum that emerged in the voluntary responses came through again in these directed responses, as did most of the minor ones—and some of the latter took on more importance, as now viewed from the perspective of the relevant classes.

The first point—that perspectives on the social structure differ according to where one ranks within it—is nothing new. It mirrors what Davis, Gardner, and Gardner (1941) observed in Natchez, Mississippi, four decades ago in their conversations about social status with people of both races and at all different levels of the structure. Essentially, what they found—and what we found again in this study—was that Americans draw more class boundary lines through the status continuum in those areas with which they are most familiar (that is, where they identify themselves as belonging) and draw fewer in areas furthest removed from their own position. The upper-status Americans we interviewed distributed people earning $15,000 a year or more through five different classes, while lower-status Americans concentrated them all in two. Then, down at the other end of the income scale, Upper Americans divided people earning less than $7,500 into just two classes, while Lower Americans spread them over four. The other side of this coin is that our hypothetical class names were "cheapened" in their assumed reference by respondents of successively lower status. To use one example, the title middle-middle was attached by Upper Americans to people earning $15,000 or more a year, usually as college graduates; Middle Americans associated it with men and women at the comfortable standard (with annual incomes centering at $12,000 and $13,000); and Lower Americans thought of it as referring to families with incomes around $9,000 or $10,000 a year. (One problematic by-product of these differences in perspective on the social structure is that we social scientists cannot in every instance pretend that our class nomenclature derives from and reflects a lay-public consensus.)

The three different perspectives on social structure that emerged from this experiment with hypothetical class names lead us to propose a more elaborate breakdown of the status ladder than was established in our seven-class division a few pages back. In this breakdown, subdivisions have been recognized in all but the top-ranked of those seven classes. Interview materials from respondents at or near the respective classes have been used to identify these substrata. The names we have attached to these groups are our own, however, borrowed from the literature and previous research, then modified on occasion to reflect the language and emotions of our respondents.

This elaborated breakdown runs as follows. On top are the old rich of aristocratic family name—otherwise to be called *upper-uppers.* Our Upper-American respondents separated such a group out from the broader world of rich and upper-status people when they presented this very narrow image of what the class title top class referred to: "That's old family money, the established names . . . the bluebloods. . . . Whatever is left of a true aristocracy in America." In contrast, the phrase next-to-top class meant "people who are different from the top class in that they have newer money—they're the first generation of achievers."

The new rich success elite—conceived broadly by Middle Americans and Lower Americans as including virtually anyone whose income appeared to be averaging $37,500 or more per year in the early 1970s— divides into two levels. One we call *lower-uppers* and the other *high-level upper-middles.* The first is the status group our Upper-American respondents identified with the phrase next-to-top class. Occupationally it ranges from "medical specialists earning $60,000 or more" (and lawyers and corporate executives of similar minimum income) up to "industrial magnates" and "the General Motors president who earns $750,000." It does not usually include that segment of success-elite men and women who were earning $40,000 or $50,000 in 1972. Such persons our Upper

Americans associated with the phrase upper-middle class rather than next-to-top, characterizing them as "successful but not super-successful"—or, more explicitly, as "run-of-the-mill doctors, not high-powered specialists" and "top-level managers, not big-wheel executives."

The college-educated professional and managerial class also seems to divide into two levels. One we call *standard upper-middles*, the other *marginal upper-middles*. In the standard category fall the lesser business and professional people that Upper Americans identified with the phrase upper-middle class (that is, those not earning $40,000 or $50,000 a year). This, in prototype, is "The average educated business or professional person, including college graduates, some with advanced degrees. . . . Their incomes would be $25,000, $30,000, or $35,000 these days [1972]." In the marginal category fall the college graduates whom Upper Americans identified with the phrase middle-middle class. Of this social level, Upper Americans said, "They're college graduates—but not earning all that much money, maybe only $15,000 or $18,000 or $20,000. . . . They're working as engineers, college teachers, middle-level civil servants, or researchers."

Middle Americans of comfortable living standards present a more complicated picture. If we include within that designation all people who are not college-educated and/or are not accepted as part of Upper America but are more than comfortable economically (that is, "they're leading the good life"), then this becomes a much larger status group than earlier envisioned, and it contains two substrata, distinguished from one another by living standard. If we go along with the Upper-American perspective and divide these people into white-collar and blue-collar categories, we would seem to have four substrata instead of just two. Probably the best way to sum up this imagery is with three strata. The stratum with high rank we will refer to as the *socio-economic elite of Middle America*. This is drawn from people that Lower Americans included in their next-to-top class, that Middle Americans included in their upper-middle class, and that Upper Americans sometimes included in their conception of middle-middle. In prototype, this class includes "people who didn't finish college but are making good money—maybe certain kinds of small businessmen, craftsmen getting top pay, and salesmen of all sorts." The other two strata we would label *white-collar middle class of comfortable living standard* and *blue-collar working class of comfortable living standard*. We would not, however, wish to imply thereby—as do Upper Americans looking down from above—that all of the first rank socially above any of the second. That would not accord with the way our Middle-American respondents spoke of status at this level, nor would it accord with our findings from the magnitude estimation experiment reported in Chapter 11. There we will see high-income blue-collar families granted higher status scores than middle- and low-income white-collar families. Ultimately, after carefully examining the behavioral patterns and social relationships of persons of this status in our sample, we came to more complicated conclusions about stratification at this level and developed simplified class names (see Chapter 9). But for the moment, while we are still dealing with status images, we will use these tongue-twisters since they reflect part of the public's view.

Middle Americans just getting along can be divided, if we accept the Upper-American perspective, into white-collar middle-class and blue-collar working-class segments. Our Middle-American respondents did not look at matters this way, however. Instead, for the most part they lumped both into one category, working class, treating that phrase as having reference to "the $9,000-a-year bracket of people getting by, paying their bills, earning anywhere from $150 a week to $200 . . . [such as] factory workers, construction workers, and lower-office workers—a hard working class of people." Lower Americans bracketed an almost identical group into their middle-middle class, saying, "They could be store help or plant workers or utility company employees. . . . They would have an income of around $9,000 or $10,000 a year."

The lower working class of people who are poor but not on welfare quite cleary contains two substrata in the eyes of both Middle Americans and Lower Americans. (Upper Americans seem too far from this socio-economic level to know anything about such a division, or to care.) The higher of these sub-strata we would call *marginal Middle-Americans*, and the lower, *people who are Lower Americans but not lowest class*. Marginal Middle-Americans are the group that Middle Americans of getting-along or comfortable living standard in our sample referred to as lower-middle class. They are "decent enough, but they average only $6,000 or $7,000 a year in earnings. They just barely make ends meet. They live in not-the-best neighborhoods, but they're not lower class." People who are Lower-American but not lowest class are, by contrast, men and women who "may make just the minimum wage, but they're working and too proud to accept welfare. Their jobs are common labor . . . and they lack the education to better themselves." Many are thought to be "members of minority groups—blacks, Chicanos, Puerto Ricans, and American Indians —who are poor and have special problems." These are the various types of people identified with the phrase next-to-lowest class by our Middle-American respondents; Lower Americans divided people of the same station into two categories, lower-middle class and next-to-lowest class, differentiating between them by saying that the former stood "a step above poverty" while the latter fell below it in living standard.

An image division for members of the non-working welfare class was suggested by most of our Lower-American respondents. This would separate "people who are on welfare but keep themselves clean" from those who are "just dirty—they don't have any pride at all." Another division—which is a special irritant to Middle Americans—might be made between people who do very well on welfare—they live as well as many people who work and welfare recipients who don't do that well. From the broader view these distinctions may not be important, and, in any event, our respondents' tendency to condemn everybody on welfare to the bottom of the status ladder may reflect more emotional-political myth than social reality.

In the above delineation of the American status structure we have drawn exclusively on the imagery about social class that people in Boston and Kansas City produced in response to our open-ended and directed questions. There are obviously gaps in this imagery, and our analysis has perhaps raised as many questions about public perception of the structure as it has answered. In Chapters 8, 9, and 10, where imagery about the three main status groups is put in close focus, we shall resolve many of these issues as we bring to bear other kinds of data from our survey—club memberships, best-friend choices, and reports by our sample members of informal social participation in the neighborhood and wider community—to portray how Americans group themselves hierarchically (and otherwise) in everyday interaction. These data, together with information about household income, occupation, housing level, neighborhood, educational background, and ancestry help us understand how and where social reality diverges from this account of class imagery.

CHAPTER 8

Social Standing
in Upper America

AT the pinnacle of Upper America, as this position is envisioned by average citizens, stand the families of greatest and longest-held wealth. The greater the wealth, and the longer it has been held, the higher they stand. At the lower edge of Upper America, said the middle-status Bostonians and Kansas Citians in our survey, is anybody who has attained a material standard of living sufficient to "live the good life." From the highest level of Upper America down to the lowest stretches a vast expanse. On a magnitude estimation scale, the distance might measure from a high of 800 or 1,000 down to a low of 130 or 140. The area between is populated with myriad forms of above-average status. For some families, the identification with Upper-American standing is essentially political; for others, it is genealogical; for still others, it is mainly cultural; for most, economic superiority is part of the picture.

How Middle Americans perceive the stratification of the people they identify with the world of Upper Americans is one story; how Upper Americans stratify and categorize themselves is another. In this chapter we shall first tell the one tale, then sketch the other, thus highlighting the differences between the two.

The Middle-American View:
Three Main Strata Differentiated by Living Standard

To the average American, status within the world of upper-income America is almost exclusively a matter of how much income a family has. As the typical Middle American sees things—and, for that matter, Lower Americans, too—the more income a family has, the more envied is its standard of living, the better the housing its members can afford, the more lavish the vacations they can take, the more expensive the recreation they can enjoy, and the greater their freedom from hard work, a 9-to-5 routine, and other people telling them what to do. Middle Americans divide the world of Upper Americans into three main categories, and often, but not always, recognize subcategories in each. The highest of the three is the top class of the definitely rich. Below that is the next-to-top class of the success elite—the people "who really have it made" in income and/or political power. The third main category consists of the people who are leading a good life: these are families "in the upper-middle-income bracket," most of whom are "college educated, with jobs in management or the professions," but some are the self-educated, prospering small businessmen and tradesmen.

The top class of definitely rich. In the Middle-American image of life at the top-class level, four themes dominate: the grandeur of their housing, the incredible ease of daily existence that their incomes permit, the extravagant forms of recreation they pursue, and their isolation—both physical and economic—from the problems of the rest of the American public.

Perhaps the quintessential definition of the grandeur of their housing was this, from a blue-collar Bostonian, "When I think of a really rich man, I think of one of those estates where you can't see the house from the road." This is how Middle Americans almost invariably envision the housing of top-class families: "They live in vast houses with fifteen or twenty rooms"; "It would be in an estate-type setting, in a secluded place"; "They live in cloisters where they are isolated from the lower elements." In Boston this means that they have "one of those beautiful farms in Dover," or "a $200,000 home in Pride's Crossing . . . on the North Shore, with a view of the ocean," or perhaps "one of those massive townhouses on Beacon Hill that's been in their family for years." In Kansas City, without so developed a tradition of country seats for its aristocratic families, the locations are more urban and more in public view: "They have a gigantic house at 63rd and Ward Parkway [a boulevard lined with mansions for nearly two miles]" or, "They have one of those show-places in Mission Hills, with lots of land around, that go for $500,000."

It is not just that people in the top class "can have anything in the way of material possessions they desire" that marks their ease of life; more truly it is that "they have butlers, maids, gardeners, chauffeurs, service people taking care of their houses and grounds . . . probably more than one per house"; that "their children would go to exclusive, private schools"; and that "they belong to exclusive social clubs," where "they can have parties that are attended by no less than one hundred people"—and, of course, all the work is done by others.

The extravagance of their recreation is illustrated in various ways. They have two or more houses, perhaps "one house in the country, another in the city," or "winter houses in Florida and summer houses on the Cape" (if they are Bostonians), or "a winter place in Arizona or on an island, and a summer place up in the Northern lakes" (if they are Kansas Citians). They "have more time for vacations—almost unlimited in the case of the wives"; "they travel to Europe regularly or see the world and take it off their income tax"; and they take "weekend jaunts to the Bahamas any time they want." Finally, "they are the people who have debutante parties—the people you read about on the society page."

For such an existence, an income of $100,000 a year at minimum (1972 dollars) is assumed by Middle Americans. A top-class family's two biggest worries—as the ordinary citizen sees things—are "keeping all the money they've got" and "wondering when someone will try to kidnap a daughter and hold her for ransom" (or, "A radical will bomb their swimming pool—that happened to a couple of those families in Mission Hills [in Kansas City]"). Such problems isolate top-class people from the press of the average family's struggles just to "pay the bills" and educate its offspring.

Occupationally, the men of the top class are primarily big business people—"board chairmen," "presidents of large concerns," "corporate heads," "big bankers," or owners of large businesses "like department stores or chains," or manufacturing plants. They may also be "the very top politicians," "the most respected specialist physicians," "the brightest lights among the lawyers," and high-income people in the entertainment industry, including sports personalities. Within this top-class world, at least four gradations of status appeared in the descriptions given by Bostonians and Kansas Citians of Middle-American status. These are gradations in levels of wealth and in awesomeness of financial position, political power, and celebrity standing.

At the summit level are "the plutocrats and billionaires"—"the ultra-ultra rich"—some of whom are "so rich they try to keep out of the public eye, like Howard Hughes and J. Paul Getty." Other names and phrases for this level, spoken over and over, were "the true upper class of old money like the Fords and Rockefellers" and "the jet set like Onassis and the Kennedys who have their own social class." These are names of fable around the world; the average American looks up at their wealth in utter awe; we can safely label this stratum *the international-legend rich*.

A step down are what might be called *the local and regional-legend rich*. These are men and families who may be worth perhaps $20 million or $50 million or rank with "that fellow who owns the Kansas City Royals, Ewing Kauffman—he's worth about $160 million." They "own big corporations"; they are "extremely wealthy," with "incomes too high to think about—maybe a million a year." In Kansas City four names dominated discussion of people of this status: "The Kempers—they have banks, family companies, and land"; "Joyce Hall, who founded Hallmark Cards and has made millions—he's a big, sensible businessman"; the baseball team owner Kauffman (who first built a fortune in pharmaceuticals); and "Lamar Hunt, who owns the Kansas City Chiefs" (who is not a Kansas City resident but a Texan, despite his football team proprietorship). In Boston, the names of local and national legend that seem to command this kind of reverence are "the Lodges, Cabots, and Saltonstalls—the old established families, quite a few of whom are in government."

A notch below this is the *presidential-and-celebrity level*. Here "the president of the United States is the top man," but placed alongside him were "the men who run the larger businesses and make $250,000 or $300,000 a year," "corporate executives whose incomes range in the hundreds of thousands of dollars," "famous actors and actresses," and "the very rich you read about: movie and TV personalities, sports figures, or one of these surgeons doing new operations."

At the lowest level of top-class status are the more anonymous very, very well-to-do. The major criterion for inclusion at this level is an income in the three-figures range, but the names of these people may not mean anything to the public at large. For the most part Middle Americans vaguely speak of them as "men who own factories," "people in finance earning over $100,000," or "the most respected physicians and lawyers." Among political figures at this level—whose names would, of course, be known—are the chief justice of the Supreme Court, the vice-president, and "the [other] politicians next to the president." Except for the political figures ranked here, this is a stratum of the moderately wealthy, which is another way of calling it the lowest level of the definitely rich.

Generally speaking, this is how Middle Americans structure the top class in their minds; they rank its members in terms of the level of their wealth, political role, and celebrity status. They do not rank all those who inherit top-class membership above the newcomers to that stratum. People at each of the four levels who inherited high position are looked upon as more to be envied than those newly risen to it but are not thereby equated socially with those in the next level up.

It is a common conviction that "education does not have much to do with this: people with good hard common sense can go as far as those with college degrees; they can make a million or more a year." It is also understood that "Doctors and lawyers would have had a good education, but the rest might only have four years of college—or not even that."

The next-to-top class of success elite. Not in the top class, but assuredly leading an elite level of existence as Middle and Lower Americans envision it, are people whose 1972 incomes were running from $37,500 up to $100,000. At such levels, "A family would have just about everything they could need or want. . . . They go out a lot, entertain a lot, have nice homes and cars. . . . They are enjoying all that life can give them. . . . They have lots of bucks, lots of doors open—they don't want for anything." Another way of phrasing it was: "They're not outright rich, but plenty well off. For them, money is not a problem." Also, "They are what you'd call lower-upper class. They can have a Cadillac and a country club membership without a struggle." In occupational terms, these are men and women whose success has been sufficient that, in the eyes of the mainstream of the American public, "they really have it made." In economic status, they are the people who are not in the upper one-thousandth but nevertheless rank among the nation's top 2 or 3 percent. In this respect, they appear to average Americans as a success elite.

The range of earnings associated with this level permits a wide variety in standards of living. Taking a closer look at our conversations with average-status Bostonians and Kansas Citians, we actually identified two subcategories. One centers on people who "make around $40,000 or $50,000 a year," and the other is composed of those who "are almost into big money; they make $60,000 or $75,000 a year." For these two categories we can delineate differences in occupational titles, political power, and the luxuriousness of existence as these are imagined by the average American.

Doctors comprise the occupation group most commonly associated with both levels of this success elite class; plainly, to Middle America, most physicians are next-to-top class, if not at the top. Indeed, it seems assumed that all but the youngest doctors and least successful general practitioners are at this level. Doctors placed at the upper level were "the specialists, but not the big-time specialists" ("That would be a less-than-spectacular physician who's still doing very well," said a Kansas Citian); those at the lower level "are just ordinary doctors, the ones in general practice, not a specialty."

Lawyers were the next most frequently cited occupational group; those identified with the upper level "are fairly prominent," while those at the lower level "have a good practice going for them—they're not just scuffling like so many in that profession." Third in volume of mention were upper-echelon corporation employees: here, "executives—but not the Number-One Man" or "bank officials making $75,000 a year" were of higher rank, while at the low edge were a variety of "bank and insurance company vice-presidents," "people in executive-type positions in a small company, not a big corporation," and "managers in big indus-tries—like a plant manager or general sales manager for a large lumber company." Among business owners, "contractors" and "auto dealers" seem to characterize the upper level, while "the smaller-businessmen doing very well with, say, a tool-and-die shop," and "owners of a clothing store—or some of the real estate people" more commonly exemplify the lower.

Especially significant to Lower Americans as part of our society's elite are "politicians." Mention of them as top class or next-to-top by Lower Americans exceeded that for any other occupational group. However, with Middle Americans, people in government or politics ranked only fifth. Toward the high end of this next-to-top class, Bostonians and Kansas Citians placed cabinet members, the governor, senators, "Mayor White" (in Boston), "Mayor Wheeler" (in Kansas City, Missouri), and Supreme Court justices. Toward the low side they put "the council-men" (in Boston), "the city manager" (in Kansas City, Missouri), "the mayor of Kansas City, Kansas," "congressmen who are less than com-mittee chairmen," "top advisors in government posts," and "all the judges."

Also associated by Middle Americans with this next-to-top class of the nation's successful people were all the following occupational groups: "college administrators," "deans," "popular scholars," "top professors," "dentists—orthodontists, really, not the ordinary dentist," "some of the high-paid scientists in research labs," "electronic engineers earning maybe $40,000 a year," "good architects," "leading clergy," "the super- intendent of schools," "airline pilots," "athletes," "TV news personalities," and "top salesmen—earning like $50,000 a year." A Boston woman of higher status expressed this succinctly: "In the next-to-top class I'd put all the people who are the brightest lights in their fields, whatever their claim to fame is—scientists, artists, educators, writers. . . . If they're renowned, they can be in the class without making six figures a year, as long as they're in the upper percentile of their respective profession and have the most respect and have been there longest." Most of these mem- bers of the success elite would rank toward the low edge, but not all, since some have succeeded well enough to live on a nearly top-class scale and have achieved prominence on the national scene equal to that of almost any governor or Supreme Court justice.

Most members of the next-to-top class have four years of college, some six or eight years, as middle Americans imagine them. This is the status group they see as "tops in schooling," more so, indeed, than the top class itself in which unique factors such as inherited wealth or "knowing how to make money" appear to count. Here, where more con- ventional skills and paths have produced a somewhat less awesome level of success, a college background is seen to have paved the way more often, and in the instance of professionals and corporate managers it has been well-nigh imperative. Only "self-made" businessmen, entertain- ment people, and some political figures are exempted from this pre- requisite for success-elite status. It is understood that among these, "many came up the hard way," through "talent, initiative, and a lot of person- ality." This exemption notwithstanding, the collegiate image dominates in Middle-American impressions of the next-to-top class; over and over the people we interviewed spoke of this group as having "flocks of degrees," and many seemed convinced that "most had a master's degree at least." (In this regard, no distinction was drawn between the upper and lower levels of the next-to-top class; both were described as having "more education than anyone else.")

The kinds of houses that Middle Americans enviously project for the success elite amount to "an absolute dream" of contemporary amenity. They feature all the latest in gadgets and push-button conveniences for in-home recreation and a work-free existence ("everything at your finger- tips," "a room-to-room intercom," "a wet bar in the game room"). And outside, of course, an in-ground swimming pool, "a couple of acres for privacy," and "a full sprinkler system for the lawn." "A true luxury spread" is what one Bostonian called this kind of home. And in Kansas City an especially opulent version was described: "That would be like Len Dawson's place [Dawson was then the Kansas City Chief's quarterback]—it has a swimming pool and tennis court, three and one-half baths, beamed ceilings all over, a three-car garage, and two Cadillacs." The adjectives people applied to such housing ranged from "beautiful," "fancy," and "plush" up to "posh," "ritzy," and "super-luxurious"—this last was reserved for houses of the upper-level success elite. At a minimum, such a home was believed to cost $70,000 in Boston (as of 1971) and $65,000 in Kansas City (in 1972). For the more fortunate, the homes they could afford would range from $125,000 to $150,000 and $175,000, with appropriate additions in space and equipment. To maintain such establishments, the upper-level success elite would "have a housekeeper come in every day," but at the lower edge, families would have to settle for "help three days a week."

Other aspects of the success-elite standard of living are seen as similarly self-indulgent and materially enviable. It is believed, for instance, that members of this class have at least two and often three cars and buy a new car every year, "usually Cadillacs or very expensive foreign makes." They "have to have nice clothes for all their social life"; the children "are sent off to camp every summer"; and the parents "regularly go out to dinner at nice places," "have parties and social doings to go to all the time," and "have a country-club type of life"—except that "they don't belong to as fancy a club as the top class." Those at the lower level of next-to-top-class status "can't afford to belong to both a yacht club and a golf club, only one." Families at the upper edge are assumed to "take at least two big vacations a year," going abroad for at least one, and possibly venturing clear "to the South Sea Islands." They "definitely have a second house" where they regularly spend either a month in summer or a month in winter. Families at the lower edge may not have a second house, but probably do. In Boston this would be "a summer cottage down the Cape or somewhere in New Hampshire," and in Kansas City it would be "a place on a lake in the Ozarks"; in any event, they "take about six weeks of vacation a year," and depending on their whim "may go to Europe or just to the Caribbean." For their recreation and vacations success-elite people were perceived to do "whatever is popular," which— in the early 1970s—seemed to mean that "they all play golf and tennis," "are big on skiing in winter" and, if Kansas Citians, "have suites at the football games." Finally, the higher up on the scale, the more "they donated a lot of time to civic affairs" and "have to go to lots of fundraising events."

This latter side of high-status life is not so attractive to Middle Americans. They have the impression that it is a stressful existence, full of civic obligations and social reciprocities, of striving to rise higher financially and/or politically, of desperate concern for public acceptance and personal reputation. If the men get to "play hard, they also have to work hard"—"life is full of business"; "the more they make, the more they probably want, they're never satisfied"; "there is an awful lot of pressure and responsibility—not too much time for relaxing; they would always have to be going to meetings, studying, and keeping up." Many a middle-status Bostonian and Kansas Citian in our sample echoed one Boston woman's verdict that:

> "Life is very hectic for those people. There are more breakdowns and alcoholism. It must be very hard to sustain the status, the clothes, the parties that are expected. I don't think I'd want to take their place."

Among Middle-American women it is commonly felt that being the wife of a success-elite husband—whether businessman, professional, or politician—must be no bed of roses: that "their husbands are not home as much as mine" and that "you find a lot of those women starting to drink, and they fuss and complain about their husbands," that "though they have a beautiful home and everything you'd think they want, they're still no happier than I am." It is, then, mainly the material rewards and sybaritic pleasures that Middle Americans envy about the success-elite lifestyle; what they see as the efforts that have gone into achieving it (and must go into maintaining it) and the pains that often result, they would just as happily do without.

People leading a good life. Within this third main level of Upper Americans, we can identify two distinctive sublevels. These sublevels are quite important analytically, even though Middle Americans generally lumped them together into a single large category of upper-middle-income and associated both with the upper-middle-class level of social standing. The higher level we shall refer to as *a very good living: the professional-and-managerial class standard.* In our magnitude experiment with three-factor profiles, families at this level were scored 160 to 249. The lower level we shall label *the good life: Middle America's hope and goal.* Families of this sort were scored 130 to 159 in the magnitude estimation test. The income range that characterized the higher level in 1972 was $22,500 to $37,500, while the lower level ranged from $22,500 down to $15,000.

A prime ingredient of the good life—and a principal proof of its achievement—is the house a family has acquired for itself. This is central to the estimate that Middle Americans make of one another's financial status—so much so, indeed, that it is questionable whether a family is regarded as a full participant in the good life, no matter what its income, if it does not own a suitable home. A Kansas City woman described it in these words: "The house would have at least one and one-half baths, a living room, dining room, kitchen, family room, and three bedrooms— seven rooms and at least 1,500 or 1,600 square feet of living space. It would have a two-car garage and should be air-conditioned." An essentially similar picture was presented by Bostonians, except they did not demand either central air-conditioning or space for a second car.

By contrast, the home of a family that had achieved a very good living, according to Middle Americans, would "have eight rooms or more," "there would be a minimum of 2,200 square feet of floor space," and "it would provide both a family recreation center and all the rest of the things they'd want, including a living room with a fireplace, a formal dining room, four bedrooms, at least a double-car garage and all the 'goodies'—a trash compactor, dishwasher, and two or more bathrooms." Such a house is thought to be "lovely" by Middle-American women and is praised as "damned good" by Middle-American men.

Going beyond the symbol of the house, what the good life more generally suggests to Middle Americans is a world of "people who are working hard but make good money—they can save for their later years and have enough to live very comfortably right now." It means "people that make more, have more, live more comfortably than most of us." A Kansas City woman said, "The good life is when you aren't up to dabbling in the luxuries but have lots more than the necessities." A Boston man said, "That's two shades above me," and a young Kansas City blue-collar worker probably spoke for all in his age and income bracket (below $10,000 a year) when he daydreamed, "If I were making $20,000, I'd think I was in Fat City."

Next in importance to a seven-room house in the suburbs as a symbol of the good life is ownership of two cars. These may be "a late model Ford and some kind of camper or trailer to enjoy over the weekends"; "a stationwagon for the main family car and a smaller one when only one person needs it"; or "one car for the husband (maybe a big Buick) and another for the wife (one of those compacts would probably be best)." Having two cars is imperative; with only one there would be a strain, and it would not be a good life in the suburbs.

In terms of recreational customs and leisure enjoyments, the good life includes "going out to dinner once a week," "occasionally eating at expensive places," "going to a movie whenever there's one you want to see," "playing bridge," "going bowling, fishing, or golfing every weekend," and "doing all sorts of things together as a family—camping and boating, whatever they prefer." The parents "have plenty of time to spend with the children," because, unlike those one step up, "they aren't always out socializing." There is, then, this distinction in Middle-American imagery between a good life and the kind of very good living associated with the professional and managerial class making $22,500 a year and up in 1972: at the very-good-living level, a country club membership is commonplace ("they use private facilities for recreation, though not quite so expensive as the top class's"), while for the good-life level it would be rare; for people at the higher level social life is very important ("they use it to promote their careers"), while for those at the lower level, the pleasure in social life is its own reward, treated as neither stepping stone nor status symbol.

The vacation patterns that Middle Americans associated with those living the good life centered around the idea that "they get three weeks of vacation a year." Ideas about how these three weeks might be spent varied from "One good trip across the United States a year, to a different state each year" to "renting a place on the Cape for two weeks in the summer and going skiing in New Hampshire one week in the winter." Of one thing regarding the good life Middle Americans were sure: "Their trips are, well, like to the Grand Canyon—not European travel" and "they aren't trying to impress people by saying, 'We went to Paris'." In this respect, again, a distinction is drawn between the good life and a very good living, since for people at the latter level, "trips to Mexico," "travel to Europe every three or four years," and "one week at a winter resort in Florida" are assumed—and also one extra, fourth week of vacation per year.

All of this represents to Middle Americans "living more comfortably than most of us." For the economic mainstream of citizens the requisites of a good life are not terribly far removed in cost or luxury from their own standard of living; these requisites are "not a maid or butler—you don't have to have that" and certainly "not private education for your children, just maybe some kind of lessons."

Middle Americans assume that a large proportion of the professional work force has reached the income levels they associate with a very good living. Included in this image would be "young doctors," "lawyers who are not well-known," "engineers making $25,000 to $35,000," "professors," "dentists," "CPAs," "scientists," and "school administrators, like a high school principal." Almost as commonly identified with this world are "people holding responsible positions in large companies," who are variously referred to as "upper-middle management," "managers in business corporations who carry out policy rather than make it," or "college graduates in managerial positions." A proprietor ranked at this level is described as "a person who owns his own business and makes $25,000 a year" or "the self-employed businessman on the medium scale." Also included in this bracket, but with less frequency, were "college graduates in sales," "a factory superintendent," and "government people at the $30,000 salary level" (in Boston this included "some of the top jobs under the mayor," and in Kansas City, "the Number-Two and Number-Three people at City Hall").

A quite different mix of occupations was associated by Middle Americans with the more moderate good-life standard of living. The four dominant types were "upper level office workers—they make $1,500 a month," "underpaid professionals," "tradesmen who are high in unions and earn a good deal of money," and "people who have a small business—like a restaurant or a grocery store that does well." Also identified with this level, though less prominently, are "salesmen of all sorts—especially insurance salesmen," "supervisors in production," "civil servants," and "lots of families where both the man and wife are working, so their combined income puts them way up there, though individually they aren't making so much." What these diverse occupations and family situations have in common, of course, is their level of earnings. These earnings, with $15,000 assumed to be the minimum in annual pre-tax income, have allowed such families to purchase the kinds of houses, cars, and spare-time pleasures that mark them as people leading the good life. To that extent, they are not only socially equal to each other in the eyes of most Middle Americans but also clearly superior in standing to people merely comfortable or just getting along.

Middle Americans believe that the great majority of those earning a very good living started adult life with the advantage of "four years of college at least and maybe more," while among the men and women who have achieved the more modest good-life standard, there is "a mix of educational qualifications ranging from high school graduates to college graduates."

To the men who have attained the professional and managerial class standard of a very good living, Middle Americans in Boston and Kansas City attributed an educational level almost, but not quite, equal to that of the next-to-top-class success elite (and possibly exceeding, on the average, that of the top class). The difference between them was perceived to come not so much from their school experiences as from their success in pursuing their careers and whether or not "they know how to make big money." The men at the very good living level were almost universally spoken of by Middle Americans as well-educated, and indeed, frequently assumed to "have degrees in abundance—graduate degrees, professional degrees, or whatever additional training was required to fit them for their positions." Even when it was said, "They're mostly college graduates, just a few self-made men among them," they were placed, in image, considerably above the average man at the good-life level. The typical view of the latter was that "they would have a better-than-average education, like a couple of years of college or more"; and, although a significant minority were thought to "have a bachelor's degree of some sort," an equally significant minority were believed to have nothing more in the way of educational credentials than "high school plus technical training." This image bespeaks a belief on the part of Middle Americans that attaining the good-life standard of living is not an unreasonable hope for those without educational advantage; it may be greatly more difficult to get there without a college degree, as they see it, but the lack of such is no insurmountable obstacle—and no great social disgrace.

This concludes the first story in this chapter: a description of Middle Americans' ideas about which of their fellow citizens rank above them in social standing, on what basis, and how far up. Now we move to the second story, which is of the social divisions Upper Americans recognize among themselves and the criteria they employ in rendering such judgments. In telling this story, we shall project it separately for the two cities in our study. There are two reasons for this. One is that our data from Kansas City are richer, based on continuous research contact and observation going back to the early 1950s. The other is that Upper Kansas City seems more simply structured and its hierarchic features perceived more readily than is the case in Upper Boston. That Boston's metropolitan area population is more than twice Kansas City's is one factor in this; that Boston's people are more diverse in ethnic origin is another; and that Boston's society is more pluralist, except at the extreme upper edge, is a third.

The Upper Kansas City View: A Multi-Level Hierarchy of Clubs and Cliques

The real keys to social standing in Upper Kansas City are "the clubs you belong to and who your friends are." That is what the people we talked to in Kansas City through the years have always said, first in 1952, most recently in 1974, and off and on in between. This is also the conclusion that observation of their behavior warrants. All along, our Kansas City informants have insisted that money—thought of either as assets or income—is not the proper measure of high status, that while "it counts for a lot," it does not explain all—"not by a long shot." Neither is lineage the ultimate clue, not even at the highest level, though it can be signal asset or critical handicap. Always playing a part are civic contributions and educational background, but again, hardly as crucial or critical. Ultimately, say upper-status Kansas Citians, social standing in their world reduces down to one issue: where does an individual or family rank on the scale of private club membership and informal cliques?

For this scale, the area's many country clubs for golf and family-style clubs for swimming and tennis are the basic indexing variable. What Kansas Citians have to say about these clubs variously suggests, or proves, their individual roles.

Standing at the summit is the First Jackson Country Club.* Regarding the First Jackson's stature, the verdict is unanimous:

> "All the ultra-elite of Kansas City are there in the First Jackson. . . . It's the center of our top-cream society. . . . Its membership has always been the best. . . . Anybody in the First Jackson is automatically considered part of Kansas City society, with a capital S. . . . That's where people who aspire to a high social position would want to be. . . . Anybody who gets invited to join First Jackson would leave Missoukana [the second-best club] to go over there. . . . Only those with less ambition are satisfied to be in Missoukana."

One step down, as implied above, is Missoukana Country Club:

> "Missoukana is the absolute number-two country club. It's the only other one that really counts socially. . . . Missoukana has some members who you'd call 'capital S'—they're definitely in Society—but most really aren't, they're next-to-top class. . . . No one needs to apologize for being in Missoukana—the members are a very fine group. . . . Missoukana doesn't take just anybody who is wealthy—it's really very exclusive. If you

* The names of all local country clubs and social clubs are pseudonyms. Quotations from different respondents are separated by ellipses.

weren't born into it, it can be very difficult to get in. . . . Missoukana's a long step above Silver Hills—there's hardly any overlap. People almost always leave Silver Hills if they get a chance to join Missoukana."

In third place on this country club ladder is Silver Hills:

"A lot of people you could call upper class—well, they're in the next-to-top class, not really the top—are in Silver Hills. . . . Silver Hills' rich members are newer families; they don't have the right credentials or sponsorship to get into Missoukana. . . . Silver Hills isn't all upper-class though. Some of its members are just the top flight of typically successful professional and business people. . . . You'd almost certainly have to have an income of $35,000 or $40,000 to join, or maybe just $30,000, if [you are] really determined. . . . Silver Hills is a very strong third among the country clubs; there's a gap between it and the mass of country clubs below. Only some of the leading Catholic families at Emerald Hills might stand as high socially as the leadership at Silver Hills."

Bunched together as a fourth step are four country clubs: Emerald Hills (with a slight edge on the rest because it is believed to have some upper-class Catholic members), Shawnee Woods, Johnson Fields, and Blue View:

"Those are country clubs for people who couldn't afford the initiation fees at Silver Hills. . . . They're what you might call the country clubs of suburbiana. . . . They're nice enough, but they're just clubs—they aren't at all in the Society swing of things. . . . The members are the garden variety of manager or professional—minor executives with smaller companies or hard-working middle-management in large corporations. . . . Most would have college degrees, but probably from ordinary schools, not the Ivy League. . . . The man would make at least $20,000 a year, more likely $25,000 or $30,000." (And top-class Kansas Citians remark, "Their members are people you never heard of.")

Down another notch are what Kansas Citians in the organizations above—from fourth rank up to first—refer to as "player's clubs," meaning that while these are private golf clubs, they lack swimming and tennis facilities and are without rooms for party-giving and party-going. In other words, they are clubs "only for golfing and golfers," with "the nineteenth-hole bar" the only other form of on-site entertainment. Their status is assessed in phrases like this: "They're just the golfing set at clubs like that. . . . They're not necessarily even upper-middle class. . . . A lot of ordinary salesmen might be members." (Below these, as a sixth notch on the golfers' social ladder, are the public links, where anyone can play "who can pay the day's fees," there is no such thing as membership.)

Proliferating on the Kansas City scene since the early 1950s have been swim-and-tennis clubs. One of these—the Portico, with "the most expensive and elaborate layout"—is socially ranked equal to Silver Hills; another two—in relatively high-status neighborhoods—are treated on a par with the fourth-rung all-facilities country clubs. Most, however, are not much above the players-only golf clubs, if at all. Kansas Citians of higher status have dubbed them "cement-block country clubs," since, as they say, "all you see is a big parking lot, a few tennis courts, a small swimming pool, and very little grass." The status attributed to the individual representatives of this type of club varies according to the character of the neighborhoods they serve. For the most part, it is assumed that members of clubs like these "might make just $15,000 a year, or, if [they are] young and on the rise, their salaries may not be over $12,000 yet."

The relationship in Upper Kansas City between financial status and social standing, as measured on this golf-and-country-club scale, is not always what middle-status Kansas Citians might imagine. There is—by knowledgeable report from people at the top—an inverse ratio between initiation fees charged by the leading three country clubs and their social rank. Silver Hills, the number-three club, is known to be "the most expensive—its initiation fee is $2,000 more than Missoukana's and $3,000 more than the First Jackson's." This upside-down price structure, with the highest-status club costing its members the least, was explained in this way: "The First Jackson likes to keep on its roster a certain number of old families whose incomes may be just $30,000 a year; it adds age and dignity to the place." Another example is that each rank of club is assumed to have a certain share of $30,000-a-year members. At the public courses, for instance, "there are plumbers and truck-drivers making that much" (said a few of our respondents); at the same level are some of the salesmen at the player's clubs, many an engineer or accountant at the country clubs of suburbiana, and "determined young professionals on the rise" at Silver Hills. Finally, as suggested above, there are financially hard-pressed second generation members at Missoukana and First Jackson.

There is, however, a basic correlation between economic standing and this country-club rank of social status (these surprises to the contrary notwithstanding). The average members of the fifth-rank clubs are, both by image and by the findings of our study, college-educated families where the husband is "not doing all that well—just making $18,000 or $20,000 a year." The average member of one of the fourth-rank clubs is, indeed, a management man making $25,000 or $30,000, and thus, the family is leading a very good life. To make it into Silver Hills without special connections or determination, an income of $40,000 or $50,000 would seem necessary; in other words, the family would qualify as one of the new rich success elite, as defined by Middle Americans. Then, to rank as one of Silver Hills' rich members, or to have one's application even considered by Missoukana (if, that is, "you weren't born into it")—an income of $60,000 would probably be the minimum. As one Kansas City executive of this status explained, "If you aren't making $60,000 or $70,000 a year, you're not in high cotton."

None of this is to say that families at each of the designated income levels are routinely accepted into clubs of the indicated rank. Kansas Citians insist that this is not the case and say, "It all depends on the individual." What this phrase seems to refer to is that nebulous thing called *personality*—whether someone is "terrific company," "fun to be around," and "socially attractive," and also whether or not they "contribute to the community." This rule is said to apply to the descendants of old families almost as much as to the newly rising.

Probably nothing changed so much in Kansas City between our first study of social standing there and this most recent one as did enthusiasm for civic contribution as the means to, and a near-requirement for, high status in its most respected forms. The number of organizations to which upper-level Kansas Citians volunteer their time, talents, and energies seems to have nearly doubled in the interim as new causes have been discovered—the zoo, amateur opera, and historic houses, to name a few—and old causes have found new groups developed in their support. The social columns of Kansas City's news organs reflect this change. As the years have passed, they have increasingly been dominated by coverage of benefit events, committee meetings to plan the benefits, and elections to office and membership on these committees. A prime result is that a reputation for contributing or not contributing has become a crucial ingredient in an Upper Kansas City family's image and rating. Contributors are invariably praised, characterized by their peers as "fantastic—she's given millions of dollars," "a real leader," "energetic and involved in the community," or "unassuming but responsible—a quiet worker." And those not contributing are as roundly damned: "He doesn't give anything to the community—he may be a millionaire, but you can't get $500 out of him"; "She's selfish—she hasn't done a thing for the city"; and "That family is not very popular—all they seem to care about is giving parties. They haven't given much else." Given these attitudes, it is not surprising to find that volunteering has extended down below the upper-class level, where formerly it was narrowly concentrated, into the upper-middle level, where now many a woman is said to be "up to her ears in volunteer work."

Causes in Kansas City are ranked like the country clubs. Contributing to the art museum has the highest status, volunteering for the zoo much lower. Moving up through the structure of ranked causes goes hand in hand with graduating up the country-club scale—and, indeed, successful volunteering is believed to be one of the best ways for the socially ambitious to gain attention and approval from those already higher up.

Beyond country clubs and causes, virtually all other kinds of associations and activities that upper-status Kansas Citians enter into, whether formally or informally, are ranked and rated. The churches they belong to are differently valued; some are said to have "pretty much a Society tone," others are "typical upper-middle class, suburban congregations." The men's town clubs are socially scaled by expensiveness and exclusiveness. So too are the women's service clubs, with an invitation to join the nationally affiliated Junior League more sought after than memberships in any of the local groups of similar purpose. The neighborhoods occupied by upper-status folk are also finely graded; addresses reflect different levels of social aspiration and self-identification. Finally, there are bridge clubs by the thousands and couples' dinner-dance groups by the score that divide Kansas Citians into smaller cliques than the formal organizations; each has a rating among those who know of it. Social standing in Upper Kansas City is the sum of all an individual's or family's associations. These fix rather precisely where persons rate and with which country club crowd they are associated in popular impression, even if, in fact, they hold no country club membership.

The best illustration of how all these ranked clubs and cliques further stratify each main social level of Upper Kansas City is found in the stair-step subdivisions of Capital-S Society. Knowledgeable Kansas Citians can identify four main levels, or rungs, as it were, on the Capital-S social ladder. (Nearly 3,000 Greater Kansas City men and women—approximately 0.3% of the total adult population—are identified with this stratum; of these some 250 are Jewish, and these Jewish members, no less than the Gentiles, are found on all four rungs.) The lowest rung on this exalted ladder is formed—in image—around the families of highest rank in the Missoukana Country Club (i.e., that segment of members cited earlier as included in Capital-S Society). Also at this level are most Capital-S families without a country club membership at all. The definitional core for the next rung up—the third—is drawn from the lowest-ranking families in the First Jackson; these are, for the most part, that club's newer, first-generation members. Another step up—and now we are speaking of people definitely in the upper reaches of Capital-S Society—are the First Jackson's middle-level families. First Jackson members of this rank are very solidly established at the Club. Often they can trace their affiliation with the First Jackson through three generations, or if not that, they have become very well-respected through a shorter time span. These families, though not at the pinnacle in status, are nevertheless thought of as top-drawer Kansas City in the most general sense of that phrase; another term often applied to their stature is *Old Guard*. These middle-level First Jacksonites, though not at the pinnacle, nevertheless rank socially in the top one-thousandth of the Kansas City public.

"Our local *crème de la crème*" is the label society columnists like to apply to the men and women of the Capital S tip-top rung. A more vulgar characterization, used by Kansas Citians of lower-upper status, is "the filthy rich—they have enormous, unlimited amounts of money with an old family name attached." To describe social-pinnacle people in the latter fashion is not, however, completely accurate, because a sizable portion are not that rich. A more appropriate view is that they are the First Jackson members with "the most flair for Society leadership"—the women are uncommonly good-looking, the men generally handsome, and the lineage almost unfailingly impressive. First Jackson members not in this elegant circle refer to it with a certain awe as "our Oak Room crowd." This is because there is a particular alcove at the First Jackson dubbed "the Oak Room," in honor of its paneling and furnishings, where these pinnacle people do their drinking, card-playing, and informal socializing when at the Club; there, it is believed, only they among the Club's membership truly feel "at home."

"We Each Have Our Niches": The Upper Boston View

When asked if there is such a thing as social classes in America, one very upper-status Boston woman replied: "I've always lived around Boston. I came out and went away to boarding school. If you've been brought up that way, it influences all your thinking, and not necessarily snobbishly. Maybe you shouldn't call it social class, but it is a niche— and we each have our niches." Several of the niches this woman and others of our one hundred upper-status Boston respondents talked about are, more truly, ranked notches: a top class, next-to-top, upper-middle, and so on. However, probably most of the categories these interviewees described are indeed niches—subdivisions among social equals or parallel groupings of people who are differentiated along lines of religion, ancestry, schools attended, politics, profession, geography, and recreational preferences, rather than by status itself.

Among these many niches, there is one about whose social standing Upper Bostonians unanimously agreed. This is the world of old, old established families who are, of course, "the tip-top—as close to true aristocracy as you find in America." This group was variously referred to as "Yankee families that go way back"; "the WASPs who were here first—they came over on the Mayflower"; "the bluebloods with inherited income —they live on stocks and bonds"; "the landed gentry—they have had money in their family a long time"; and "that group from illustrious backgrounds, where for several generations their people were recognized as leaders." Names of national renown such as Adams, Lodge, Saltonstall, and Cabot—all known for public service—were cited as examples. But less famous persons were also described as representative of this status:

> "One family would be the Leonards [a pseudonym]. They live on Clyde Street in Brookline [a street lined with some of Greater Boston's most impressive in-town mansions]. The husband is chairman of the board of several businesses. They're on museum boards and belong to the Brookline Country Club. They go to Europe every year. All the daughters had debuts."

> "A heart surgeon who is from an old, moneyed Brookline family. Streets are named after them. Professionally he's very successful. He's a Harvard graduate, also the Harvard Medical School. He has an active social life, a general air of great sophistication. He is associated with socially prominent people."

> "There is a bank president in this neighborhood who owns a yacht and travels around the world. He's only about forty-five, but he has a very old Yankee background, and I'm sure he has a very high income."

Many of these old, old established families are believed to be continuing to assume a leadership role in business, public service, and education, but of others it is said, "They lead frivolous lives; their jobs are only nominal; they just do whatever pleases them." And while it is believed that the incomes of families in this circle "might range from $40,000 a year up to $500,000," it is also acknowledged that "some have family connections without much money." There are other characterizing images: "They belong to the best clubs; the women, to the Vincent Club and Junior League, the men, to those groups where the membership is passed from father to son"; "They are big on civic projects, like the Symphony and philanthropy"; "They were educated at the prestigious private schools"; and "They have the *Social Register* type aura."

The top class old families of Boston are not narrowly identified by the public with just one or two neighborhoods, as is true in Kansas City. Rather, their presence was noted in many different places by the Upper Bostonians in our sample—in exurban Concord and Dover (where "they have country estates"), in suburban Milton and Dedham ("you still find some of the upper-uppers here in Dedham"), "on Brattle Street in Cambridge," and "in beautiful homes on Chestnut Hill in Newton." They also live in "mansions in Brookline," "in portions of Beacon Hill—though that's going down," and "along the North Shore, where they have those big estates right on the water, like in Pride's Crossing." This geographic dispersion of the established old families, which exists in fact, as well as in image, is closely associated with differences in life style and is part and parcel of the Upper-Bostonian perception that "we each have our niches." The many clubs that established old Boston families are affiliated with— women's clubs, men's town clubs, country clubs, hunt clubs, yacht clubs, and arts-and-culture clubs—also separate these people into niches and, as in Kansas City, into ranked notches. We know this, however, not from anything told us by our sample members (who are largely unaware of and uninterested in such fine lines of distinction), but rather from society-page reporting in Boston's newspapers and from the writings of social historians who have lavished attention on Boston (Amory, 1947; Birmingham, 1958; Kavaler, 1960).

When asked about classes below the established old families, upper-status Bostonians presented characterizations essentially similar to the Kansas City descriptions. The next-to-top class, as they spoke of it, was "a mix of highly successful executives, doctors, and lawyers with incomes of $60,000 a year at least, many, $100,000 and more. . . . They have help in the house, fancy cars, frequent and expensive vacations, and at least two houses. . . . They're not considered top society because they don't have the right background—they're newer money, with less tradition in their life style." In turn, the upper-middle class was envisioned as "college-educated managers and business people earning $25,000 or $30,000 on up to $50,000"; and the middle-middle class as "college people not doing so well, or still on their way up."

The most noteworthy difference we found between upper-status Bostonians and upper-status Kansas Citians in their portraits of these several high strata is that Bostonians much more frequently cited professors, scientists, researchers, and college graduates in the arts as their occupational examples. Indeed, it was not unheard of for high-status Bostonians to identify "the professional people who are service-oriented, Harvard professors, research doctors, and some of the performing artists like Arthur Fiedler [director of the Boston Pops Orchestra]" as next-to-top class alongside—or even instead of—the *nouveau riche* executive elite. More commonly, however, this group was described as virtually a class unto itself, "the intellectual class," and was characterized as "the more remunerated group of liberal professionals, all highly educated: university people, architects, artists, poets, performers, and writers. . . . They have time to think. . . . They may not be rich but have incomes of $20,000 or more. . . . They enjoy their own prestige." Many an upper-status Bostonian would say, "I'd place myself there [in the intellectual class]— I tend to associate myself with people of similar interests, so conversation can be reciprocal." Looking at the representatives of this intellectual class (self-designated or otherwise) who fell into our sample, we would conclude that they constitute not so much a separate sub-class as a series of ranked niches. Collectively they form Upper Boston's intellectual wing (or niche, if you will), but individually they are of equal standing neither within that wing nor in their positioning by the wider community of Upper Bostonians, since they are distributed up and down the hierarchy according to their particular merits of family, fame, or fortune.

Social divisions created by religion and ancestry are also much more talked about by Upper Bostonians than by Upper Kansas Citians. To a large extent this, too, is a matter of niche more than notch, with each major group described as "socially sticking to themselves." But the status dimension is not entirely absent, since Jews and Catholics in Boston feel excluded by religion alone from certain upper circles and generally "looked down on a bit" by the old Yankee Protestants. Bostonians are very conscious of the geographic concentrations of these groups, treating this as important proof of the social division. Time and again the men and women we interviewed spoke of "the rich Jews out in Newton and Brookline," doing so half in envy and half in hostility; similarly, certain suburbs or sections of suburbia were considered to be favored by the "better-off Catholics," with the whole South Shore commonly called "The Irish Riviera." Clubs were also acknowledged to be sharply divided along these lines. Country clubs, for example, were categorized as "all Jewish," "mainly Catholic," or "predominantly WASP" (those in the last category were further characterized as having admissions policies of "no Jews allowed, and Irish Catholics kept to a 15- to 20-percent quota").

Politics and ideology are also understood to create divisions among Upper Bostonians. To a certain extent this is rooted in occupation, with

the liberal intellectuals and professionals on one side and the conservative business people on the other. But the division also has to do with
religion and ethnicity. Boston's Jewish population is noted for its liberal
stance on virtually all public matters. Catholics are closely identified with
the Democratic party but are known to be less liberal on many social
issues. Protestants are thought to be Republicans generally, but those
who are Unitarians or Quakers are often among the leaders in humani-
tarian reform causes.

Finally, there is a geographic component. Upper Bostonians commonly choose a suburb according to their conception of its ideological
atmosphere; Newton residents, for example, will say, "Newton is closer
to my feeling about politics; it's not so conservative"; while those in
communities of opposite atmosphere will say, "I could never live in
Newton." Important in this respect are the schools. Some of the Boston
suburbs—Newton certainly, Lexington, and Lincoln, to name but three—
are known for their progressive schools, and they attract parents who
prefer this approach; other upper-status suburbs are known as bastions
of traditionalism and attract parental advocates of this educational
philosophy. This division of towns by ideological stance is reflected in
organizational affiliations and recreational patterns. In the "liberal"
suburbs, cause-conscious and cultural organizations are most popular; in
the "conservative" towns, country clubs, boating, riding, and tennis-and-
swim clubs exert a greater appeal.

Differences in educational background are yet another force that
Upper Bostonians recognize as dividing them—in this instance into
notches as well as niches. A difference especially important to Bostonians
who are lifelong New Englanders is the secondary school background.
Men and women who did not go away to boarding school when in their
teens are very conscious of a distinction between themselves and those
who did, and those who did distinguish among themselves according to
the social ranking of the boarding school they attended. People who did
not go to boarding school but attended a highly reputed private day school
are in turn distinguished from those who attended a public school, and
both are conscious of a difference between themselves and those who
went to local parochial schools. Another educational distinction of considerable importance refers to where the undergraduate collegiate years
were spent, as reflected in such status-placing statements as, "He's college
but not Ivy." In the highest of Boston social circles, the college attended
and the club joined as an undergraduate far transcend degrees earned
as a factor in determining which niche is occupied. In less elevated ranks,
professional achievements count for more, but the collegiate background

in all its aspects—undergraduate experience, graduate and professional schooling, and the where of both—has symbolic significance; it seems always to remain in the background as an image factor and status ingredient in the way Upper Bostonians deal with, and speak of, one another.

The Social Scientist's View: Two Classes, Five Substrata

The Upper Kansas Citians and Upper Bostonians we interviewed were in essential agreement, thematically, in their portrait of status divisions in their respective communities. In both places, the phrase *top class* summoned up visions of established old families, still socially important. The designation *next-to-top class* meant new money. The title *upper-middle* seemed to embrace a very wide spectrum of college-educated managerial and professional people, possibly even two sublevels, with incomes from $22,500 up to $60,000 a year in the early 1970s. And the label *middle-middle* suggested "college graduates not earning all that much money and people who didn't finish college making good money."

When we weigh the imagery inspired by our hypothetical class titles against all else that upper-status Kansas Citians and Bostonians said about differentiations in social standing in their world, the conclusion we reach is that there are five thematic status groups in Upper America. Two of these rank so high that most upper-status people recognize them as upper class. The other three can be considered subdivisions of upper-middle-class America.

The higher of the two upper-class strata is most commonly entitled *capital-S society* in Kansas City. Sometimes in Boston it is labeled "people listed in the *Social Register*." For the present purposes we will refer to this stratum as *upper-upper*. This title seems appropriate to the extent that it traces back to Warner's Yankee City volumes (1941 on); now, as then, its reference is to a stratum most of whose members are at least second-generation in high status.

To the lower of the two upper-class strata, Bostonians and Kansas Citians most commonly applied the somewhat derogatory phrase "nouveau riche." *Lower-upper* sounds better, so that is what we will use. Thematically this is the stratum of socially accepted newer money. People in both Boston and Kansas City seemed to think that an income of at least $60,000 a year was ordinarily required of aspirants to this status, but it was no guarantee of acceptance. (Less than that is "possible, if the family is really popular," said Kansas Citians.)

The highest of the three upper-middle-class strata we shall call *upper-middle elite*, continuing a class-naming practice from Coleman and Neugarten's earlier Kansas City study (1971). (*High-level upper-middles* or *upper-middle specials* are other possibilities.) These are the upper-middles that Middle Americans would identify as next-to-top class, not merely upper-middle; in living standard and professional accomplishments they impress the average person as being part of the success elite. An upper-level Kansas Citian clarified their status with these words, "They are not just ordinary upper-middle class; they make more money, they live better, they have a higher social standing, but yet you couldn't call them upper class." Upper Bostonians identified a significant segment of their city's intellectual, academic, and artistic community with this status level. Upper Kansas Citians would include many of the more successful volunteers to causes in this group, as well as local leaders in culture and the arts. Both could rank here with or without the $37,500-a-year income ordinarily associated with this level.

The middle of the three upper-middle strata we shall call *upper-middle core*, again borrowing from Coleman and Neugarten. Thematically this is the average or standard college-educated professional or business family. The income range associated with this group in 1971 and 1972 was $22,500 to $36,000. For full, unquestioned acceptance at this level, a college degree seemed expected of husbands by our Boston and Kansas City respondents; only "some college"—ideally at a school of solidly respected status—was expected of wives.

The lowest of the upper-middle strata we designate *upper-middle marginal*, and we turn to behavioral data supplied by our Boston and Kansas City samples for suggestions as to how its membership can be differentiated from the top level of Middle Americans. There—in the evidence of self-reported community participation and leisure-time pursuits—the most crucial thing we note is the existence in both Boston and Kansas City of two quite separate social networks, one Upper American in orientation and the other Middle American. Paralleling this is a distinction in life styles. Central to the distinction are differences in educational background, but the split does not entirely rest on this. There are college graduates—especially from lower-status colleges—in our two samples whose social relationships are with the Middle-American network, and there are people who did not graduate (and some who did not even attend) who relate upward to the Upper-American world. Indeed, neighborhood choice is as good an index as educational background to participation in one network or the other. Our conclusion, then, is that this differentiation between Upper-American and Middle-American social networks and correlated life styles gives us our key for distinguishing which middle-middles are to be considered upper-middle marginal Upper Americans, and which should be identified as some kind of elite Middle American.

To give some more detail on this, let us compare the recreational customs, associational memberships, and church activities of respondents in our sample whom we would call marginal upper-middle with those whom we think of as Middle-American elite. As one example, we find the associations that men in the first group are most involved with are professional groups—an Advertising Council, teachers' associations, the Weed Science Society, and so forth. Those that men in the second group care most about are more social—the Knights of Columbus, Elks, American Legion, and Lions Club. As another example, the evening meetings that couples in the first group report attending are Vital Issues discussion groups or the ecology-conscious Wilderness Society; those that the second attend may be the Neighborhood Protection Association. Couples in the first may also participate in "a local dramatic group," while couples in the second "get together with our square-dance club." Women in the former are often active in the League of Women Voters and "like to go to the art gallery" on spare afternoons; some are Headstart volunteers. Women in the second group more often are members of church guilds and "just go shopping or talk on the phone with their friends." For sport, men in the first group enjoy tennis, squash, and handball; men in the second like bowling and playing pool in their basement game rooms.

The denominational preferences of upper-middle marginals run toward Episcopal, Presbyterian, Congregational, Unitarian, or agnostic Protestant; those who are Jews tend to be Reform if they are active. The Middle-American elite tend much more often to be Lutheran, Methodist, Baptist (in Kansas City), fundamentalist, Orthodox, Conservative if Jewish, or Catholic. (Catholics of the Upper-American group are almost exclusively of northern European ancestry, while those of Middle-American status run the gamut.)

The neighborhoods favored by upper-middle marginals are those physically closest to the areas where families of upper-middle-core status live. These are usually suburbs (or census tracts) where the 1970 U.S. Census reported that the median years of schooling for adults twenty-five years of age or over was one or more years of college, and at least 80 or 90 percent of employed men were in white-collar occupations. Middle-

American elite respondents, in contrast, usually lived in neighborhoods where the median level of schooling was only high school graduation and only 70 percent (or perhaps 50 percent) of employed men were white-collar workers. Some of the neighborhoods where Kansas Citians of this Middle-American elite group had their homes were referred to by upper-status respondents as "a hick place to live," "a redneck stronghold," and "like a small town."

In educational credentials, the differences between the two groups were, as expected, marked. The typical marginal upper-middle man is a college graduate; nearly half the women are also. Among the Middle-American elite, the average woman is only a high school graduate, and the median man in our sample reported only two years of training past high school, some in business school or technical institutes and others in regular college. Where the two groups are *not* different is in economic status; indeed the difference here, such as it is, favored the Middle-American elite. In our sample, their median income was $20,300 while that of the upper-middle marginals was $19,500. To sum up, both groups had incomes sufficient to provide a good life, as this is conceived by Middle America, but they were leading that good life in very different ways.

From this analysis, we may set forth the following image of upper-middle-marginal families (which image is, by the way, a social science product; it does not come from respondents). The male head of these families is usually a college graduate whose earnings are below the doing-very-well level but seem sufficient to provide for a good life. The largest portion of these men work in the less remunerative professions—teaching, the ministry, social service, and the arts—and the rest usually occupy semi-managerial positions in corporate or governmental bureaucracies. Educationally, both men and women of this status are almost equal to people of the upper-middle core. Some of the men have advanced degrees in education, religion, the humanities, or social science; women have usually attended colleges of at least medium rank, or perhaps schools of art, music, or dance. They tend to live in the best neighborhoods that they can possibly afford. In formal and informal socializing, they interact upward with upper-middle-core families rather than downward with Middle Americans. The long and short of it is: Upper-middle marginals rank higher culturally, behaviorally, and in social orientation than financially—they "have more class than money."

CHAPTER 9

Levels in Middle America

A KANSAS CITY woman of middling income said, "You can't speak of social classes anymore. It used to mean what level of society you were in. Now, everything is judged by what standard of living you have." In so remarking, she gave succinct summary to what most Bostonians and Kansas Citians of similar socio-economic status seemed to believe about the social divisions among themselves, as well as about stratification all up and down the scale: namely, that standard of living is the most critical variable.

In line with this understanding, our sample of Middle Bostonians and Middle Kansas Citians verbally divided themselves into three status levels, each based almost entirely on economic position—two main, truly Middle-American groups and a third of marginal standing. The higher of the two main groups we can think of as *people at the comfortable standard of living*. That they are comfortable in housing and income is the key fact about their social position; it is the unifying theme, regardless of what name might have been used by sample members in speaking of them. Sometimes they were labeled "high-income working-class people" and other times they were characterized as "Middle Americans at least average in standard of living or a little above— they're not hurting at all." Among the social class titles suggested by our questions, middle-middle class was the one most commonly associated with people of this socio-economic level. The other of the two main groups is most aptly called *people just getting along*. Working class was the hypothetical class title most frequently associated with them. More descriptively, they were referred to as "Middle Americans making do with what they have" or "the working class who get by, but with a struggle." The third group—the one marginal in the world of Middle Americans—can be designated as *people who aren't lower class but are having a real hard time.* The class title lower-middle was most frequently applied to families in this economic condition, but lower-working class was also an often-volunteered name. When Middle Americans talk about people of this status, they say, "That's the lowest part of the working class that you might not mind having as neighbors."

People at the Comfortable Standard of Living

To have a comfortable standard of living, Middle Bostonians and Middle Kansas Citians thought a family needed an income of $11,000 a year in 1972. If a couple with two children had such an amount of money at its disposal, or perhaps a little more, they could—it was believed—have a good life in terms of marital happiness, modest contentment with their lot, and the knowledge that they were at least solidly average in financial standing, even if they were not sharing in all the material comforts of the good life that people with incomes above $15,000 a year would seem able to afford. Families with less than $11,000 a year in income were generally identified as just getting along and only able to think of themselves as comfortable or having a good life to the extent that they were resigned to never doing any better and thankful that things were no worse.

From the standpoint of Boston and Kansas City families in this latter condition who were just getting along financially, what having a comfortable standard of living would mean, in contrast to their own lot, was "having everything you need" with much less "scrimping" and budgeting; experiencing very little if any, "worry about meeting your financial obligations"; and "saving a few dollars to build up a reserve." People who were themselves at the comfortable level said, "We have enough, but we can't splurge" and "We have to think twice about buying anything major." The pride they expressed in their position usually centered around their ownership of a house and what they were doing for their offspring. One woman said it this way: "We have everything we need, but not an abundance. I have a car, my own home, and commodities in the home. If I want to go on a vacation, I can. We can afford to enjoy ourselves. We can take the kids places." Certain limitations were acknowledged. "We can't live lavishly," "We don't dress extravagantly," "We do without some of the conveniences of the upper-middle class," and "We don't have any real luxuries—luxurious vacations are out." But these deprivations were placed in this perspective: "We do have nice clothes," "We are buying our own home in a nice neighborhood," "We eat well— We don't have to worry about feeding our families," and "We can afford to educate our children."

Being comfortably housed is well-nigh essential if a family is to be included without reservation by other Middle Americans in the category of people at the comfortable standard of living. The prototype of such comfort is a single-family home with six regular rooms, plus one and a half baths, which the family owns, not rents. It is up-to-date in fixtures and kitchen and bath equipment, neatly and completely furnished, and located in "a quiet, suburban neighborhood." There is a gardened yard with "plenty of space for the children to play in, and a minimum of 1,050 or 1,100 square feet of finished living space" in the house. Bedrooms number three at minimum—in the two-child family this means that "each child has his own bedroom and the parents, theirs"— or more, ideally, if the family is larger so that in any event there are "not more than two children per bedroom." The house does "not necessarily have a dining room if the kitchen is big enough to eat in and if they have a separate family room," but if there isn't a family room, then "they would want a recreational area of some kind—either a good basement or a finished porch or breezeway." Ideally, this house should "not be over thirty years old"—but, whether it is or isn't, at least "it is adequately filled with all the modern conveniences and home devices that make your life easier." In addition, Kansas Citians place great store by air-conditioning—at least in room units, if not central. A garage, a patio, "a fenced-in yard," and "a lot measuring at least 50 by 150 feet" are also treated as important features of the comfortable home.

Upper Americans tend to describe this level and style of housing as "ticky-tacky"; they criticize its post-World War II manifestations as "tract housing—ordinary ranches or split-levels where you see rows and rows of them all alike." But Middle Americans regard "the newer housing additions" as the ideal setting for comfortable housing, for it is in such places that one is most likely to find "everybody in the neighborhood owning his own house and keeping up his property." Indeed, these two things—(1) "nice neighborhoods with no deterioration and no substandard housing nearby," and (2) home ownership—are main ingredients of the comfortable standard of living (especially ownership of the home). To Middle Americans in our Boston and Kansas City samples, it was extremely questionable whether a family with children of school age at home can truly consider itself comfortably housed— or, for that matter, comfortably situated in the more general sense—if it is still "shelling out rent money each month" instead of paying off a mortgage. It is an almost universal conviction that "you have a lot more when you own your own place—you can be more at ease." In Boston, the market price in spring, 1971, for houses that met most of these criteria for family comfort ranged above and below $25,000 by $4,000 or $5,000 (Bostonians typically said, "$25,000 would be about average for that kind of house"). In Kansas City, in the late fall of 1972, the cost of purchasing one was usually pegged by respondents as "in the low twenties" (more broadly, from $17,500 up to $25,000).

When middle-status Bostonians and Kansas Citians talked about the neighborhood setting of the comfortable life, six phrases dominated their descriptions: "suburban," "outside the city," "safe," "quiet," "newer," and "not crowded." Chief among these were "suburban" and "outside the city," these two tending to promise the rest. There was virtually no difference between Boston and Kansas City in this respect; in both places, respondents treated the words *suburban* and *comfortable* as virtually synonymous. In our Boston sample we found almost everybody who lived in the suburbs insisting, "If you want to be comfortable, you've got to get out to the suburbs, away from the city"; many still in the city seemed to agree, complaining, "I don't know of any good places to live in Boston anymore—it's just too dangerous." Similarly, our Kansas City respondents were firm that for comfortable living, "you can live anyplace in the suburbs—north, south, east, or west—but not in the center of the city." One man spoke for many when he said, "That would be almost anywhere except in Kansas City itself, judging from the crime rate and what I hear about the schools." In the least demanding view, all that is required for residential comfort is "a quiet street with nice children for your kids to play with," where—in the words of one Boston woman—"there are more trees and houses instead of apartments." Ideally, though, a comfortable neighborhood is more than just one or two isolated streets of safety and quiet; it is a considerable expanse—indeed, a whole school district or suburb of tranquil existence, "like in Melrose, Stoneham, or Reading [suburbs to the north of Boston] where there are whole sections of one-family houses in a row—not really rich, but nice, just a little over average."

In terms of what is inside the house of a family at the comfortable standard of living, Middle Bostonians and Kansas Citians in our sample established the following guidelines: "They [people at the comfortable level] would have a dryer as well as a washer," "They might have an automatic dishwasher—but not necessarily," "They definitely have a color TV," and "They have better furnishings—good quality, but not costly." As for their transportation equipment, it was generally believed: "They have a medium-priced, later model car"; this might be either a Chevrolet, Ford, Plymouth, or Buick Skylark—"but no Cadillacs"; a new one would be bought "every four or five years," meaning that as a collective average, "they're driving a two-year-old or three-year-old car." In Kansas City—where 37 percent of all area families had two cars according to the 1970 Census report—it was rather widely expected of a family in comfortable circumstances that "maybe they'd have a cheap second car, bought used." But in Boston, where only 26 percent of families were two-car owners, people said that having two cars was rare at this economic level.

The picture Bostonians and Kansas Citians have of a comfortable family's home life and recreational pleasures features these elements: "They watch TV a lot, and usually enjoy it," "They keep their lawns mowed and the hedge trimmed—their yards really look nice," and "They do a lot of barbecuing on the backyard grill." It was assumed that "recreation is mostly with neighbors or friends from business or work," that "they entertain at home mainly—just visiting or playing cards," plus "going on picnics and family things in the summer." They would "only go out to dinner every now and then, where the budget allows, but not to any place very expensive." As for movies, "they have money to spend on shows—when they can find one that is suitable for family entertainment." They could also afford "taking in a professional sports event from time to time." Indeed, all told, "they could go out twice a month, inexpensively," to one or another of the above activities: dinner, movie, or game. In addition, they "most likely go to church"; the men "belong to the American Legion, a lodge, or a bowling league"; and the women "spend time with the PTA, or with some neighborhood organization."

Just as three weeks of vacation a year were considered standard for the good life, a two-week vacation was deemed the norm for families at the comfortable level. And while it was understood that people of this economic status "couldn't take elaborate vacations," it was an almost universal conviction that "they *should* be able to go away" for the period. In Boston, what going away usually means at this level is "renting a cottage for two weeks down the Cape," or perhaps "in New Hampshire on Lake Winnipesaukee" or "up in the mountains." Every third or fourth year "the family might take a trip up to Canada"; plus which, on weekends or holidays during the year, "they would take local trips to points of interest." In Kansas City, going away means "down to the Ozarks," "visiting relatives in other states," or "camping, fishing, and vacationing in parks and recreation areas in the Rockies." Many Middle Americans in both cities said, "They could go camping—we do it," but not all shared their enthusiasm; indeed, the majority would say that the kind of vacations a comfortable family should, or could, take, "all depends on what their idea of a good time is." For some at this level, when they described their own vacations a good time was sightseeing in cities and distant states; for others, it was visiting old friends who live elsewhere; and for a third group, it was physical activity in lake, forest, stream, or mountain.

Occupations associated with the world of Americans having a comfortable life in the early 1970s were drawn equally from blue-collar and white-collar categories. That such an indiscriminate mix characterizes this socio-economic level was the common wisdom of our Middle-American sample members. Time and again they specified this in their descriptions of this stratum, as in these examples:

> "That would be a mix of big union wage workers and white-collar lower-management—and what I'd call quasi-professionals, like teachers."

> "They're high-paid blue-collar workers or some kind of technician or teacher, or they're in small businesses."

> "He would have either an office job, maybe a college-type thing, or a fairly highly skilled working-class job."

> "It's the average working American, with a job in construction or selling."

> "That is good blue-collar jobs or medium white-collar jobs."

The medium white-collar jobs most commonly associated with the comfortable standard of living were the following (listed by frequency of mention): "the normal office worker—bookkeepers, bank clerks, accountants"; "schoolteachers—they don't make much money, but they have the education"; "salesmen—like clerks in retail stores, car salesmen, office supply salesmen"; "managers, small-time management in businesses," "lower management in the utilities"; "lower-level administrative bureaucrats"; "shop owners—with little concerns like gift shops," "cleaners or hardware storeowners," "the guy who has a franchise for a gas station"; "technicians—like in electronics," "people technically trained"; and miscellaneous "quasi-professionals" (nurses, social workers, pharmacists, and ministers).

Counted most often by Middle Bostonians and Kansas Citians as having "good blue-collar jobs" were, "men in trades unions, electricians, plumbers, carpenters," "workers fairly high in factories," and all the following: policemen, foremen, over-the-road truckdrivers, mechanics, power-plant engineers, tool-and-die makers, busdrivers, machinists, TV repairmen, firemen, inspectors, telephone employees, and postal workers. The common thread defining all these blue-collar and service jobs as "good" was that "They're better paid"—which in most instances meant, "they have the best unions—they're in the unions with the highest scale pay." Less common as an explanation for their relatively high occupational status was this notion: "They're blue-collar workers who use their heads rather than just their hands."

The educational background most typically associated with people at the comfortable level by Middle Americans was: "high school graduation at least, and usually a little something more." Some men and women at this level—the schoolteachers and quasi-professionals, for example— were assumed to "have finished college and maybe even have a master's degree." For the rest, however, if they went to college at all, "they maybe went for just a year or two," and likely as not "to a junior college, not a regular four-year college." But the majority probably did not do that much, since the general understanding was that "you don't have to have been to college at all" to be in this class. Mostly the kind of educational experience beyond high school attributed to people of this stratum has taken place at a technical institute, business school, "in night school," or "in some special trades training program." It is hard for Middle Americans to imagine that a family could have attained the comfortable standard of living without such an educational extra. A high school diploma does not seem enough by itself; most people just getting along are believed to have one of those, these days. More seems needed or else "you wouldn't have anything going for you," no competitive edge.

When Middle Bostonians and Kansas Citians of comfortable living standard spoke of their own position in society, they liked to say: "We're the people who make the world go around, the part of the population that the country can't get along without. . . . We pay the bulk of the taxes and do most of the work." They emphasized their occupational stability—"My husband has been twenty-two years in the same job as an electronics technician"—and talked proudly of their financial prudence, acknowledging all the while the difficulties of saving enough (given their moderate incomes) to "send the children to college and have enough left over for retirement."

When men and women just getting along talked of these Middle

Americans who are comfortable, they usually reflected envy of what the latter had achieved in living standard. Often as not, though, they traced the difference not so much to merit as to luck—as in, "That's a guy with a good union leader," or "They had the advantage of a better education," or "They're working two jobs." When Lower Americans—the folks way down the scale living in poverty or having an extremely hard time—described people at the comfortable level, they seemed most impressed that the latter "don't have the kind of money worries the rest of us have." Knowing that "they aren't exactly the blue-bloods," Lower Americans nonetheless looked very much up to the comfortable as "people who have tried to better themselves" and in consequence "are making a very good income." They called them upper-middle class.

When Upper Americans in our sample talked about people who are comfortable—merely comfortable, that is, and not prosperous or well-to-do like themselves—they sometimes drew this distinction: "They [the comfortable people] work hard to get ahead, but they're not like the upper-middle class because they don't have as much ability." More in condescension than as a compliment, they characterized parents of the comfortable class as oriented toward their children—"They hope their children go to college; they can't do enough for them"—and suggested the reason that "education is so important is that they expect their children to rise above them." Upper Americans also said of people who are comfortable—in words of seeming praise—that "they treasure the traditional values of American life"; "they are imbued with the work ethic; their houses are never in need of paint; there are no holes in their walls." Then, in a tone of deprecation, they would conclude, "But a narrower outlook goes along with that."

People Just Getting Along: The Slightly-Below-Average Part of American Society

For a family of four to be just getting along, Middle Bostonians and Kansas Citians felt that an income of $7,500 would be rock bottom (in 1972). They thought a family would not really be in the mainstream of the ordinary working class unless its earnings were closer to $9,000, but it could still get along if it had at least $7,500 coming in through the year. With less than that, the family would have to be considered as having a real hard time. Of such a family our sample members said, "They have licked the survival problem where the lower class hasn't"— but "It's a daily struggle, and ends don't always meet." To be just getting along, "they have adequate housing and food—not luxuries, but all the necessities," and "with careful budgeting, they can make ends meet." Also, to be getting along instead of having a hard time means, "It's a normal family life. They can eat, clothe themselves, and live on a steady schedule."

When Americans who are comfortable imagine what life is like for those just getting along, their vision is one of constant scrimping, budgeting, and careful shopping; they see such fiscal strategies as imperative if a family with only $7,500 or $8,000 a year is indeed to feed, clothe, and shelter itself adequately (and hardly less important for families with incomes of $9,000 or $10,000 a year if they are ever to enjoy any extras). Time and again our Boston and Kansas City respondents of higher status said of people just getting along, "They'd have to be do-it-yourselfers in most ways. They'd be real thrifty. The husband couldn't throw money away on anything he doesn't need. The woman would have to be an economist. A clever mother could do it; she would have to sew and be an expert in shopping." As for their food, "they would have plenty to eat, but it'd be the plainest type, hardly ever anything extra-special. . . . They'd use the cheaper meats, lots of hamburger and lots of Hamburger Helper." Regarding their attire, "they have enough for clothing, but it wouldn't be expensive clothing—few new clothes, no extra clothes, nothing faddish, because it wouldn't last." All told, then, just getting along means a life—as Upper Bostonians and Kansas Citians picture it— of almost no luxuries: "They have to stay within the necessities. They have to live within their means, keep everything in moderation."

When people having a hard time or who are in poverty talk about a life of just getting along, they look up in mixed envy, exasperation, and self-pity. They say of people at this higher level, "They have some of the nicer things in life. They don't have to sweat buying groceries. They can probably just pick up what they want at the grocery store instead of shopping around to save money like I have to. They have more peace of mind, they're not constantly bickering over bills." A Kansas City woman near poverty said, "I think my life is only half as good as theirs." And a Boston woman of similar status remarked bitterly, "They have everything they need. . . . They look down their noses at their neighbors on welfare and people who are poor like us."

When people just getting along describe their lot, they tend to emphasize that while they are not poor, neither are they rich. The first is a major pride. It means: "We don't live in a ghetto—we live in a decent neighborhood" and "I'm not on welfare or anything like that, 'cause I can get everything I want." The second fact—that "I'm not rich; I don't have a lot of extras"—is a fact long lived with and tolerable, apparently, as long as the sufficiency of essentials continues; as long, that is, as "we have enough to eat and wear and enough of everything else we need." The central concern is that a run of sickness, trouble, or sudden unemployment could take away that sufficiency, temporarily or permanently. One Boston man typified this fear when he gave this picture, from personal experience, of what life just getting along is like: "You don't have money to throw around. You have to worry about bills. You live on a tight budget. A sudden expense would really cause trouble." That their present sufficiency of life's essentials might be imperiled by their history of modest income and lack of savings seems to be the major worry, the deepest fear of people just getting along. Over and over, the men and women in our sample of this economic status reflected this anxiety, reporting that "if something sudden comes up, like if the car breaks down or a kid gets sick, you're in trouble," that "if you got hit with something big, you couldn't make it." In other words, continuing to just get along depends on having no inordinate bad luck—and bad luck means winding up down with the people having a real hard time.

Probably nothing is so important as housing in communicating to the wider society that a family is just getting along instead of being comfortable or having a hard time. If a family's home or apartment is of the kind commonly associated with this getting-along standard, then that will be the income status attributed to the family unless there are overwhelming signs to the contrary. The prototypes for this level of housing vary somewhat from Boston to Kansas City. In Kansas City, the image is of "average wood-frame houses," either "a small, little bungalow with two bedrooms, living room, dining room, and kitchen," or "an older, six-room house on a not very large lot, with three bedrooms and just one bath"; if the first, the house has "approximately 900 square feet of living space," and if the second, as much as "1,000 or a little more." In Boston, just-getting-along housing is usually "one floor of a two-flat or three-decker house—five rooms with a porch," rented, not owned by the occupants. When, in the less common circumstance, families at this level own their housing, then they "might have a tiny Cape or ranch house," but more likely "a two-family or three-family house where they live on one floor and rent the rest for income." A middle-level Boston man, now comfortable, characterized just-getting-along housing in these words:

"I think of a house worth about $18,000—or, if they were renting, nothing more than $150 a month. It would have at least two bedrooms for a family of four, and three if more. It's adequate. It keeps them out of the cold in the winter and out of the heat in the summer. It's something the children may not be happy to bring their friends home to. It's not everything the parents would like it to be. But I think you could call it 'standard and decent housing' for a blue-collar worker and his family."

The psycho-social impact of just-getting-along housing is almost certainly the same in Kansas City: it is "adequate, but not everything [its occupants] would like it to be" and not really something that the parents take pride in any more than do their children—but it *is* standard, not substandard, and it *is* decent. It tells the world that here live people who are at least getting along; they are *not* having a hard time.

Much of what Middle Bostonians and Middle Kansas Citians had to say about this level of housing stressed its difference from substandard. Thus, of the houses and apartments occupied by families just getting along, it was said: "It's not like those substandard places where not everything works; these people have cold and hot running water available at all times"; "The electric wiring is safe and adequate to their needs, and the plumbing is in good working order"; "It is warm, well built, with no air coming in around the doors or windows"; "It has good air circulation, though no air conditioning"; "The foundation would be secure and not deteriorating"; "There are no leaks in the roof"; and "The house, if made of wood, is kept up, not rotting." By general conviction, just-getting-along housing "is more modern than the lower class could afford"—which in Kansas City tended to mean not more than 50 or 60 years old and in Boston not more than 70 years old—or, if that old, then "remodeled to current standards." Ultimately, though, it was agreed that "age isn't so important, but clean is," that the houses of people just getting along would at least "be kept up—repairs are made on whatever needs to be repaired," and that the occupants, whether owners or renters, "are taking care of the property, not letting it fall apart." When this housing was compared with comfortable places, the distinctions made were more of size and cost than condition and basic equipment; just-getting-along housing was spoken of as "modest," "simple," "plain," "basic," "enough," and "just ordinary"—all in all, "at the low end of the fair scale."

Market values associated with this level of housing in Kansas City centered around $13,500, some Kansas Citians saying that "bungalows like that would cost $12,000 plus" and others referring to it as "small houses worth $15,000 or a bit less." Public impression that the typical

Kansas City family at this level was buying, not renting, is probably valid; certainly the 1970 U.S. Census records a majority of Kansas City families whose incomes in 1969 ranged from $7,000 to $9,999 as belonging to the category of homeowners. For those renting, a monthly average of "$125—plus you pay all the utilities" was imagined in Kansas City; this would be, as a range, $130 to $180 a month in gross rental expenses. Middle Bostonians assumed that most families just getting along there were renters, since "they'd really have to scrimp to get the down-payment together" to buy and most would never quite manage it. Again, public impression seems valid, inasmuch as the Census report shows that the majority of families in Boston at this income level in 1970 were renting. The market value of a single-family house for people just getting along in Boston was generally identified as $15,000, $16,000, $18,000, or $19,000; the kind of two-family house people at this level might own was believed to cost $25,000. Rentals for this level of housing also ranged higher in Boston image than in Kansas City; $145 a month was considered typical without utilities included, and $170 or $175 typical with. Housing is thus imagined to cost Boston families of low-average income more than families similarly situated in Kansas City, and they have less to show for it.

A prime requisite Middle Bostonians and Kansas Citians established for the neighborhoods where people just getting along would live was expressed this way: "They're clean areas, not rundown . . . the yards are clean . . . people are keeping their property up." If a neighborhood does not meet these standards visually, it is associated with the world of people having a hard time—or worse. Another criterion was that "the neighborhood is not threatening in terms of crime. . . . It's a decent place for parents to bring up their children." Ideally, virtually all the housing is of at least the quality associated with this getting-along standard, and some is better, but it was understood that the areas where people of this income level typically find themselves contain a few examples of substandard dwellings mixed in with standard. The most likely locale for these neighborhoods is, in public image, "closer in— [since] people who make less money generally have to stay closer in"; but they are not too close in; "They're not near the downtown area."

In Boston, these general principles of "clean" and "closer in" but not too close were translated by respondents into these specifics: "communities that border on the inner city—Medford, Malden, Everett— but aren't in the city," "the nicer areas of Somerville or Cambridge— the tripledecker areas of two-family or three-family homes," and "parts of Boston itself that used to be nice—Roslindale, Hyde Park, Jamaica

Plain—but now are slipping." In the main, these are the inner-ring suburbs, stretching from Quincy on the south to Revere and Lynn on the north. Neighborhoods beyond the inner ring that belong in this category are the areas of oldest settlement in what used to be "country towns"; here, too, two-family and three-family housing dominates and renters outnumber owners.

In Kansas City, the neighborhood settings for people just getting along were variously characterized as "scattered all around, wherever they could afford—but not in Johnson County," "a settlement of older, smaller houses," "just an average area—maybe northeast or the better parts of the East Side," "in areas about five miles from downtown," and "not anywhere in the inner city but the neighborhoods next to it."

The home appliances and furnishings associated by the Middle-Boston and Middle-Kansas City publics with just getting along as a standard of living are a palpable cut below those attributed to the comfortable level. It was assumed of people just getting along, for example, that "they wouldn't have a stereo," "they might have two black-and-white TVs, but few would have color," "they'd have a clothes-washer at least, but probably no dryer," and "you'd almost never find a dishwasher in their kitchens." As for their furniture, "they would have all the essentials—the basics—but nothing extra"; "It would be regular, inexpensive stuff from a place like Sears"; and "Some of their pieces would be banged up a bit, getting ragged around the edges." However, unlike people lower on the scale, families just getting along can at least buy new furniture instead of used, "they don't have to shop for Salvation Army recycled"; what they have "is not just sticks"; and "they've got carpets on their floors, not linoleum."

Owning a car is absolutely essential if a couple is to be considered part of the Middle-American world of people just getting along. The phrases our respondents gave this requirement illustrates the extent to which it is imperative: "They wouldn't be without an automobile"; "They have dependable transportation that gets them where they want to go"; "They can afford what they need—and you need a car." The car people just-getting-along would have, as Middle Bostonians and Kansas Citians imagine it, is "probably five or six years old—nothing too new," and it was likely bought second-hand." It is a "fairly decent car" and "its gotta have a good engine"; the family might even "keep it till it gives out." Whatever else, though, it is *not* what the neighbors would call "a junker" and for maximum respectability it should not be "a Cadillac like some of those idiots drive who don't have another thing to their name." Ideally, it is "just an all-around practical car . . . maybe a Ford or Chevy . . . [and] they take fairly good care of it."

As for the recreational and vacation habits of people just getting along, the dominant conviction among those better off is that these are very restricted: "They can't do very much that costs anything. . . . After the bills are paid, there wouldn't be much money left." In this image, recreation is a mix of "Sunday rides with the family," "neighborhood bean suppers," "eating out occasionally at McDonald's," "drive-in movies as a family because it's free for the children," "seeing sports on TV instead of at the stadium," "watching games in neighborhood parks" (and sometimes being a player there), "swimming in public pools and beaches," "seeing relatives," and "maybe bowling in a league." Husbands, it is imagined, "have a night out with the boys once a week or so," when they probably "play poker" and/or "drink beer" ("they drink more beer than liquor on that income"), possibly "at a Veteran's post" (or "the Moose hall") or maybe "at a neighborhood tavern." They might go hunting or fishing on weekends or their days off, "since that doesn't cost too much if they go someplace close." Some wives "take part in church activities" and may "play bingo," but many are assumed to do nothing except stay home, "drink coffee with a neighbor lady," "care for the children," and "do what the husband needs." The "kids [if they are old enough] can go roller skating and to movies oftener than their parents." The phrasing in this impression may at times be condescending, but it is probably a fair assessment of how people just getting along socialize and entertain themselves. Some in our sample at this income level described a life of greater fiscal austerity and more Puritan pursuits, saying, "You can go out to supper or a movie occasionally, but you really have to plan for it" or "You can go to a show—something that comes to town—about twice a year; this is from my experience on an income like that." But when characterizing their own lives and describing the lives of others at this level, the majority presented a picture much like the above, emphasizing both its pleasures and its limitations and acknowledging the ever-present possibility that the former must from time to time be sacrificed "when extra bills pile up."

The restrictions on vacationing that result from having just enough income to get along range, in public impression and reported fact, from "working an extra job instead of taking the time off," through "just taking day trips in the area," to "going away for just one week—and never very far away." The only way, it was supposed, that people just getting along could spend more than one week away from home base was by "visiting relatives or going fishing—that doesn't cost too much money." Otherwise, maybe "they go out of town one year and then stay home the next two" or stay inside the budget by "taking a long weekend at the lake once or twice a year." Bostonians and Kansas Citians who themselves were just getting along said that many of the people they knew with incomes like their own "didn't really take what you'd call vacations"; that "when they get their two weeks, they work somewhere else so as to pay some bills and get a little ahead." Or, if not that, then "they use their vacation time every year to do repairs on their house." Indeed, fixing up the house may well be the most prevalent—if not exactly the most popular or preferred—vacation-time activity for people just getting along.

Occupations associated with this status level by our Boston and Kansas City respondents were mainly from the blue-collar field, but the white-collar world was represented by mention of "lower-income office workers," "some of those government clerks," and "men with sales jobs at Sears and Montgomery Wards." From the blue-collar world, factory workers—variously characterized as "people with factory jobs," "semi-skilled mill workers," and "men that work in plants"—constituted the prime examples. Also cited with fair frequency were construction workers, truckdrivers, utility company employees, and workers for the city ("like mechanics on the MBTA [Massachusetts Bay Transit Authority]").

Blue-collar workers at this level were differentiated from those lower down the scale in three ways: (1) skill—"They have jobs that require more know-how than the lower class; it's not menial work"; (2) unionization—"They belong to unions, and in this way they're different from the lower class which hasn't made it into unions"; and (3) higher pay. Women of this economic stratum, if they worked, were generally thought to be employed as waitresses, in hospital work, clerking in a supermarket, filing in an office, or "doing something for the telephone company."

More important than these job types and descriptions—in popular characterization—of the work done by people of this stratum was the pay level. These people, if hourly-rate workers, were said to be "just getting paid $4 or $5 an hour"; if employed at weekly pay jobs, their take-home was "only $150 or $200" each paycheck; and if, as in the case of office workers, they were paid by the month, their salaries "would run no more than $800, as an average." As an annual total, "That's like my son—he drives a truck and made $7,800 last year." It was with this income factor in mind that many Middle Bostonians and Kansas Citians, when we asked what jobs they associated with the phrase working class or the status of getting along, avoided occupational designations entirely and spoke instead of the toil involved and the relatively disappointing end result:

> "They have all kinds of jobs. . . . They're ordinary people trying to make a living, who don't earn too much."

> "That's the hard-working, underpaid class of people."

> "That's anyone who has a job of any kind and earns enough to support himself and his family and doesn't have anything left over."

> "It's just the general working man who doesn't earn as much as he'd like. . . . He doesn't have one of the better jobs."

> "Sometimes you can work your head off and still just get by—that's what it means to be in the working class.

Ultimately, then, what the men and women just getting along have most in common, in public image, is not *what they do* for a living, but *what they get paid* for it—which isn't as much as they'd like; it's just enough to get by.

The educational level commonly attributed to people just getting along is high school graduation—nothing more and possibly less. The rationale behind this—that "high school education would be as high as they got"—is twofold. On the one hand, "That's all they need for the kind of jobs they have," and on the other, "They couldn't afford more . . . they had to quit and go to work." A distinction is frequently made that "the younger ones finished high school, but they didn't used to." "The younger ones" in this instance most properly refers to people born in the 1930s and after, since it is for these generations that high school graduation has become the rule, not the exception. Those who "didn't used to" refers most clearly to people born before 1920. Among Americans of that age—they were fifty or older at the time of our survey— less than a majority finished high school; ninth, tenth, or eleventh grade was the more common point for termination of schooling when they were growing up, especially among youth of working-class origin and no special ambition or expectations.

Upper Bostonians and Kansas Citians in our sample were inclined to refer to people just getting along as "the Wallace vote." They described them as "people who do not have too much expectation for themselves or their children." Many assumed that these families fall where they do on the economic ladder because "they don't have as much ability as the people doing better. . . . They don't have as high an I.Q." They suspect that parents in this class do not especially encourage their children to go to college, that "they mistrust education."

People in Boston and Kansas City who were themselves just getting along saw things differently. They complained of their lot in life in many ways, even while claiming, "we can make our own way . . . at least we don't lead a hand-to-mouth existence like the lower class." One frequently voiced complaint was that "we don't have enough money to send our kids to college." Another was that "we're helping pay the bills of the country . . . we're paying the taxes for the bigshots." A third was that while they were the people "who actually get the job done," it was "the boss who's getting the credit for the job being done." And a fourth complaint—the most common—was this: "We've worked hard but don't have a lot to show for it." Individually and collectively, they feel, people just getting along "have plugged away and never really gotten anywhere."

People Who Aren't Lower Class But Are Having a Real Hard Time

There are two ways to think about the social position of this group of Americans. One way is to focus on the idea that they are *not* getting along economically; that—as far as public appearances go—they are worse off than that. Indeed, they seem, in common parlance, to be "having a real hard time." From this standpoint their position would be defined as below, and hence outside of, the middle-majority mainstream. Upper Americans often take this view, though singling them out as the highest stratum within that category. The other way to think about their standing is to share with Middle Americans the attitude that "they're really the same as the working class, except that they would be the lowest part of it."

This second view emerged when the middle-status Bostonians and Kansas Citians we interviewed insisted on making two status groups, instead of one, of people having a real hard time. To the higher group they variously applied the labels, "lower-middle class," "lower-working class," and "the lower part of the working class"; the lower, they described as "a lower class group but not the real lowest part of the lower class." This distinction was rendered as much on the basis of style of living and values as on standard of living—though, inevitably, anyone living in poverty and most people just barely above poverty were relegated to the lower stratum while families almost getting along were more apt to be placed into the higher. Crucial in this division were these ideas: the higher group—the people having a hard time who aren't lower class—"have too much pride to live in slums or in public housing"; "They're still striving. . . . They're probably a little cleaner—they're trying a little harder to better themselves"; "They have steady jobs. . . . They're almost never unemployed or on welfare"; their jobs "aren't common labor . . . or real dirty work, like trash collector"; and "They may not have the money to keep their property up so well, but they try . . . [so] you wouldn't object to their being in your neighborhood."

Clearly, to Middle Americans these distinctions matter more than income in determining which people of lower economic standing than themselves they are willing to include—albeit at bottom rank—in their own broad social world. That this is their view is reinforced by our observation of the differences they in turn emphasize between people having a hard time who aren't lower class and people just getting along. These differences are almost exclusively monetary—matters of income level and manifest standard of well-being—not of mores and manner. Thus, comparing the two, they mainly said of the lower: "They have to struggle a lot harder to meet their budgets"; "They have less in the way of material things"; and "Their standard of living is lower in terms of housing, food, and income."

The income levels that our Middle-American respondents associated with the world of people who are having a hard time but aren't lower class averaged closer to the minimum they specified for getting along than to the figure they perceived as the poverty line. This latter, in our sampling, was $4,500 a year (1972 dollars). People who aren't lower class, said Middle Americans, "would not be right down at poverty." In line with this understanding, they explicitly excluded families whose incomes were only $5,000 a year from this stratum, saying, "That's a bare subsistence wage—you can't really do anything on that." (Of the same significance were exclusions from this class phrased in terms of weekly incomes—"They wouldn't make less than $100 a week"—or of hourly rates—"He'd have to earn more than $2.50 an hour.") The lowest-income Middle Bostonians and Kansas Citians seemed willing to concede families who aren't lower class was $5,200 a year, which one man said was "$2,000 less than the experts say a family needs to get along."

In turn, to be well-established in this category of people having a hard time who aren't lower class, it was thought that "the guy should be averaging $6,300 a year" (of which amount it was said, "and that's not easy to live on, if you have a family"). Other characterizations of the incomes expected of people having a real hard time who aren't lower class, phrased in weekly, hourly, or monthly rates, were: "That's the man who is making probably $125 every week"; "He'd earn $3 an hour"; and "They'd average $500 a month."

Life on such an income, as Middle Bostonians and Kansas Citians who were getting along or comfortable imagined it, is "drab," "very plain," and "really repetitious—with nothing to look forward to." In this impression, families so situated economically "would have to manage their money very, very carefully"; they "would have a hard time making ends meet and keeping out of debt." They "would have enough money for daily subsistence, but nothing whatsoever to save for the future," and "they probably wouldn't have charge accounts." As for their food: "They'd have enough to eat, whether or not well-balanced. . . . It would have to be less than the best, just a sufficient amount. . . . They wouldn't be eating meals of roast beef too often." Their furniture "wouldn't be the best—and the way it looks depends on how the children have been brought up to take care of it." They would have "enough money for new clothes every now and then," but "they wouldn't be able to afford good clothing." Finally, with respect to transportation, in Kansas City "they would have some sort of car . . . [since] everybody has a car these days," but in Boston they might not; if they had one, "it would be an early model, more than seven years old, bought second-hand, for sure."

It is their housing, rather than any of the above, that is reckoned as the main sign, the most visible, unequivocal evidence that families are having a real hard time. For, in one way or another—and, indeed, generally—the places they occupy are substandard as judged by the Middle-American public; this more surely than almost anything else marks off families of this economic condition from people just getting along.

In Boston, the prototype of substandard housing (as of 1971) was a flat or apartment in a multi-family structure that had been built in the 1880s, 1890s, or very early 1900s; it was located in a neighborhood densely packed with such buildings and was operated by an absentee landlord—but it had been maintained sufficiently through the years that it was "not yet a slum." The principal variant was "a public housing project for low-income families"; this too, unless it had fallen into disrepair, ranked in Boston as substandard, but it was not considered a proper residential setting for people who aren't lower class though they're having a hard time, since such a family should "have more pride" than to accept even that much charity. A third form, occasionally acknowledged, was "one of those shanties like you see near the railroad tracks or down by the water in Quincy or Weymouth."

In Kansas City, there was no prototypical version of substandard housing, but many different possibilities were embraced within the image. These ranged from "a small, government-subsidized prefab on a tiny lot" through "one of those mobile homes" to "cheap, rented apartments in less desirable sections" or "a small, inexpensive, older house worth around $6,000 or $8,000."

The neighborhood associated by Middle Bostonians with this world was visually characterized in phrases like these: "It's congested—there's too much traffic . . . and the houses are too close together"; "They have mixed zoning—residences intermingled with businesses"; and "There's not much yard—you see very little trees or grass." Areas that look like that are mostly found "wherever you have those aging three-flats." Another clue commonly offered for where this class would live was "as far away from Roxbury [the center of Boston's black population] as they can afford." Middle Kansas Citians said that families of this status in their city "wouldn't live in or near the slums," that "they would avoid what are called blighted neighborhoods," but would nevertheless have to settle for "an older, or borderline, area . . . not in the best section of town." Many families of this stratum are more fortunately located than that—indeed, they live in the same neighborhoods as people just getting along, occupying the substandard housing that such neighborhoods usually contain to a moderate extent. Not many are worse off, because to reside in slums or the worst of substandard areas is to risk identification with one or another of the categories of people who are lower class.

One phrase—"They have low-paying jobs"—is at the center of the way Bostonians and Kansas Citians of all classes characterized the employment situation of this stratum of people having a hard time. The occupations most often cited in illustration were "low-grade factory workers," laborers, janitors, gas-station attendants, and waitresses. But many respondents offered no such examples, saying instead: "They could be in almost any trade where you don't earn much money"; "No certain jobs—just low-paying ones"; and "It's just work they're doing to get by." Beyond this, the thrust of imagery about what this class does for a living established both the people and their jobs as superior to those found in Lower America but not up to the level associated with people getting along. They were said, for example, to be "less skilled" than the latter, but "not completely unskilled like the lower classes." As one Boston man pegged them, "They're what you'd call semi-skilled; they're on the assembly line just putting the bolt on." They were also said to "have to work harder with their hands than the working class," but "not do the real menial, physical labor that the lower class has to." In specific comparison to people and jobs of higher status, the possibility was raised that longer hours of toil may be required ("They may work from 9 to 9 just to make ends meet") and/or that the hours might be odd ("They may work a graveyard shift. . . . It's like shiftwork in the plants"). Then, in comparison with people and jobs of lower status, a crucial point registered in their favor was that "they have steady work . . . they have security on the job," so that "they're never on welfare"; and a second distinction was, "It's decent work they do, not jobs like garbagemen or streetsweepers—no one would want those."

As for the educational background of these men and women who aren't lower class but are having a hard time, Middle Americans assume that "most likely they didn't finish school," that, indeed, some may have "quit as early as ninth grade for lack of funds," and that certainly "they went no further than their junior year." This, in the common view, is "where their problems began." For, without a high school diploma to their credit and with no vocational training to help them, it has been almost inevitable that "the only jobs they can find are ones that don't pay much."

An especially bitter consequence of having jobs that don't pay much, as the middle-status Bostonians and Kansas Citians in our sample pictured life at this stratum, is that expenditures for pleasure must be cut practically to zero. "Vacations," these respondents said, "are nonexistent": "On an income like that, they sure can't afford to get away"; "The only kind of trips they would take are to relatives' funerals." Even in town, they hardly have any recreation: "They do mostly what they can do for nothing"; "The Lions Club or the Knights of Columbus wouldn't have them"; and "They watch TV mostly." "Outings would have to be a picnic in the park, a church social, a swim at the closest public beach [in Boston], a visit to the zoo"—"whatever they can find to do that's free, and there's precious little of that in Kansas City." A Kansas City woman of this economic level concurred: "Recreation for us is pretty much just watching TV and going to friends' houses once in a while. We never go to anything that you have to pay for. We watch the ball team with the YMCA that plays in Wyandotte County park. We couldn't go see the Royals."

All in all, then, for people having a hard time, "life is no bed of roses"—no more in their own view than in the eyes of those better off. Of the families at this economic level who aren't lower class, the Middle Americans we sampled were inclined to say, "They're different from the lower class because they have some sort of order in their lives." Many are thought to be in these economic difficulties through circumstances beyond their control; maybe "illness forced them into economic straits" or perhaps "their parents couldn't afford much schooling, but they've done the best they could with what little they got." They are redeemed from being lower class because somehow, despite adversity, they have approximated Middle-American standards of behavior, attitude, and appearance, or, more negatively stated, they are *not* "bad people or criminals," they are *not* "white trash," and they are *not* "on the dole."

Further Observations: Two Main Divisions by Life Style and Social Networks

In the preceding chapter on social standing in Upper America, we presented two stories. One told how Middle and Lower Americans in Boston and Kansas City projected their assumptions about the critical role of economic status onto their rankings of people much higher in standing than themselves; the other story told, in contrast, how Upper Americans divided and rated one another in much more complex ways, assigning less-than-critical importance to standard of living. Again in this chapter we are going to tell two stories. This time, however, the two stories do not reflect differences in view between two groups, outsiders and insiders; rather the differences are between ordinary citizens on the one hand and professional status analysts on the other—between what our Middle-American respondents publicly pronounced about the divisions in their midst and what we, as social scientists, have observed in our data. In telling *our* story, we would, for example, challenge the Middle-American pronouncement that differences of status in their world are almost exclusively matters of income level and standard of living; in doing so, we would suggest that this view has been overly influenced and simplified by the deep envy which these differences in material well-being arouse. Our basis for this challenge goes beyond that, however, for when we look closely at the friendship patterns, organizational memberships, and neighborhood locations of the 600 Middle Bostonians and Middle Kansas Citians whom we interviewed, we find these people associating with one another selectively in ways which suggest that similarity in standard of living does not produce the kind of equality in social standing our respondents were inclined to assume.

The selectivities in association that we note from our interviews with Middle Americans relate to many things. Income is definitely one

of them, and an important one—but not the fundamental one—or, at
least, not as we analyze things. Type of occupation also serves as a se-
lecting principle and is important—but not much more so than income.
Other sources for selectivity in friendship choice and feelings of social
equality include ancestry, church affiliation, cultural level, and language
patterns. The list is nearly endless. Ultimately, these many grounds for
selectivity seem to divide Middle Americans into two main groups. One
of these we choose to label *middle class*, the other *working class*, drawing from the traditional sociological meaning of these phrases. The first
has historically been referred to as *lower-middle class* to distinguish it
from *upper-middle class*, but now that we find so many citizens associating that label with the very lowest stratum of Middle Americans, we
find it difficult to continue using it as a designation for persons who represent the upper half of that category.

    We cannot absolutely prove from our research that these group-
ings—middle class, working class, and three substrata of each (high,
middle, and low, as we shall subsequently detail)—amount to the real
truth about status differentiation in Middle America, transcending divisions between the comfortable and just getting along in importance.
Nevertheless, we would propose that this is the case, and in so doing,
we would hark back to how much in the way of non-economic factors
Bostonians and Kansas Citians admitted bringing to bear when socially
rating one another in actual face-to-face contact (see Chapter 4). Also,
in the magnitude estimation experiment, income was not the sole variable
respondents employed in judging status of families in the middle range;
education and occupational type counted for as much as 40 or 45 percent of the score assigned (see Chapter 11).

    Out of the total 625 Middle-American respondents in our two-city
sample, we identified 295 as essentially middle class and 330 as working
class. The typical middle-class respondent was living comfortably, but
nearly one-fourth were not. Most of these latter were young couples; retired people; or widows, divorcées, and otherwise single women. The
typical working-class respondent was just getting along, but nearly 40
percent were comfortable, and there was even a handful—some 6 percent—leading the good life. Our division of respondents into these classes
was not based on any one thing; all variables that we had come to think
of as relevant were weighed in, and a "best judgment" was made for each
person and family with this question always in mind: "In life style and
social network, does this respondent seem more middle-class or working-
class, as these categories have been defined historically and as we have
brought them up to date in our research here?"

To illustrate what this difference is between middle-class and working-class Middle Americans, we would like to turn now to a detailed comparison of a specified subsample of both. These will consist of mature married couples (age range for husbands is 32 to 64 years of age) whose standard of living falls in the comfortable range as judged by both their neighbors and the wider society. There were 68 families in our sample whom we would call middle-class and who fit this specification, and 90 families whom we would identify as working-class. These two groups of sample families were virtually identical in declared income, both ranging by just a few thousand dollars up and down from medians of $14,000, and seemed essentially equal in standard of living. To all appearances they spent approximately the same total amount annually (though distributing it somewhat differently) on their housing, the appliances and furnishings in their houses, their clothing, their cars, and their recreation and vacations. The impact of these expenditures was to place all cases, in the public eye, at the comfortable level of living. These two sets of families have been distinguished as middle-class and working-class by no one special criterion—as we said before and as will become clearer shortly—but rather by the entire fabric of their daily existence. In the comfortable middle-class sample, 28 percent of the male heads of families were employed in occupations grouped in the blue-collar category by the U.S. Census; in the comfortable working-class sample, 19 percent of the male heads had occupations classified as white-collar. Thus, whatever else, these are not occupationally determined strata.

A central sign of the difference between these two groups is that the comfortable middle-class families have spent relatively more on their housing, especially for its neighborhood setting, than have the comfortable working class. They have almost totally avoided regions of their respective cities—Boston and Kansas City—where the average resident is just getting along; they have chosen in marked degree to live in neighborhoods where white-collar workers are numerically dominant; and for those who are parents of schoolchildren, a special consideration has been location in the so-called better school districts. In contrast, 80 percent of the comfortable working-class families we sampled were found in neighborhoods dominated by blue-collar workers, and 40 percent lived in areas where most of their neighbors were just getting along. In this single, specific act of neighborhood selection, these two sets of identical-income, Middle-American families revealed strikingly different reputational priorities.

A second sign of difference was in the houses themselves and what was inside them. Comfortable working-class houses tended to be older;

they had more often been brought up to standard by do-it-yourself projects. Comfortable middle-class houses, while neither larger nor any more modern on the inside, showed more care expended on exterior appearance, and their yards were more attractively landscaped. Middle-class families appeared to have spent relatively more on living-room and dining-room furniture, judging from our interviewers' comments, but they had spent relatively less on appliances, especially passing up the higher-priced models of television sets, stereos, and refrigerators that so many working-class families seem attracted to when they reach a comfortable income level.

A third sign of difference was automotive equipment. The cars owned by our comfortable middle-class sample members tended to be smaller and represent the more moderately priced makes, both domestic and foreign. The cars of comfortable working-class families ran the gamut from older to brand new, but in any event they tended to be the more expensive models and brands; also trucks, campers, and vans were greatly more numerous. Further, there was a notable visual difference between middle-class and working-class neighborhoods regarding cars. In working-class neighborhoods, cars and trucks of all sorts were to be seen in great volume and clear view at all hours of the day and night, parked in front yards as well as in front driveways and at the curb. In middle-class neighborhoods, autos tended to be discreetly out of sight, placed in the more recessed areas of owners' driveways if not hidden in the garages.

Another mark of difference was in the patterns of community participation and choice of friends. The comfortable middle-class men and women in our sample reported many more memberships in formal associations than did their income peers in the working class. Indeed, about two-thirds of the former belonged to at least one club while a majority of the latter belonged to none at all. The middle-class men who were active were often Masons; they supported the Boy Scouts; they belonged to a local unit of the Lions Club; they were in church men's groups; and they held membership in occupational associations (such as The Blue Goose Insurancemen's Club). Working-class men were more commonly members of a Moose Club or Eagles Lodge than of the Masonic orders; they belonged to clubs celebrating their ethnic origin—the Sons of Italy, "a Polish brotherhood," or "a Portuguese men's group here in the neighborhood"; they were in gun clubs or sports clubs (with names like Chippewa Athletic Club), or perhaps the Police Relief Association. The women of both classes were mainly involved in PTAs or church guilds, if they were active. The difference, then, apart from that of number of memberships, was to be found in the social standing and neighborhood location of the school groups or churches with which these women were affiliated.

We asked the people we interviewed in Kansas City to "tell us who the people are you see or visit most often." Comparing the answers of middle-class and working-class respondents, we found that two-thirds of the people named by the former (compared to only one-half named by the latter) were neither relatives nor neighbors. There were other differences. For example, 40 percent of the people seen most often by comfortable middle-class Kansas Citians were said to have obtained one or more years of education past high school, while only 14 percent of working-class best friends had gone that far; furthermore, the majority of men named as friends by middle-class people (71 percent) were credited with white-collar occupations, compared to only 26 percent of the men named by working-class respondents.

To sum up, two different social worlds (or networks or orbits) seem represented in these samples, the question of hierarchic rank aside. These patterns of difference in material goods consumption, in social milieu, in community participation, and in friendship choice consistently distinguished the people in our Boston and Kansas City samples whom we would think of as middle-class from those whom we have designated working-class. They apply no less to representatives of both classes who were leading the good life or just getting along than to the people we examined who were comfortable. To a large extent these are differences of social aspiration. They also relate back to differences in educational background and ethnic identity, as well as to differences in work role.

The differences in educational background are especially noteworthy. Among the comfortable middle-class men in our sample, 68 percent had had some schooling beyond high school—collegiate, commercial, technical, or paramedical—as had 50 percent of the comfortable middle-class women. In our comfortable working-class sample the comparative percentages were only 26 percent for the men and 22 percent for the women. Indeed, the number of working-class men and women who had quit before finishing high school was greater than the number who had gone beyond—36 percent of the men and 23 percent of the women.

The differences in ethnic and religious identity between the two groups were as follows. Protestants were more heavily represented in the middle class, Catholics in the working class. Ancestors were overwhelmingly from northern Europe and the British Isles in the middle class; southern European and eastern European ancestry were fairly common in the working class. Very few middle-class comfortables re-

ported themselves to be the children of immigrants, but 29 percent of
the working-class sample classified themselves as such.

Whether the Middle-American families in our sample whom we
have identified as middle-class in life style and community network stand
socially superior in the eyes of self and society to all whom we have
declared working class is not conclusively answerable from the data of
our study.[1] Only occasionally did middle-class respondents openly admit
feelings of social ascendancy vis-a-vis working-class families of equal or
superior financial standing. One instance of this occurred when a Kansas
City woman said,

> "I consider myself middle class. My husband works for a construction
> company in the office. Many of the construction workers make a lot
> more than he does. But when we have parties at my husband's company,
> the ones with less education feel out of place and not at ease with the
> ones with more education. I think of them as working class."

Sometimes working-class respondents hinted at the same kind of social
differentiation, but from a different perspective. A Boston man of comfortable working-class status said,

> "I'm working class because that's my business; I work with my hands. I
> make good money, so I am higher in the laboring force than many people
> I know. But birds of a feather flock together. My friends are all hard-
> working people. . . . We would feel out of place with higher-ups."

At this point, having considered all the evidence about status differentiation in Middle America unearthed in the present study—evidence, that is, both of image and behavior—and then having placed this
evidence in the context of findings from previous in-depth studies, we
are ready to delineate a thematic six-fold division as our story of how
Middle Americans rate and relate to one another socially. Three of these
divisions are in the middle-class sector; we call them *elite*, *core*, and
marginal. The other three are in the working-class sector, and we call
them *special*, *core* (or *average*), and *marginal*. The sector herein designated *middle class* should be thought of as lineal—hence, a contemporary parallel—to the *lower-middle class*, as this was titled and defined in
prior publications. Similarly, our *working-class* sector is lineal (and
thereby today's parallel) to the stratum called *upper-lower class* in some
earlier works. This class "ancestry" is important to our analysis in Chapter 12 of the volume and direction of social mobility in the past thirty
years.

The Middle-American elite. This is the social top-flight of Middle-
American families. There is no single occupational prototype for this

level. Male household heads are variously small-business owners (average number of employees is four to seven), moderately prospering salesmen, government or corporate bureaucrats at the lower-management level, and professionals in the lower-status fields (optometry, pharmacy, chiropractice, public school teaching, and the ministry). The head's earnings in most cases have been sufficient to provide a good life for his family, or maybe even a very good life. The family, however, has not translated this into Upper-American social status and participation. (In a small number of cases—where the head is a college-graduate professional—his earnings may not be up to good life average, but the family is regarded as among the Middle-American elite by virtue of this professional identity and educational background.)

Some form of post-high school education is typical for both men and women of this social position, if not at a regular college, then in a junior college, technical institute, business school, arts school, or nurses' training program. College graduates—who would be rare among people born before 1930 but are increasingly common among those younger—usually have received their degrees from institutions of the lowest rank (teachers' colleges, for example, or small, low-status denominational schools) or in night-school programs.

It is rare to find families headed by blue-collar or service workers—electricians, plumbers, truckdrivers, or milkmen—treated as part of this highest Middle-American social group even though many earn enough money to rank this high on purely economic criteria and by manifest standard of living. Some of these families rank no higher than working-class specials (or superspecials), as suggested by their neighborhood choices and associational and church memberships. Others, depending on their aspiration level and how they present themselves socially, may be accepted at the middle-class marginal or middle-class core level, as non-prototypical members of those strata. Precious few, if any, rank up here, however. As one Kansas City respondent phrased their problem, "You find a lot of those union guys earning plenty, our milkman for example—but, well, he just wouldn't be in [this] class; he's still Joe, the milkman."

The middle-class core. The prototype family head is a white-collar worker—salesclerk, civil servant, small-business owner (one or two full-time employees), manager of a small office or store, bookkeeper, or technician—whose income and living standard are at the comfortable level, as this is defined by the American mainstream. (In 1972 dollars this meant an income of $10,800 up to $14,900 for a family of four.) More important for this status than the occupation or living comfortably, however, is realizing a life style that is in the middle-class tradition—really lower-middle class—as this has been characterized by sociologists going back to the first Lynd study of Muncie in the 1920s (1929). A central value is propriety. Living in a neighborhood on the better side of town is one sign of this; participation in churches and clubs predominantly white-collar and professional in membership is another.

Educational standards for this stratum vary by age. For men and women born before 1920, high school graduation without any education beyond is the norm; for those born in 1920 or since, one or two years past high school would be expected—at a business school or technical institution, if not a regular college; for the youngest (born 1940 or after), an associate of arts degree from a junior college is becoming the rule.

Middle-class marginal. The thematic prototype for this status level is a white-collar family not fully comfortable economically, yet middle class in life style and associational choices. Not fully comfortable as in the case of these families could mean one, or all, of three things: family income below $10,800 (1972 dollars), or possibly above that yet not sufficient for comfort because there are more than two children; living in too small or too old a house; or residing in a neighborhood that once was prosperous but has become too near inner-city problems for the full comfort of its residents.

Families with a blue-collar head and a comfortable living standard may also be of this social standing if, through ambition to rise above working-class status, they have acquired the proper lower–middle-class symbols in neighborhood location, church and club memberships, cultural and recreational tastes, and personal presentation (grooming and language).

Women of this middle-class marginal stratum are usually as well educated as those in the core and elite levels. Indeed, it is commonly a wife's educational background that has keyed the family's ambition to be middle class socially despite the handicaps of either below-average income or blue-collar occupational identity. (Educational qualifications of marginal men are not up to those of the Middle-American elite, speaking as an average, but they are closer to those of the middle-class core than to what we find among the working-class specials.)

The occupational dimension in class identification. The occupational differences between middle-class and working-class Middle-American men must be clarified as differences of degree, not differences of category or absolutes. Certain principles obtain, however, in explaining which blue-collar workers are middle-class in highest frequency and which white-collar workers, as defined by the U.S. Census, are most often working-class. As for the former, the men who are middle-class usually do relatively "clean" types of blue-collar work, hardly ever "the dirtier jobs"; they also, as one said, "use their heads as well as their hands"; and finally, many "give orders instead of doing the work." As for the latter— the men who are working-class though classified as white-collar—a few examples of occupations from our sample may illustrate the point: ship- ping clerk, collector for the Massachusetts Bay Transit Authority, postal sub-station supervisor, filling station operator, and ditching contractor. These men are more truly "gray-collar" than white-collar. Their clerical functions are performed not in an office but in a shipping room, ware- house, or subway car; those with managerial or proprietorial functions perform them in plants, in filling stations, or at construction sites. (An- other occupational distinction worth noting is that many men in the working class work odd hours—at night "on the swing shift" and/or on weekends—and while this is not an absolute rule, it is much more common than for men in the middle class.)

The work that women of the two classes do is also differentiating. Over half of the women identified as working-class in our sample were employed at jobs or in settings not conventionally middle-class—that is, they worked in school cafeterias as cooks, in dime stores as salesclerks, in restaurants as waitresses, on assembly lines as stitchers, in stock rooms as packers, and in homes for the elderly as practical nurses. Women in the middle class who work almost never do any of those kinds of things; they eschew service or industrial jobs and seek only "ladylike" em- ployment.

Working-class specials. These are families definitely comfortable in living standard whose neighborhood choices, recreational habits, and social participation patterns would be judged working-class as this life style has been characterized by sociologists since the 1920s. In the present era this means that inside their houses, appliances and modern conveniences have been given expenditure preference over furniture; also that second cars, when owned, are more apt to be trucks, vans, or campers than compacts or station wagons. Further, despite their pros- perity, these families usually live on the wrong side of town—either in post-World War II workers' suburbs or in "old country" ethnic enclaves.

Most household heads are blue-collar or service workers, but some are white-collar workers who, along with their families, prefer a working- class life style. Men and women born before 1920 rarely completed more than eighth or ninth grade; those born in 1920 or since have usually gone further than that, but often not past twelfth grade.

Standing at the pinnacle of this stratum are people we might call superspecials because they are more than merely comfortable: to all appearances they are leading the good life. They drive expensive cars (as one Boston man in this bracket said of himself, "My friends think I'm upper-class because I drive a Cadillac"). Some own boats, even second homes. The men who are avid fans of professional sports may be season-ticket holders to follow their favorites. But they aren't socially accepted by middle-class Middle-Americans because they are too uncouth and unlettered—often insufficiently Americanized. They may be contractors, union officials, fire chiefs, or small-businessmen, or perhaps very well paid truck drivers, heavy equipment operators, or plumbers. They live in industrial suburbs of low status or inner-city neighborhoods that are ethnic ghettos. Superspecial wives are commonly quite uneducated; interviewers tended to describe them as "extremely overweight—from cooking and eating too much spaghetti," or "healthy and large-boned; looks like she was brought up on a farm."

Working-class core (or average). The prototype family head is a blue-collar worker from "the rank and file"—on an assembly line or in service occupations (as taxi drivers or bartenders, possibly)—whose earnings are only sufficient to provide a just-getting-along standard of living. Struggling self-employed men with cleaning shops, repair services, or corner groceries also fit into this category, as does many a deliveryman or mechanic, and the lowest-paid salesmen and clerical workers.

In the life style associated with this level we find the models for what journalists sometimes call "T-shirt and pin-curler America." The men like to hunt together; fishing is another favorite out-of-the-city sport. Many of these men work on each others' cars and go to the auto races. Both men and women play pinochle, dominoes, bingo. The most devoted churchgoers tend to be members of Protestantism's fundamentalist denominations, or else are Catholic.

People of this stratum born before 1920 are usually not high school graduates, and many did not go past eighth or ninth grade; those born since 1930 more often than not finished high school, but few went beyond.

Working-class marginal. These are the people having a hard time who are socially accepted by Middle America as part of its world in broadest definition and not treated as lower class despite their economic difficulties. A favorite phrase among Middle Americans for people of this status is, "They're poor but white and decent, not trash."

A significant share of families of this status in our sample have been plagued by health problems, with the result that an unduly large share of past and present income has been committed to medical bills, leaving relatively little for housing and furnishings. In other instances, an income that ordinarily would have been enough for a getting-along existence was being strained by too many mouths to feed, including dependent older relatives as well as children.

Whether all families housed in a substandard manner (as were these) and who are therefore identified as having a hard time economically are treated as social marginals, as less desirable companions, by people who are housed in standard manner is questionable. Looking at the other side of the coin, we can propose that a certain portion of families who would seem to be getting along economically may rank as Middle-American marginals when it comes to reputation and social interaction; that is, they may not truly have any higher social standing than the average family having a hard time. Then, to go a step back up the ladder, we must similarly suspect that not all working-class families exhibiting a comfortable standard of living rank above all who are merely getting by, when the ranking is rendered in purely social terms of who looks at whom as socially equal, inferior, or superior.

These issues and all others regarding precise social position in the Middle-American world require for their resolution socio-metric studies of clique behavior and personal reputation. Such studies, using neighborhoods and work settings as a base, were outside the intentions of this research into public images of factors in social standing. A multi-factored social arithmetic test—in magnitude estimation format—might be the best solution for measuring prestige as such. Elaborate profiles could be constructed and pictures of houses (possibly even of families) could be shown to respondents; this would be far better for indexing status in the real world than the three-factor profiles used experimentally in this research.

CHAPTER 10

Images of Lower America

THE Bostonians and Kansas Citians we interviewed readily separated the people of Lower America into two status subdivisions: *people at the bottom of the ladder* and *people who are lower class but not the lowest*. They distinguished between these two layers of Lower Americans on four criteria: dependency, employment, living level, and effort. Effort served as the crucial dichotomy. People at the bottom of the ladder were pictured as making no effort to be anything but bottom rung in social standing, while people who are lower class but not the lowest were believed to be trying to rank better than that. The bottom group was labeled *the welfare class* and its members damned for usually or always depending on public aid or charity for their income; the people of the higher group were accorded their superior standing because "they're never on welfare" or "only occasionally" (and "if on, they're trying to get off"). People at the bottom were said to "live in messes," to present to the world a level of living below the poverty line, while those in the class above appear merely "semi-poor"; that is, they live in "substandard places, but not bad slums or public housing projects that have gone to pieces." The men and women of the bottom class were imagined to be "usually out of a job and not interested in finding one"; those of next-to-lowest standing were, in contrast, envisioned as "always employed or out there looking for employment when they're not."

In all these distinctions the people of the next-to-lowest class were defined more by what they are *not* than by what they are. They are not the polar extreme; they are not the worst-off Americans; they are not the social nadir—but they are not really very far from it. They are close to poverty; they are almost in dependency; the work they do is unskilled and very poorly paid, and their housing falls far below mainstream standards in cost and type. In the eyes of all above them in the social ladder, they have more in common with people at the bottom than with the Middle-American marginals. They, too, as with people at the bottom, have "often had a lot more children than they can support." They too "live in the neighborhoods you wouldn't want to live in if you could help it." They too are "in many cases members of the racial and ethnic minority groups." And, as distinguished from marginal Middle Americans, "they don't try as hard to better themselves." Or, if they are trying, their problem is "they don't have as much skill or competence" with which to pull themselves up. Ultimately, then, there is a neither-nor quality to the Boston and Kansas City definitions of the next-to-the-lowest class: its members are neither accepted as Middle Americans nor yet so vigorously condemned as the bottom category of Lower Americans. There is no question, though, that as Middle and Upper Americans see things, they belong to the latter broad class rather than to the former; and we suspect that this is because their political and economic interests are perceived as being at odds with those of Americans in the Middle and of a piece with those of people at the bottom.

People at the Bottom of the Ladder: Welfare Cases and the Poverty Group

Lower Americans, when defining status within their world, almost invariably discriminate between two types of people at the bottom. One category consists of people who, though poverty stricken and/or on welfare, are physically and morally "clean"; the other is of people who are "not clean" in either respect. This second category is referred to as "truly the people at the bottom" and the first called "the next-to-lowest class." (To people whom the rest of Americans call next-to-lowest class, Lower Americans tend to apply the titles "lower working class" or "lower-middle class.") Upper Americans hardly ever so discriminate. They tend to lump together all who by government definition fall below the poverty line with all who are on welfare as "those unfortunates at the bottom of the ladder"; they do not bother with differentiations within the group on the basis of moral character or public cleanliness, except perhaps as occasion for expressing sympathy or withholding it.

Middle Americans tend to follow the same definitional tack as Upper Americans except that they distinguish between people at the bottom and those in the next-to-lowest class more on the basis of appearance than on a theoretical definition of poverty. By this standard, people at the bottom are those poor whose homes, clothes, and possessions are so visually offensive—"dirty," "raggedy," "broken-down," and "torn-up"—that an insufficiency of care in their maintenance is suggested, not to mention of income. Meanwhile, people who—though they fall slightly below the poverty line financially, nevertheless manage to present a picture of self-discipline, some effort at cleanliness, and regular employment—are usually identified by Middle Americans with the next-to-lowest class, not with the bottom.

On the question of who ranks at the very, very bottom of the ladder—almost below its first rung—Americans of all classes seem agreed: these are "skid-row type characters," "bums," "the indigents who are drunkards," or "those men on the Bowery." One step in social standing above the skid-row stratum, as Bostonians and Kansas Citians in our sample imagined things, are people who are destitute. This state of affairs was associated with family incomes of under $3,000, "maybe just $200 a month," or "as little as $1,500 a year." Other phrases for it were "people that have practically nothing in terms of money," "they're real desperate, real hardship cases," "they're in total poverty," and "they barely have enough to survive." People who are destitute were differentiated from the men and women of the skid-row stratum and ranked above them, largely on the grounds that there is more order in their lives, a fixed place of residence, perhaps even a family structure. But their living quarters were envisioned as the worst imaginable.

The poverty standard of living. Most people that Bostonians and Kansas Citians placed into the poverty group are not so desperately poor or in such dire hardship as the skid-row stratum or people who are destitute. Rather they are, as one Kansas Citian said, "in mid-poverty—that's not total poverty, but it's definitely poor." Sometimes this state of affairs was described in terms of hourly earnings: "Their income is just the minimum wage of $1.60 an hour" or "They don't make over $2.00 an hour when they work." For someone fully employed and drawing pay forty hours a week for fifty-two weeks a year, that would come to an annual total of $3,328 up to $4,160. Sometimes this status was spoken of in terms of weekly wages: "[Earning] $60 or $65 a week would be poverty" or "They wouldn't make more than $80 a week—they'd be ditch-digging or dishwashing, something like that." That would amount to as little as $3,120.

Most commonly our Boston and Kansas City respondents characterized poverty standing in annual incomes, saying: "They only have $3,000
or $4,000 to go on"; "That's families of four with incomes around $5,000
or less"; "They can't earn much of a living—maybe $3,500 is all they get";
or "Their income is from welfare and runs $3,000 to $4,000, depending on
what program it is." The upper extreme of poverty status, as suggested
by our respondents, was anything less than $7,000 a year, but very few
drew this line, and all who did were themselves very, very upper-income.
Respondents from the lower half of the income spectrum tended to name
$4,500, $4,000, or $3,600 as the line. Summing these impressions, we have
chosen to speak here of $4,500 a year as the public consensus poverty
line. Families of four who appear to earn more than that we refer to as
people who are bad off but not in poverty, and families of similar size
who appear to have less we say are operating at the poverty standard
of living, as popularly conceived.

As the people of Middle- and Upper-American status look down at
life on the poverty standard, they acknowledge with a mixture of sympathy and horror that it is "really rough going." The men and women
in our sample phrased their impressions variously, while invariably making the point that "it is a miserable existence":

"They just live terribly."

"It's living day-to-day in a continual depressing state."

"These people are just existing—that's all. They really don't know what
it is to have anything. You really can't talk about what they have because
it isn't much."

"It means they can't make it on their own. They need help from the
government, from churches."

More specifically, life is hard for people at the poverty standard to the
extent, as higher-status people imagine, that: "Many suffer hunger and
malnutrition. . . . Children sometimes go to bed hungry. . . . Sometimes
there's no food in the refrigerator—they have food one day, but not the
next. . . . A lot of time they have to get food stamps in order to eat. . . .
They wouldn't have the right kind of food—they always have to buy
the cheapest grades of everything." As for their furniture and clothing,
"they can't ever have anything new or nice." Often, "it's just cast-offs
from various volunteer organizations." The furniture is "used" and/or
"broken-down" and "clothes for the kids is mostly hand-me-downs";
further, "there's not enough money to keep things clean." A car "probably couldn't be afforded—they'd have to rely on public transportation."
If they owned one anyway, it most likely would be "an old junker." A

Boston woman, contemplating this living standard, said, "God help them, I don't know how they do it."

Slums—both individual dwellings and whole neighborhoods of such —were the symbols of this standard of living most richly verbalized by the Bostonians and Kansas Citians we interviewed. These represent poverty in its most dramatic, starkly physical, readily visible form. All Americans housed in such fashion seem identified by that very fact as people at the bottom. That they live that way is taken as a sign of their being "the laziest" and "the dirtiest" of the poor, if not necessarily always the poorest. That they are willing to so present themselves to the world condemns them to this lowly social status far more than does their income level itself.

Slum-level housing, as identified by our respondents, comes in three forms: "dilapidated" multi-family buildings, "falling-down" single family structures, and "government projects that were new a few years ago but are already torn up."

Public definition of what makes for "slummy neighborhoods" includes everything that is bad about slum-level housing units and much more. As spoken of by our Boston and Kansas City respondents, they are a melange of overcrowding, disrepair, decay, danger, disease, filth, apathy, and abandonment—and are always "ugly" to the eye. Boarded-up warehouses, smoke-spewing factories, and all manner of grimy, decaying commercial structures may be on the scene, often vying with transit facilities for physical dominance of the environment. Refuse is overwhelming and everywhere: "Garbage is on the sidewalks . . . thrown out the windows." The animal population is cause for concern: "stray dogs and cats are running loose," "rats live in the gutters and sewers," and inside, the apartments themselves are "veritable breeding grounds for mice and other vermin."

Plainly, then, slums are "a terrible place to bring up children" and the children who are there represent a special form of horror-of-the-slums to Middle and Upper Americans. They are invariably pictured as "raggedy . . . very poorly dressed . . . clothes all torn, never mended . . . never washed . . . half-starved . . . not properly fed . . . just running wild . . . neglected and ill-kept . . . all dirty from playing in the streets." And worst of all, "they are growing up without hope," already the victims of their parents' apathy, which is itself a crucial feature of the slum image. Over and over Bostonians and Kansas Citians in our sample said:

> "Slums remind me of people who don't give a damn. . . . The yards are dirt and filled with garbage. People don't clean up. Nobody seems to care."

"Slums are nothing more than what people make them. . . . You can't get rid of the slums by putting people in new buildings—it's people that make the slums."

Thus is the slum neighborhood ultimately perceived to be a world of people as abandoned in aspiration and care as the buildings and material that surround them have been abandoned in use and maintenance. It is a world of brokenness—broken human spirits and broken, worn-out products of other men's machines and craft.

The locational referents for these slum neighborhoods where people at the very bottom live were phrased the same in Boston as in Kansas City: "the inner city," "ghetto situations," "the worst crime areas," and "projects that have been wrecked by the residents." Translated into geographic specifics, this meant in Boston the areas immediately to the south, southeast, and southwest of the downtown; also included would be the northern third of the area known to all Bostonians as Roxbury (the center of the black population). In Kansas City, it meant the areas surrounding the business districts of both the Missouri-side central city and its Kansas satellite plus the oldest black neighborhoods, closest to the downtown centers. In addition, it is recognized in Kansas City that there are patches of "neighborhoods about as bad as you could find" further out, following along the valleys of the Kaw and Blue rivers, as they flow into the Missouri.

The welfare way of life. The word used most often by our sample members to characterize the life style and income source of people at the bottom was *welfare*. For a great share of the Bostonians and Kansas Citians we interviewed, the answer to our question, "Who is at the very bottom of the ladder?" was quite simple: "It's the welfare person. . . . The lowest class is people on welfare." The phraseology for this condition varied somewhat—"they receiving public assistance," "that's the public aid group," "people on government handouts," "the person on relief," "those on the dole of some sort," "charity cases"—but the concept did not vary. The principle enunciated in any case was that *the welfare class* and *people at the bottom* are nearly synonymous terms, that any American for whom welfare has become a way of life is thereby to be accounted among the nation's lowest-class citizens.

The Boston and Kansas City people we interviewed were frequently harsh in their indictment of this group. Labels such as "chiselers," "freeloaders," and "parasites" were commonly applied. A special aggravation is the notion that life on welfare "is not so bad these days," that "some people do very well on relief," that many on welfare indeed "live better than people who work." For many a Middle American in our sample it is incomprehensible—and in fact "wrong"—that "the government gives the man on welfare money for rent so that he can have the same kind of house the man has that works." This level of public largesse is seen as exacerbating the problem, encouraging people to "go on welfare instead of working." For people with this view, the welfare class ultimately amounts to an enemy class—an enemy, because its members are "living off the middle class," "costing the rest of us lots of money," and "causing trouble when they don't get enough."

Another notion about welfare that our Boston and Kansas City respondents found cause for grave concern is that "it is a cycle system." In this image, "the people on welfare just go on and on and on and their children go on and on living on welfare"—or, in other phrasings: "It's a kind of chronic thing in that their condition is repeating itself, their father and mother lived in the same way"; "The mother has lots of kids, then the older daughter has her first child on welfare, and the wheel just starts to turn all over again."

In the midst of all this denunciation of the welfare system and of the welfare person, we found most of our middle- and upper-status sample members making a distinction between people for whom welfare has become their way of life and those for whom it is only an occasional resort. The latter—people who are only sometimes or partially on welfare—were usually recognized as standing above the former socially, possibly a full step up the ladder. It was only when people were totally and always on welfare (or usually and mostly), that they were identified as being on the ladder's bottom rung. If "welfare is what gets them through life," if "they have no income aside from government aid," if "they get all their commodities from welfare—subsidized food as well as subsidized rent," if "they wouldn't have housing without government help," if "they're able-bodied but have chosen to go on aid instead of work"— if any or all of these conditions apply, then Bostonians and Kansas Citians said they were people at the bottom.

Indifference and incontinence: the self-victimizing vices. A title for this lowest stratum that would reflect how most Middle Americans in our sample spoke of its members would be people who don't try to rise above the bottom level and deserve to be there as a result of their folly and bad habits. Time and again opinions like these were expressed: "There's no reason to be lowest class unless they're handicapped. . . . The bottom class is people who don't care how they live and don't care to change things. . . . They don't want to try to better themselves—they don't care just so long as they have a roof over their heads. . . . They are more or less satisfied to be at the bottom. . . . They like it this way. . . . There's usually some way to work out of the bottom if you want to. . . . The bottom is people who've just given up."

In short—and surprising though it may seem, given the horrors envisioned for life in the slums—it is a common image of people at the bottom that they are indifferent to their condition. Or, if not truly indifferent, that they do not mind it enough to be willing to put out the effort required to escape it. They are "just lazy"; they "lack ambition," "don't care about anything," "don't want to work hard," "have a nonchalant attitude—no purpose in life," and "just wait for nothing to happen."

When our Boston and Kansas City sample members were asked what occupations they associated with people at the very bottom of the ladder, the impressions they registered in response ran this gamut: "They have no skills to speak of—they're unemployable"; "They just can't find jobs—they're usually unemployed"; "The only work they can do is the most menial"; "They can't hold a job—they haven't picked up the right habits"; "They only work from time to time when the spirit moves them"; "They usually aren't working—they don't like to"; and "They won't even look for work—they don't want it." These impressions reduce down to two main themes. One is that people at the bottom have very little or nothing in the way of occupational competence to offer prospective employers, and the other is that they are too indolent and indifferent to bother. This latter, of course, is corollary to the proposition that these are men and women quite willing to remain in the bottom class; it constitutes proof, as it were, that they deserve to be there.

Alongside this image that people at the bottom dislike work, cannot find jobs, and/or earn very little when they are gainfully employed, there is another image (or understanding, we might call it) that not all persons at this social level can be so characterized, that a certain portion of people at the bottom do not object to work, work steadily, and earn wages palpably above anybody's poverty lines, yet are slum-dwellers all the same and appear in the public eye to be living at the poverty standard. Their problem, as described when they are singled out for separate indictment, is not one of insufficient income but rather of incontinence in its use; that is what explains their low status. These are the people Boston and Kansas City interviewees called to our attention with phrases and stories purportedly proving that "they don't know how to manage their money." Of them it was said: "They have beer and whiskey around their house all the time. . . . You see a new Cadillac parked out in front of their shacks. . . . They have a color TV and an antenna on their roof, but what they're living in is a slum. . . . Go inside and you'll find expensive toys lying around getting broken. . . . They have no sense of responsibility about money; they're always broke, while others making the same are making ends meet and able to live decently." (As can be imagined, the same judgment was commonly made about the spending habits of most persons with incomes below the poverty line, that is, "There's not always money left for the right food in poverty families because they have spent money on things they don't need, like big television sets and cars.") It was in line with this understanding about who does or does not live in the slums and in poverty that many Bostonians and Kansas Citians said in effect (as did one in fact), "If [the family is] making between $5,000 and $7,000 a year, it depends on how they spend their money whether they are in poverty or not. It's mostly a matter of management."

Going beyond matters of occupation and money, this world of people at the bottom is imagined by Middle and Upper Americans as a tangle of social and behavioral pathology; of sexual misbehavior; of unstable, squabbling, and broken families. It is a world of people "who have no standards at all . . . they don't try to keep up their property . . . they don't mind if their houses are crummy . . . they don't teach their children anything." And almost invariably "they have far too many kids . . . eight or ten per family . . . some illegitimate." More often than not "the father is missing . . . he ran off . . . the mother's been left with a lot of children and had to go on ADC." If the husband is still home, "he and the wife would be hitting each other all the time," since, as people above the bottom have heard, "in poverty, there's lots more fighting in the family."

No handicap was more widely attributed to people at the bottom than "limited exposure to education." Over and over our sample members said of this stratum: "They lack education," "They didn't get too far in school," "They probably quit school at a very young age," and "Their basic education is the lowest." The typical translation of this into actual school attainment was that no more than eight grades were completed: "Few of them ever made it to high school. . . . They'd have an eighth-grade education at most. . . . You'd doubt some of them got through grade school. . . . A lot would be just sixth grade or less." Three interpretations were offered for this early termination of formal education. One is essentially genetic, that "they are the least intelligent. . . . They're not educable—you just can't teach them. . . . They're mentally deficient. . . . Many are retarded." A second can be called environmental in that it points to family history as the problem: "Their parents didn't care about school and insist that they go" or "Their father and mother didn't try to teach them anything at home; they didn't set an example." The third is characterological and accusatory: "They didn't care about an education. . . . They didn't want to go to school," with—as one variant— the notion that "they're just lazy and haven't utilized whatever education they got."

To Middle and Upper Americans, the most unfortunate aspect of the handicaps of ignorance, low intelligence, and limited education is that those who suffer them seem thereby doomed, regardless of their character and desire for employment, to work at the least-respected, lowest-paid, most menial of jobs—if, that is, they can find work at all. Thus it is that the occupations our Boston and Kansas City respondents associated with the workers in this stratum were all either extremely unpleasant in image—garbage collectors, ditchdiggers, streetsweepers, dishwashers, and clean-up help were most commonly mentioned—or characterized as "unskilled work . . . just plain labor—not a brainy job at all."

For men and women more marginal in ability and drive, the occupational prognosis rendered by our sample members was worse than that. The best that many could hope for, it was believed, was "part-time work . . . just transient, situational cleaning jobs . . . nothing that is steady." In part this prediction was based on the assumption that a number of the jobs people of this level have held in the past are "being phased out these days." And in part it was predicated on the proposition that "you can't train them for anything . . . they're unable to function in a job." The employment possibilities for persons of rural, bottom-class origins who have come into urban settings was deemed especially questionable to the extent that "they haven't learned the social skills that are required" for non-agricultural employment; "they don't have the right habits." Regarding the most extreme cases of mental and physical handicap, the judgment of their occupational potential veered toward verdicts that "they have no utility . . . they are perpetually unemployed and unemployable; they are really dysfunctional to society as a whole."

People Who Are Lower Class But Not of the Bottom Layer

Much of what Bostonians and Kansas Citians said about this next stratum—that "they're working and trying," that "they're usually not on welfare"—cannot be construed as true praise and compliment of its membership; rather it mainly constituted a definition and damnation of people at the bottom. That such is the case becomes clear when one observes that the people one stratum up—Middle Americans having a hard time but who aren't lower class—were regularly distinguished from these lower-class people not at the bottom in much the same way. As respondents said over and over when differentiating the two, "basically it's a matter of ambition and drive." By this accounting, the men and women of this next-to-lowest stratum "are just too lazy to move up" and they "don't work as hard as the working class to bring themselves up in the community"; in contrast, marginal Middle Americans have shown "more ambition to better themselves" and have "applied more effort" to accomplishment of that goal.

More meaningful characterizations of this stratum and an explanation of its position in the social hierarchy were established by our Boston and Kansas City respondents through six clusters of imagery. These define people who are lower class but not bottom layer as follows.

They are "bad off" economically, but not so much so that they have to live like people in poverty. They are only semi-poor in the public eye.

They live in bad housing, but not in real slums. Their homes are definitely substandard and the neighboods are "sort of awful," clearly worse than Middle Americans would ordinarily tolerate, but not the very worst.

They have "lousy jobs" that "don't pay much" and "don't give them much security." But the men and women of this stratum, unlike those below, are "all employable and willing to be employed."

They may sometimes find themselves resorting to governmental assistance, but not regularly, and they are "too proud" to let such assistance become their way of life. Living in public housing projects may be "the only form of welfare they take."

Almost all are handicapped in one way or another—educationally, linguistically, ethnically, racially, and possibly physically—but they have not been utterly crushed thereby as have many who are one step down at the bottom. These handicaps do, however, constitute a barrier to their social acceptance by Middle Americans.

Further, they are believed to be distinguished from Middle Americans in most instances by behavior and appearance: "their speech is not very good," their houses, cars, and yards are generally "junkier," in dress "they're not so neat" and possibly are "odd." In turn, however, they can usually be separated from the stratum below because they are "not as dirty"; in Middle-American imagery, they are hardly ever as disgusting

to the eye, ear, and nose as the bottom layer. And that, of course, is ultimately why they are not of the bottom layer, though indubitably lower-
class.

   Low-edge subsistence: the standard just above poverty. Two phrases
most aptly summarize how Bostonians and Kansas Citians characterized
the economic position of people at this level: "It's very marginal—what
you'd call the low edge of subsistence" and "They're plenty bad off, but
at least they're not in poverty." Impressions about how much income
these families had to live on ranged in the main from $4,500 a year to
$6,000 (in 1972). This is what respondents who phrased their images in
hourly earnings seemed to have in mind; the rates of pay they suggested
were, variously, "$2.50 an hour," "around $2.75," and "$3.00 at maximum."
(Such rates project to $5,000, $5,500, and $6,000 in annual totals, at full
employment.) The same placement was suggested by respondents
accustomed to thinking of economic status in terms of weekly wages,
they focused on $100 a week as what earners of this class would be paid,
thus: "They make $100 a week, or a bit less"; "He'd be earning around
$100 a week, not much more"; or "They make under $120 per week, and
in lots of cases only $100." (The annual total from fifty-two weeks' pay
at $100 per week is, of course, $5,200.) People who talked in terms of
monthly pay usually said "at least $400" but "no more than $500 a month."
Those who used annual totals tended to estimate $5,000 or $6,000 a year;
several, however, made statements like this: "That's anywhere from
$4,500 on up—they could be making $7,000 or more and not spending it
right."

   The income levels attributed by our sample to this group overlap
with the range associated with people having a hard time who aren't
lower class (as reported in Chapter 9). They averaged $1,200 less,
however: $5,300 as compared with $6,500. This may look like a small
difference, but both Middle Americans and Lower Americans treated it
as consequential, marking off two recognizably different levels of subsistence living. The lower was just one step above poverty and the higher
a palpable two or three steps up, closer to getting along than to poverty.
As respondents in our sample imagined life at the lower level (which we
shall refer to as the *low-edge subsistence standard*), it is a "bare" affair
of "just scraping by" and "everything minimum"; thus:

   "They just scrape by. They're probably doing without some things they
   actually need."

   "Everything is minimum for them; they can't have very much in the way
   of property or pleasure."

"They can pay their bills and rent, but just barely; there's nothing left over."

That, in general terms, is the quality of life associated with the stratum of people who are one step above poverty.

Beyond this, life at the low-edge subsistence standard was imagined by our Boston and Kansas City respondents as a series of minor and major deprivations, about which the only good thing to be said was, "It's better than poverty or being on welfare." With respect to food, for example, families at this standard were commonly differentiated from those in poverty on two counts: "There's always food on the table" and "They don't usually have to buy it with food stamps." (A minor deprivation they were believed to suffer when compared to mainstream families is that "they could never go out for dinner—they can't even afford a hamburger at McDonald's.")

Families at this level with a male head were expected by our Boston and Kansas City respondents to own a car more often than not; without a male head, though, it was assumed they would rely on public transportation. As for the kind of car that a man of this status might have, impressions were on this order: "It would be an old clunker . . . at least ten or twelve years old . . . real beat-up . . . bought second- or third-hand. . . . He might not have insurance on it, even if a state law requires it." All worthwhile spare-time pursuits requiring a sizeable outlay of cash were considered out of the question for people at this income level. The major form of recreation attributed to them was "capacious amounts of TV watching." Another widely mentioned form was "frequenting taverns more than they should." A third was going to parks and playgrounds. Vacations, it was unanimously conceded, "would be limited to things they could do in the local area"; most assuredly "there'd be no traveling, no motels." The happiest thought was that "They might get to go fishing once in a while if they are lucky."

Finally, the housing associated with families of this level was at the low edge of substandard in the public image, much closer in quality and appearance to slum level than to the house that any Middle American would occupy. Bostonians and Kansas Citians repeatedly made the point: "They live in places that are a little better than slums, but not much. . . . It's poor housing, not bad slums. . . . It's not slums yet, but soon to become slums." More broadly spoken, the deficiencies in this level of housing are four-fold: size, age, general appearance, and state of repair. The housing is variously characterized as "inadequate," "too small," "minimum," "crummy," "shabby," "poor looking," "run-down," "too old," "not modern or kept up," and "kind of worn out." That "paint is needed" both inside and out is a universal verdict, and that the plumbing, heating, and electricity are all in some way "faulty," "bad," or "poor" is also understood. As for the deficiencies in size, there are two. One is that units are too small ("They don't have more than four rooms, all small"), and the other is that there is overcrowding ("They have less space than is adequate for normal family living"). That "all the children are crowded into one bedroom" is assumed to be an all too-common condition among families at this low-edge subsistence standard of income and housing.

It is taken for granted that virtually all housing of this lowly status is rented, not owned by its occupants. This follows from the assumption that the occupants, who appear to have so little regular income to spend on housing, would almost certainly also have too little in the way of credit, collateral, or savings to make ownership possible. The prospect they face, then, as our Middle- and Upper American respondents imagined things, is that "unless they come into sudden money, they're going to be renting all their lives."

The lowest stratum of working Americans. Nearly as important as standard of living in the distinctions our Boston and Kansas City respondents established between two levels of Lower Americans were images of difference in employment history and attitude. In the more vivid wording of these images, praise of sorts was paid the men and women of the higher stratum for their drive and spirit, for their determination not to rank at the bottom:

> "That's the guy who's not going from day to day without work or without looking for work. He wants to work."

> "This class has made the first step up the ladder. They have begun to work."

> "They are not skilled, but they're still trying to do the best they can. They want to pull themselves up."

> "They will take any kind of job, even scrubbing floors, to get out of the slums and have a better place to live."

> "The big thing is that they work. Maybe it's only menial labor, but they are working. And that's a big difference from being a charity case."

The general view, of course, is that these people are too close to poverty and too different from the mainstream in behavior, appearance, and speech to be considered anything but lower class, no matter that they are willing to work and regularly have jobs. Ultimately, then, that they are part of the work force and off the welfare rolls seem almost the only things they have in common with the people who stand above them socially.

An alphabetic listing of types of employment attributed by significant portions of our sample to the men and women of this lowest stratum of working Americans would read as follows: busboys, common laborers, dock workers, factory workers paid minimum wages, filling station attendants, food service workers, handymen, hotel help, laundry workers, loaders, park maintenance men, railroad laborers, restaurant workers, stockworkers, waitresses, and yardmen. The forms of ill repute associated with these jobs are essentially three: they are "dirty work," "hard work," and/or "dumb work." Beyond this they are deemed undesirable to the extent that they are generally poorly paid, not unionized, and insecure.

Educational deficiency is another serious problem attributed to people lower class but not bottom layer. By the near-unanimous judgment of our Boston and Kansas City samples, this is a central factor in their income difficulties. "If they were better educated, they could get better work and make more money." Or, as otherwise declared: "Their lack of education is holding them back. . . . Their schooling is low and limited—it's not as good as the working class has. . . . If they had a halfways decent education they wouldn't be in the class they are." The number of years they spent in school is believed to have been whatever was the minimum required by law. This could mean that they quit attendance as early as age thirteen, but maybe not until sixteen, depending on when and where they grew up. In any event they almost surely completed no more than seven, eight, or nine regular grades. And, most importantly, what they missed out on was vocational training or other kind of specialized training that could "ensure them a job."

Other problems and handicaps associated by the Middle-American public with second-layer lowers are essentially moderated versions of the deficiencies in character, behavior, and continence attributed to bottom-layer lowers. They too, for example, are believed to "have had too many children for their small incomes." Six, seven, or eight children are assumed to be the rule, not the exception. Also assumed is that they have marital problems, that much family fighting occurs, that there is more divorce, and that they "aren't as stable in their family life as the working class." Husbands are thought to "squander money on things they don't need, like gambling and drinking, depriving the family of what they should have." In the worst instances, wives are seen as joining the men in folly: "They stick their kids in the door and say, 'I'm going out.' They hit the beer joints a lot and don't use their money very smart." It follows, then, as Middle Americans imagine things, that "the parents don't teach their children how to be worthwhile. . . . They don't encourage their children to get a better education. . . . They let them grow up ignorant of the better things." Thus it is that while second-layer lowers are understood to have at least tried and worked enough not to be down at the lower-class bottom, they are still said to be "different in motivation from the working class." They are accused of having "less ambition and drive," of "being relaxed about things," of being "selfish" and "unwilling to make sacrifices" that might yield long-term improvements in their living conditions and social standing—in short, that they pursue present pleasures at the cost of possible elevation into working-class status.

Images Lower Americans Have of Themselves and Their Place in Society

Nine hundred people were interviewed for this study. Among them, we estimate that some seventy-two (thirty-two in Kansas City and forty in Boston) would qualify as Lower Americans by the definitions of this status set forth above. They would be so judged, we believe, in response to their speech, appearance, and living standard. Of the seventy-two, thirty-seven reported themselves to be receiving transfer payments or some other form of government subsidy at the time of our study. Many of the other thirty-five acknowledged having been the beneficiaries of such at some time in the past. Blacks constituted almost half the total, numbering thirty-five. Five Mexican-Americans brought the sample representation of minority groups up to forty. Among the other thirty-two, sixteen can be counted as white ethnics—they were either born abroad or are the children of immigrants from Italy, Portugal, the Balkan states, Near Eastern countries, or Ireland. The other sixteen identified themselves as "just plain Americans" or "old Yankees"; one told of ancestors who "came over on the Mayflower."

This sampling is an under-representation. Census data on occupational distribution, income, educational background, and housing suggest that somewhere between 12 and 13 percent of adults in the two cities are of this status, not a mere 8 percent. Plainly, our interviewers avoided the worst of houses and neighborhoods, even when sent on assignment in their general direction. It would be reasonable to conclude, then, that the Lower Americans who were recruited into this sample were more often second layer, instead of bottom layer, than a proper sampling would contain. We cannot, therefore, in this section purport to tell how *all* varieties of Lower Americans feel about their lives and place in society; we can speak only for the segments represented by the men and women who came into our sample.

Self-declarations about social standing on the part of these Lower Americans are primarily correlated with race. Further, there is astonishingly little relationship between the classifications we have rendered of their position and the way any given Lower-American respondent chose to define his or her position when asked to do so by the interviewer. These two conclusions are drawn from these observations: Most whites in this Lower-American sample refused to call themselves lower class, even those in the bottom layer; most blacks accepted a lower-class designation for themselves, whether on the bottom or not. Some of the most elevated self-placements were voiced by respondents who have dwelt socially on the lowest rung their entire lives—and are still there; oppositely, some of the lowest self-placements were selected by persons not on the bottom at all, who had slipped down to Lower-American identification from an earlier membership in a Middle-American status group.

The white Lower Americans in our Boston and Kansas City samples avoided identifying themselves as lower class or lowest class in a variety of ways. The most common was to point to slum-dwelling blacks as a group far lower in status. Over and over they found comparative comfort in their own condition by saying, "At least I don't live in places ready to fall down like over there in the colored-town district," or "I'm not in dirty poverty the way the blacks are who live in real slums like in New York City and Chicago." Another was to point to other whites who were worse off in housing and income and proclaim in mixed relief and gratitude: "I'm not on Skid Row," "I'm glad I'm not in a housing project," "I don't live in places that aren't kept up—windows boarded up and stuff like that," or "I don't live in a junk yard or in one of those apartment complexes where there are eight or nine people in just three or four rooms." Clearly, for most whites in our sample who did not live in a slum-level dwelling, this one fact of their lives was taken as sufficient by itself to elevate them out of bottom-class standing into some broad, all-American middle category.

A third approach, widely used by the worst-housed of whites as well as the best, was to assume an attitude of moral and behavioral superiority. In some instances this was voiced as a generalization: "Lower-class people are those who have no morals" or "The bottom of the ladder are people who don't try. They live in the slums and don't care about anything." And in other instances it was voiced as a specific derogation of neighbors: "Some people around here on welfare don't even keep their kids clean; the kids have to come to my place when they want to get clean" or "That family across the street has problems. . . . The father won't work and the children have done some stealing—they've been in jail." Or, "There's some people around here who have loud parties and the cops are here all the time having to quiet them down." In such words, the point was established: *Really* lower-class people are lacking in the will "to try," they are "unclean," and "immoral," they "steal," and the police are very much part of their lives, sometimes carting them off to jail, other times "quieting them down." The speakers (usually female) implied that since none of these applied personally, they were therefore not truly lower-class. A young Boston mother on ADC, maintaining a fairly neat apartment, said plaintively: "I consider myself working class, not lower class. . . . I try to better myself; I don't try to go backwards, I try to go forwards."

Many of these men and women, when speaking of their past and their parentage, said, "I used to have it worse." A considerable portion told of growing up in families where "there were nine of us kids"—or ten, or twelve, or thirteen. A goodly number had lived for a while in projects. Several remarked that "at one time we were on welfare," then half congratulated themselves, "but we managed to get off." Some of these and others described their families as having been "dirt poor during the depression"; a few told of fathers who "worked for the WPA [Works Progress Administration]." There were instances where men who had been "unemployed" at some point in the past spoke of themselves as "definitely working-class now" (though their jobs paid little and were near the lowest in public regard). In similar fashion we found women, and men too, who had formerly lived in "real slums" or in government housing saying of the somewhat better places they had moved to, "This ain't a bad neighborhood. I'd rate it average, 100." It was from such a perspective, of having graduated up from lower economic status, that so many white Lower Americans spoke when they referred to themselves as "plain, working, family people, just average" or "ordinary people, just middle-class, not upper-class."

There was one young woman in the sample with an opposite vantage point. She had grown up, as she described it, "in a $25,000 house in the suburbs, where we had two cars and everything else you could want." But she had quit school at fifteen to get married and by the time of our study had fallen two or three rungs down the ladder. She had been abandoned by her husband, was living in a "scroungy" apartment on the waterfront, working part-time as a nurse's aide, and getting further support for her children from ADC. Regarding her status, this woman said, "My kids and I would be considered lower-class—that would be our place in the community—but I used to be middle-class." She was able to see herself through the eyes of Middle Americans, and she knew that there was nothing "middle" about what she saw. Carefully she worded her statement of place, "would be considered lower-class," defining it from the viewpoint of those above.

Some of the Lower-American women in our sample, denying that money could measure happiness, said, "I'm having a good life." Always these were women who had the financial support of husbands fully employed and the spiritual comfort of children at home who had not yet disappointed them. One in Boston said, "We are poorer than people having a good life economically. We have to watch every penny we spend. But I think I have a better family life. I think poor families have better children and they have a closer relationship. I have this comfort of my family relationship, so I guess this is more satisfying to me than if I had more money and not such a close relationship." And one in Kansas City said, "I would describe my life as low in a money sense. I'm poor. I don't have a car. I don't take vacations. I don't own a home. I'm classed way down, I suppose." She placed herself as lower-middle class, above both the next-to-lowest class and people at the bottom. "But my kids give me a good life. I live for them. I don't have to have money. I just feed and clothe my kids and keep them warm."

The very poorest white man in our sample—the only one living in a project, thirty-seven years old but long disabled—replied when asked about his status, "I'd say I'm middle-class; it's the systems that have put me here; the situations have put me in the lowest class." The situations that he referred to were his disability (a blood disease) and his lack of education—he had quit school during seventh grade. He was saying that "what you see here is not reality, not the real me." The truth of his being and of his social standing, as he suggested to the interviewer, were to be found back in his happy childhood. "There were twelve of us. We lived in the country and fished and hunted frogs all day long. . . . My daddy made a good living." But now, he concluded, "The systems have put me here, and there's no way to get out." In less dramatic fashion, others of the poorer whites in our sample, both men and women, absolved themselves of blame for their lowly condition. They looked upon their situations as an unkind accident of fate. They treated their unfortunate economic status as not a true definition of their class as human beings. They said, in effect or in fact, "I'm lower-income, but not lower-class."

The black Lower Americans in our sample who avoided identifying themselves as lower-class did so in all the same ways as the whites. One in Kansas City, with eight children and occupying "the worst apartment" in the sample, called herself middle-class, even though earlier she had been asked what she thought the phrase *bottom class* meant and had described her own condition perfectly: "People who are not working and are living on welfare and have no husband and they live in a cheap apartment and they have not finished high school." A young woman in Boston, with only one child instead of eight and living in a "surprisingly well-kept place," spoke more realistically of her situation: "I'm poor now, but I am in a government program. . . . I like to think I am not lower-class. When I'm through with my training, I guess I'll be working-class."

It was not so much the rule, however, for the blacks in our sample of obviously lower status to deny a lower-class identity. Typically they treated the question of their status almost indifferently, as if it were one of the givens in their lives. A woman would say, "I am poor and uneducated. . . . I have no husband to give me support for my kids, and I am just making ends meet." And a man would say, "I am in the low class, because I am not working." Few looked around to find someone lower to look down upon. They did not make a point of being martyrs to centuries of oppression; rather, they spoke matter-of-factly as realists living in the present. Occasionally one was defiant—as was a young black man in Boston, for example. Living in an apartment that was not really a slum, just "rather bare of furniture except for a good stereo set," when asked where he would place himself, he spat out: "Shit, man, I'm lower-class; I'm black; I live in this slum. What else do you need to know?"

CHAPTER 11

How People Calculate Social Standing

Fathoming the outlines of the American class structure is one thing; determining the position of each and every person in it is another, and far, far more difficult. The greatest part of the difficulty stems from a dimly understood truth: an incredible variety of families and individuals are to be found at most every income level. This variety is what frustrates easy conceptualization of the hierarchy. The average citizen has to ignore it for the most part when formulating an impression of the structure. Images of the social order must be built around prototypes—families who fit general expectations of how education, occupation, and income go together. Prototypical families then become the core for each status level. But in the real world, prototypical families are only a fraction of the total.

We cannot fully understand the social structure until we see how families not prototypical—who, unfortunately for easy comprehension, are the majority—are related to it. Toward this end, we conducted one more magnitude estimation experiment, this time to determine how people use social arithmetic to place families. We borrow this phrase *social arithmetic* from Leonard Reissman (1959:129), who employed it in the following manner:

> There is the likelihood that judgments made of an individual's total social position in the community represent a balanced assessment of all relevant characteristics that might set an individual's position in the prestige hierarchy—personal characteristics, occupation, education, organizational memberships, community participation, family background and life style.

This social arithmetic depends on an intuitive balancing and weighting of the individual's relative standing according to several prestige dimensions simultaneously. These values are summed by a special social logic that can handle each dimension as if it were comparable to all other dimensions. Only by these methods can income be added to occupation, family background to power, and participation to life style.

In our experiment we tested the social arithmetic involved in weighting the three status dimensions that were assessed singly earlier in the interviews: income, education, and occupation.

The method in our experiment is identical to our magnitude scaling of the individual status continua. The only difference is that instead of asking respondents for estimates of status from a single variable, we asked for estimates from three-factor profiles of hypothetical families. In 1971 we presented our question in this fashion:[1]

Compared to the Mims' 100, based on the clues given, estimate the *general standing as most people would see it* of each of the following families:

The Mims Are 100. How Much Are . . .	Less than the Mims (0–99)	More than the Mims (100 or more)
The Joneses—he is an electrician who earns $10,800 a year and has an eighth-grade education.		
The Smiths—(and so on.)		

Himmelfarb and Seun (1969), Hamblin (1971a), and Shinn (1974) had all conducted such magnitude estimation experiments with small samples, using three factors instead of just one in the inquiry, so we were not without precedent. The only difference is that we attempted it in a large-sample survey, with a cross-section of the lay public as our respondents, and we used a much wider and more representative set of profiles—129 in all.

In our 1970 survey seven profiles were given each respondent to judge; we used twelve different sets of profiles; approximately fifty respondents judged each set. This gave us a total of eighty-four hypothetical families rated in the first study. The interviewer read these profiles to the respondent and recorded their answers on the form. In 1971 the magnitude estimation questions were printed on a self-report form—the respondents read the questions silently, then wrote in their own answers. In 1971 we increased the number of profile items per respondent to fifteen. Three sub-samples of one hundred persons each rated different sets of these profiles. This gave us a total of forty-five hypothetical families rated in 1971, none of which were repeated from the 1970 experiment.

The results of this social arithmetic test are presented in Table 11-1. The 129 tested profiles have been rank-ordered by geomean status estimate. The year of survey is indicated to show which profiles were judged by 50 respondents (those in the 1970 survey) and which by 100 (1971).

The Relation of Qualitative to Quantitative Status Evaluations

The status estimation approach elicited from members of the community numerical estimates of the magnitudes of status associated with particular socio-economic resources or, in the case of the profiles, with a pattern of socio-economic resources. In the qualitative study, members of the community were asked a wide-ranging series of questions about their images of both single status dimensions and the pattern of resources they believe characterize different positions on the continuum of social standing. From this complex pattern of responses the researcher abstracted a set of images of ranked groups.

The most straightforward way, given the data available to us, of relating these approaches, was to compare the classes into which the qualitative analyst would place the profiles of 129 families used in the two Boston surveys with the magnitude estimations of those profiles provided by our Boston sample.

We have previously described a number of different ways in which the status continuum can be divided into more or less homogeneous groups in terms of social standing. For the purposes of analysis here, each of the profiles was placed in one of thirteen social status levels. Two of these levels are subdivisions of the upper class and three are subdivisions of the upper-middle class (see Chapter 8). Six of the levels are subgroups of Middle Americans, three from the middle class—a high, middle, and low—and three from the working class (see Chapter 9). The final two are subgroups from the lower class. Richard Coleman classified each of the profiles into one of these thirteen levels, the placements representing

TABLE 11-1

Magnitude Estimates of General Standing for
Hypothetical Families Based on Three-Factor Profiles

Occupation, Title and Description	Level of Education	Annual Income	Status Estimates (Geomean)
Unemployed	02	$ 500	16
Garbage collector	04	1,900	16
Unemployed*	02	800	17
Laundry worker	02	300	17
Dockworker	04	1,100	17
Laborer in furniture factory	11	1,200	20
Shoeshiner	06	1,600	23
Gas station attendant	06	600	27
Janitor	08	1,100	27
Shoe repairman	08	1,400	27
Hospital attendant	12	2,500	28
Loom operator	12	2,200	29
Truckdriver	12	2,100	31
Spraypainter	12	2,600	31
Brickmason	12	2,700	31
Barber	09	2,200	33
Bulldozer operator	09	2,100	38
Janitor*	10	2,700	41
Personnel director	07	4,400	41
Truckdriver	05	2,100	43
Laborer in furniture factory*	12	3,000	43
Ditchdigger	08	4,600	43
Auto repairman	12	2,500	45
Glass cutter	09	3,700	46
Laborer in a bottling company	08	5,700	46
Expediter	08	3,900	47
Gardener	08	4,200	47
Shipping clerk	08	4,200	48
Restaurant waiter	10	3,500	48
Machine operator in bag company	05	4,100	48
Hospital attendant*	08	3,300	50
Dockworker	08	4,300	50
Glass cutter	05	3,700	51
Ditchdigger	03	8,500	52
Janitor	03	8,700	53
Grocery clerk	12	4,800	53
Machinist	06	5,200	54
New car salesman	14	3,900	56
Hospital attendant	08	5,500	56
Laundry worker	08	4,200	57
Truckdriver	05	7,500	57
Railroad freight inspector	07	9,400	58
Shoe repairman	08	9,700	58
Traveling salesman	12	4,800	63
Insurance salesman	12	4,800	64
Auto repairman*	07	5,100	65
Stock clerk	06	7,400	66
Hardware clerk	14	7,400	67
Laborer in furniture factory	08	6,300	68
Printing press operator	05	7,600	68
Assembly line worker*	11	5,700	69
Construction foreman	10	6,000	72

TABLE 11-1 (continued)

	The Three Factors in Profile Specification		Status
Occupation, Title and Description	Level of Education	Annual Income	Estimates (Geomean)
Hardware clerk*	14	$ 5,400	73
Gardener	11	8,100	73
Bulldozer operator	12	7,500	74
Laborer in bottling company	05	9,400	74
Radio-TV repairman*	13	5,400	79
Airplane mechanic	07	9,700	79
Spray painter	05	10,700	79
Clothes presser*	10	7,800	81
College professor	M.A.	4,200	82
Mail carrier*	12	6,300	82
Parts checker	13	12,300	82
Railroad freight inspector*	12	6,300	83
Airplane mechanic	12	9,700	83
Auto repairman	05	11,100	83
Printing press operator	05	11,600	83
Airplane mechanic	12	6,000	84
Restaurant cook	04	9,600	84
Taxi driver*	06	10,900	85
Fireman	12	11,900	85
Airplane mechanic	07	6,000	86
Gas station attendant*	12	8,400	86
Machine operator*	06	8,800	86
Factory foreman*	14	6,200	88
Metal grinder	05	8,300	88
Physician	M.D. + Ph.D	4,600	90
Loom operator	09	9,200	90
Machine operator in bag company*	07	9,500	92
Loom operator*	11	11,100	92
Owner of drycleaning store*	14	7,100	93
Shoe repairman	04	9,700	93
Assembly line worker	10	10,600	93
Stock clerk	13	10,700	93
Dockworker*	10	13,200	94
Fireman*	09	9,100	96
Insurance salesman*	M.A.	7,800	97
Manager of a small store*	12	8,000	97
Government accounting clerk	B.A.	8,500	98
Shipping clerk*	09	10,500	98
Carpenter*	12	9,800	99
Printing press operator*	12	10,200	99
Barber*	07	11,200	99
Plasterer	09	12,700	100
Machinist*	14	9,500	103
Electrician*	08	10,800	103
Chemist*	13	9,600	108
Restaurant cook*	13	11,700	108
Bookkeeper*	B.A.	11,100	109
Accountant*	M.A.	8,400	112
Government accounting clerk*	13	12,000	112
Accountant	B.A.	7,500	114
Construction foreman	12	14,300	120
Assistant manager, office supply co.	M.A.	11,700	121
High school teacher*	B.A.	10,500	124
Tool and die maker*	12	14,700	125
High school teacher*	15	13,300	128

TABLE 11-1 (continued)

| Occupation, Title and Description | The Three Factors in Profile Specification | | Status Estimates (Geomean) |
	Level of Education	Annual Income	
Factory foreman	14	$ 18,200	130
Accountant	12	19,200	130
Truckdriver*	13	21,000	130
New car salesman*	10	20,500	132
High school teacher	M.A.	13,300	138
Department head, state gov't.	Ph.D.	12,000	143
Office manager, moving co.	B.A.	23,400	144
Owner of drycleaning store	06	22,600	145
Owner of drycleaning store	12	22,600	150
Department head, state gov't.	M.A.	10,300	156
Salesman for electrical manufacturing company	B.A.	23,400	162
Civil engineer*	13	29,100	173
Chemist	B.A.	21,000	174
Department head, state gov't.	M.A.	22,800	203
Owner of factory*	B.A.	33,500	205
Owner of factory*	10	60,000	225
Traveling salesman*	12	90,000	233
College professor*	Ph.D.	30,000	238
Physician*	M.D. but no B.A.	40,000	276
Board chairman	B.A.	200,000	370
Manager of large factory	M.A.	200,000	425
President of a billion-dollar corporation	Ph.D.	2,000,000	537

*Profile in both 1970 and 1971 questionnaires.

his best estimate of where families with these characteristics would rank in terms of the status structure proposed in the previous three chapters.

These class placements are obviously only a very rough approximation of the kind of rating that would be made for the profiled families were more data provided. Missing from these profiles—but vital, as we have learned from the images our respondents offered for different social classes—is information about the housing and neighborhoods in which these hypothetical families live, their voluntary group participation, and the education of the wife as well as of the husband. In addition, the act of rating these profiles is not exactly the same as rating a real family, whether done by a researcher or by members of the community, since in the real situation data are generally available with which to explain and interpret status inconsistencies. (Coleman and our respondents were in a similar state of ignorance about our made-up families. If Coleman and the respondents shared similar conceptions concerning what other status-related characteristics are likely to go with the three included in our profile, then the fact that information about the families given in the profiles is inadequate should not detract from the agreement between the respondents and the researcher.)

The next thing we did was compute a mean magnitude estimation score for the profiles Coleman had grouped into the thirteen levels. These means are shown in Table 11-2. They were weighted for census-indicated real-world distribution of each profile. Table 11-2 shows that the ranking of profiles by Boston survey respondents and by Coleman are essentially similar: the group means are successively higher. Coleman and the respondents differed, of course, in ranking of specific cases. The correlation between Coleman's placement into thirteen levels and respondents' magnitude estimation geomeans for the 129 profiles was 0.92.

TABLE 11-2

*Mean Status Estimates for Thirteen Subclasses
(Census weighted regression)*

The Status Groups	Magnitude Means
Upper-Class Upper Americans	
Upper-Upper	537 (one case)
Lower-Upper	397 (two cases)
Upper-Middle Upper Americans	
Upper-Middle Elite	242
Upper-Middle Core	185
Upper-Middle Marginal	139
Middle-Class Middle Americans	
Middle-American Elite	130
Middle-Class Core	116
Middle-Class Marginal	106
Working-Class Middle Americans	
Working-Class Specials	102
Working-Class Core	92
Working-Class Marginal	69
Lower Americans	
Not the Lowest	55
The Bottom Layer	35

It seems reasonable to conclude that the qualitative approach to social class placement derived from the open-ended interviews produces essentially the same ranking of individuals as that provided by a sample of members of the community using magnitude estimation techniques to estimate general social standing. In turn, Coleman's classifications represent simply an updating of an earlier approach to social class placement, as in Coleman's 1950s Kansas City research and that of Warner and his colleagues earlier.

Having concluded that these two different approaches place individuals in similar ways, we can now ask what is the relationship between the ordinal placements implicit in the qualitatively derived social classes and the ratio estimates provided by the status estimation techniques.

Even though we cannot put too much weight on comparisons of adjacent regression coefficients, the overall pattern of the coefficients is instructive.[2] We note first that there is a middle-status group for which respondents in our sample, on average, saw quite small differences in general social standing magnitudes. The two higher groups in the working class and the two lower groups in the lower-middle class, which together account for over half of the census weighted profiles, represent a quite narrow band of status magnitudes ranging from 92 to 116—the higher number being only about a quarter greater than the lower. It might well be that within this range there would not be the same level of agreement as that reflected in the overall correlation between social class placements and the status estimations. The narrow range of status estimates for these four groups is consistent with the common assertion by our respondents that there is a very broad middle class that includes a heavy representation of typical blue-collar as well as white-collar workers. At the lower end of the scale it is clear that the profiles that fit images of a lower class are seen as quite far removed from the average working-class group.

Above this broad middle group, we see that the solid upper-middles are also perceived as quite distant from the middle group. If we could have confidence in the accuracy of the regression coefficients we could conclude that our Boston respondents saw the profiles that Coleman placed in the marginal upper-middle group as basically much closer to the higher-status lower-middles than to other upper-middles. (If this kind of result held up under further exploration, it would suggest the usefulness of a status category called middle middle.)

At the extreme high-status level, the upper-class groups, represented here by only three profiles, are seen as quite distant not only from the middle-class group but also from the upper-middle-class group. How well this result applies to the broader range of upper-class types, and how much it is a function of the fact that the three profiles Coleman characterized as upper class were also ones with extremely high incomes, is difficult to know given our limited data. A great many people who fit into

one or the other of these two upper classes in fact do not have incomes
as divergent from those of typical upper-middles as our three upper-class
profiles do (all $200,000 a year or more).

The Relative Importance of Income, Job, and Schooling

The major objective in this experiment was to study how each factor
of the three under consideration independently contributes to general
status judgments. To achieve this, we deliberately minimized the intercorrelations of the three within the profiles; this facilitates disentangling
the effects. This meant that many of the profiles we tested were of non-
prototypical families—families in which the three variables were mixed
in less-than-commonplace ways. Of course, we also wanted some prototypical families in our test, both for control purposes, as it were, and also
to give respondents the feeling that these could be real families they were
rating.[3]

A continuum of status scores from 16 as low to 537 as high was
produced by the two administrations of this experiment. In the 1970
survey when only fifty persons gave estimates for each profile, inversions
in status estimate occasionally cropped up, reminding us of the hazards
of small-sample research. For example, a geomean estimate of 86 was
recorded for an airplane mechanic with seventh-grade education earning
$6,000 a year, while an estimate of 83 was recorded for an airplane
mechanic with twelfth-grade education earning $9,700. Oddities like this
aside, we count the experiment a success in suggesting how much more
heavily weighted is income, in the average American's social arithmetic,
than education or occupation. This is especially true of people's intuitive
weighing and dividing when incomes are extreme. Very low incomes are
almost invariably a source of very low ratings of general standing. Very
high incomes are not quite so invariably translated into equally high
general status, but at least they always seem to place their recipient far
above the common man.

Robert Hamblin, who was the first to perform an experiment of the
sort described here, hypothesized that the magnitude estimates for the
status of such profiles would have a regular relationship to the magnitude-
estimated status of the components of the profile (Hamblin, 1974).[4]
Having found power functions to be the best mathematical approxima-

tion for his income, job, and education status continua, Hamblin proposed that the regular relationship between profile status and the status of the income-occupation-education components of the profile would take the form of a "multivariate power function":

$$S_G = K(S_E{}^{n_E})\ (S_I{}^{n_I})\ (S_O{}^{n_O})$$

where

S_G = General Status, S_E = Status of Education, n_E = Exponent for educational status, S_I = Status of income, n_I = Exponent for income status, S_O = Status of Occupation, n_O = Exponent of occupational status, and K = An empirical constant. When we take logarithms of each variable, this equation takes the form of a multiple linear regression equation:

$$\text{Log } S_G = n_E \log S_E + n_I \log S_I + n_O \log S_O + \log K$$

In this sort of research, as contrasted with Warner's or Hollingshead's method of index construction, the criterion for the weighting of a status dimension in the index is its efficiency in prediction, not of the classification based wholly or in part on a researcher's expert judgment, but of the consensus judgments of a set of lay persons. However, as we have shown, the expert's judgments and the sample's average judgments are in our case essentially the same. This means that using the multiple regression technique to discover the coefficients for each of the three status factors, the exponents, according to the consensus judgments of the respondents, also tells us the coefficients that the expert implicitly uses in applying what has been learned from what the respondents have said in their open-ended comments—as it should be, of course, if our qualitative and quantitative methods and analyses have both been valid.

We analyzed separately the eighty-two 1970 profiles and the forty-five 1971 profiles, and then combined them into one analysis.[5] The results are quite consistent. They suggest that income is the most important factor—a coefficient of 0.57 for the combined data—with job next most important (0.29) and education trailing far behind (0.10). The coefficient of determination was very high for the 1971 data (0.982), lower for the 1970 data (0.912) where sample sizes per item were under fifty persons, and not much higher for the combined data (0.927). However, the coefficients are hardly different; it seems reasonable to conclude that the errors are random and do not bias the coefficients.[6]

So, it would seem that for the wide range of social standing represented by our profiles, general social standing increases with slightly more than the square root power of income status, the one-fourth power of job status, and the one-tenth power of education status. That means that a doubling of each of the status resources would have quite different effects. Holding the other two constant, doubling would have these effects on general social status:

Doubling income   = 49% increase in general status
Doubling job   = 22% increase in general status
Doubling schooling — 7% increase in general status

Examination of the profiles suggests that, as foreshadowed in earlier chapters, schooling loses explanatory significance at the higher ranges of income and job status and that this accounts for its very low coefficient. It would be a mistake, then, to take our one-tenth power exponent as a good measure of the influence of education at the low to medium-high ranges of status (say up to 250).

In order to see whether the disproportionate number of higher-income profiles were distorting the influence of schooling at lower ranges we computed the regression again after weighting each profile so that it reflected roughly its proportionate share of the population. This "census weighted" equation almost doubles the schooling coefficient without much change in the other two.[7] Now, income has an exponent of 0.543, job of 0.273, and education of 0.184. This tells us that general standing is the product of these three variables in approximately this relationship: the square root of income status, the three-tenths root of job status, and the one-fifth root of schooling status. Overall, it appears that variations in income status account for almost two-thirds of the variation in general social standing, and that schooling status and job status split the remainder about evenly. Income is of overwhelming importance in how Americans think about social standing. It is unfortunate that sociologists have paid so little attention to it.

Translated back into the original units of dollars of income and years of schooling, the regression coefficients for income, job, and schooling mean that wide variations in schooling have remarkably little direct effect on the status assigned an individual by peers' knowledge of that schooling (but see Chapter 15 for the large indirect effects). If job and income are held constant, increasing schooling from grade school (geo-mean score of 47) to high school graduation (geomean of 93) increases general standing by only 13 percent. Going from high school to college graduation (geomean of 160) represents only a 10 percent increase. Another way of pointing out the small effect is to say that a person with four years of college has only one-fourth more general standing than someone with just an eighth-grade background—unless, of course, the additional schooling has also paid off in the job and income attained (as respondents kept telling us—see Chapter 4).

A comparable job variation would be from garbage collector up to truckdriver up to owner of a small but reasonably successful store. Holding income and schooling constant (as unreal as that may be), a change from garbage collector up to truckdriver would increase general standing by just 20 percent, and a further move up the line to storeowner (with geomean rating of 160) would represent another 16 percent increase in general standing—for a total of 40 percent from garbage collector up to storeowner.

Income increases over the same geomean range—from about $4,500 (in 1971) to $9,200 up to $17,500—would increase general standing by 45 percent for the first job and an additional 34 percent for the second, for an overall gain of 94 percent.

When we relate these possibilities of change in job, education, or income to our social class schema as developed in Chapters 8, 9, and 10, we find that changes of great magnitude in schooling or occupation status seldom make a difference of more than one subclass level—marginal to core, or core to elite, or elite of one class to marginal of the next. Changes in income of the magnitudes we have been discussing, on the other hand, have a much stronger effect, often moving the profiled family at least two or three subclasses and sometimes four or five, and more often across class lines than merely within.

Income inequality and mobility, then, are clearly the most dynamic aspects of status inequality however we probe the issue—whether with questions like "What does class mean to you?" or by asking for status estimates of profiles.

PART III

ATTAINMENT OF
SOCIAL STANDING

CHAPTER 12

Images of Opportunity and Social Mobility

THAT America has been a land of great opportunity for socio-economic mobility during the twentieth century's middle decades is the conviction of our Boston and Kansas City respondents. The majority have witnessed it in their own lives. All have seen mobility in the lives of many relatives and acquaintances. And most think this has been a saving grace of the American status system, as well as one of the most thrilling aspects of individual destiny in our society. There is a deep worry, however, that mobility will not be so commonplace in the future as in the past and that perhaps as much of it—or even more—will be downward instead of up. In the past, most has been up.

In this chapter we shall examine public images of opportunity and social mobility from three different perspectives. First we take up our respondents' own social mobility stories. Here the perspective is apparently autobiography; yet the story is as much one of sharing in a national upsurge in standard of living as one of personal accomplishment. Next we take up respondents' views of how friends and kin have fared, and why. Here the perspective is popular interpretation of mobility processes. From this perspective we can project the American public's image on the general rules for rise and decline in class position—the who, how, and why of social mobility in the society at large. The view is essentially characterological; status destiny is largely a matter of individual differences in energy and effort. Finally, we look at mobility from a third perspective: how will the future compare with the present and the past?

From this perspective we see the anxieties that the idea of declining opportunities brings to the fore. These anxieties are both individual and national, for the idea is that America itself will no longer be advancing with such giant steps as characterized the century's middle decades.

Everyman's Personal Success Story: "Easier," "Better-Off" Living in Post-Depression America

Among Bostonians and Kansas Citians who had been adults for at least a decade by the time we interviewed them in 1971 and 1972, a clear majority (60 percent) classified themselves as higher in socio-economic standing than their parents, when we asked them to make such a comparison. Another 31 percent said that they were essentially of the same rank, then almost always added in clarification, "But I have had an easier life than my parents; I've been better off, if you judge material-wise." Only 9 percent referred to themselves as of lower status.

This finding and others about how our Boston and Kansas City sample members compared life in the United States in the years of their adulthood—the 1940s, 1950s, and 1960s—with what life had been like for their parents, emerged in their answers to this complex of questions: "What social class were your parents part of when you were growing up? What was life like for them at that time? How do you believe your present position compares with your parents'? And why do you feel that way—explain the differences and similarities, if any."

Almost a finding itself is how readily and richly our respondents poured forth their replies. Several who had difficulty talking about classes and status in the abstract suddenly spoke easily. To many, this question seemed the favorite. And for almost all, it was a question to which they related with marked emotion. Those who believed themselves to have risen in status expressed pride in the accomplishment, even while crediting it (more often than not) to parental push and dreams. Those who believed themselves to have fallen treated the question as a moment for rueful self-examination. Those who thought themselves the same in status seemed dissatisfied yet relieved. In sum, this response suggests that comparisons on socio-economic standing of self with parents are for the average American very much a central feature in "the story of my life."

Intertwined in the comparisons our sample made of present with past and self with parent are two ultimately separable stories about "easier," "better-off" living. One is of society-wide improvement in which at least 90 percent of our respondents acknowledged a share; the other is of individual elevation in socio-economic rank, which 60 percent—as mentioned earlier—claimed to have achieved. These are, from our view, two quite different stories of change and, not surprisingly, were usually recognized as such by the respondents themselves.

The first story was told in its purest form by that 31 percent of men and women in our sample who considered themselves to be of the same social rank as their parents. Over and over, the men said: "My life is a lot easier—I don't have to work so many hours to make the same kind of living. . . . I have more free time to do what I want." With equal frequency the women said: "I have a better life. . . . I have all the modern conveniences of home that my mother never had—more push-button things. . . . They had wringer-washers then and no automatics. . . . I don't have to can food like my mother did. I am sure she worked harder." For the non-mobile, then, the sense that they have experienced a marked improvement in the physical conditions of living, even without social status advance, was strong, and was related centrally to the reduction in labor required of women for house-keeping and to the reduction in hours on the job required of men for earning a decent wage. Beyond this, two advances in material well-being were widely emphasized: the replacement of radio by television as the principal home amusement and the likelihood of a family's having two cars today instead of one—or one instead of none—as in the parental decades, the 1940s, 1930s, and 1920s.

Two other changes were often reported by non-mobiles. One quite commonly remarked on by average-income working-class and middle-class respondents, when they compared their present life style with their parents', is a change in attitude toward money and the care of possessions. Of the parents, it was said, "They made things last," and "Thrift was a byword in our home." The other, mostly observed by the offspring of Upper-American families or the most prospering of Middle Americans, is that their parents "enjoyed the niceties in life later than I have." What they meant was that in the parental generation such evidences of the good life as resort vacations, foreign travel, second homes, second cars, and private club memberships were not commonly experienced until the male household head was well past forty-five years of age—or often past fifty-five; in contrast, the respondents themselves had often begun attaining these luxuries while in their late thirties and early forties.

More generally, we find that for each parental social status level except the highest, life was pictured as definitely more austere in the

pre-World War II period than it has been since, with the remembered
hardships varying from minor to major depending on the years involved
and the class level spoken of. The very worst deprivations were remembered, of course, by those in our sample who referred to their parents as
lower class. Variously these respondents told us of growing up in homes
"heated only with oil lamps," of having to "go outside to the toilet," of
"eating rabbits and berries," of having "just one pair of shoes," of not being
able to "get clothes when we needed them," or there being "too many of
us kids for our parents to support," and (often) of the early death of one
or both of the parents.

A Boston man, now of solid working-class status, speaking of such a
childhood, said: "As I look back, we were worse off than people on welfare today. We did without medical and dental care that they receive.
We wore a lot of hand-me-downs; we hardly ever had anything new."
Also vividly remembered were the difficulties experienced by parents
who had emigrated from non-English-speaking countries. The first years
were almost always "very hard" as they struggled to get a foothold in the
new country. Men and women who grew up on a farm also tended to
remember their parents' lives (and their own lives as children) as "hard,"
as "lacking in modern conveniences," and filled with "long hours of back-
breaking physical labor" (as one Kansas City man said, shaking his head
in memory of it, "On the farm, there's no end to work, daylight to dark
almost all year round").

One change that many respondents pointed to as having altered
the circumstances of working-class life significantly over the past thirty
years is that "the unions are much stronger now." For union members the
benefits have been manifold. For one, their hourly pay rates have esca-
lated to the point where a much higher percentage of blue-collar families
can lead lives at the comfortable or good-life level than could a generation ago; in addition, job security has been increased, the retirement
years are better provided for, and paid vacations have become the rule
rather than the exception. All in all, a middle-class life style has been
made more attainable for those who wish it.

Images of personal mobility. In some instances of our second story
of "easier," "better-off" living—the story of individual elevation in socio-
economic rank—the gains reported by our sample members were by their
own reckoning bewilderingly impressive, on the order of four-step or five-
step leaps up the ladder. When this was the case, our respondents would
speak of their status histories in this vein: "I'm wealthy compared to
what I was as a kid. . . . I have more than my parents could ever have
dreamed of having. I drive a Cadillac and they never even had a second-

hand Ford" or "There's just no comparison between the way I live today and the way my parents lived. They would think of this as a $100,000 home." About one in fourteen of our Boston and Kansas City sample members made this kind of extreme comparison between their parents and themselves in standard of living.

In other instances of self-declared upward mobility, the ascent claimed was more on the order of just one step or only half a step. When this was the case, the gain would be phrased in this fashion: "My folks were—well—sort of middle-working-class, and I'm what I'd call upper-working-class" or "My parents would be lower-middle-class and I've gone up a bit to middle-middle." One in seven sample members gave themselves credit for this much upward mobility.

For the rest of the 60 percent of sample members who placed themselves above their parents (now we are speaking of 38 percent of the total sample) the gains they claimed were some place in between. They amounted to at least two steps, or three, up the economic ladder, and one full class or more up the social ladder. In these instances, the comparisons of own status with parental status were of this order:

> "I own my own home, and they never did. It's in a better neighborhood than I grew up in. I have more possessions, and a good job."

> "There is a distinct and definite increase in income level and living standards. . . . The ability to educate my children has been much greater for me."

> "Our housing and general mode of living is considerably higher. . . . In travel, recreation, and vacations—all the things that you consider—our life is different from our parents'."

> "We can educate our six children and clothe them and take care of them in a better fashion. We take vacations, and my husband has more time to spend with his family."

Over and over, four points were made as proof of the improved status: a higher-paying job, a better house and neighborhood, more money available for education of the children, and more for recreation—for travel, vacations, and going out to eat.

Always, when self-proclaimed upward mobiles thought about the ways in which their lives have been easier and better than their parents', they interpreted the difference as exceeding societal norms for improvement between the two generations. The 31 percent of men and women in our sample who believed themselves of no higher *social* status than their parents did not so interpret whatever improvements in *standard of living* they had experienced. The difference between upward mobiles and non-

in this regard is most clearly revealed when we look at how the
oke of their present income and living standard compared to
rents'. A lifelong upper-middle class Boston man said: "My
father's standard of living and mine would be about the same relative to
the times. . . . My salary is twice as great as his at his peak, but it
doesn't have any more purchasing power." And a lifelong middle-class
Middle American in Kansas City said: "I'm earning more money than my
dad ever saw, but it only buys a similar type of life."

Most of the Bostonians and Kansas Citians in our sample who professed upward mobility rested their case for higher rank solely on advances in income and standard of living. Whatever differences there may
have been between themselves and their parents in education, type of
occupation, or cultural attitude, they left unmentioned, as if irrelevant
to the proof of higher status. This was how two out of every three upwardly mobile people told the story of their rise in social position.

In marked contrast were the other one-third. They seemed eager to
credit education as crucial to their status gains, giving their schooling
central attention in the story of how their lives had become easier and
better than their parents', and often as not lauding their parents for
launching them with this advantage:

> "I have gone to college and have a professional job. My father was just
> a tradesman. He wanted me to do better and sacrificed for my education."

> "I'm in a higher bracket, society-wise, than my parents because of
> education. . . . I have an M.A. and my father just finished high school.
> This has meant that I am able to engage in higher-paying areas of
> employment."

> "I have had twice as much education as my parents and my income is
> much higher—my education accounts for the difference."

> "The big difference is that my parents didn't have a high school education
> and I did—and now I'm giving my children college."

Almost invariably, when improved social rank was credited to education,
economic gains were also indicated. In the rare instances where they
were not, then the higher social rank was explained as a matter of change
in mind-set and cultural outlook. An example of this was a spinster
college professor of foreign language whose father had been a prosperous
dairy farmer; of the change in her status she said, "I'm no better off
financially than my parents, but I'm culturally more advanced—I have a
less traditional point of view." Usually, if there had been elevation in
education without subsequent escalation in income, no upward social

mobility was claimed. In short, higher education without an economic payoff was rarely treated as socially beneficial.

The 9 percent of men and women in our sample who identified themselves as lower in social class than their parents all cited the same circumstance: a much lower standard of living. The historical accounts of how this had come to pass varied—one woman had "lost all that I inherited," another had rebelled against parental "plans for my life," a third had "married below my class—and my husband isn't financially able to give me everything my father did"; one of the men had "married too young and dropped out of college . . . so I don't earn nearly as much as my father, who's a doctor," and another whose father was also a doctor chose to teach school instead and so is "far below my father in income and how the community sees me."

Analytic estimate of class mobility. From 200 members of our sample, half in Boston and half in Kansas City, we acquired a sufficient amount of information about their parents that we could pass a judgment for ourselves on parental class position. Comparing this with our reading of the respondent's social standing at the time of interview, we reached our own conclusions about how far or how little—and in what direction —each of these 200 persons had moved from class of origin.

Our findings from this sample, referring now only to those in the group who were ten years into adulthood when interviewed, are as follows: 42 percent had moved up at least one class from class of origin, 49 percent were in the same class as their parents had been during middle adulthood, and 9 percent had sunk to a class below the parental level. Upward mobility by two class levels—from Lower-American status up to middle-class Middle Americans, for example, or from working-class Middle American up to professional-managerial Upper-American standing —was strongly indicated in 7 percent of the histories. Two-class downward mobility was suggested in 2 percent.

At first glance this analysis of the status histories of our sample may seem to differ from the way the respondents interpreted events, by our crediting fewer with upward mobility than claimed it for themselves. That is not really the case, however. For we would say that in addition to that 42 percent who had moved up one or more classes from class of origin, another 18 percent had improved a bit upon the parental social status without crossing into a higher class. An example of this kind of within-class upward mobility would be climbing up from a childhood as working-class marginal to adult status as either working-class average or working-class special. Both forms of within-class upward mobility were frequently observed among our sample members. When instances of within-class upward movement are added to the volume of cross-class moves that we recognized, the total—60 percent of persons who we say have been upwardly mobile in some measure—is equal to the volume of self-proclaimed improvement on parental status.

This is a small sample and hardly representative statistically speaking; yet the story it suggests on the volume and direction of social mobility in the United States is not thereby to be discounted. Indeed, it is sufficiently in line with other yet-unpublished findings from much larger, more representative samples that we are tempted to project the following class mobility estimate for the whole cohort of Americans who were in the thirty-two to sixty-four age group as of the early 1970s: 42 to 44 percent upwardly mobile by one or more class levels, 48 to 50 percent stable, and 8 to 10 percent downwardly mobile.

Two things that have happened simultaneously are the primary factors in this impressive volume of upward class mobility. Only one, however—"better job opportunities," as our Boston and Kansas City respondents put it—is part of the lay public's understanding of recent American history. The other—a striking differential in birth-rate by class in the 1910s, 1920s, and 1930s—is virtually unnoticed as a factor by the ordinary citizen.

The statistic most relevant to the first factor is that, whereas in 1940 only 29 percent of men in the American labor force were employed in what the U.S. Census Bureau classified as white-collar jobs, by 1970 this had grown to 41 percent. This rise in white-collar employment of American men—the sort of employment most closely associated with middle-class status—has paralleled a decline in farm employment from 18 percent down to 6 percent. Among urban workers alone, the percent in white-collar employment has not increased so dramatically but nevertheless has gone from 38 percent to 45 percent. Taking into consideration these changes in occupation distribution of male workers and placing them in the context of changing life styles and educational levels, we have made the following estimates on the changing portions of Americans identified with each of the major classes, first in 1940, then in 1970. The upper class has expanded hardly at all—from 1.2 to 1.3 percent. The upper-middle class has enlarged considerably—from 8.3 to 11.0 percent. And the lower-middle class has grown from 29.0 percent to 32.7. The three upper-half classes have, thus, expanded from a combined 38.5 percent in 1940 to 45.0 in 1970. Meanwhile, the working-class share has declined slightly—from 39.0 percent to 37.5; and the lower-class share has declined sharply—from 22.5 percent to 17.5. If the American class distribution has indeed changed in the fashion we project, this change by itself would have required a net excess in upward class mobility of 14.4 percent. That is the percent needed to fill the openings that appeared in each higher class. This is not quite half the total net excess of 34 percent that we project from our studies.

The fertility differential by social class explains more (see Kahl, 1959). The studies on this differential are scant in number and their samples are small, but the findings coincide to suggest that the reproductive rates have been of this order: the upper class averaged slightly more than two children per family in the 1910s, 1920s, and 1930s, the upper-middle averaged slightly less than two, the lower-middle averaged between two and three, the working class averaged between three and four, and the lower class averaged five. Projecting these fertility averages against our estimates on class distribution suggests shares-by-class of children born in the early twentieth century approximately on this order: for the upper class, 0.8 percent; upper-middle, 5.5 percent; lower-middle, 23.7 percent; working class, 40.3 percent; and lower class, 29.7 percent. This distribution by class of origin for adults in the age cohorts we have studied, when plotted against our early 1970s estimates for share-of-population by class, would make for a net excess in upward class mobility of 33.7 percent—which is almost exactly the excess our recent studies of mobility have suggested.

To sum up, if our estimates are approximately correct—of the changing class distribution, of the birthrate differential, and on the volume and direction of social mobility—then that total of 43 percent upwardly mobile can be interpreted in this fashion: 9 percent has compensated for downward mobility, 14 percent represents expansion of the higher classes, and 20 percent came about in consequence of the differential in reproductivity.

Other things beyond the upgrading of the male occupational distribution and the birthrate differential have made it possible for far more than half of all Americans to feel they have had an easier, better time of it economically than their parents. One is that job opportunities for women have opened up, with the result that in the early 1970s far more families than ever before were benefiting from having two wage-earners. Many of the examples in our sample of within-class upward mobility were just such two-income families.

The improved standing and standards of many born at the lower edges of the working class and lower class can be traced to the in-migration of sizeable numbers of Puerto Ricans and Mexicans who, in such large measure, have been given the lowest-paying, least desirable occupations. This has been the history of many immigrant populations: the first generation starts at the bottom, then the second and third move on up when they are supplanted at the bottom by a new wave of immigrants.

Tales of Upward and Downward Mobility:
Ubiquitous Proof of the Open Class System

We asked 200 of our Boston and Kansas City sample members two questions about status changes that they had observed in the lives of people around them. One was: "Tell us about some people you know who are in a higher class than their parents—and how you think they did it. . . . These can be people you know from your school days or people you've met since you've grown up or children of friends—anyone you know." The other was: "Tell us about people you know who have gone down in class from that of their parents—and tell why you think it happened." The ease and enthusiasm with which our respondents answered these queries suggested that Americans generally are every bit as aware of class mobility in the lives of their fellow citizens as in their own, and that they know dramatic changes in status—acquaintances who have climbed three or four classes up the ladder or have fallen into disgrace by parental standards—as the stuff of real life in this country, not just as plotlines for novels and movies. Virtually everyone in the sample cited instances of family members—anyone from brothers and sisters to cousins and nephews—and schoolmates, former friends, new friends, neighbors, and employers as examples of definite class mobility, naming some in each category who had moved up and others who had fallen down. Further, they viewed these changes as more than merely interesting stories; they treated them as proof that America is a fluid society in which "effort" and "drive" are rewarded more often than not and lack of the same is usually punished.

Downward mobility exerts a special fascination on its beholders. It is spoken of in tones of "Thank the gods it didn't happen to me," mixed mock-horror, and secret satisfaction. Mentioned most commonly as a cause was alcohol. Often this was stated in flat generalization, as in such statements as: "Liquor mostly—yes, I'd say liquor has been the number-one cause of people going down in class from their parents . . . starting to hit the bottle and not trying to change," or "Several people I have known threw away all their advantages by drinking to the point where they couldn't keep a steady job." This conviction was expressed at all levels of society. Upper Americans in our sample cited it as the prime cause, both as a generality and in specifics, time and again mentioning "a fellow I knew in college who even got a master's degree, and then went down because of alcohol," or "a family friend who was born wealthy but became an alcoholic, and ended up in potter's field." Middle-American men are most conscious of it as causing the downfall of fellow employees, frequently telling of "cases at the office of men who were demoted because of drunkenness" or of "a guy who used to work with me who went out and started drinking. . . . He didn't have a wife or anything else before long." Middle-American women seem to have experienced the problem mainly through a "girlfriend who married someone that drank up all the household money"—never, incidentally, the woman herself becoming a drunk. Lower Americans described the problem from a more frightening perspective: "Drinking too much—that's the biggest cause of men going to the bottom. . . . All they want is a bottle—then they'll rob and steal for a drink."

In like fashion, in nine of every other ten stories our Boston and Kansas City respondents told us of downward mobility, flaws of character or imprudent behavior are held at fault. For women who have fallen below their class of origin, this is usually due to some kind of mistake in marriage. In many instances it is the marriage itself—to a man down a class or two from the parental level—that has accounted for the status decline: "One of the girls I was friends with in school, who came from the higher middle class, married a boy who didn't finish college—his parents were only working class—and now she has to watch her money." In other instances, the man "turned out bad" later on, becoming an alcoholic or "a deadbeat" or perhaps getting in trouble with the law. Sometimes this potential for difficulty was obvious from the beginning to all but the woman herself: "One of my girlfriends fell in love with the wrong kid. . . . He went to jail and she's had a terrible time." But the wrong man is not always the problem; frequently it is simply "too many children," or, even worse, "too many too fast" and/or "too early," as in these illustrations:

> "Some of the women I know who are not as high as their parents had a baby right off after they got married, and their husbands were young. They had insecure jobs, and they've had nothing but problems. Some have had to go on welfare."

"I know a girl who had six children fast, then the bills started rolling in and she just kept going down."

By contrast, blame for downward mobility of men is rarely placed on mistakes in marriage. (If so, the problem cited is apt to be of the sort where the wife "spends all her husband's money that she can get her hands on, and even runs around on him, too.") Rather, the fall is usually traced to mistakes the man has made outside marriage, as in this Boston example: "I know one guy that got mixed up with two women at the same time. . . . So, rather than tending to business, he was chasing around and lost all that he had built up." In Kansas City, too, "too much attraction to the opposite sex" was accounted from time to time as the source of male class decline. (This may not be a problem for entertainment-world stars, but apparently for men on Middle-American incomes, it's a bit too much to manage!)

Beyond alcohol abuse and marital mistakes, the defects in character and behavior that our Boston and Kansas City respondents most enjoyed associating with downward mobility bore such labels as "laziness," "a don't-care attitude," "unwillingness to work at anything," "not enough drive," "no self-discipline," "no initiative," and "lack of ambition." Illustrations offered were in this vein:

"My ex-brother-in-law is one who has fallen from where he started. He has no ambition. He did not finish school. He cannot hold a job, so my sister divorced him. He just won't work or try to help himself."

"A friend of mine whose father was an accountant has definitely gone down in class. He now works in a gas station. It was just a lack of ambition on his part."

"There is a couple down the street where the husband just sits around and doesn't work. His wife won't work either. They'd rather take welfare. Their parents weren't like that at all."

In a goodly number of instances, the parents are held partially to blame for their children's failures to put out the effort or do the kind of work necessary to maintain the original position; they are said to have "spoiled" them. The stories here run to tragic extremes:

"I know this guy who could speak five or six languages. . . . Now he's a dishwasher. He was a spoiled, only child and just didn't want to work. He lost every one of his good jobs. His mother has now quit giving him everything, but he hasn't changed."

"I have one friend who has no ambition or sense of responsibility. This was because his father wanted to give him everything. His father makes probably $30,000 or $40,000 a year, and I think my friend makes just $7,000 to $10,000."

"My brother is one who has gone downhill. He came at the end of the family and was very spoiled. He was always used to having everything handed to him without working, and he'd like to get away with the same thing as an adult. Now he's run into hardship and can't cope."

In other examples, "a nephew went through his dad's business like water—sold everything to get the cash and now he's broke," and "a girl whose parents were very wealthy could never learn to manage her money so she lost everything she inherited."

In these instances of downward mobility for which some blame is assigned to the parents, the children are not truly excused. They are sympathized with only in part, but the final verdict is always implicitly that they "should have changed once things got tough," that by not doing so they have victimized themselves; now, they more than half-deserve their fate. The only cases of downward mobility where almost unquestioning sympathy is extended to the victim are those ascribed to either "a terrible, disabling disease" or an inexplicable mental illness. To fault persons who have suffered socio-economic loss from this kind of cruel fate would apparently seem unkind.

Turning now to the instances cited by our Boston and Kansas City respondents of people higher in class than their parents, we must first note that stories concerning kin were most popular. Sometimes these stories were told with undimmed pride—by a daughter of her father ("My dad's parents were dirt poor, but he acquired a trade and became a contractor on his own"), by a wife of her husband ("My husband finished high school, and his father was from a family of eight and did not have an education"), or by a mother of her sons and daughters ("I think all my children have done better than me. . . . They've all graduated from high school, and two boys are going to college—one is a Vietnam veteran, the other is working his way through—and I didn't finish the grades"). At other times admiration was mixed with rueful envy in the telling. An older brother, for example, pointed to both of his younger brothers as examples of upward mobility ("One brother became a dentist from the G.I. Bill and the other became a lawyer—I came up earlier and didn't go to college"); a maiden aunt cited the offspring of a married sister ("I have two nieces and a nephew who put themselves through college—they've each made a nice life for themselves"); and many a nephew and niece referred to "my rich uncle," obviously drawing upon memories from childhood of how these uncles had been so different in standard of living from everyone else in the extended family circle.

That social standing in America is widely recognized to be more a matter of individual achievement than inherited family status could not possibly be better illustrated than in the answers produced by our Boston and Kansas City sample to our questions on social mobility of self and friends. Not only did most of these people express the belief that they had experienced a change away from parental status in their own lives, but more often than not, when illustrating upward and downward mobility in the lives of others, their references were to blood relatives. This would seem compelling evidence of how little importance kin group has in conceptions of status in this country. The American public seems to know full well that adult siblings are not identical to one another in social standing any more than they are individually in the same class as their parents before them. Indeed, it almost seems taken for granted that the various adult members of a kinship circle will *not* be of the same status, that individual destinies more often separate relatives socially than unite them. This is very much one of the perceptions about life in this country that our respondents were operating with when they said that classes in America are "not rigid," that "we have an open system." In public ideal, social mobility is more rule than rarity.

Next to the rise of relatives, the upward mobility stories most favored by our sample were those involving two-class or three-class jumps by friends. In many of those, the status gains are portrayed as the product of ambition and hard work by both parent and child. A black mother, for example, always in domestic service, had sacrificed comfort to send her daughter through college, and the daughter had earned an advanced degree in social work. Or first-generation white parents, themselves earning very little, had "scrimped and saved" so that their children could have the education they did not get, and now the children "live in much better houses out in the suburbs." In other instances, the stories are of exceptional, individual talent developing itself without noticeable parental push: "A fraternity brother of mine is an orthopedic surgeon and his parents are just working-class people—now he's upper-class," or, "I know a guy who grew up on a farm in North Dakota. . . . He won a scholarship to college, now has a Ph.D., is a professor here at the university and is part-owner of a consulting service. . . . His parents were just struggling farmers and all his brothers are still working on the farm—with him, it was just a matter of individual drive." In still other instances, "hard work," "initiative," and unbridled "ambition to make money" are said to have fueled the upward movement, with special or professional education no part of the picture: "A man who was our neighbor started building houses, worked eighty hours a week, and just kept on building his business up—with the rising price of houses he's really made money" and "Three men I knew in high school whose parents are in the lower-middle class have become multi-millionaires through their own initiative—they really wanted to make money and found the opportunities."

In these stories, the upward mobility has seemed to the teller sufficiently out of the ordinary as to be rarity not rule; yet the emphasis in their telling was on opportunities taken advantage of, not on impediments overcome. They were told in a spirit of illustrating the eminent possibility of such dramatic upward strides, of proving how "green the pastures are in America" for status advance.

Another question about upward mobility that we put to a cross-section of our Boston and Kansas City respondents—a different group from those whom we asked to cite and explain instances of cross-class advance—was this: "From all that you've read or heard or seen, what do you think is the most effective way for a person to improve his social standing in America?" The responses pointed to four ingredients: "parental encouragement," "a better education," "ambition to get ahead," and "plenty of hard work." Permeating this imagery were two basic premises: first, that there are many opportunities available in this country for those who want and seek them and second, that with education and hard work there are few limitations on an individual's ability to advance.

The nice thing about parental encouragement as an ingredient in the recipe for upward mobility is that it makes the parents heroes and heroines quite as much as their children—if not even a bit more. It suggests that it was the parents who made it all possible because it was "their wish—they wanted their children to be more than they were." Acting on this aspiration, they gave their children "a solid start in both education and ambition," they "set aside money for their children's future," and they "worked to give them the passport of college to higher status." And now—when surveying the results, if favorable—the parents can believe they have scored a vicarious triumph in the American class drama; through their children's ascent, some of their most treasured dreams in life have been fulfilled.

The important thing about the ingredient of a better education is the occupational opportunities it opens to the aspirant for upward mobility. In the case of the highest-paying professions, where entry absolutely depends on acquisition of the proper credentials of schooling, it can even be a crucial ingredient; law, medicine, and dentistry are examples of this. In exhortations to the young, the role of education was sometimes phrased quite idealistically by our sample: "First get an education—that will get you a better job and that will lead to higher social standing, because you will then be making more money." Most of our Boston and Kansas City respondents recognized, however, that such happy results are not inevitable; they acknowledged that in the final analysis education's role is only as an entry ticket to the contest for higher status, that it is no guarantee of winnings. In the crucible of adult life competition, they said, ambition and hard work count for more.

Hard work is working-class America's favorite recipe for well-deserved succcss—or, at least, so it would seem from our study. When our Boston and Kansas City respondents of this status talked about people they knew who had been upwardly mobile, the phrases they most freely applied in explaining how it had happened were "pure effort," "persever-ance," "just plain hard work," "sheer work," "work, work, and more work," and "he wasn't ever afraid of working." The heroes of their tales had often worked two jobs instead of one; they had worked double-time whenever they could; they had not taken vacations; they had worked nights and weekends beyond the thirty-five or forty hours a week most people put in, especially if self-employed and trying to build their business up; they had "tried to become the best at their jobs," working harder to "learn all the ins and outs"; they had "not just sat back and stayed on the line," they had "worked themselves up to being supervisors—they wanted the responsibility"; and always they had "kept their noses to the grindstone." In many an instance "the wife went to work too and worked just as hard." This is how individuals and families from their world had risen from just getting along up to leading the good life. This is how men they knew had become "bosses not workers," or "bigtime contractors" instead of "little one-man operations." And, often as not, their only educational advantage had come from learning more than their fellow Americans in the open-admission School of Hard Knocks.

Ambition seems something else. It is more than merely the inner push to excel, of which effort is an outward manifestation. It may include special talents and cunning—an "eye to the main chance"—as com-ponents. In any event, along with "motivation," "desire," "determination," and "drive," which seem its synonyms in the public lexicon, it was the trait that Upper Americans in our sample most often attributed to the upwardly mobile people of their acquaintance. Especially did they talk of ambition in its most extreme forms as a force that distinguished the success elite in their midst from those of average income and the economically marginal. Of the most astonishingly successful, our re-spondents would say, "They wanted to make money—lots of it—and if you want to make lots of money, it isn't hard. . . . You just have to be money-motivated." Implicit in all this is that diffcrences in ambition are taken as the prime accountant for differences in the occupational destinies of persons with equal talent. The highly ambitious are identified as having always used their time and energies to career advantage; they are said to be "more aggressive in pushing to get ahead," they have "the stronger desire to improve their standard of living," and they have decided what they really wanted to do and have done it.

Implicit in the way our Boston and Kansas City respondents have interpreted the processes of upward and downward mobility is that the American status system is an *effortocracy*. The people who rise in this system—in our respondents' idealized view—are those who have been the most determined to do so, who have put out the greatest efforts toward that end. The people who fall—again in this idealized view—are those who have lacked the character, the will, and the enterprise even to maintain the social position they inherited. The surprise in this portrait of status change is how little notice was given "talent" or "quality" or "contribution," the status assets associated with a meritocratic system. In such a system, natural superiority and excellence of performance are, along with effort, the keys to high status; destiny is largely prefigured in the genes or early childhood. That was not quite how the people we talked with in Boston and Kansas City chose to illustrate and explain mobility in the United States through the past thirty years. Our society, as they talked about it, has been much more open to self-choice in destiny than that. In the competition for status, ambition, energy, and application are seen as the prime virtues, dereliction the prime defect. For such a social system—where victory goes to the vigorous and loss to the lazy—the most fitting name is effortocracy. This, in its most positive connotations, is how our respondents wanted to see America.

Harder Times Ahead: The Rise of Falling Expectations

Up to this point, the changes in individual social and economic status that we have been discussing in this chapter refer to the experiences of persons born before 1940. We turn now to analyzing what our Boston and Kansas City sample members have noted and anticipate for Americans of later birth. Here our analysis derives in part from the experiences, attitudes, and aspirations of those in our sample who themselves were born after 1940—that is, from how they chose to look at their own lives and goals in comparison with their parents' and what they told us they expect will happen as they pass on through adulthood. But that is only one part of our concern; the other is with how the older members of the sample, as well as these younger people, look at the future of social mobility in America. For this, we depend for our understanding primarily on responses to this question: "As things are going in the United States, do you think it is going to be easier or harder for the younger people growing up now to change their class from their parents' class?" The response of young and old alike to this question coincided with forecasts of the American future made elsewhere in the interviews to suggest these two predictions: first, easier, better living is not going to be the typical experience for upcoming generations that it was for Americans born between 1900 and 1940, and second, upward mobility will be harder, the opportunities for it much diminished.

A prime factor in this forecast that upward mobility will be harder for the young people growing up now is a general pessimism about the American future. This was given its most vocal expression by the older members of our Boston and Kansas City samples. The basic premise behind their pessimism is that industrial growth can no longer be taken for granted in the United States, that increasingly it will be constrained by limitations in natural resource and by societal concern about harmful environmental impact. Following from this is deep concern that the era of "American plenty" is over, that the average family's standard of living will not be as high in years to come as it was in the late 1950s and early 1960s. Just one token of this is a conviction that cars will be smaller and that we may have to revert to greater reliance on mass transit. Much graver is the spectre of possible shortages in food and energy. Over and over, our respondents—especially those past forty years of age—voiced gloomy auguries like this:

> "The world is going to be a harder place to live in. . . . We lived in the good times. It's not going to be so easy in the future."

> "We've had a great leveling off in the last few years, and there's no place to go."

> "Everything costs more money. We're having inflation in costs without inflation in earnings. Our standard of living is going down instead of up."

> "The economy is worsening. . . and taxes are eating away the fruits of our labor."

There was even a sprinkling of predictions that "the system is falling apart," that "society is breaking down." Our younger respondents did not generally look so bitterly at the future; they treated these prospective changes more as challenges to innovative response than as disappointments to be suffered and cursed. Even so, hardly any anticipated the kind of increase in ease of life that the older members of our sample claimed to have experienced in comparison to their parents' generation.

Of great concern to the young themselves is what they perceive as a likely scarcity of good jobs relative to the number of aspirants; this, not a scarcity of goods, is what most commonly inspires their pessimism about the future. Those in our sample whose age marks them as products of the post-war "baby boom" showed themselves extremely conscious of their membership in this birth cohort, and they interpret it very much as burden, not boon. Time and again the young adults we interviewed anticipated adverse affects from this, saying variously that "the competition is rougher from just the sheer numbers"; "We're having it harder because there's more of us—there's going to be too much competition and it'll get worse"; and "The opportunities may be as many as in our parents' day, but there are more people fighting for those opportunities." For reasons that are not entirely clear, they seem obsessed with a notion that there are "fewer new fields opening up" and "fewer frontiers" to explore than in former years, with the result that "competition in every field will be keener" and "more people—more educated people—will be looking for the same jobs," competing to rise. Ultimately, what we see behind these prophesies by the young of widespread frustration among their generation in career pursuit is more than worry that an easier life is not to be theirs or that upward mobility has been rendered more difficult; there is considerable fear of a definitely harder life, of absolute loss in status compared to the parents, of downward mobility itself.

A third phenomenon widely cited as complicating forecasts on the volume and direction of class mobility is expanding educational credentialism. Older and younger respondents pointed to this in equal numbers. The problem, as understood in general terms by the public, is this: ever-higher levels of education are being required for entry into many occupations, but the number of people attaining these required levels has been exceeding the number of openings available, with the result that meeting the requirements has been no guarantee of entry. As stated in the vernacular, the situation is a two-edged sword: "You need a lot more education than ever before; without it you'll be a dead duck"—*yet*— "Education doesn't help that much anymore; so many educated people can't find jobs or positions." Almost everyone in our sample seemed to have heard that "the market for college degrees has been saturated." And many said that "education has been oversold—society just cannot function with everyone wanting to be white-collar." Still, though, most advised that "if you don't get an education, it will be even worse." The irony in this is double: as higher education has opened its gates wider, its value as mobility route has quite probably narrowed; as degrees and diplomas have become ever more imperative credentials in the race for class standing, the success promised their holders has become ever less (G. Boudon, 1973 and 1975).

Generally regarded as exceptions to the rule that life in the United States might be harder for the next generation and class change more difficult were young black people and the children of other minority groups. For them the future was expected to be brighter, the standard of living much higher on the average than what their parents had experienced, and mobility up from the bottom strata easier. This conviction was expressed by whites and blacks alike, the latter with extra pleasure. A young black woman in Boston, herself enrolled in a training program and enthusiastic about her future prospects, said, "We have more educational opportunities and many nice job programs that our parents did not have. If you improve yourself, there are better positions for you." A black man in his late 30s in Kansas City who had become a successful business-man after a childhood "close to poverty," said almost exultantly: "I can't speak for the white people, whether it's going to be harder for them to change class or not, but we have greater opportunities today than when my parents were growing up. . . . The racial barriers are down, or coming down."

CHAPTER 13

Resources Among American Men

I N previous chapters we have reviewed much evidence indicating the importance of income in determining a family's social position as assessed by community standards. From the qualitative and quantitative approaches used to investigate the views that Americans hold concerning social standing, we find that income stands out as more important than such factors as education and occupation (which have taken up much more of the attention of sociologists concerned with social stratification than income). In our status estimation experiment we find that income accounts for almost two-thirds of the variance in social standing of the sample profiles; the balance was accounted for about evenly by occupation and education. In the qualitative analysis of the open-ended material, the role of income, particularly in the form of standard or level of living, was foremost in the views of men and women at all social class levels.

For these and other reasons, if one is to understand their class situation, it is of considerable importance to understand how people come to have the economic resources they have.

Ideally, we would like to have a much more inclusive measure than income of the actual socio-economic resources used by individuals in pursuing their lives. However, relatively little work has been done on ways of measuring the many non-pecuniary resources that are important in people's lives. Similarly, very little work has been done on how one might aggregate and add up the well-being values that separate resources represent. If such conceptual and empirical work had been done, we could then attempt to develop a model of the "social income" or "social happiness" of individuals and families.

Tinbergen notes, for example, the inadequacy of attending only to the distribution of pecuniary resources and observes that in economic theory attention to the welfare of individuals requires broader focus:

> For economists welfare is identical to utility in its broadest sense, and it's also identical to happiness in a restricted sense. The happiness meant might be indicated as "social happiness," that is, happiness as far as it is dependent on social variables and parameters, or variables and parameters as far as they are relevant for the individual's *role in society*. It excludes such entirely personal elements as friendship, love, or religion; and there are more. The frontier between personal and social may be a matter for debate and may also shift over time. Clearly we are up against a realm of analysis hardly opened up yet. [1975]

Even though we would like to have a much broader measure of socio-economic resources, a focus on income is at least a good starting place. It is likely that the correlation between income and any more inclusive measure of "social happiness" or well-being would be very high indeed. Therefore, in the exploration reported below we feel justified in assuming that the general pattern of relationships among various factors during the individual's life cycle and his well-being would be similar to the pattern we find when we look at income alone. But looking only at income will probably yield an underestimation of the impact of various social factors on well-being, since in their life choices people trade off pecuniary and non-pecuniary benefits against each other. Therefore, focusing on the relationship between a given variable and income will often minimize the role of that variable in the individual's overall well-being. One study by G. Duncan, using the same data source that will be analyzed below, makes an effort to explore "non-pecuniary work rewards" and discovers that a characteristic such as years of schooling, for example, is more highly associated with an overall index of pecuniary and non-pecuniary rewards than it is with wages themselves (1974). Duncan also finds that the wage rate correlates 0.95 with his best composite index of a series of job related rewards. (It is of considerable interest to note, however, that the correlations were lower among blue-collar employees.)

We will be interested, therefore, in income as a component of overall well-being and, with much less precision, in income as an index of overall social resources.

Another compromise with the ideal is made in this analysis. If we are interested in income, then we really should be looking at family income and seeking to develop a model for the economic resources available to families. However, even a brief look at family income as a dependent variable impresses one with how incredibly complicated the issue of the amount and sources of family income is. Therefore, we have preferred to begin with one component of family income for one type of family. In this analysis we look at the head's income in families that are male-headed. That means that our analysis ignores female-headed families. It ignores the other sources of income in male-headed families, and it ignores the few males in the age range examined who are not heads of households. For the households involved, head's income is, of course, far and away the most important component of family income (and our preliminary efforts to develop a model similar to the one outlined below with total family income as the dependent variable indicate that the results would not be markedly different from those we found for head's income alone). For the male-headed families in the sample analyzed, head's income amounts to about 80 percent of total family income.

Much of the qualitative research on social class suggests that, to the extent that income and standard of living are the paramount factors in the way members of communities place each other, this relationship holds most strongly during the middle of the life cycle—that is, the years in which men and women are in their thirties, forties, and early fifties. In the earlier adult period, social position is more a function of income expectations than it is of current income. It is not so much the standard of living a twenty-five-year-old enjoys that others attend to in forming impressions of his or her social standing as the standard of living the individual and his family are believed likely to have some ten or more years hence. It is understood that much of the payoff from the getting-established period may be deferred.

Among individuals past the broad middle period of their life careers, it is similarly understood that present income will be much affected by the choices they make from among the possibilities available to them. Children grow up, leave home, and are no longer a financial burden on parents. Misfortunes in the form of illnesses and disabilities are increasingly likely to befall individuals as they get older. Older people may well have built up considerable social capital in relationships with others, as well as wealth, which they can draw on to sustain a given social position even though their incomes decline or fail to keep pace with the incomes of their contemporaries.

As a result of such factors, income is more central to the definition of social standing during the middle years of the life career and, perhaps for that very reason, it is more readily accounted for by a model of the socio-economic career.

We will utilize a data set that has unique advantages for exploring income, a method developed by Otis Dudley Duncan (Blau and Duncan, 1968) and applied by him and others since to study the socio-economic career. More recently Jencks (1974) and his co-workers have extended and applied these methods to a wide range of factors hypothesized to play some role in income determination.

One of the problems in relating income as measured in survey research to the role people ascribe to income and standard of living in social ranking has to do with the variability of income from year to year. When individuals describe a given family as having a high or low or average standard of living, they are observing and referring to the net effect of the income stream the family has enjoyed over a period of several years. We know that individuals have similar conceptions of their own income. Their current behavior is determined not only by their current income but by income in the recent past and by income expected in the near future. Economists have analyzed the role of income over time on consumption by using the concept of permanent income (Friedman, 1957; Modigliani and Brumbert, 1954). To explore the determinants of the income as it relates to social standing requires a measure of permanent income rather than income in a given year.

One particular, widely available national sample survey provides a measure of permanent rather than one-year income and gives very careful attention to collecting its income data. We have chosen to analyze this data set for a particular group of male heads, those who were thirty-five to fifty-four years of age in 1972. The survey we have chosen is the Panel Study of Income Dynamics, conducted by the Institute of Social Research of the University of Michigan under the direction of James N. Morgan.[1]

The Panel Study of Income Dynamics (P.S.I.D.) involves a national sample of nearly 5,000 households interviewed annually since the winter of 1968.[2] The families who were interviewed in 1968 were interviewed, if possible, in each subsequent year through 1972 (and later, but the data that we are analyzing here ends in 1972). If a member of a sample household had moved out of the household during the previous year, an effort was made to interview him or her also. These, the so-called split-offs, exceeded the number of households lost in each year's re-interviews so that by 1972 there were 5,060 households represented in the sample.[3]

We selected for our sample of male heads men with the following characteristics: were household heads from 1968 to 1972, were thirty-one to fifty years old in 1968, were in the labor force in all five years (that is, were either employed or unemployed—not retired or totally disabled —at the time of each of the five interviews), and were not farmers in 1968. There were 1,147 such men. Below we will refer loosely to our sample as representing men, but it should be understood that we are talking about non-farm men (actually 0.1 percent of the men had become farmers by 1972) who were continuously in the labor force and who were household heads.[4]

The dependent variable for our analysis is the head's taxable income plus the asset income of the wife. From the point of view of social stratification, income from assets is a central element in the distribution of life chances.

The analysis that follows is divided into three parts. In the first part we examine the relationship of the men's income to other aspects of their current socio-economic situation. In the second part we analyze the relationship between head's income and the related socio-economic characteristics to the education of the man and, when he is married, of his wife. This we take to represent the relationship between the "launch phase" of the adult career and the man's subsequent situation. Finally, we examine the influence of factors determined during the subject's childhood on his education and current socio-economic situation. Here we are particularly concerned with the effect of parental social class on subsequent socio-economic resources.

It should be noted that it is not our intention to offer the model as a causal model but rather as a descriptive one. While there is a large literature on structural equation models as causal models, we are uneasy with such a claim, at least in the case of these data. We seek only to show how different characteristics are related. To the extent that some characteristics occur earlier in time than others, there is, as O. D. Duncan notes, a reasonable basis for arguing causality. However, these models do not tell us anything about how or why given earlier characteristics have an effect on later ones. A different kind of research is called for to answer such questions.[5]

The men in our sample received an average income from labor and assets of $58,647 between 1967 and 1971, an average of $11,729 per year. The standard deviation of their taxable income was $35,594. These men's income is quite positively skewed—that is, the mean income is considerably higher than the median, and there are more people with incomes in excess of a given amount above the median and fewer that same amount below the median. As has been observed by many others, the distribution of the logarithm of income is much more normal. In the case of the five-year total it has almost no skew at all, and even in the case of single years the skew is fairly slight. For this and other reasons we have taken the logarithm (base 10) of income as the dependent variable in the analyses reported below.[6]

We start the development of our descriptive model by looking at the relationship among income, characteristics of the individual's relationship to income-producing institutions, and the economic opportunities in the geographic area. We know that some areas of the country have higher average incomes than others, even when one controls for the differential distribution of jobs from one to another. Therefore, part of describing a person's socio-economic resources involves describing the kinds of resources that the area makes available. In terms of a person's position in the organization of income-producing institutions, there are two major types of characteristics, one having to do with the kind of work done and the other with the terms of employment and employment experience. We will refer to these three aspects of his situation as *area resources* or advantages, *job resources* or advantages, and *employment resources* or advantages.

In a world in which the perfect kind of data to develop our descriptive model existed, one would be able to look up in a table the typical (mean or median) income of persons in a given area with a particular kind of job (understanding a good job classification to include elements of both occupational and industry classifications).

We would, therefore, be able to describe each person in terms of the expected income for a person with that kind of job living in that particular city or economic area.[7] Actual income could be viewed as the product of expected income and a proportionate variation from that expected income. Thus, an individual whose job and area combination would be expected to net $10,000 but who only earned $8,000 a year would have as one component of income the expected income of $10,000, and as another component the proportional variation from it, a factor of 0.8. Our task of analyzing the dynamics of income determination could then be separated into two tasks. One would be concerned with explaining the expected income of the aggregate of persons defined by the combination of a particular job and residence in a particular labor market. The other would involve analyzing the factors associated with individual variations from expected income.

A considerable portion of the literature on labor markets is concerned with the first of these tasks. That part of labor economics concerned with institutional factors has paid particular attention to the fact that the same kind of work will have different wage rates in different industries and locations. Thus, one may find that in one city a beer-truck driver makes quite a bit more than a laundry-truck driver, whereas in another city the reverse is the case (Dunlop, 1957).

To the extent that such interactions between area, industry, and occupation are important, the model that we will use below will not be able to capture the full association between income and these characteristics. Ours is a simple model that views the relationship between area, job, and employment resources as multiplicative. We do this recognizing that, in reality, even though the relationships may be mainly multiplicative, there may well be sectors of the labor market in which the effects are additive and other sectors in which there are various kinds of ceilings or more complex interaction effects.

We will estimate a structural equation model to describe the relationship between income and three types of variables: area resources (A), job resources (J), and employment resources (E). We will scale the measures of resources in each area in such a way that they represent relative advantages over the average person; thus, if an individual lives in an area where incomes average 20 percent higher than nationally, his area resources score will be 1.2. Similarly, if job characteristics average 1.5 times the national average, the job resources score will be 1.5, and so on. Thus, at a time when the national geometric mean for men in our age group was $12,000, for a person who lived in an area with 20 percent higher incomes, had a job with 50 percent higher income, and acquired employment experience with 10 percent higher income, predicted income would be 1.98 [1.2 x 1.5 x 1.1] x $12,000, or $23,760. If the actual income was $26,000, our "error" would be 1.09. The product of those four ratios multiplied by the national mean then would equal the person's income.

We will use regression analysis to analyze the relative role of several different aspects of a person's situation with respect to each of these resource types. Thus, area resources will be represented by a vector of five characteristics of the area in which the person lives, job resources by a vector of four characteristics of the person's job situation, resources related to terms of employment by a vector of four aspects of the individual's employment experience over the five-year period.

Job Resources

People have jobs; social scientists and others group those jobs into occupations. As the division of labor increases in complexity, the task of assigning all jobs to an occupation becomes increasingly problematic. The highly refined systems of occupational classification in use in the United States meet this challenge remarkably well. However, the grosser categories of occupations that normally must be used in social research introduce an undesirable degree of heterogeneity into the occupational classes that they define. Ideally, in an analysis such as the one developed here, we would like to keep all possible detail about occupation and characterize each occupation simultaneously in terms of the individual's relationship to the productive process (self-employed, salaried, and so on) and also in terms of the nature of the particular job (see Goldthorpe and Hope, 1974).

In the case of the data set we are examining here, the occupational information available for the first five years is of the grossest kind. Respondents are categorized only in terms of such categories as "professional, scientific, and technical workers." But we also have certain additional information about the individual's job situation that allows us to make a reasonably adequate composite indicator of the economic resources associated with the job. We know the industry in which the individual worked for the last three of the five years; we know whether in each year he or his family owned a business enterprise of any kind, and whether that business was incorporated or unincorporated. We know whether the individual is a member of a union, and we also know whether the individual's job involves hourly pay or not—we have called this last variable *wage worker*.[8]

First, we combined the P.S.I.D. code for main occupation with a question asking whether the individual was self-employed or worked for others, to create ten occupational groups. Using the Current Population Survey report on money income in 1972 of families and persons, we characterized each occupation in terms of the percentage of the average income for all year-round full-time male workers ($11,304) that the mean individual in each kind of job earned. These scores ranged from 225 for self-employed professionals to 55 for farmers.

In order to make use of the industry data we calculated an "industry advantage ratio." This is the ratio of the mean income for particular occupations in an industry to the income of all men with that occupation. Using the same Current Population Survey document we were able to calculate these ratios for industries using four gross occupational groups: professional and managerial workers, clerical and sales workers, craftsmen and operatives, and other workers.[9]

We recoded each individual's occupation, using the occupation income ratio for each of the five years, and then averaged these five ratios to characterize occupational resources (OCC). We did the same for the three years for which data are available to create the industry advantage ratio (IND).

We have built the factor of self-employment into our occupational income ratio measure, but there are two other aspects of the individual's economic class for which data are available and which turn out to be quite important in relation to income. The first has to do with whether the individual or family is at least part owner of an incorporated business. We computed the probability that the men in our sample had had an ownership interest in a corporation in a given year (CORP).[10]

We experimented with several ways of making use of the variables having to do with union membership and with whether the individual was compensated in an hourly way or not. Several dummy variable regressions using these variables suggested that it was the *joint* occurrence of not being a union member and being paid on an hourly basis that had the greatest impact on earnings. Therefore, we counted the number of years in which the respondent had been a non-union wage worker and divided that by five, arriving at a number that is the probability of the person's being a non-union wage worker in a given year (NOUN).

We estimated the following equation:

$$\text{Log income} = \log a + b(\log \text{OCC}) + c(\log \text{IND}) + e(\text{CORP}) + d(\text{NOUN})$$

(Table C-1 in Appendix C presents relevant statistics for these measures of the economic resources represented by jobs characterized in these four ways.)

An average 5.4 percent of the men in our sample were corporation owners in each year and an average of 24.22 percent of them were non-union wage workers. The balance, an average of 70.4 percent each year, were either self-employed or salaried or unionized wage workers. The multiple correlation of the four factors with income is 0.662. We were able to capture nearly half (43.9 percent) of the variance of income with these four characteristics of the jobs the respondent had. Occupation alone accounts for 37.5 percent of the variance.

The occupational income ratio has the lion's share of the influence but both the probability of being a corporation owner and the probability of being a non-union wage worker also play an important role. The unstandardized coefficient for the corporation owner variable is very interesting indeed. It tells us that an individual who was at least a part owner of a corporation for all five years had on the average one-and-a-half times the income of a man who was not a corporation owner, *holding constant* the individual's occupation and industry. Without holding the other factors constant, the corporation owners were receiving two-and-a-half times the income of the non-owners. Similarly, holding occupation and industry constant, non-union wage workers are expected to receive 80.6 percent of the income of other workers. Without holding these factors constant, they would be expected to receive about two-thirds of other workers' incomes.

Resources Associated with Terms of Employment

If one cannot find a job, one cannot earn a living. If one can only find work for half of the year, one is not likely to be able to earn as much as if one could find work for all of the year. Therefore, it is to be expected that how much a person is able to work will be related to how much income is earned. At a less gross level, terms of employment also affect income. A job in which the individual continues to be paid when ill should result in greater income on the average than one without the benefit of sick pay.

In addition, individual choices of how much to work can affect earnings. Some individuals will take on extra jobs to earn money, others will work overtime when overtime is compensated. It may be that even among salaried workers those who are more willing to put in extra hours of work are more likely to receive pay increases.

For all of these reasons one would expect that the proportion of the year a worker has a job will affect income, that the number of hours worked per week (when working) will affect income, and so on. After experimenting with a number of different specifications we chose four variables that seem to represent reasonably well the measures available in the P.S.I.D. data that capture employment resources.[11]

We have chosen to estimate first the number of weeks in the five-year period during which the individual was not unemployed, that is, the number of weeks he had a job, whether he worked at the job or not. We have included the time spent on vacation and any time that the worker was ill, although the Michigan data allow us to look at those two components of time employed separately. We will call this *weeks employed* (EMP), understanding it to represent the number of weeks an individual considered himself to have a job, that is, not to be un-employed. The second variable (HOUR) involves an assessment of the mean hours per week the individual worked when he was actually work-ing (that is, not on vacation or ill). The third variable is the proportion of the weeks the individual was employed when he was well (WELL). Finally, it seems possible that there might be a significant non-linearity in the weeks employed variable; we have represented that by adding a dummy variable that has a value of one for individuals who have had zero hours of unemployment during the five-year period and a value of zero for those who have had at least some unemployment (ALEMP).

Preliminary analysis for a number of subgroups suggested that there was an important difference between non-union wage workers and other workers in the extent to which employment resources are related to income. Therefore, we present in Table C-2 the results of regressions run separately for the approximately one-quarter of the sample who were non-union wage workers and the three-quarters of the sample who were either self-employed, salaried, or members of a union. We estimated for each group the following regression equation:

$$\text{Log INC} = \log a + b(\log \text{EMP}) + c(\log \text{HOUR}) + d(\log \text{WELL}) + e(\text{ALEMP})$$

The coefficient of determination for the non-union wage workers is quite a bit higher than for the other workers—almost 50 percent higher (0.30 compared to 0.21).

All of the unstandardized coefficients are higher for the non-union wage workers than for the others, suggesting a pattern of greater re-sponsiveness of their incomes to terms of employment than is true of the other workers. The difference is small and not statistically significant in the case of mean hours worked per week, but for two of the other variables the differences are significant and of moderate size.

Non-union wage workers' incomes are much more responsive to how much of their employment time they have been well than is true of other workers. Presumably non-union wage workers, when ill, are much less likely to be paid even though they continue to be employed—that is, they have the right to go back to work when they are well. The unstandardized coefficient of 1.66 indicates that a non-union wage worker who was well only 80 percent of the time over the five-year period would be expected to earn 69 percent as much as he might have, given his other employment characteristics, while another worker who was sick that much would be expected to earn 73 percent as much—a 6 percent disadvantage for the non-union wage worker. The non-union wage worker who has always been employed is expected to earn 27.4 percent more than a comparable worker who has experienced some unemployment, whereas in the case of other workers he is expected to earn only 17.4 percent more—a 57 percent disadvantage.

It is in the number of weeks that the worker had a job that the largest difference between non-union wage workers and other workers exists. This weeks-employed variable and the always-employed variable, of course, reinforce each other. Taking the two together, let us compare a non-union wage worker with another worker, both of whom experienced one quarter (13 weeks) of unemployment in the course of the five years. The non-union wage worker would be expected to earn 67 percent of the amount earned by a comparable worker, and the other worker would be expected to earn 79 percent as much. In other words, the non-union worker's disadvantage is about 15 percent. If we take workers of the two groups who experienced two quarters of unemployment (that is, 26 weeks) the non-union wage worker would be expected to earn 56 percent as much as a fully employed non-union wage worker, whereas the other worker would be expected to earn 73 percent of the income of a fully employed other worker. The disadvantage at this level of unemployment for the non-union wage worker is 23 percent.

It is easy to reason after the fact and explain these differences between the experience of non-union wage workers and those of others, but we would be happier if there were direct survey data that sought to measure the different fringe benefits that are available to these different classes of workers. For example, we can well imagine that non-union wage workers have received very little in the way of severance pay and, therefore, experience more of an income loss when they become unemployed. They may, in particular, be unlikely to receive severance pay if they quit their jobs, whereas other workers may receive the pay whether they quit or are let go. If that is true, then two workers from the two groups, each of whom look for work for one or two months, would have quite different income experiences since one worker is receiving severance pay and the other is not. (Remember that unemployment compensation is not included in our variable of taxable income.)

Area Resources

The simplest index of the advantages or disadvantages associated with living in a particular place would be the median income of people in that place. This variable is not available on the tape with which we worked, and therefore we have used several indicators that seem to be associated with how high or low incomes are in a given area. These variables are:

BUD: The budget index—a cost-of-living index for the county in which the respondent lives.

WAGE: The unskilled male wage rate in the county in which the respondent lives. These data were collected by the Institute for Social Research using questionnaires to employment officials in each area in which a sample household lives.

SMSA: Whether or not the respondent lives 50 miles from the center of a standard metropolitan statistical area.

CITY: Whether in 1968 (the only year for which this variable is available) the respondent lived in one of the twelve largest SMSAs.

POP: Mean city size in each of the five sample years—an average of the size of the cities in which the respondent lived (if he lived in the same city all five years this measure does not change, but if he moved, the variable is an average of the size of the cities in which he did live).

The equation we estimated was:

$$\text{Log Income} = \text{Log } a + b(\text{Log BUD}) + c(\text{Log WAGE}) + d(\text{SMSA}) + e(\text{CITY}) + f(\text{Log POP})$$

Overall, our five indicators of area resources correlate 0.356 with income (see Table C-3). About 13 percent of the variance in income lies between areas characterized in this way, while the lion's share of variance is within the areas.

Of the five characteristics, only city size does not have a significant regression coefficient. Apparently the other characteristics succeed in capturing just about all of the co-variance of income and city size.[12]

There are no surprises here. Big cities and expensive cities tend to have higher incomes, as do cities with higher typical unskilled male wage rates. Living far from an SMSA tends to depress income. An important issue has to do with the social significance of income amounts in different areas. Presumably when members of a community place each other income is discounted in terms of the expected income for a given area. Thus, an individual with an income of $10,000 in a community where incomes run 10 percent below the national average might be expected to have higher social standing by virtue of income than an individual earning $10,000 in a community that has average incomes 10 percent above the national average. One might want to use these results, therefore, to discount income before examining the relationship between income and other status-related factors.

Our main interest in area resources in what follows has to do with the extent to which they are related to other types of resources in the individual's current situation, and the extent to which they are a product of earlier characteristics connected with education and family background.

The Interrelation of the Three Types of Resources

Having constructed multiple indicators of resources associated with three aspects of the individual's socio-economic situation, we can now look at their interrelations. Using the regression equations outlined in the previous section we constructed composite scores for each individual to represent the income advantages associated with the area in which he lived, the kind of job he had, and the kind of employment experience he had had over the five-year period. The constant in these equations was adjusted so that the mean would be one for each composite variable. An individual's score on each variable, then, represents his proportionate advantage or disadvantage over the average member of the sample.

The means are arbitrary, but the standard deviations continue to be meaningful. The variable with the greatest variance in terms of the advantages different individuals possess is the job variable. The variable with the least variation is the geographical one. The coefficient of determination of the three composite indicators with income is 0.578; thus 42.2 percent of the variance is unexplained by our model.

There is very little association between the resources conferred by particular geographic areas and those conferred by jobs or employment experiences. There is a strong association between job and employment resources, as one would expect, since certain kinds of occupations have a much higher risk of unemployment than others. Starting with a simple index of occupational resources that correlates 0.612 with these men's relatively permanent income, the addition of other measures of resources associated with one's labor market situation increased the correlation to 0.760. Expanding our measure of job characteristics from occupation alone added 0.064 to the coefficient of determination of income. Including a measure of employment resources added another 0.064. The combined job and employment resources variables accounted for half of the variance of permanent income. The advantages associated with area added another 0.075, making a total coefficient of determination of income of 0.578. This fuller measure of labor market resources explains over half again as much variance as the simple occupational scale. We believe that even if the occupational scale were more detailed, the broader measures would improve the correlation almost as much.

It seems likely that had we presented a wide menu of job characteristics for judging occupational standing to our Boston respondents, they would also have attached considerable weight to such things as being a union *versus* a non-union wage worker, or experiencing unemployment, or working in a low-income area. If occupational prestige is mainly an assessment of the general desirability of jobs, then the more concrete the description of jobs the more variance there is likely to be in people's assessment of occupational standing. The standard deviation of our occupational scale based on correlations with income increases by 24 percent as we add more specifications of an individual's labor market situation. We would expect a subjective occupational standing scale to increase at least this much with additional information available to the status evaluators. Of course, if we were also able to include in job descriptions their holders' nonpecuniary advantages, we would expect the variance in job prestige to increase even more. For the purposes of our study, however, we will regard our overall measure of labor market situation as an adequate occupational scale for the analysis of the role of schooling and family background that follows. We begin that analysis with the understanding that about sixth-tenths of the variance in men's mid-career permanent income can be associated with their measured labor market characteristics, and that about 40 percent seems associated with some combination of measurement error and unmeasured factors.

CHAPTER 14

Schooling and Family Background in Adult Attainment

Iᴛ ɪs ᴄᴏɴᴠᴇɴɪᴇɴᴛ to think of the adult career as launched during the period immediately following completion of schooling. This makes for a nice model. Family of orientation factors affect the personal traits a young person has when going to school, and they affect aspirations. They can affect the amount of schooling and grades while in school. All of these things in turn have an impact on the first job a person takes, and then they—along with that first job—have an effect on occupation and income in the later career. If one is looking only at the skeleton of the socio-economic career, then, one wants measures of family background, of schooling, and of the socio-economic resources conferred by the first full-time job. Unfortunately, people's actual careers are not as neat as this model suggests.

It is particularly difficult to characterize the early work experience of the individual in a simple but meaningful way. The Panel Study of Income Dynamics (P.S.I.D.) inquiry, for example, asks of each head of the household, "Thinking of your first full-time regular job, what did you do?" After several efforts to make use of the responses to this question (which were coded into the same nine gross occupational categories that were used for present occupations) we decided that as a meaningful measure of launching a career in the labor market, this question was really not useful. The correlation between the first job and later jobs was quite low, and the correlations of education with this variable were similarly low—lower in fact than the correlation between education and later occupations. We believe that a more detailed line of questioning and coding would be necessary to capture those factors about early work career that are important for the later career. Indeed, to deal adequately with the connection between family background, the launch period, and later periods of the socio-economic career, one should ask a set of questions that provides an understanding of what went on in the person's life at this time.

For those who have attended college, the interrelations between going to school and work are especially complex. At a minimum, we would want to be able to identify (1) those individuals who went more or less straight through college with only minor work experience (part-time and summer jobs) and then took a "real job" to launch their careers, (2) those who worked their way through college by working full-time and perhaps did not attend college full-time, (3) those who worked at full-time jobs and then decided to go to college—either continuing to work or stopping work and attending college full-time, and (4) those who used schooling—particularly graduate schooling—to improve qualifications in a career on which they were already launched (such as teaching or city planning). The returns to college training might be expected to be rather different for such different college experiences.

In the case of those who did not attend college at all, one would want to know something about not just the first job but also the work career during the first few years after the completion of school.

Since we do not have these kinds of data, we must confine our analysis to the role of schooling.

The Role of Schooling

We will use the level of schooling completed by the husband and by his wife as indices of the socio-economic resources available to the family at this early career point.[1] We believe that the variable of a wife's schooling can add somewhat to what we learn about the family's social position at this time, partly because wives bring resources to the couple that may be helpful in career pursuit and partly because in choosing whom to marry, women may make acute assessments concerning the potentialities of the possible husband, and therefore the schooling of the woman provides us with an indirect additional measure of the man's resources at this time.

Husband's and wife's years of schooling are, as we might expect, rather highly intercorrelated (0.665), but by no means overwhelmingly so (see Table C-5). Well under half of the variance in the one is predictable with the knowledge of the other. As would be expected, the husband's schooling correlates more highly with the various components of his income than does his wife's schooling, and the addition of her schooling as a variable increases the correlation between schooling and these components of income only very slightly. On the other hand, all of the regression coefficients for wife's schooling remain significant after controlling her husband's schooling.

Let us first consider the pattern of correlations and coefficients for head's schooling. A man's schooling has a strong association with his income—the correlation is 0.602. That association is transmitted mainly by job resources. The association with employment resources is only about a third as strong and that with area resources is really small—schooling accounts for only about 4 percent of the variance in the latter. The same pattern is present in the cases of wife's schooling.

We have phrased the relationship between years of schooling and income in a similog specification, that is:

$$\text{Log income} = \log a + \log b \text{ (years of schooling)}$$

The coefficient b specifies the rate of increase per year of schooling in much the same way as interest compounds. Thus, if the coefficient's anti-log were 1.10, we would know that the prediction is that each year's schooling nets the individual 10 percent more income than the previous year.

In fact, the unstandardized regression coefficient for head's schooling is 9 percent—that is, each additional year of schooling on the average increases income 9 percent over the lower level of schooling. This overall effect on income breaks down to approximately a 1 percent per year effect from area resources and employment resources, and a 6 percent effect from job resources.

Effects at Different Levels of Schooling

The above specification of the effect of schooling on income imposes the condition that one year of schooling has the same effect, whether one considers the difference between five and six years of schooling or fifteen and sixteen years of schooling. It could well be that there are different incremental effects at different levels of schooling. In order to investigate this possibility, we carried out a dummy variable regression for each of the nine levels of education provided in the data. It yielded a correlation of 0.608. The regression coefficients indicate that up through some college, there is an extremely regular percentage increase in the payoff from an additional year of education. Through some college, each additional year of schooling, without controlling for other variables, adds 8 percent to income.

High school graduates with no additional training are predicted to earn 97 percent of the geometric mean of the sample. A person who completed the eighth grade would be expected to earn 71 percent, and a person who completed some college (assumed to be two years on the average) would be expected to earn 114 percent of the sample's geomean. The same 8 percent increase in income per year of additional schooling seems to apply to postgraduate schooling compared to college graduation (on the assumption that the postgraduate group averages two years of additional schooling). The college graduate coefficient of 152 percent, compounded at 8 percent for two years, comes to 178 percent.

However, a college graduate coefficient of 152 percent is higher than would be expected on the basis of an 8 percent per year increase over high school graduation (or some college). At that rate, the regression coefficient should be only 132 percent. Thus there is a 15 percent bonus for college graduation over and above the number of years of schooling graduation represents.

When other variables are controlled, we observe that the rate of increase in income by years of schooling declines.[2] If we control for family of orientation and present place of residence, the 8 percent rate that applies to up to some college declines to only 5 percent.

However, preserving dummy variables for college graduation and postgraduate education suggests that this decline is not as great at these two higher education levels. For the unadjusted dummy variable regressions, college graduation had a regression coefficient 15 percent greater than would be predicted on the 8-percent-a-year rate. Therefore, adding 15 percent to the regression weights for college graduates and postgraduates predicted on the basis of 8 percent per year brought them into line. As we control for other variables, however, this bonus has to be increased. For a college graduate, when we control for family of orientation and place, the bonus for college graduation has to be increased to 22 percent, and there is now a small 6 percent bonus for postgraduate schooling.

The sample sizes for these categories are small enough that these differences may not be significant. But they are worth noting to indicate that controlling for other variables may shift the pattern of relationship between education and income in other than simple linear ways. In the case of postgraduate education, controlling for other variables does not reduce the proportionate increase in income over college graduation. In the case of the increase in income from some college to college graduation, controlling for other variables does reduce the proportionate increase —without controls the college graduates earn one-third more; controlling for family of orientation and place, they earn 26 percent more. However, this decrease (about 20 percent) in the difference in earnings is not as great as it is at lower educational levels (nearly 40 percent).

Effect of Differences in Colleges

As more and more people attend and graduate from college, differentiation among colleges may become an increasingly important factor in accounting for social status and for income. Unfortunately, the P.S.I.D. provided no information about the colleges that respondents attended until the 1975 interviewing year. The Productive Americans study does provide a categorization of selectivity of colleges from which respondents graduated (for a description of this study see Morgan, 1966). The regression coefficients from a dummy variable analysis of these data suggest that selectivity is an important variable. We have collapsed the more detailed categories available into three—ordinary colleges rated as either unaccredited or not selective (about 40 percent of the male graduates in our age range attended such colleges), selective colleges (45 percent attended such colleges), and very selective colleges (15 percent attended those).

Despite small samples, the regression coefficients for different types of colleges are significantly different from each other. What they suggest is that completing a college that is not at least selective confers no income advantage over simply attending college for a few years, but that graduating from a better college does confer a considerable advantage, one that is not simply a reflection of family background. Attending a selective college increases income by 52 percent, and attending a very selective college by an additional 32 percent—a doubling of income as we move from ordinary to very selective college graduates.

When we introduce controls for father's education, place of birth, and race, the differences are reduced but persist—40 percent from ordinary to selective, 21 percent from selective to very selective or a total of 69 percent.

A thorough measure of the individual's income advantages at the beginning of the work career would certainly include, therefore, a measure of the income advantages accruing by virtue of the particular college attended. It would be interesting to have these selectivity measures not just for those who completed college but also for those who completed some college. More detail on the college years might serve to tap some of the heterogeneity of the actual socio-economic situation that is buried in the categories *some college* and *college graduate*. We cannot do a very good job of controlling for family background from the data available in the Productive Americans tape, and therefore the above figures may represent an exaggeration of the advantages accruing to attending particular kinds of colleges (implicitly including family), but they are suggestive of the possible importance of education variables other than simply years of education.[3] We do note that, as would be expected, addition of controls for family background reduces the coefficients most for very selective and selective colleges and least for ordinary colleges.

Overall, these probes into other characteristics of schooling than simply number of years suggest that a more refined categorization of schooling is not likely to produce a much higher correlation between years of schooling and income, but it does tell us with greater precision what the effects of particular kinds of schooling in the post-high school years are. However, as more and more young people attend college, the income variance within the college group will represent a larger and larger proportion of the total variance in income. As that proportion increases, it is likely that taking into account variations other than simply years of college will significantly increase the correlation between the schooling variable represented in this more complex way over one represented simply as number of years of schooling.

The Direct Effect of Schooling on Income

We can conclude by observing that husband's and wife's schooling together do not have a large direct effect on income. Considering that our measure of occupation is quite gross, one might have expected schooling to add significantly to the representation of "human capital" in our model. Overall, the addition of the schooling variables increases the coefficient of determination of income from 0.577 to 0.612, only a 3.5 percent addition.

It could be, of course, that different levels of schooling have different patterns of effect on the components of income we have identified. It is not hard to imagine, for example, that the higher levels of education have more effect on job advantages than the lower levels. The reverse may be true for area and employment resources, that variations in the lower part of the range have a greater effect than variations in the upper part of the range. We have not investigated these possible interactions.

Parental Social Class and Other Childhood Resources

We complete our exploration of the model of mid-career men's socio-economic resources by considering resources that derive from the pre-adult period of the individual's life. Some of these are resources of a purely ascriptive kind, such as the identity conferred by being born into a particular racial or ethnic group. Others may represent so-called human capital, such as knowledge and other psychological attributes that may be an advantage for an adult individual. Most resources, particularly in the form available to us in a data set such as the Panel Study of Income Dynamics, represent an indeterminate mixture of advantages that are external to the individual and advantages that have to do with the kind of person the adult individual has become.

For example, how are we to interpret the advantage conferred by being born in a city as opposed to a small town or rural area? To some extent, this may simply mean that individuals born in cities tend to stay in cities, and wages are higher in cities. To some extent, it may mean that people born in non-city areas are in some ways discriminated against. Or city dwellers may have had superior schooling and exposure to generally more sophisticated cosmopolitan ways. Finally, it might simply be that city-born people are more interested in making money. Therefore, as with the other variable indexing resources that we have considered, we must look on the results of this exploration of parental social class and other childhood resource variables as pointing a direction for searching out the actual causes of adult success, rather than as being themselves measures of those causes.

We have been particularly interested in assessing the social class of the family in which the individual grew up. Compared to the rich variety of information that we would want, the data that are available to us are skimpy. The P.S.I.D. data tape provides information about father's schooling, father's usual occupation when the individual was growing up, and the respondent's answer to the question: "Were your parents poor when you were growing up, pretty well off, or what?" We would like much richer detail on parental occupation. We certainly would like to know the family's financial circumstances with more exactness. Granted that one can hardly expect valid answers to a question about parental family income, we could build a much more reliable index of family financial circumstances if we had answers to questions concerning the housing and other possessions of the individual's family during childhood and adolescence. Therefore, we can expect that the relationship between parental social class and the individual's current income or occupation will be underestimated. Depending upon how inaccurate our measures of parental social status are, this relationship could prove to be markedly underestimated.

Much work on the socio-economic career has sought to estimate the differential impact of father's occupation and education and other indices of parental socio-economic status on the individual's adult achievements. It seems to us that placing a heavy interpretive burden on different path coefficients for father's education and occupation could be misleading. To make use of such findings we would want a model of the process by which father's schooling affects adult status, as opposed to the effects of the particular kind of work the father did. In fact, most discussions that make use of the path model approach do not specify such a model. The two measures generally seem more alternative indices of overall social status than anything else.

We chose here to pursue a different course. We have used the information about father's schooling, occupation, and family financial circumstances to construct an overall index of parental social class. In order to link our measure of parental social class to the work in the qualitative tradition discussed in the earlier chapters, we made use of the relationship between social class as developed in Coleman's qualitative analysis and the profile of general social standing scores described in Chapter 11. There we developed a scale of status estimation magnitudes to correspond to Coleman's ordinal social class scale ranging from lower-lower to upper class.

In order to place the fathers of the men in a social class, we cross-tabulated the father's schooling by father's occupation, by family financial circumstances, and by two age categories. Those cross-tabulations were then coded into one of thirteen class groupings by Coleman, based on standards he has developed in terms of the age cohort of the individual and the time for which the placement is being made.[4]

Coleman's class placements were converted into a parental social class score for each individual, using a rounded set of social class magnitudes derived from the analysis in Chapter 11.[5] These scores were then used to scale the categories of father's schooling, occupation, and family finances in terms of their status significance. A dummy variable regression for each characteristic was run; the resulting regression weights could then be used to characterize the probable class significance of an individual's father's schooling, father's occupation, and his characterization of the family's financial circumstances. (The scores associated with each of these characteristics are given in Table C-6.) Since Coleman made a social class placement for each family if there was any information at all about the father, the regression weights also tell us the social status associated with no information about a given variable.

Overall, Coleman relied most heavily on father's education in making his placement, as indicated by the multiple correlation of 0.843 between the dummy variables for schooling level and his placement score. He found father's occupation and family financial circumstances about equally important in making his overall placements; the multiple correlations are 0.636 and 0.650 respectively.

We were interested in determining the extent to which an overall index of parental social status accounts for as much of the variance in such adult characteristics as schooling and income, as could be accounted for by the three parental socio-economic status variables in a multiple regression. In order to simplify this test, we computed a new social class score that was the average of an individual's score on each of the three variables. We then subtracted that score from the individual's score on each single variable to obtain a discrepancy score for each. Thus, if an individual had an average on the three variables of 100 but his father had graduated from college, his parental schooling discrepancy was +63. If, on the other hand, his father had completed six to eight years of school, his parental schooling discrepancy score was —20.

A multiple correlation of the average score and the discrepancy scores for each of the three variables with head's schooling and income (all in logs) tells us the extent to which more than the single overall index of parental social class is necessary to account fully for the variance that can be explained by these three family background characteristics. If none of the three discrepancy scores are significant, then it is not unreasonable (at least with the data available) to conclude that we should speak only about the general effect of parental social class position on subsequent career. This, of course, would fit with our earlier stated preference for identifying a single status dimension to which different socio-economic resources make contributions. In fact, none of the discrepancy scores add a significant contribution to that of their average (which is, of course, more reliable than they are singly).[6]

There are four other aspects of the individual's childhood situation that have been used in the analysis reported below. The first variable we call *majority*. This variable has a value of one if the individual is not coded as black or Spanish-American, Puerto Rican, Mexican, or Cuban on the P.S.I.D. computer tape.[7]

Another set of variables characterizes the type of community in which the respondent was born. We have retained two dummy variables from several more elaborate explorations of community and region grown up in. The dummy variables—"grew up in a rural area" and "grew up in a large city"—seem optimal in terms of simplicity of the model and yet captured most of the variance of more elaborate characterizations.

We have used the number of siblings as another characterization of the individual's childhood resources. Much earlier research has suggested that, controlling for parental social status, children from smaller families have an advantage in terms of adult economic success over those from larger families.

Finally, we have constructed an index of the social mobility of the individual's siblings as an indirect measure of status-related characteristics of the family environment during childhood. We constructed this index in a way similar to that for parental social class. The Panel Study tape provides information concerning the schooling of the respondent's oldest living brother and a response concerning how well he is doing financially (coded into these categories: "very well," "all right," and "not so well"). If there is no living brother, then the respondent is asked the same question about an oldest living sister. We cross-tabulated the answers to these two questions, and Coleman assigned a class placement in the ordinal scale of lower to upper class to each cell in the cross-tabulation. As with parental social class, this placement was then translated into a class magnitude score for the sibling. Variations above and below one represent proportionately greater or lesser mobility on the part of siblings. The scale is a scale of the relatively greater or lesser mobility by an individual's siblings than would be expected of an average member of his cohort.[8]

As such, this scale can be thought of as representing several possible aspects of the family environment relevant to economic success. First, we would expect this variable to pick up some of the errors in our measurement of parental social class. In that sense we are not really measuring the mobility of the siblings at all; instead the variable is simply another indicator of parental social class. In addition, however, we would expect this kind of variable to pick up some aspects of the family environment that were conducive to economic success in the children's generation, even though not producing the same level of economic success in the parental generation. For example, we would expect this variable to be a useful index of the extent to which the individual's family was more or less oriented toward school accomplishments on the part of their children than others of their class.

Our analysis of resources stemming from childhood then rests on five variables: majority (MAJ), parental class (CLASS), number of siblings (SIBS), sibling mobility (SIBMOBIL), and size of community (RURAL and CITY). The latter involves two dummy variables, so that the regressions reported below have made use of six variables to describe family background.

We estimated the equation:

$$\text{Log INCOME} = \text{Log } a + b(\text{RURAL}) + c(\text{CITY}) + d(\text{MAJ}) + e(\log \text{CLASS}) + f(\text{SIBS}) + g(\log \text{SIBMOBIL})$$

Table C-6 presents the means and standard deviations and regression coefficients for these variables. The coefficient of determination of adult characteristics ranges from a low of 6.5 percent of the variance for employment resources to a high of 36.9 percent for the variance of head's schooling.

The area resources, as would be expected, are significantly associated with the size of community in which the individual grew up. None of the other family background characteristics seem to have an effect on it. The coefficient of determination is 0.168, almost all of which is a product of "rural" and "city."

Job resources, on the other hand, are affected by all five variables— most strongly by parental social class. These five variables correlate 0.508 with job resources. Employment resources are very weakly related to family background characteristics.

Most of the effect of family background on the incomes of these men comes through the impact of each type of characteristic on job characteristics, and from the impact of the size of the community grown up in on the area resources. From unstandardized regression coefficients we get some idea of the magnitudes of the effects of these background factors.

If a man was born into a majority family he is expected to have two more years of schooling and his wife one more year of schooling than if he were not born into such a family. His job resources will be about 23 percent better; his terms of employment about 10 percent better. Overall, his income is expected to be about 43 percent higher, even controlling for other family background characteristics, some of which are certainly themselves in part caused by majority group membership—such as parental social class.

People who grew up in rural areas are expected to live as adults in areas where incomes are generally only 90 percent of the national average. Those born in cities are expected to be about 22 percent better off in terms of income, a combination of the more advantageous areas they live in and the more advantageous job and other resources they have access to (in part because they will have achieved almost one additional year of schooling, controlling for other family background characteristics).

The coefficient of parental social class on head's and wife's schooling is not easy to interpret directly. Roughly, for every 12 percent increase or decrease in parental social class (holding other factors constant) one expects a one-year increase or decrease in head's schooling. For every 30 percent increase or decrease in parental class one expects a one-year increase or decrease in wife's schooling.

Job resources increase as an approximate two-thirds power for parental class—a doubling of parental class increases job resources by 58 percent and employment resources by 21 percent. Income resources increase almost but not quite linearly (0.875 power) with parental class—doubling parental class increases income by 83 percent.

The number of siblings has the expected effect. Each additional sibling is associated with a decline of about a fifth of a year in both head's and wife's schooling, and each additional sibling costs the individual about 1.5 percent of the income he would otherwise have. Our sibling mobility variable has a strong relationship mainly with head's schooling, and as we will see when the schooling variables are included, all of the significant effect of this variable is discovered to be transmitted through its effect on the schooling of the head.

Examining the joint effects of schooling and family background characteristics on current resources measures (see Table C-7), one discovers that a number of the significant coefficients in the previous regression are no longer significant, indicating that most of the effect of the background variable is effected through one or the other of the schooling variables. Even after including the schooling variables, however, the majority variable continues to have a strong effect on job resources—majority individuals are expected to have about an 11 percent advantage. The direct effect has been approximately halved by the addition of education. As noted, the sibling mobility variable no longer has a significant coefficient. In the case of the number of siblings there remains only one significant coefficient, that for wife's schooling—suggesting that the effect of the number of siblings on adult socio-economic resources is achieved primarily by its effect on the schooling of the head and his wife.

Overall, our exploration finds a moderate effect of the set of family background characteristics on adult socio-economic achievement, as indexed by the overall correlation of 0.53 between all six of our family background variables and adult income. Given the very rough-and-ready way family background is measured in even a careful survey such as the Panel Study, we can expect this to be a rather considerable underestimate, but only research that directs itself very carefully (and with considerably elaborated measurement) to family background characteristics can adequately test this hypothesis.

In order to examine at the same time the several different characteristics of current and childhood situations we have discussed above, we will simplify again in order to reduce the number of variables to be dealt with. We will combine into an overall index of family background resources all the variables we have just examined except majority (the effects of majority or minority group membership are exercised throughout the individual's lifetime by the behavior of others toward him). With this simplification we are now able to characterize (1) the individual's childhood situation in terms of two variables, majority and an omnibus variable of family background; (2) his situation at the launch period using two variables, his and his wife's schooling; and (3) his current socio-economic situation represented by three components, the resources of area, job, and terms of employment. We can use the technique of path analysis to display the relationships among these various points in the socio-economic career.

In scaling family background we have weighted the five separate variables in terms of their overall contribution to income just as we have done in decomposing income into a number of different resources. Thus the family background variable is the individual's predicted income, given his family background characteristics:

$$\text{Log INCOME} = \text{Log } a + b(\text{RURAL}) + c(\text{CITY}) + d(\text{log CLASS}) + e(\text{SIBS}) + f(\text{log SIBMOBIL})$$

We arbitrarily set the family background variable at a mean of 1.0 to represent the average (geometric mean) family background resources in our sample.[9]

A recursive model allows a summarization of all of the effects we have been discussing in this and the previous chapters. Table 14-1 uses an accounting device developed by Alwin and Hauser (1975) to display the patterns of direct and indirect effects in a recursive system of equations. In order to present the results in this way we stipulated the causal order of the variables as follows: majority and family background "cause" head's schooling achievement; these three in turn "cause" wife's schooling achievement; these four, area resources; these five, job resources; these six, employment resources; and all seven "cause" income.

TABLE 14-1

Decomposition of Effects of Independent Variables on Income

Dependent Variable	Predetermined Variable	Total	Head's School-ing	Wife's School-ing	Area	Job	Employ-ment	Direct
					Effects on Income via			
Head's Schooling (R² = 0.373)	Majority	.175						.175
	Family Background	.551						.551
Wife's Schooling (R² = 0.393)	Majority	.150	.087					.063
	Family Background	.427	.274					.153
	Head's Schooling	.497	–					.497
Area Resources (R² = 0.171)	Majority	−.029	−.001	.001				−.022
	Family Background	.416	−.026	.005				.437
	Head's Schooling	−.047	–	.016				−.063
	Wife's Schooling	−.032	–	–				−.032
Job Resources (R² = 0.402)	Majority	.188	.082	.006	.0			.100
	Family Background	.438	.258	.014	−.010			.176
	Head's Schooling	.467	–	.047	−.009			.429
	Wife's Schooling	.095	–	–	.0			.095
	Area Resources	−.024	–	–	–			−.024
Employment Resources (R² = 0.161)	Majority	.117	.051	.004	.003	.022		.037
	Family Background	.205	.160	.012	−.050	.039		.044
	Head's Schooling	.290	–	.040	.007	.091		.152
	Wife's Schooling	.079	–	–	−.004	.021		.062
	Area Resources	−.114	–	–	–	−.005		−.109
	Job Resources	.217	–	–	–	–		.217
Income (R² = 0.619)	Majority	.210	.078	.009	−.005	.043	.009	.076
	Family Background	.445	.247	.020	.090	.077	.011	.0
	Head's Schooling	.448	–	.065	−.013	.181	.038	.177
	Wife's Schooling	.132	–	–	.006	.042	.015	.069
	Area Resources	.208	–	–	–	−.010	−.028	.246
	Job Resources	.431	–	–	–	–	.094	.377
	Employment Resources	.251	–	–	–	–	–	.251

The table shows for each successive variable in this recursive system the total effects of the independent variables in the form of standardized regression coefficients, and it decomposes this total effect into components that are direct effects on the dependent variable (the path coefficient directly from the independent to the dependent variable) and those that are indirect, operating through the given independent variable's effect on intermediate independent variables. Thus, we read in the second panel of the table that the total effect of majority on wife's schooling (controlling for family background but not for head's schooling, because that is subsequent to it in the recursive system) is 0.15. That effect is the sum of a 0.063 direct effect of wife's schooling and a 0.087 effect that operates through the effect of majority on head's schooling and the latter's effect in turn on wife's schooling. In this way a patient person can trace out the pattern of effects in the complex system represented by even such a small set of variables as these eight.

This table sharpens the impression gained from the earlier presentations of the data. Area resources are affected in a major way only by family background—by where the individual grew up. Area seems relatively independent of the other factors in our model. Job resources are most strongly affected by schooling, family background, and majority. Almost 60 percent of the effect of family background is channeled through its effect on head's schooling, as is 44 percent of the effect of majority.

Employment resources are less strongly affected by other factors than job resources. The principal effects are those of family background, schooling, and job, with majority having a moderate positive effect and area a moderate negative effect. As with job resources, family background affects employment resources primarily through its effect on schooling (78 percent of total effect) while the independent effect of schooling itself is primarily direct, with a modest indirect effect through job resources.

It follows that the effects of childhood resources on income are exercised heavily though indirectly by way of head's schooling. There continue to be important direct effects of family background on area and job resources, however. The direct effect on income is reduced to zero. Majority continues to have a notable direct effect on income, equal to more than one-third of its total effect.

Childhood and schooling factors seem to affect mainly the role of job resources, not changing the effects of area and employment resources much. Controlling for earlier factors reduces the total effect of job resources from 0.579 to 0.431. This is primarily as a result of the influence of head's schooling. This suggests that there are aspects of the job situation highly correlated with schooling that we are not picking up in our measure of job resources.

Given that we have good reason to believe our measures of family background are not as good as they might be, the strong effect of childhood factors on income is impressive—almost a third of the variance of income is accounted for by factors settled in childhood. Those settled by school leaving time account for slightly over 40 percent of the variance. With more adequate measures of both childhood and launch-stage factors, these would surely turn out to be underestimates.

Conclusion

The number of variables we have dealt with to represent three stages of the socio-economic career—childhood, launch stage, and middle —to some extent obscure the simplicity of the model. Let us summarize the main points about the connections among family background, schooling, and adult resources by simplifying the model still further, dealing with one overall family background variable (by adding in majority status), schooling, one overall occupational resources variable (combining area, job, and employment resources), and income. We are interested in the extent to which the two types of adult resource, occupational or labor market resources and income, are accounted for by childhood and launch-period resources. The answer is schematized in Figure 14-1. Overall, family background and schooling have the same level of association with labor market resources, but the latter has a stronger association with income (0.61) than the former (0.53). As discussed above, all the family background characteristics explain just under 30 percent of the variation in income, and about 37 percent of the variation in labor market resources. (Our measure of labor market resources is constructed by correlating the set of labor market characteristics with income. Here, however, we want it to stand for all the resources the individual gains from labor market participation. We feel that it can stand for this more inclusive variable, since it seems likely that it would correlate very highly with a more inclusive measure.)

In the status attainment model, family background causes both schooling and adult career resources and can affect those latter resources either directly or indirectly through its influence on educational attainment. We want to know how much of the effect of schooling is merely a transmission of family background effects, and how much is an inde-

FIGURE 14-1

Simplified Path Diagrams for Mid-Career Resources

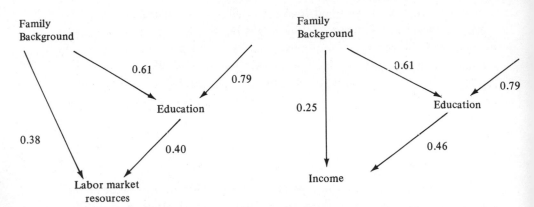

pendent effect of schooling over and above that of transmission. The issue is a vital one in any discussion of the effectiveness of schooling in increasing equality of opportunity and reducing the degree of social inheritance.

We observe that, when the schooling variable is added to family background, this two-variable model now accounts for 49 percent of the variance in labor market resources and 41 percent of the variance in income. Schooling adds 10 and 13 percent to the explanatory power of family background alone. This means that, taking into account the full effect of family background, one standard deviation more schooling increases occupational resources 0.32 of a standard deviation (0.79 x 0.40) and income 0.38 of a standard deviation (0.79 x 0.46).

Without controlling for family background, schooling increases occupation resources at the rate of 7 percent for each year of schooling, and income at the rate of 9 percent a year. But the independent effect of schooling over and above that of family background is only 3.5 percent for occupational resources and 5 percent for income. Without taking into account the full effects of family background we would observe a 31 percent increase in occupational resources and a 41 percent increase in income as a result of a four-year increase in schooling. But after removing the effect of family background, we find that schooling independently increases occupational resources by 15 percent and income by 22 percent for a four-year increase in schooling.

By this estimation of the "unique" effects of schooling, we obtain an estimate of the extent to which educational attainment can compensate for the efforts of families to pass along their advantages to their children. Our estimates assume that families would find other ways of passing along their advantages if schooling no longer served as a transmission belt for privilege. Under this strict assumption, the gain to schooling is small indeed, in addition to its being a risky investment as shown by the low correlation between it and resources.

A high estimate of the true effect of schooling on resources comes from the assumption that leaving out family background biases our estimate of the gains from schooling merely because of a spurious component to the correlation between schooling and resources, because we have not controlled for the direct effects of family background on occupational resources (0.38) and income (0.25). Here it is assumed that if families with more advantages did not send their children to school, those children would not do as well as adults, and therefore the total effect of schooling is the sum of the effects of family background transmitted by schooling and the unique effects of schooling. In our diagrams these effects are 0.40 and 0.46. Thus, instead of true schooling effects on occupational resources and income being merely 50 and 57 percent of their apparent effects, we find them to be 63 and 75 percent of those biased estimates. By this estimate the true effect of four additional years of schooling on occupational resources is a 19 percent rather than a 15 percent increase. In the case of income the true effect involves a 30 rather than a 22 percent increase.

This latter approach assumes that families are passive to changes in the educational opportunity structure; the first approach assumes they would have the same level of success (indexed by the correlation between family background and resources) even with an increase in educational equality. The truth for American society today is probably somewhere in between, with the true occupational resource gains from schooling slightly less than 4 percent per year, and the gains for income about 6 percent per year. (However, our results for college *graduation*, reported above, suggest more of a gain than these rates would indicate.)

The effect of relatively poor measurement of family background is that we are probably still overestimating the total and independent effects of schooling on adult resources, but not by very much. The main error is probably an underestimation of the direct effects of family background factors on adult resources. We proceed in the next chapter on the assumption that our model of objective resources is close enough to the true situation to make it worthwhile to explore the connections between resources and social standing.

CHAPTER 15

Translating Social Resources into Social Standing

Tрше BULK of the evidence presented in earlier chapters supports the hypothesis that social standing, or social status, is assigned by Americans on the basis of perceptions of how well off they believe particular individuals and families to be. Thus social standing and social well-being are essentially synonymous. It comes as no great surprise to find that the three most obvious components of being well-off, as judged by our respondents, are income, job, and schooling. These are the three most straightforward clues to the general desirability of an individual's life situation, because they are regarded as the three principal resources for the attainment of a given level of social well-being. These three represent general dimensions that run from high to low and have their impact at all social class levels. Although in the qualitative data one finds hints that the relations of these three to one another and other factors may vary somewhat in the high, middle, and low status regions, in none of our quantitative analyses have these kinds of interactions seemed to be important. It may be that the manner of speaking about social status varies from one level to another but that, in the actual process of making judgments, people at different status levels in fact use overwhelmingly similar sets of decision rules. (This also seems to apply to the sociologist approaching data about families. In further study of the Panel Study of Income Dynamics data, in which an effort was made to take into account all of the data in seven years of interviews with a sample of individuals, it turns out that almost all of the variance in the social class ratings based on the whole body of the data can be accounted for by a model making use only of schooling, job characteristics, and the various income sources of the families.)

We have developed in Parts I and II a status evaluation model that captures the way each of these three major resource variables is converted from its "natural" units into a subjective perception of the social status associated with particular positions on that variable. Thus, we have shown how dollars of income are converted into units of income status, how years of schooling (or age at the completion of schooling) are converted into units of schooling status, and how particular job titles are converted into units of job status.

We found that income status increases in direct proportion to income up to an amount almost half again that of the median family. How dollars of income represent one unit of status of course varies over time, depending on the general level of affluence of the country. Above a point about half again the median income, status increments increase in less than direct proportion to increases in income—they increase in proportion to the square root of the income; thus the higher the income the more rapidly diminishing the status gain for given proportionate increases in income. The one-for-one proportionate increase holds for the approximately 80 percent of the population that has incomes below one and a half times the median.

We found that schooling status increases very rapidly with years of schooling. For example, a 10 percent increase in the age at which an individual completes schooling produces an almost 30 percent increase in schooling status. The overall effect is that high school graduation is worth about 60 percent more than grade school completion, and that college graduation is worth about 60 percent more than high school graduation. As a rough rule of thumb each additional year of schooling seems to increase schooling status by about 16 percent.

There are, of course, no natural units to describe occupations. Using a representative selection of census occupations, we find that occupational status has a wider range than schooling status, because the highest status jobs have higher status than the highest status education (such as a Ph.D. degree). Income status, of course, has the widest range of all.

We find that when Americans make judgments of overall social standing based on knowing an individual's income, schooling, and jobs, income is the most significant factor in their judgments, while schooling and job are of lesser importance (but equal to each other). For a representative sample of profiles, general social standing seems to increase in proportion to roughly the square root of income, whereas it increases in proportion to only about the 0.3 and 0.2 powers of occupational and educational status.

In the last two chapters our focus shifted from status evaluation to the objective distribution and interrelations of these three resources. We dealt with a particular population—men during their thirties, forties, and fifties. We made use of a unique data set that allowed us to estimate a model of the interrelations of schooling, permanent job, and permanent incomes.

This resources model conforms quite well to the model that our respondents seem to carry around in their heads. Respondents believe that there is a considerable amount of social mobility in society—a social free-for-all—and we find that family background characteristics, while accounting for a significant proportion of the variation in schooling, job, and income attainments, did not come close to accounting for even half of their variation.

Our Boston and Kansas City respondents told us that they considered schooling an important "cause" of social standing, but that they thought other events and motivations in people's lives (particularly effort) accounted for more of the variation in job and income success. We find that schooling plays an important role in accounting for occupational and income status, both as a transmitter of family background influences and on its own, but that, indeed, most of the variation even in more permanent or average job and income attainment seems related to contemporaneous factors.

Having developed separate status evaluation and social resources models, we are now in a position to integrate the two and thereby to trace out the effects of social resources on general social standing. We do this by applying the status evaluation model to the resources model for the Panel Study sample of men in mid-career. Thus, we use schooling, five-year average job characteristics, and five-year average income estimates to calculate the relatively permanent schooling, job, and income status of these men and their relatively permanent general social standing.

Our status evaluation model states than an individual's general social standing is a product of the simultaneous evaluation by fellow citizens of the status due the individual's level of schooling, job, and income. Our resources model views an individual's income as a product of job, schooling, and—more remotely—family background. Job resources are a product of schooling and more remotely of family background. Schooling, finally, is a product of family background.

These two models provide answers to two somewhat different questions about an individual's situation. The status evaluation model answers the question: "How is an individual placed by fellow citizens, on the basis of current status characteristics?" The social resources model answers the question "How do individuals come to have their particular social resources characteristics?" When we combine the two models, we are then able to answer the question: "How do individuals come to have their current social status?"[1]

We will examine the combined model in two steps, first attending only to schooling, job, and income resources and later introducing the role of family background. Figure 15-1 presents a diagram using standardized path coefficients to show school, job, and income effects on general social standing. We insert a path coefficient of 1.0 between each resource characteristic and its twin status characteristic, reflecting the "errorless" translation of resource stimuli into status evaluation. The diagram makes explicit the assumption noted earlier that there are no direct effects of the resource characteristics on social standing, that resources achieve their effects only through their effects on the correlated status characteristics. Thus, there is no direct effect of schooling on general social standing, or on job status or on income status. Schooling can affect these three only by its effects on schooling status, job resources, and income resources.

We have observed that income status has the strongest effect on general standing. An increase of one standard deviation in income status (and except at high income levels this is tantamount to saying a one-standard-deviation increase in income itself) increases general standing by 70 percent of a standard deviation. One-standard-deviation increases in schooling and job statuses each produce only a 20 percent increase in general social standing. A simultaneous increase of one standard deviation in all three kinds of status produces approximately a one-standard-deviation increase in social standing.

Now we want to assess the ultimate effects of the three kinds of social resources on general social standing through their direct and indirect effects on the three kinds of statuses. Clearly, income can only affect income status. Job, on the other hand, affects not only job status but also, because it has an effect on income, indirectly affects income status as well. So there are two paths from job to general social standing. In the case of schooling, there are four paths of effect on social standing.

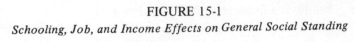

FIGURE 15-1

Schooling, Job, and Income Effects on General Social Standing

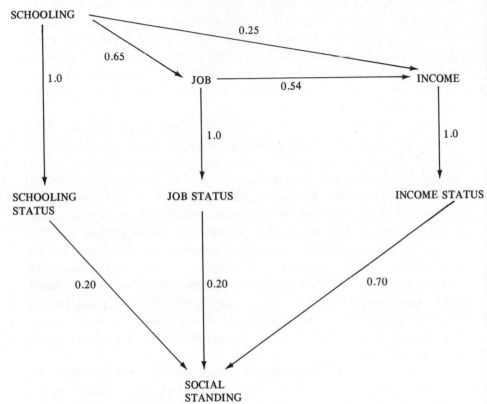

Schooling affects schooling status; it affects job, and through job both job status and income status. It affects income, and thus income status. Thus, the total effect of schooling resources on general social standing is a summing up of these four different kinds of effects. Similarly, the total effect of job resources on social standing is a summing up of their effects on job status and their second-hand effects on income status.

When we judged the relative importance of the three status variables, we noted that income status seemed the most important. Now when we look at the effects of the three kinds of resources, however, we get quite a different picture. Although the direct effects of schooling and job (about 0.2) are much inferior to those of income (0.7), their total effects come much closer. The total effect of schooling on general social standing is actually greater than the total effect of income (0.75 versus 0.7), and the total effect of job resources (0.58) comes close to that of income. Thus, a one-standard-deviation increase in schooling resources produces a total effect of 75 percent of a standard deviation's increase in social standing. That total effect is compounded of a 0.2-standard deviation (SD) increase in general social standing through schooling status, a 0.11 increase in general social standing through job status, and a whopping 0.42 SD increase through income status. Similarly, the 0.58 total effect of job resources on general social standing is composed of a 0.2 SD effect on job status and a 0.38 SD increase via income status.

Saying that income is the most important factor in general social standing is to describe what people rely on in arriving at their judgments about an individual's general social standing. It is not the same as saying that income is the most important cause of an individual's social standing. The difference between the relative role of these three characteristics as "cause" and "component" of general social standing is highlighted by a decomposition of the sources of variance in general social standing. Table 15-1 presents such a decomposition. In Panel A we decompose the components of the variance of general social standing without taking into account the role of family background. We have observed that some 68 percent of the variance in general social standing is accounted for by income status and the remainder of the variance more or less equally by income and job status. In the table, we show the proportion of variance accounted for by each of the three resources through each of the three status variables. Thus, schooling resources account for all of the variance in general social standing accounted for by schooling status—15 percent. But, in addition, schooling resources account for 10 percent of the variance through job status and 33 percent of the variance accounted for through income status, for a total of 58 percent of the variance in general social standing. Job resources account for the balance of the 17 percent of the variance accounted for by job status (7 percent), and there is an additional 12 percent of the variance accounted for by the effect of job resources on income status, making a total of 19 percent. Income contributes the remaining 23 percent of the variance in social standing by its effect on income status independent of that part of income resources accounted for by schooling and job resources. Thus, our impression that income is the most important and schooling the least is exactly reversed. Now schooling resources seem the most important.

We have a paradox. Income is the most important *component* of general social standing, but schooling is the most important *cause*. But this paradox is more seeming than real. In the first case, we are focusing on the factors that people use in judging an individual's social standing, and in the second we are focusing on the relative role of different kinds of resources in producing the social standing an individual comes to have. The paradox is resolved when we observe that schooling is as important as it is because it has a strong effect on income resources, which in turn have an effect on income status. We note that over half of the total contribution of schooling resources to the variance of general social standing comes from the contribution of schooling to income status.

TABLE 15-1

Proportion of Variance in General Status Accounted for by Four Resources as Transmitted by Three Kinds of Status Evaluations

Source of Status Evaluation	Family Background Resources (%)	Schooling Resources (%)	Job Resources (%)	Income Resources (%)	Total (%)
A. *Without Controlling for Family Background*					
Schooling status	–	15	–	–	15
Job status	–	10	7	–	17
Income status	–	33	12	23	68
Total		58	19	23	100
B. *Controlling for Family Background*					
Schooling status	7	8	–	–	15
Job status	7	4	6	–	17
Income status	23	12	10	23	68
Total	37	24	16	23	100

Many researchers have shown that we get a very misleading understanding of the effects of schooling on adult position if we do not control for family background. Therefore, let us move on to a four-resources model in which we take explicit account of family background. This model is diagrammed in Figure 15-2. We have simplified the model by developing one omnibus measure of family background advantage that combines family socio-economic background, number of siblings, race, and the kind of community in which the respondent grew up. (One could, of course, work out a more elaborate model in which each of these is treated separately, as they were in the previous chapter, but such a model is more complex than we really need at this point.) Direct and indirect effects of our four resources on the three kinds of status and on general social standing are presented in Table 15-2. Family background

FIGURE 15-2

Family Background, Schooling, and Adult Resource Effects on Social Standing

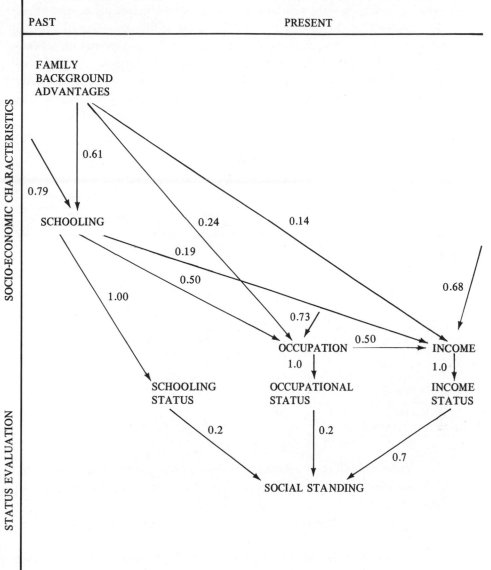

has a total effect on general social standing of 0.61. That is, a one-standard-deviation increase in family background advantages increases social standing by 0.61 standard deviation. The channeling of that effect through the three kinds of status breaks down as follows—0.12 SD of this effect is accomplished through the effect of family background on schooling status, 0.11 SD of the effect proceeds from job status, and 0.38 SD of the effect proceeds from income status. This latter effect is not primarily a direct effect (only 0.10 SD is) but is rather a result of the transmitted effects of family background on income through schooling and, to a lesser extent, job resources.

TABLE 15-2

Effects of Resources on Status Evaluations

		Effect via			
Status	Total Effect of Resource	Schooling Resources	Job Resources	Income Resources	Direct
Schooling					
Family Background	.61				.61
Job					
Family Background	.55	.31			.24
Schooling	.50	–			.50
Income					
Family Background	.53	.27	.12		.14
Schooling	.44	–	.25		.19
Job	.50	–	–		.50
General					
Family Background	.61	.37	.14	.10	–
Schooling	.61	–	.28	.13	.20
Job	.55	–	–	.35	.20
Income	.70	–	–	–	.70

The total effect of schooling resources on general social standing, once we control for family background, drops from 0.755 to 0.610. The total effect of job resources is not much affected by the addition of family background advantages to our model, nor of course is the total effect of income.

A picture of the relative importance of these variables in accounting for the variance in general social standing or social class is perhaps best captured by Panel B of Table 15-1. There we find that the independent contribution of schooling resources to the variance of general social standing is much reduced by the inclusion of the measure of family background resources. Family background accounts for 37 percent of the variance in general social standing. Schooling and job statuses each transmit 7 percent of this effect, leaving 23 percent transmitted by the various paths from family background to income and income status. Thus, the primary impact of family background resources on general social standing comes through its effect ultimately on income status.

The independent contribution of schooling is reduced from 58 percent of the variance to 24 percent of the variance now, but it is still as important a cause of an individual's general social standing as is income. As with family background, the most important effect of schooling resources is on income status rather than on schooling status or on job status.

When we focus on the past we see that some 61 percent of the variance in these men's general social standing was settled by the time they entered the launch phase of their careers. The past accounts for all of the effect of schooling status (15 percent), for most of the effect of job status (11 percent), and for slightly over half of the effect of income status (35 percent).

Job mobility up or down from the status platform established by family background and schooling resources adds another 16 percent to the explanation of the variance in these men's general social standing. Thus we see that some three-quarters of social standing variance is accounted for by non-income resources, even though the judgments made by people in their placement of individuals rely primarily on their information about an individual's income—or, more broadly, standard of living. Understanding why individuals are placed where they are by their society requires that we look primarily at income-related factors and secondarily at jobs and schooling. Understanding how particular individuals end up with the general social standing that they have requires that we pay particular attention to their family background and their schooling.

We believe that our analysis based on the Panel Study of Income Dynamics data still seriously underestimates the effect of family background on these men's present social class or social standing. A correlation between family background and present social standing of 0.70 to 0.75 is probably closer to the truth than our 0.61. A more accurate measurement of family background would probably decrease somewhat the effect of schooling resources on later resources and, through them, on general social standing. Our guess is that this better measurement would only marginally reduce the effects of job and income, however.

Our estimate of the combined effect of family background and schooling on general social standing is probably only slightly low; an increased effect of family background would be compensated for by a reduced effect of schooling so that the combined explanatory power of the two for accounting for social standing might increase no more than from our 61 percent to around 65 percent. That is to say, we believe that about 65 percent of the variance in the social standing that men have in their mid-career periods can be accounted for by resources accumulated at the time they begin their work careers—a one-standard-deviation increase or decrease in the combined advantages of family background and schooling would be associated with an approximately 80 percent increase or decrease in mid-career social standing, a powerful effect indeed.

Even so, a society characterized by this degree of social inheritance plus the effect of schooling would by no means be one in which there is not a great deal of movement during adult life. The "social free-for-all" that our respondents are so fond of, their images of considerable up-and-down movement from the status platform of the beginning of the work career, are consistent with the variance still to be explained after taking family background and schooling into account. Our figure of 65 percent of the variance accounted for by the end of the launch period still means that two random men with the same family background and schooling would be expected to be about 0.6 SD apart on general social standing. That much of a dispersion in general social standing is equivalent to the distance between being in the middle of our Middle-American group and being a marginal member of the Upper-American group, or to the difference between being an average person in the traditional working class—a person who is at the just-getting-along point—and being a marginal member of the traditional lower-middle class.

We have seen in Chapter 12 that our respondents have both lively and highly moralistic ideas about what accounts for these differences in the adult social standing of persons who start their careers in similar stations. Thus we have seen the emphasis that respondents place on the role of effort, which eventually may affect job and income statuses favorably, and on the contrary, on the effects of laziness and personal pathology (such as alcoholism) that are expected to have deleterious consequences.

Further research would be needed to match more precisely the actual connections between resources and general social status as mapped in this chapter with Americans' perceptions of how much these resources are intercorrelated. Such an exploration of their "ethno-sociology" would allow us to move from our relatively qualitative characterization of the public's picture of how the stratification system operates to a more quantitative one, one that could produce a diagram like Figure 15-2 representing the public's perception of the effects of various resources on later resources in the socio-economic life career. For now, all we can say is that the integrated resources/status evaluation diagram of Figure 15-2 does not glaringly contradict the impressions that most of our respondents seem to have about how the stratification of life chances operates in American society.

The status evaluation model that we have developed tells us how the distribution of social standing can stay relatively unchanged even though (in at least two of the components) there are major changes in resource levels. We have seen that people seem to be quite good at discounting increases in average income so that they reproduce at each time basically the same distribution of income statuses, each income status unit costing more each year as average incomes increase. No wonder our respondents have the sense that the standard of living has somehow not increased nearly so fast as has nominal, or even constant dollar, income.

Much the same kind of discounting process probably operates with respect to schooling. (But as we have discussed in Chapter 4, the time period in which estimates of schooling status have been collected does not allow us to estimate an equation for schooling status that makes use of relative schooling differences.) On the assumption that there is that kind of stability, we have argued that there has probably been a quite marked discounting of the status value of given levels of schooling over the past thirty years and have suggested that there is likely to be a continued, though not as dramatic, discounting over the next thirty years.

All of the research on occupational standing suggests that the prestige of almost all occupations has stayed roughly the same over the past half century. That may be true of occupations judged simply by their titles, but both our qualitative and quantitative data would suggest that a slow process of change may be going on as a result of relational changes in wages—some occupations gaining, others losing. To the extent that these changes are known, they should bring about a change in the social standing attributed to occupations. They clearly produce a change in average social standing in those occupations. One could estimate the extent to which such changes have taken place given reasonably detailed data on the distribution of income within occupations.

Taking all of this together, the implication of the model developed above is that the distribution of general social standing will not change more than very marginally in the foreseeable future. Most discussions of likely developments in inequality of income distribution suggest not much change on that score. This means that inequality of income status can be expected to remain the same. We believe that people are quite adept at discounting increases in schooling, so that in all probability the distribution of educational status as opposed to years of education will change only very slightly in the remainder of this century. Assuming that the occupational distribution as it relates to status considerations does not change very much, then we would expect no significant change in the variance of occupational status. The variance of general social standing, then, should remain at about the same level it is today. (We would feel much better about such a prediction had we measured a wider range of resources by taking into account the fact that family income is increasingly produced not just by male breadwinners but also by women, either in the role of wives or as sole household heads, and the increasing role of public transfers.)

How do our respondents think about the question of likely evolutions of the social classes and of the social standing distribution? We turn to this issue, and to a discussion of how social science research on stratification issues should evolve, in the chapters that follow.

PART IV

A CHANGING

CLASS SYSTEM?

CHAPTER 16

Public Images of Change

THIS CHAPTER is constructed around responses of people in Boston and Kansas City to two research issues: Is social class less important, or more important, than it used to be? and What changes in social class do Americans want in the future? An evaluative, as well as a predictive, view of the status system emerged from these responses. Thus in this chapter we offer not merely prescriptions for change, but evaluations of the past and present. The faults Americans find in the social structure, as it is at the moment, are discussed; so too do we describe what they find satisfactory about it—or, if not fully satisfactory, then at worst ineradicable. Predictions of change—and hopes for change—are predicated upon these evaluations of what is good and bad, what is changeable and what is not, and what should not be changed.

What we have to say in this chapter also represents a continuation of themes from Chapter 12, "Images of Opportunity and Social Mobility." For, as it turns out, a major proof advanced by our sample for the impression that social class is less important is how commonplace an experience social mobility has been for the present generation of adults. The idea is that if class—in the old-fashioned sense of a very conscious, rigid placement of people—were still so important, mobility could not have occurred in such volume. As for the future, a major recommendation from the people of Boston and Kansas City is that the opportunities for social mobility be broadened beyond their present dimension.

Ultimately, as we proceed through our analysis, what becomes clear is this: social mobility—both the possibility of it and the fact of it—is what Americans like best about the nation's status system. Social mobility is given much of the credit for our individual and collective high standards of living. The opportunity for change in status—and the reality of its frequent occurrence—is regarded as the incentive for invention and productivity.

Is Class Less Important Than It Used To Be?

Among the several general questions about American life that we asked in our survey, few elicited any higher level of agreement in response than this: "Do you think social class is getting more important or less important in America these days than it used to be?" Well over two-thirds of our respondents—including nearly 90 percent of those under thirty years of age—pronounced a verdict of "less important." Elation and enthusiasm marked the response of this solid majority. Not very many in the sample took the opposite position that class is getting "more important," and the few who did seemed definitely angry about it. A much larger group, numbering just over 20 percent, took the middle position that "class is as important as ever." They were consistent (consistently cynical, that is) in all their answers to questions about change. To each such question they responded, in fact or in effect, "Today and yesterday are the same." To this question in particular, the spirit of their reply was, "We're still a competitive society; people are still trying to get ahead of the next person; and if that ever changes, it won't be America anymore."

The most persuasive proof to our Boston and Kansas City respondents that class is less important than it used to be is the social mobility they witnessed in the first twenty-five years after World War II. That so many Americans appear to have moved up, down, and away from the class they originated in during those years seems to demonstrate that "class doesn't count for so much as it did when our parents were young." Serving this image of change is a belief, uncertain in source, that Americans in previous generations did not escape their family backgrounds so often, that social position was far more a born-into-it-die-out-of-it matter. That, in extreme form, is what Americans consider a "true class system": a rigid society where class membership is "fixed by birth." This is the definition of class and the image of the American past that so many of our respondents had in mind when they said that "we don't have social classes like that anymore," that "class based on birth is less important nowadays."

All kinds of barriers to social mobility—to leaving the class of one's origin—are believed to have fallen in the last thirty years. Everything seems more open than before to all comers regardless of family background—jobs, schools, neighborhoods, private clubs, and personal friendships. Among these changes, the end of job discrimination by race and minority was given most attention by our respondents. (A Boston businessman, almost unable to believe the results, illustrated them in this fashion: "You should see the U.N. I have working for me . . . blacks, Indians, Puerto Ricans, you name it! . . . That couldn't have happened years ago.")

Decline in prejudice related to ancestry and religion was another popular case in point. (A Boston woman whose parents had emigrated from Italy said, "People don't hold so much by ethnic background any more. . . . When my parents came here, they still had religious distinctions.") Opening up higher education "through scholarships to children of all races and classes" was a third point. Time and again our respondents expressed the belief that "a person now can get however much education he wants, no matter whether his parents are poor or in minorities." What all these changes have accomplished, as perceived by some of our sample members, is that "people are now accepted on their merit—you're hired regardless of which class you came from if you can do the work." Previously, according to this interpretation of American history, "there was a class status involved in obtaining lots of jobs. . . . Background and family were more controlling of what people were allowed to do."

Changes in income distribution in the post-war years, especially changes in the comparative standing of occupational groups, are believed to have played another of the major roles in this socio-historical drama. Our Boston and Kansas City respondents illustrated the contribution of these changes with comments like this: "Incomes are evening out—there isn't such a difference between people in various occupations as there used to be"; "With trade union people making up to $35,000 a year, it is difficult to maintain a frozen sense of classes"; and "Working class is no longer synonymous with lower income and lower status—now it's part of the middle." Implicit here are a series of related assumptions: first, that in previous eras there was a marked differential between blue-collar workers and white-collar workers in income level; second, that as a result of labor union activities, this differential had largely ceased to exist in any predictable fashion as of the 1970s; third, that blue-collar workers used to be thought of as belonging to a different social class than white-collar workers, with the aforementioned income differential the prime, or sole, factor behind the differentiation; and fourth, that with the disappearance of the income differential there are no longer any grounds for putting blue-collar workers into one class and white-collar workers into another. Finally, there is the assumption, this time only partially related to the above, that whenever you combine two classes into one, the importance of class is resultingly diminished. It is as if, by throwing away a social dividing line, you reduce the incidence of snobbery.

Important beyond the imagined equalization of blue-collar and white-collar is a conviction that more Americans than ever before are included now in the middle-income, middle-class category; further, that the standard of living associated with this position is more comfortable compared to the life of upper-income Americans than was ever the case in eras past. A Middle American in Boston pronounced this verdict in this fashion: "Until recently the affluent people had access to more material things, but these things are more widely available now. More people are making it comfortably." One in Kansas City said, "The middle class is getting more and more wealthy—I think we're almost meeting the upper class, or maybe they're coming down toward us." Other Middle Americans illustrated the spread of comfortable living with examples of this order: "People who don't have much education and just ordinary jobs can buy homes in the suburbs"; "The things our parents considered status symbols, like trips to Europe, are now available to everyone"; and "There are more cars now, and everybody has television and most of the automatic appliances. The standard of living is so much better for most people than it used to be." The old dichotomy of "haves *versus* have-nots" seems to have moved down in its reference to a point where Lower Americans alone are the true "have-nots." With everybody else counting themselves relatively among the "haves," it may just be that "class lines are disappearing," as several Middle Bostonians and Kansas Citians proclaimed.

This brings us to yet another widely cited sign that class is less important: to wit, that not only do the upper classes seem less distant from the middle than in years past, but also (a) their membership is no longer so interesting to the ordinary citizen and (b) individually they are not deemed so worthy of respect and adulation. A Boston woman in her middle 50s, a perfect example of the type called "lace-curtain Irish" in that city, gave succinct perspective to this when she told us, "My mother was up on Boston Society—she knew all the names, watched them from afar . . . but my sister and I have never been interested in that. I couldn't name a one."

Other women of Middle-American standing, in Kansas City as well as Boston, spoke similarly of themselves as "not interested in following the doings of society people," managing to suggest that "we're getting away from that, from setting upper-income people aside from others." Several applied this more broadly to entertainment-world celebrities, saying, "When I was young the movie stars were idols. Now nobody even cares." Such protestations of disinterest, that nobody cares, must be taken with a grain of salt even though a measure of truth is granted. After all, the nation's major media—newspapers, magazines, and television—still treat the trials and triumphs of celebrities as of consuming public interest, hardly less now than thirty or fifty years ago. The difference seems to lie not so much in the level of attention as in attitudes. Persons of purely local upper-class status, however, are almost certainly not read about so avidly as formerly. There is very little now of awe and worship in the way Americans look at these people on top. More nearly they are followed with a spirit of detached amusement; the approach has much in it of acquiring the coin of conversation, of "keeping up" so as not to be left out of what "people are talking about." Accompanying this is a heavy dose of skepticism that the important and rich are all that much more deserving and honorable or happy than the average man; and especially is such an attitude displayed toward politicians and business-men. (Entertainers have always been of dubious propriety, which image has enhanced their fascination.) As often as not, our respondents spoke with venom and deprecation of these figures from the high worlds of money and politics, accusing them of "having gotten much of what they have illegally" and/or "scheming to beat someone else out of the top, so they can get in." Over and over the judgment was rendered, "To me, they have no class."

How all this relates to the perception that class is less important is that for many people class in its richest meaning refers to the classiness of a society's classiest, uppermost citizens. There is a deep yearning in the public for those occupying the summit positions to be reckoned the most excellent, the most admirable, of the population—indeed, for them to be aristocrats, above the requirement of ambition; inherently, ineluc-tably superior. When Americans begin saying—as did so many in our sample—that "the so-called upper class is not being looked on as superior people like they used to be," it follows that soon they will be saying "class is in decline." The equation is clear: class becomes less important when-ever there is less of it at the top. Traces of disappointment were registered by our respondents that such a change would seem to have occurred, that "there isn't much aristocracy left," and that aristocrats, such as they still exist, may not be quite so aristocratic. A Boston woman said wistfully:

"The rich today aren't like the Saltonstalls used to be." And a Kansas City man said, also half in sorrow: "The people you used to think were marvelous aren't marvelous anymore."

Finally, a significant portion of our sample from all status levels and age groups expressed the belief that, individually and collectively, Americans had become less class conscious in the last decade or so. People of upper status pointed to relaxation in dress codes and greater tolerance for diverse behavioral standards as illustrations of this proposition. A Kansas City woman described the transition quite personally: "Entertaining is a lot more casual, at least in our circle. You don't dress for dinner or drag out your silver; often as not, you wear slacks." Others spoke more generally of increasing freedom in Upper-American life styles, saying: "We have changed so much in dress and manner that there are no set rules for anything anymore"; "There's a great deal less social pressure—we have more options on how we wish to spend our time and money"; "We're not so bound by convention; attitudes are so much more relaxed"; and "There are so many variations and so many exceptions— just look at the more flexible attitudes toward deviants, like the artists." At the Middle-American level the change was explained more simply, characterized in these terms: "There's not so much keeping up with the Joneses"; "You never hear talk of class anymore"; "Social standing doesn't mean as much"; and "People are more democratic today."

It was young Americans of all status levels who took credit (and were given it by their elders) for the most dramatic instances of disappearing class consciousness. (Our survey, it must be remembered, was conducted in Boston in 1971 and Kansas City in 1972, when the "youth revolution" was at its peak.) Almost to a person, the Boston-area graduate students and college-dropouts in our sample proclaimed themselves "totally disinterested in class." Further, they boasted, "none of the people I know consider class seriously—they laugh at it." Concluding, they predicted: "Class distinctions are not what the people of my generation will base their lives on." Our other younger respondents in Boston and Kansas City, though not inclined to such rhetorical extremes, nevertheless usually characterized themselves as "not as much interested in social standing as people of my parents' generation." Many of our older sample members professed themselves "bewildered at the young people we have today" and, not entirely sure it was a good sign, said, "It's certain that *they're* not concerned with social class." More than a few, though, were congratulatory. A woman in Boston euphorically exclaimed, "Look at our youth, how free of snobbery they seem to be!"

How Should the Social System Change?

No question in our survey so fully tapped the gamut of public feelings about differences in status as this one: "What sort of changes in social class in America would you like to see in the future, and why those?" At one extreme of response were vituperative attacks like these: "Social class is the dirtiest thing I have ever heard of"; "It's rubbish"; "It's all hogwash"; and "It's totally wrong—I've always resented it." At the other extreme were ringing endorsements: "It's a challenge to any red-blooded American," and "Having an upper class gives the middle classes something to strive for." In between were all manner of more cautious postures, some registering approval, others disapproval. Prescriptions for change varied accordingly. To the one side were advocacies that "social class should be exterminated." To the other were pronouncements that "no change is needed—it's fine the way it is." Toward the middle were proposals for income redistribution and/or for further reduction of barriers to social mobility; some of these were quite modest in their intended impact, others definitely substantial. The essential truth to grasp is that prescription always followed from diagnosis, that changes proposed in social class always reflected the ills or wrongs observed.

The wrong most frequently diagnosed in the present system is that too many Americans take differences in income and ancestry as a chance to judge—and to treat—other members of the society as less than equals, or that "some people think they are better than others just because they have more money or because their skin is white." Every prescription for change that followed from this diagnosis was in one fashion or another to this effect: America should be a land of equal standing for all (except, perhaps, for those of less-than-satisfactory character). Some respondents made this point by calling for outright elimination of social class and all associated forms of interpersonal inequality, thus:

> "There shouldn't be such a thing as social class. Everybody has the right to be treated the same."

> "Social class as a way of treating others should be eradicated. People should be treated equally."

> "I say we are all created equal, and we are not supposed to think we are better than the next person. . . . I would like to see social classes done away with."

"We should have a breakdown of social class. We should treat everybody as equal. We wouldn't have the struggle between classes then. We would all have the same goals."

"I would like to see everyone accepted as equal, period. . . . Social class is really just a state of mind. It has no right to be."

Others proposed that we start judging people by "what they are, not for what they earn," or, more broadly, that "we should start accepting people for themselves, as fellow human beings":

"I think everyone should be judged as a person, not by his job or how much money he has. Judging that way is the main thing wrong now."

"There should be less emphasis on making money. We should have more acceptance of people, not what they have in material things."

"We should evaluate each person for his intrinsic value, rather than for his income or color."

"We should take a man for what he is—as a person—not for what he has. Take people as you find them. God made us all."

A few elevated character to the final criterion for status:

"There are good people and bad ones in every class. That is how people should be judged, not by their money."

"A man should be classed for his respectability and honesty. . . . The only classes I believe in are two—the good and the bad."

And the largest number urged a unification of all Americans into one class, of "everyone getting along with everyone else, regardless of the income difference":

"I hope the time will come when everyone will get along as one class without regard for race, creed, and color, and all these extraneous things like income and material well-being."

"The main thing is that everyone should learn to love everyone else . . . no class distinctions, no race distinctions."

"I'd like to see better understanding, better personal relationships, with people learning to get along with one another—which is a big order."

These prescriptions for change represent a species of millennial thinking in that the prescribers hope for, and even seem to foresee the possibility of, a social order free from the foibles and follies of mortal personalities. One-third of the people we interviewed in Boston and Kansas City voiced these aspirations. More women did so than men. More were from the lower half of the social ladder than from the upper half. Almost equal portions of young, middle-aged, and old were represented in this advocacy. Astonishingly, none of this third of our sample proposed any reduction in economic inequality. The entire thrust of their prescribed change was toward reputational equality, income differences notwithstanding.

Almost all of the advocacy for a classless future in the United States was found in this one-third of our sample. An additional 2 percent of our respondents proposed that we achieve classlessness through making everyone equal in economic standing. Another 6 percent suggested a modified leveling of the income differential, but in so doing they recommended nothing approaching either total equality or eradication of social classes. So, of the "enemies" of class in our sample, it can be said that most were pietists, not pragmatists, in their opposition. They put forth no programs to advance their cause, only preachments. They hoped for revelation, not revolution.

A quite opposite view on the possibility or desirability of change in social class was taken by another sizeable group in our sample, in this instance approximately one-fifth of the total. In this opposite posture, hierarchy is a veritable "law of life." Societies are said to require leaders and followers—"all equals wouldn't work." As a Kansas City man put it, "You can't have everyone middle or upper class—there would be too many chiefs and no Indians." Further, by this accounting, differences in income are not only inevitable but positively beneficial—if, that is, they are accompanied by the possibility of status mobility. When this is the case, income differences motivate a society's individual members to work hard and try to get ahead. The cumulative result of this individual effort at status advance is that the whole society's standard of living—speaking of it now as an Everyman average—is pushed ever higher. An inherent human tendency toward laziness has been curbed. The American social class system of reward for effort and punishment for its lack, of leaders and followers determined by talent and energy, is thus—by this interpretation of societal purpose and human nature—the best yet devised. That individual Americans do not treat one another or judge each other as social equals is defined as a "natural" by-product of the system, hence nothing to be condemned or changed. After all, as a Bostonian said, "When you have a range in salaries and money, you are going to have social classes."

This proposition that the present system of status and income distribution needs no restructuring was most commonly put forth by the older members of our sample; those under thirty years of age almost totally adjured it. Men were somewhat more often its adherents than women, Middle Americans more commonly than either Lower or Upper.

Much of its appeal is that it seems the wisdom of the ages, a truth for all times, something that always holds. Over and over the respondents who espoused it established this point in their arguments: "There'll always be a pecking order," "The system has always been like it is," "The Bible says the poor will always be with us," and "Social class will always be important."

Among the programmatic changes advanced by our respondents, the most widely endorsed was a reduction to the vanishing point in whatever restrictions to social mobility may still exist, be they restrictions based on race or religion or class of origin. All told, 20 percent of our respondents set this forth as a change in social class they would like to see in the future, some as their sole suggestion, and others as a secondary proposal. Whites in Boston and Kansas City suggested this in almost as high proportion as blacks, and among both races, upper-status respondents proposed it relatively more often than lower. The Upper Americans who advocated this change centered their attention on the idea that "more mobility gives more chances for self-fulfillment to all people"; they also professed eagerness to "get rid of our racial stress and prejudice." Middle Americans placed special emphasis on "having the same educational opportunities for everyone," including "a college education for all students who want it but whose parents can't afford it." Working-class respondents whose parents had suffered handicaps of ethnic origin urged that "the melting pot should work better; democracy should be workable for more people." Black respondents hoped for "an absence of racial discrimination," saying "it would make for a much more flowing society."

That higher-status Americans should so favor this particular change —broadening of opportunities—and that it should be generally the most popular of proposed programs, should come as no surprise, since after all it is an essentially conservative idea, not altering the status quo in any profound way. No reduction in inequality of results is proposed, only a reduction in inequality of initial opportunity. The hierarchy is to be retained without restructuring. Only the total volume of social mobility is to be altered, and "more mobility in both directions" is expected. Implicitly, the purpose of this increase in mobility is getting the right people into the right places on the social ladder—that is, the place each person deserves by his or her ability to contribute to the nation's standard of living and/or what can be earned by efforts toward that end. Explicitly, the purpose is elimination of the frustration and injustices that result from a closed system or from special instances of closure, as in racial discrimination. As a Boston man explained, "Broader opportunities, without restrictions on degree of achievement by any social barriers, would increase the stability of society. . . . For the individuals involved, it would lessen pressures." In sum, this particular change has much to recommend it, pleasing many different tastes. It promises (depending on what a person cares most about) an increase in domestic tranquility, a more democratic society, a more effortocratic reward structrue, and/or a more meritocratic social positioning.

The only other programmatic change to command the interest of more than 15 percent of our sample was getting rid of poverty. Nearly half as many people opposed this, however, as favored it. Anything more serious in the way of redistributive schemes found very little advocacy. A mere 2 percent went so far as to urge near-total equalization of income, and this 2 percent came entirely from one population sub-group, Boston's radicalized young. A somewhat larger, though still insignificant, portion of respondents—6 percent, as mentioned earlier—proposed other, less extreme forms of economic leveling. Typically these were on the modest side, as in this example: "I would like to get a more or less balanced type of thing; we should reduce the income difference between the extremes." In another instance the wish was phrased like this: "Maybe we should have fewer very well-to-do people and fewer people who can just barely make a living. . . . That means a larger middle class, but I think that would be more fair for everyone concerned." Only a few respondents wanted to take substantial amounts of money away from the rich. Clearly, leveling from the bottom up—that is, reducing the extent of poverty—is more comfortably advocated by the typical American than leveling from the top down. Truly remarkable, in fact, is how little of its money or position Upper America is urged to give up, how rarely a request for real sacrifice is voiced.

Opposition to the elimination of poverty is largely silent. When put into words it is usually masked in such phrases as, "Only those who are willing to work should be given a living wage." Hardly anyone says out loud that poverty should be kept around as a punishment for those who refuse employment. Almost always left unstated is what level of living should be allowed those unwilling to work. There is no question, however, that most Americans believe there must be a recognizable differential in standard of living between the idle and the employed. The issue of just how great this differential should be is a thorny one, and usually it is evaded.

One way of evading it is to prescribe work as the proper punishment for people with tendencies to idleness. This is what many a Bostonian and Kansas Citian in our sample did, in effect, when the change in social class they urged was that "anyone on welfare who's able to work should be put to work, whether it be fixing roads or whatever needs to be done and is available." Especially did working-class men and women advocate this change. A favorite cry among them was, "Get the free-loaders off of relief and into jobs." From the standpoint of its advocates, this idea of everybody working and off relief has two advantages: it justifies "a living wage" for virtually all Americans—all those working, that is—and it reduces the tax burden, since the only citizens left on welfare are children and the totally disabled.

In the final analysis, the deepest and broadest source of opposition to a major change in the American class system, and especially to the elimination of a lowest class, derives from devotion to the effortocratic ideal. A middle-status man in Kansas City summed it up: "No one should get a free ride through life."

CHAPTER 17

Social Capital
and Social Consumption

IN THIS CHAPTER we pull together the various threads followed in the previous chapters, suggesting first an integration of the perspectives elaborated there, and then, on the basis of that integration, outlining what seem to us some of the dominant issues in stratification research and theory for the coming decade.

Social resources are to be understood as the result of an individual's participation in the struggle within society for the control of whatever surplus the society produces. That is, social resources represent the power the individual is able to bring to bear in the "battle of man with man" in society. The phrase is Max Weber's, used to characterize a market economy but readily generalized to characterize the kind of mixed economy called the welfare state (or any other kind of state, for that matter). It is only necessary to understand that the economy encompasses governmental operation also and that the rewards struggled for are not solely to be counted in terms of amounts of goods and services received. Weber's characterization was as follows:

> In a market economy every form of rational calculation . . . is oriented to expectations of prices and their changes as they are determined by the conflict of interest in bargaining and competition and the resolution of these conflicts. . . . No economic system can directly translate subjective "feelings of need" into effective demand, that is, into demand which needs to be taken into account and satisfied through the production of goods. . . . A need may fail to be satisfied not only when an individual's own demand for other goods takes precedence, but also when the greater purchasing power of others for *all* types of goods prevails. Thus the fact

that the battle of man against man on the market is an essential condition
for the existence of rational money accounting further implies that the
outcome of the economic process is decisively influenced by the ability of
persons who are more plentifully supplied with money to outbid
others. . . . Money prices are the product of conflicts of interests and of
compromises; they thus result from power constellations. Money is not a
mere "voucher for unspecified utilities". . . [it is] primarily a weapon in
this battle, and prices are expressions of the battle; they are instruments
of calculation only as estimated quantifications of relative chances in this
battle of interests [Weber (1968), pp. 92f., quoted in Marcus (1975),
pp. 59f.].

Money is one and by far the most important counter in the battle,
but there are others ranging from the politician's headlines to respect or
lack of it accorded to the welfare mother by caretakers. The long-term
capacity of the individual for a given level of winnings in this battle we
can term *social capital*. Winnings in a given period of time represent
social income for that period (Becker, 1975). Social capital in turn
represents some combination of an individual's economic and social
wealth. (If the term *human capital* did not already have an established,
and much narrower meaning it would be preferable to social capital for
our purposes.)

One can look at individuals or families as engaged in a productive
enterprise designed to combine resources (social capital), time, and labor
to produce a product we will call *social consumption*, that is, the total
pattern of rewarding activities in which the individual or family engages.
Our research suggests that different bundles of the social consumption
product are valued differently by representative members of the society.
When people rank individuals they rank them in terms of the value of
their social consumption product, or at least they would if they were
intimately enough acquainted with the individual or family.

Since in fact we are intimately acquainted with only a few people
(and those generally are persons who are roughly equal to us in status),
the rankings of individuals in society are done not so much in terms of
their social consumption products as in terms of the resources for social
consumption that the individual or family might reasonably be expected
to possess. The operation an individual ranker performs is essentially
that of imagining the social consumption product that could be produced
by a representative person who possessed the resources that a given
individual or family is thought to possess.

In making these rankings, we inevitably use clues about persons,
since we never know everything that may be relevant about them.
Important empirical questions for the sociology of stratification are what

clues about persons are most salient and how much weight different kinds of clues have in the judgments that people make.

What we have said so far is that general social standing (S_g) in the eyes of other members of a society is a function of an individual's social consumption product (SC_p), that is, of the individual's participation in activities differentially valued by members of the society.

$$S_g = a(SC_p)$$

(S_g is a very close neighbor to the economist's utility.)

These are activities that can be carried out alone or with others; they can involve no apparent or immediate expenditures of economic resources; or a major component may involve the expenditure of money. Almost all activities, however, require some combination of economic and non-economic resources.

Since the product of social consumption is not readily observable except by persons who are intimates and who are also around a lot, most judgments about social standing are based on conceptions of the normal social consumption product an individual can achieve with a given level of resources, since social consumption product (SC_p) is a function of social consumption resources (SC_r).

$$SC_p = b(SC_r)$$

Making the appropriate substitutions, we arrive at social standing as a function of social consumption resources.

$$S_g = c(SC_r)$$

But what are social consumption resources and what are their relative weights? We can conveniently divide social consumption resources into two types: economic resources that produce a stream of income that in turn can be used in combination with non-economic resources, time (T), and energy (E) to produce a social consumption product and other, social. resources. If we call the first resource *economic wealth* (EW)—understanding that to mean some summation of human capital, physical wealth, and access to credit—perhaps we are entitled to call the residual resource *social wealth* (SW).

$$SC_r = d(EW, SW, T, E)$$

We might even be willing to draw analogies to the economic capital realm by saying that there are some aspects of social wealth that are permanent once conferred (such as belonging to a given race, being a Nobel prize winner, or being a known ex-convict), while other aspects of social wealth, like human capital, can be actualized only through the expenditure of energy and thought (the people one knows, personal charm, developed leisure skills, and tastes).

From living in the society, its members have an understanding of how much social consumption product can normally be gained from a given set of social consumption resources. If a member were to be particularly refined about social status judgments (refined at a level that involves very detailed knowledge of individuals' life styles), that member would undoubtedly observe that some individuals and families get more out of a given set of resources than others because of differences in the amount and efficiency of their "social consumption labor." Among persons who know each other well, part of their images of one another has to do with how successful they are at translating their resources into social consumption. Pursuing this line of speculation, one would undoubtedly arrive at the point where one problem of interest in social stratification study would be that of the differing tradeoffs individuals make between those activities more or less broadly valued in society, and other more highly individual pursuits that, while they may prove gratifying, are regarded as having either no implications for social consumption or negative implications. Some forms of deviant behavior, for example, consume resources but produce a negative product—like alcoholism or compulsive gambling.

If we wish to focus on social consumption, therefore, we may take the distribution of economic and social wealth as given and trace out its uses by individuals and families in the society. Similarly, we may try to chart the connections that members of the society make between given patterns of social consumption resources or social consumption products and the social standing that they assign to persons who possess those resources, or who participate in the activities that are the products of social consumption.

Another set of problems involves the question of how persons who possess given stocks of social consumption resources came to do so. For this, we will want to take elements of social consumption resources separately or together as dependent variables and move into the production dimensions of the social stratification space, to examine what characteristics of current and past economic and social situations of individuals and families seem to account for the resources they currently possess. We would investigate, for example, the role of such factors as income (I), occupation (O), education (E), location (L), family background (FB), and minority status (M) as causes of economic or social wealth.

$$EW = e(I, O, E, L, FB, M)$$
$$SW = f(I, O, E, L, FB, M)$$

It is easier to do this with economic resources since they are measurable in familiar units of dollars and cents. It is much more difficult to operationalize the concept of social wealth.

We may also go beyond the issue of the individual distribution of opportunities for resources and look instead at the structure of positions that have implication for the stratification of social consumption resources. We might wish to examine the institutional sources of the structure of wages, for example, or institutional sources of the unequal distribution of knowledge and taste in society.

Finally, one may shift the rather static focus the above approach involves to a perspective that takes into account the fact that social consumption resources and products exercise a direct influence on members' subsequent economic and social wealth. Individuals make choices as to whether to devote their economic and social wealth at any given time to furthering their careers or to enjoying themselves. A businessman may invest his savings in his business or in a country club membership. If he does the latter and thereby gains the social consumption product that input makes possible, he may simply enjoy the associated status, or his club membership may in addition affect his business in the future through contacts made at the club. Depending on the type of business, one man may get nothing but social consumption from his membership, while another gets not only the same level of current consumption but, by expanding his business through contacts, also gains a higher level of resources, social consumption, and status in the future. Thus, resources at time two are affected by consumption at time one.

$$O_{t_2} = g(I_{t_1}, O_{t_1}, SC_{t_1})$$
$$I_{t_2} = h(I_{t_1}, O_{t_1}, SC_{t_1})$$

As we have seen, however, it proves difficult enough to deal with these matters in relatively static models.

Some Unresolved Issues in Understanding the American Stratification System

In the course of this book we have sought to advance understanding of the social logics by which Americans judge their own and other people's social well-being. It is clear that the resources that are important in the production of social well-being are highly varied. Although it is not difficult anecdotally to draw attention to a fairly wide range of such resources, sociology and economics have done little to develop a systematic inventory of resources. One of the reasons that this is difficult to do is that such an inventory should be based on an equally systematic inventory of the kinds of rewards that are valued in the society, the kinds of rewards to the production of which individuals devote their resources.

Therefore in many ways the most pressing issue in advancing understanding of the stratification system is to develop an orderly and relatively complete system for describing the range of rewards individuals are able to enjoy by virtue of their social position. We have emphasized the central importance of income in understanding social standing from the perspective both of image and reality, because the role of income in providing a wide range of rewards—consumption—has not received sufficient attention among sociologists. But that emphasis should not obscure the importance of paying attention also to the range of non-pecuniary on-and-off-the-job rewards received by workers.

The family in stratification. There is also the question of better understanding of off-the-job rewards and how these vary depending on the individual's relation to the income the family receives, that is, whether the person is an employed husband or wife or a non-earner spouse or a child. Husbands, wives, and their children occupy somewhat different positions in stratification space; much more systematic attention needs to be devoted to the interaction between family/sex roles and the individual's access to resources of various kinds.

A focus on (family) income rapidly directs our attention to the variety of sources of income for families. There is good reason for believing that source of income may well represent a resource quite aside from that represented by amount of income. It is quite likely that a dollar of asset income, a dollar of welfare income, and a dollar of pension income are regarded by Americans as different in their social meanings and in fact produce somewhat different consequences. A richer characterization of individuals and families in terms of the rewards they gain from their positions in society would make more worthwhile an effort to characterize the resources individuals have in a much more exact way. We need a much better mapping of social capital as it is derived both from work and non-work situations.

A fuller characterization of position in the social relations of production. Because of its overwhelming importance, it is probably here that the greatest effort should be made. If we define an individual's position in the world of work—job, occupation—broadly enough to include all of the individual's involvement with factors of production (that is, to include investment income even if it comes from coupon clipping), then it is reasonable to say that a richer characterization of individuals' market positions is necessary in order to advance our understanding of how the stratification system operates. The occupational categories used by sociologists—both the detailed classifications and the uni-dimensional scales dealt with in this book (the prestige scales, the scales by mean income)—are simply too rudimentary to provide a reasonable starting point for a better understanding of how class operates (Wright, 1976).

We need a better way of characterizing class position. Such a characterization will require not a single score or assignment to a single category; instead, individuals must be described in terms of a vector of characteristics that are relevant to the rewards they are able to gain. The Hope-Goldthorpe occupational scale represents one small step in this direction. It advances our characterization of individuals from a single value to a vector of two values, one representing a dimension of high to low standing or general desirability of the job, and the other representing the individual's relationship to economic activity—economic status. A little thought and an exploration of existing surveys that provide information concerning several aspects of individual jobs suggest directions we might want to take in developing a richer characterization of the individual's position. They include attention to such issues as industry, security of tenure, role in supervisory hierarchy, size of firm, membership in a union, membership in constituencies of greater or lesser bargaining power, and the like.

More attention needs to be paid to the role of industry as well as to occupation traditionally conceived. We have observed that, in terms of income, the relative advantage of a given occupation varies considerably from one industry to another. It is quite likely that other advantages vary also. Furthermore, the relative position of given occupations in given industries may change from time to time. Some industries are better to be in at some times than at others, as any unemployed aeronautical engineer or community action worker is well aware. A more systematic charting of how good given jobs in different industries are at different times might help us understand better the macrosocial dynamics that affect the resources available to individuals and also add precision to our efforts to understand social mobility.

The increasing role of the state. Related to this latter point, but at a more macrolevel, is the issue of the role of government in social stratification. Most traditional stratification texts pay heavy attention to the role of the state in social stratification in pre-industrial times and then shift attention to the role of the economy in industrial times. The rapid rise during the post-World War II period in the proportion of the gross national product that is channeled through government makes systematic attention to the role of government crucial. Daniel Bell's reiteration of Schumpeter's call for a "fiscal sociology" is a beginning along this line, as is his development of the concept of "the public household" (Bell, 1976). From the point of view of the stratification of life chances' resources and rewards, we need only observe that since 1929 the proportion of the gross national product acquired and spent by federal, state, and local governments has tripled from about 11 percent to about 33 percent. During that time the types of government expenditure and the kinds of receipts have, of course, also changed dramatically with increasing reliance on income taxes, individual and corporate, and increasing proportions of expenditures involving transfers of one kind or another. This three-fold increase is the result of complex political, economic, and ideological forces, and it has great impact on the life chances of the citizen.

The impact of this government influence on economic activity—and consequently on the distribution of life chances—is of course not confined to government receipts and expenditures. Very similar in effect to tax collections and expenditures is the category of tax expenditures that result from exemptions from tax written into the law, and the tax deductions individuals and corporations are able to take. The value of tax expenditures amounted to as much as 7 percent of the gross national product (GNP) by 1978. We can say, therefore, that the distribution of at least 40 percent of the GNP is very directly affected by government operations—either positive operations in the forms of collecting and spending or permissive operations in the forms of tax exemptions and deductions. Who gets what in American society (and other welfare capitalist states in the modern world) is thus deeply affected by the exercise of political and governmental power. For those interested in social stratification to fail to devote commensurate attention to the government is to live in a never-never land of a private market economy that simply does not exist. (The role of government is of course even larger than that suggested by this 40 percent of GNP, since the whole legal structure of the state entitles individuals differentially to various kinds of resources for the pursuit of well-being.)

Perhaps a better way of conceptualizing the role of government is to say that research on stratification, at the macro level in particular, should attend to the interrelationships between the governmental and non-governmental sectors rather than concentrating, as has tended to be the case, on the private sector. Government spends some 22 percent of the GNP on goods and services. In that way it deeply affects the life chances of employees and proprietors in the private sector, from the highest to the lowest levels. It transfers about 10 percent of the gross national product directly in the form of money to beneficiaries (both the rich farmer and the poor ADC mother), and in addition it uses a little over 1 percent of the gross national product to pay interest on various debts.

Governmental and political processes that confer advantages differentially on different industries, sections of the country, and the like have their impact eventually in the resources that are available to individuals. Governmental activity similarly confers greater or lesser rewards in the form of prestige and honor on some citizens and less on others. For any given resource that can be identified, then, it becomes important to trace out not only the distribution of the resource and its consequences in terms of different kinds of social reward, but also to develop an understanding of the social-political-economic dynamics that produce that particular distribution of resources to various persons in the society.

It is likely that the explicitly political or governmental component of resources will increase dramatically over the next several decades, even if the rate of growth in the proportion of GNP that is channeled through the government receipts and expenditures does not increase as it has. As more and more people wish to enter the labor market—not just an increasing population but also higher proportions of women wanting to work for more of their adult lifetime—the pressure on government to insure availability of positions will rise. This can be done through spending or through mandating various kinds of activities—that is, through control, through "standards."

Individuals and groups will commit themselves to a struggle for the creation of these opportunities and for the level of reward to be associated with them. It would be a challenging task to analyze each governmental initiative in terms of its stratification implications. To do so on other than a gross and impressionistic basis will require, however, the development of much more precise and detailed models of the likely purchasing and payroll implications of given government initiatives in order to answer the question of who will get what.

Public views and the politics of stratification. Finally, our results provide only suggestions for a fuller portrait of how Americans conceive of the justice and value of the stratification system as it exists. In Chapter 16 and in an earlier book (Rainwater, 1974) we have tried to suggest some of the ways in which one might move toward better understanding of the chain of connections between the basic world views Americans hold concerning the nature of life in this country and of opportunities for developing a meaningful life, on the one hand, and the views they hold concerning various existing and proposed policies, on the other. One's conceptions of the public's views are, of course, inevitably biased by one's own political preferences. This bias is reinforced by the sketchy and often misleading impression one gets of the complexity of people's views when those views are tapped through simple public opinion polling questions. Social scientists need to beware of making the public out to be "conceptual boobs" by virtue of using boobish methods. It is clear from our research, as well as from that of some others, that a great many Americans are quite sensitive to the world around them, that they give that world a considerable amount of thought, and that they struggle to try to bring into congruence their views on the nature of the world, the worth of their fellow citizens, public policy, and a more just society. It is important both for sensible development of public policy and for more basic understanding in the social sciences that this complexity be appreciated, rather than obliterated, by our research efforts.

The Interview Sample

NINE HUNDRED depth interviews are the heart of this investigation into public imagery about social standing in the United States. Each interview combined structured questions with conversational ones. Six hundred of the interviews were conducted with residents of the Boston metropolitan area and three hundred with residents of the Kansas City metropolitan area. The qualitative and quantitative data discussed in Chapters 1 through 12 and Chapter 16 come from these 900 interviews.

The 600 interviews with Boston-area men and women were conducted first, in the late spring of 1971 (May and June). (Prior to that survey, some of the structured questions had been pilot-tested in a 1970 Boston Area Survey. Both surveys were conducted by the Survey Research Program, a facility of the Joint Center for Urban Studies of M.I.T. and Harvard University; findings from this pilot were from time to time referred to in the text and integrated with the follow-up survey.) Midway through our analysis of the 1971 Boston interview results, we determined that a comparable group of interviews should be gathered in Kansas City, where one of us (Coleman) had studied social status imagery in the early 1950s. Thus, in the late fall of 1972 (November and December), the Kansas City interviews were added to the research sample.

The purpose of the interviews was put to each of the 900 respondents in this way: "We are conducting a public opinion survey on people's attitudes toward how life is going in the United States these days and what they expect in the next few years. We would like your views. We're interested, for example, in how people feel about their situations, and how they compare their situations with those of other people. . . . We're also interested in what people think about different standards of living."

The only question asked of all 900 respondents was the first question that followed this introduction. This question was, "What is the smallest amount of money a family of four (husband, wife, and two children) needs to get along these days in the Boston/Kansas City area?" Respondents were allowed to specify the amount by week, month, or year. This question has been asked annually by the Gallup Poll since the 1930s. All other questions in our study were asked of subsamples varying in size from 300 respondents to 150 respondents. In both Boston and Kansas City six different forms of the interview were employed, with 100 respondents interviewed with each form in Boston and 50 with each in Kansas City.

The Boston sampling was designed to provide appropriate representation from all parts of the Boston Standard Metropolitan Statistical Area (S.M.S.A.), comprising nearly ninety townships. The Survey Research Program refers to its method as "a random area probability sample of block groups." One hundred sampling points were chosen, from each of which six interviews were gathered. Survey Research Program interviewers were instructed to proceed, when in the field, to a randomly selected starting point marked on a map of the block group to which they had been assigned. Once there, they were to proceed from housing unit to housing unit in a specified skip-pattern until they had obtained six interviews, three with men and three with women. Any adult appearing to be under sixty-five years of age was eligible to be interviewed; so too was anyone at least eighteen years of age not living with a parent or parent substitute. No call-backs were required. Virtually all of the interviews were conducted either in the homes of the respondents or, if not precisely inside their homes, in the yard or on the porch or driveway, or by appointment at the respondent's place of employment.

The demographic composition of the 1971 Boston sample—race, sex, age, and judged social status—is shown in Table A-1 under the column "Boston." The age distribution is somewhat skewed toward the young end—probably because so many of the Survey Research Program interviewers were themselves young and found it easier to gain entry into young households; the upward skew in the status distribution came about in much the same way. The racial composition is not skewed; it mirrors the Greater Boston population quite well. The 1970 U.S. Census classified the Boston population as 94.8 percent white, 4.3 percent Negro, and 0.9 percent other. This Boston sample—while not a perfect cross-section of the Greater Boston population—is sufficiently representative for the present research's purposes; its deficiencies have been kept in mind during our analysis.

TABLE A-1
Composition of the Research Sample

Demographic Variables	Boston Sample	Kansas City Sample	Total Sample	Percent (Total)
Race				
White	566	262	828	92.0
Black	32	37	69	7.7
Other	2	1	3	0.3
Total	600	300	900	100.0
Sex				
Male	295	150	445	49.4
Female	305	150	455	50.6
Total	600	300	900	100.0
Age				
Under 30	188	79	267	29.7
30-39	143	70	213	23.7
40-49	110	70	180	20.0
50 and older	159	81	240	26.6
Total	600	300	900	100.0
Judged Social Standing				
Upper-class	14	6	20	2.2
Upper-middle-class	144	39	183	20.3
Middle-class	193	102	295	32.8
Working-class	209	121	330	36.7
Lower-class	40	32	72	8.0
Total	600	300	900	100.0

Interviewing for the 1972 study in Kansas City was assigned to a commercial polling-and-survey firm. A sample design similar to our Boston approach was developed, using fifty sampling points, representative geographically and socio-economically of the Kansas City S.M.S.A. From each sampling point six interviews were gathered, with age specifications built into the quotas as well as sex distribution. At each sampling point one younger man and one younger woman were to be interviewed, with "younger" variously specified as being under thirty or under thirty-five, depending on the age distribution in the block group as reported in the 1970 Census. One older man and one older woman were to be interviewed, with "older" variously defined as being fifty and up or forty-five and up, depending again on area age characteristics. The third man and third woman in each tract were to be drawn from a "middle" age bracket. No respondent under twenty-one was to be interviewed, nor—ideally— was any over sixty-five.

The demographic composition of the Kansas City sample is shown in Table A-1 under the column "Kansas City." The race composition in this sample is almost identical to Census report: 12.1 percent Negro, for example, in 1970. The age distribution mirrors the real breakdown for Kansas Citians between twenty-one and sixty-five years of age equally well; the status distribution is only slightly skewed toward the upper end.

The social status judgments rendered for respondents in this survey reflect the authors' rethinking of the status continuum that came about in the course of this research. The class groupings are as described in Chapters 8, 9, and 10; they are based partially on public imagery and partially on detailed analysis of social orbits and life style variables. Respondents have been classified as either middle-class or working-class according to evidence in the interview protocol as to how they spent their money and spare time, who their friends were, and how they would be treated and rated by neighbors, workmates, acquaintances, and anonymous observers. (So too, here respondents have been classified upper-class, upper-middle, or lower-class from the evidence of the interview, as this fits into the schema developed from community imagery.) Income levels, housing conditions, neighborhood location, occupation, educational background, ethnic identity, and community participation have all been considered in these status judgments, in an effort to mirror the community evaluation described in Chapters 1 through 10.

Status Scales
and Status Magnitudes

Our CONCERNS in developing a new approach to status scales were of two kinds. Methodologically, we were seeking to develop a metric and a field method that would permit ratio measurement of status continua. Our substantive concern was in understanding the links between the objective facts of income, schooling, and occupational inequality, and the subjective images and abstractions of these facts that people carry about in their heads.

The objective aspects of stratification, the unequal distributions of wealth, power, and position are dealt with in one set of studies, while another body of empirical investigation has dealt primarily with more subjective topics, such as class consciousness. Each kind of research assumes the other. We think it worthwhile to study the distribution of objective status categories because of assumptions we make about their subjective relevance. Similarly, we consider it important to study the subjective aspects of stratification because we assume they will bear the impact of the economic, political, and social processes that determine objective inequalities.

The problem for the empirical researcher, especially one interested in status measurement, has not been in recognizing the significance of the subjective for the objective or vice versa. The problem, instead, has been to isolate from the plethora of status dimensions and symbols things that are observable, countable, or classifiable, and that relate in a regular way to subjective social understandings of stratification. Thorstein Veblen's (1934) acidic recital of the way in which nearly every area of social life has been invaded by "invidious distinctions" related to "standards of pecuniary decency" is probably the classic statement on the subject of status symbolism, but his view that all these symbols coalesced in the behaviors and possessions of a single "leisure class" was an overstatement of the case. How does one choose from the multiplicity of only partially consistent status factors those that go to the heart of the stratification system; and how does one put numbers to these factors in ways that reflect the social understandings of their meaning? These are important questions in any endeavor to measure social status or prestige.

Scales for the Measurement of Social Status

One of the early sociological strategies for coping with the multistrandness of objective social status dimensions was to create scales for the possession of certain cultural artifacts. A notable example of this approach was F. Stuart Chapin's "Living Room Scale" of social status, first constructed in 1928 (Chapin, 1933). Much later James A. Davis (1956) confirmed that living room furnishings did indeed correspond with subjective understandings of status; he found that a sample of housewives could arrange a series of pictured living rooms along a status dimension in a consistent and uni-dimensional fashion. Scales based on cultural artifacts have gradually fallen into disfavor for a variety of reasons. One is the problem of arbitrary weightings for the components of the scale. Louis Guttman (1942) demonstrated that some of the items Chapin included in his living room scale had a negligible or slightly negative correlation with the overall scale score, while other items were underweighted. Another problem was that the living room scale would have had to be constantly revised to take into account changing fashions in home decor. Moreover, the requirement that a trained interviewer have physical access to a family living room somewhat limited the usefulness of such scales. Finally, objections to scales based on cultural artifacts could be raised on theoretical grounds. Many sociologists would regard these life style artifacts as peripheral to the more importantly causal factors of stratification, such as occupation or family wealth and background.

An approach to social status measurement having a much greater impact on current methods is the approach pioneered by W. Lloyd Warner and his associates (Warner, Meeker, and Eells, 1949). Warner developed the concept of social class as networks of equal rank. His social class system was based on these propositions:

that those who interact in a social system of a community evaluate the participation of those around them, that the place where an individual participates is evaluated, and that the members of the community are explicitly or implicitly aware of the ranking and translate their evaluations of such participation into social class ratings that can be communicated to the investigator. It is, therefore, the duty of the field man to use his interviewing skill to elicit the necessary information and to analyze his data with the requisite techniques for determining social class, thereby enabling the status analyst to determine the levels of stratification present and to rank any member of the community [Warner, et. al. (1949), 35].

At the core of each social class was the pattern of social relationships in which members of the community engage. It was the ranking of persons based on their participation within the community that was definitive for social class. All other status characteristics were simply correlates of these patterns of relationships. This meant that traditional measures of socio-economic status such as occupation, education, and income were regarded as correlates, perhaps as necessary conditions for but not definitions of social class.

The techniques used to distinguish between social classes depended heavily on the subjective ratings of individuals by community informants, as well as on objective data about the individual's association memberships and other indicators of interaction patterns. Because Warner recognized that his method of "evaluated participation" was time-consuming and expensive in a small community and seemed impossible to apply in large cities, he developed the Index of Status Characteristics (I.S.C.) as a way of predicting social class membership. Warner used the correlation between various social and economic characteristics and social class status in the development of his I.S.C. For each of six status characteristics —income, occupation, education, house type, dwelling area, and source of income—he constructed a seven-point scale from high to low. For a sample of 300 families who had been placed by his technique of "evaluated participation," Warner and his co-workers then intercorrelated the families' ratings on the six socio-economic characteristics and carried out multiple regression analyses to determine which factors did the best job of predicting social class membership. Warner finally included four of the variables in the I.S.C.—occupation, source of income, house type, and dwelling area (weighted 4, 3, 3, 2, respectively). The occupation variable was, in actuality, a composite variable, a combination of Alba Edwards' (1938) occupational groups (the familiar census categories) cross-cut by information about wages or salaries. Hollingshead (1949; Hollingshead and Redlich, 1950), following in the Warner tradition, produced a similar index called the I.S.P. or Index of Social Position. It consists of a linear combination of three variables: occupation, education, and residence area (weighted 9, 5, and 6). The seven-point occupation scale was derived with a few changes from the Edwards census categories. A seven-point division of the education continuum formed the education variable. The residence scale distinguished six levels of neighborhood status, as derived from an earlier study of New Haven area housing. The criterion of validity for the I.S.P. was how well it predicted placement in the researcher's five-class analysis of the community stratification system.

Richard Coleman's Index of Urban Status (I.U.S.) is a descendant of the Warner and Hollingshead indexes (Coleman and Neugarten, 1971). Coleman developed eight different dimensions in his index. He declines to specify weights, suggesting instead that the analyst treat the index as a profile, to be evaluated qualitatively on a case-by-case basis. Another social status index in current use is that developed by William Sewell. It places families on a status scale from 1 to 99 by a factor-weighted comcombination of occupation, husband's and wife's education, and several economic indexes. (For a description, see Sewell and Shah, 1967.)

The *ad hoc* aspects of the construction of status indexes would hardly be grounds for criticism were it not for the fact that indexes have tended to take on a life of their own apart from their theoretical underpinnings. While Warner and Hollingshead envisioned the stratification system as having a limited number of classes with definite boundaries, indexes based on a linear combination of variables have lent themselves just as easily to an interpretation of social status as a uni-dimensional continuum without sharp class divisions (see Lenski, 1952; Landecker, 1960). Taking seriously the view that the status indexes were a good description of the stratification system led sociologists to consider the differences between different combinations of status dimensions that yielded identical status scores, and thus a whole literature on status inconsistency came into being. (See Lenski, 1954. See also Laumann and Segal, 1971, and Nelson, 1973, for recent bibliography on status inconsistency.)

The principal alternative to the multi-dimensional index approach in measuring social status has been to concentrate on making precise measurements of the status of occupations. Indeed, to some the concepts of social status and occupational prestige have become virtually synonymous. The fact that Warner and Hollingshead both found occupation to be the best single indicator for social class placement probably encouraged later investigators to focus upon occupational status, but the biggest boost to this approach came from the functionalist theories that were becoming predominant in American sociology in the 1940s and 1950s. (Another not insubstantial reason for the efforts to establish a highly articulated scale of occupational status was the fact that occupation differed from the other most important dimensions of social status, income and education, in lacking a natural scale or metric. Income could be conveniently measured in dollars, education in years of schooling, but how did one measure the differences between occupations?)

Kingsley Davis and Wilbert Moore (1945), in their classic statement of the functionalist position, argued that it is necessary for the survival of a society that it motivate the most capable of its people to train for and perform the duties of the most important occupational positions; that this process of motivation can only be accomplished by an unequal distribution of status, income, and other societal rewards; and that differences in status are thus a direct outcome of the differences in the functional importance of occupation (as well as the scarcity of suitable personnel to fill the positions). Davis and Moore conclude with the statement, "It is therefore superficial and erroneous to regard high income as a cause of a man's power and prestige, just as it is erroneous to think that a man's fever is the cause of his illness."

Within two years of the appearance of the Davis-Moore article, Cecil North and Paul K. Hatt conducted a study designed to provide a definitive measurement of the prestige of occupational positions in American society (NORC, 1947). A number of other occupational prestige scales had appeared in the previous quarter-century (see Davies, 1952, for a summary of this literature; Counts, 1925; Smith, 1943), but the North-Hatt NORC scale was unique in that it produced prestige scores for a relatively large number of occupations (ninety) and was normed on a national sample.

A good deal of recent stratification research has depended neither on occupational prestige scores alone, nor on a status index such as the I.U.S., but on what is usually termed a multi-dimensional approach. The individual's positions are measured separately on the various social status dimensions such as occupation, income, and education, and the patterns of correlation between these dimensions are taken as problematic. Representative of this approach are the path models developed by Duncan and his followers (Blau and Duncan, 1967; Duncan, Featherman, and Duncan, 1972; Jencks and others, 1972; Hauser, 1973). One major issue inherent in such an approach is theoretical meaning of the natural continua for the income and education dimensions, which—besides occupation—are the two most commonly used factors. Seven-point category scales are anachronistic in the era of high-speed and large-capacity computers, but it is by no means clear, as Nelson and Lasswell (1960) have pointed out, that the natural continuum of years of education or dollars of income will serve as an interval scale for the status of these dimensions either (see also Conte, 1972). On the contrary, there is reason to suspect that an added thousand dollars of income would mean more in status terms to the person in the $9,000 income range than to the person making $90,000, and that, by the same token, the worth in status terms of an added year of schooling would depend to some extent on which year it happened to be.

Approaches to Measurement of Status Magnitudes

The issue of the relationship between status continua and natural continua has been raised most forcefully in the work of the handful of sociologists who have applied the technique of magnitude estimation to the problem of constructing status scales. Robert L. Hamblin (1971a, 1971b, 1974) began experimenting in this area in 1962, and his work on status measurement has been replicated by Allen M. Shinn, Jr. (1969, 1974). Both Hamblin and Shinn came to the conclusion that status, as measured by the magnitude estimation method, is not a linear function of the income or education continuum. The mathematical relationship that seems to hold was what is known as a power function,

$$\alpha = c\ \beta^n$$

where
α = status
β = the natural continuum
c = an empirical constant
and
n = an empirically determined exponent.

The exponents that Hamblin and Shinn found for the education continuum indicated that status is an accelerating function of education. Each year of education brings a greater increment in status than the last. Income status, on the other hand, was found to be a decelerating function of the dollar amount.

Jones and Shorter (1972), using slightly different measurement procedures, found a similar power function for the status of income, but suggested that an exponential function (another kind of accelerating curve) gave a better fit for their data on the status of education. David

Schmitt (1965) conducted yet another magnitude estimation study on the status of income and education, but he did not publish fitted equations for his results.

The magnitude estimation technique was borrowed from psychophysicists (psychologists who attempt to measure the intensity of response of the various human sensory mechanisms as a function of the intensity of the physical stimuli that provoke the responses). Psychophysics, though not one of the better known branches of psychology, is relatively old among the psychological disciplines. The pivotal figure in nineteenth-century psychophysics was G. T. Fechner. He first formalized what has become known as Weber's Law, the proposition that errors in discrimination between stimuli increase in proportion to the intensity of the stimuli. In other words, two lights must differ more in intensity for a person to be able consistently to tell them apart if both lights are fairly bright than if they are fairly dim. Psychophysicists say that the size of the "just noticeable difference" (jnd) increases with the intensity of the stimulus.

Fechner's other principal contribution to psychophysics was a law of his own: that human sensory response to a stimulus varies with the logarithm of the stimulus. In mathematical terms this relationship is called a logarithmic equation (or sometimes a semi-log relationship).[1]

Fechner's theories, and the voluminous research he produced to support them, have been enormously influential in the field of psychophysics. They have led, for instance, to the creation of the familiar decibel scale of sound intensity, which is logarithmic in form. In recent years, however, a competing paradigm has arisen, developed mainly by the late S. S. Stevens.

Stevens' new formulation grew out of experiments in which he asked respondents to attempt to estimate the ratio of the sensations caused by two different levels of a stimulus. Stevens and his co-workers found that if they increased the intensity of the stimulus by a constant ratio, the reported strength of the sensation increased by a constant ratio, too, although not necessarily the same one. For instance, throughout the range of response to light (from lights so dim they were barely visible to lights so bright they could almost cause injury), any nine-fold increase in the actual intensity of the light would cause observers to report an approximate doubling of its brightness. For sound, it only took a stimulus ratio of about 2.8:1.0 for subjects to report that the apparent loudness had doubled (see Stevens, 1972). These results were inconsistent with Fechner's logarithmic hypothesis. They indicated instead a mathematical power function relationship between stimulus and reported response.

Experiments with a number of other sensory continua yielded results consistent with the power function formulation (Stevens and Galanter, 1957), and Stevens eventually formalized it as what he called the *psychophysical power law* (Stevens, 1957).

Stevens' actual experimental procedures were a little more complex than we have indicated. Instead of increasing the stimulus intensity each time, he would present stimuli of greater and lesser intensity in a random order and ask his subjects to assign numbers to each stimulus. He found he could average out apparent individual idiosyncrasies and measurement errors by pooling the results from a group of ten or fifteen subjects given the same task. Stevens found that his subjects could do as well or better at the task of estimating ratios if they were directed to work with numbers rather than fractions. For instance, he would tell his subjects to pick a number to represent the intensity of the first stimulus and then assign numbers to successive stimuli to represent the ratio of stimulation they perceived. If the stimulus seemed twice as great, they were to assign it a number twice as large as the first; if one-half as great, one-half as large, and so on. This, in essence, was the origin of the magnitude estimation technique. Other experiments with magnitude estimation using the drawing of lines rather than numbers, or the squeezing of a hand-grip, produced equally useful results.

Robert L. Hamblin has applied magnitude estimation scale-building methods to a wide range of phenomena of interest to sociologists. His original experiments with status measurement conformed closely to the model of the psychophysical experiment. Hamblin used small groups of about twenty to thirty homogeneous subjects (one group of college students and another of Navy seamen).

Our object in adding magnitude estimation sections to the Boston Area Studies was not just to replicate Hamblin's (and Shinn's) work on status, but to extend the data base of this work in at least two directions. One was to gauge the extent to which the results that obtained in Hamblin's and Shinn's experiments also held true for the larger and more heterogeneous metropolitan sample. Our second object was to use a wider and more representative spread of status stimuli—particularly with regard to occupations and to the income-education-occupation profile combinations that could then be used to estimate the strength of the factors in a joint-status estimation. (We also were seeking to discover whether or not the magnitude estimation techniques could be taken from the laboratory and applied to large-scale sample survey research.) If successful, the results would give a better idea of the public's understandings of the shape of status distribution and a better idea of the extent to which such understandings are shared among different social groups.

The data reported here come from two sample surveys of the Boston metropolitan area carried out in 1970 and 1971, respectively. In the 1970 study, the questions covered a wide range of subjects, none of which focused on social status. The 1971 study, on the other hand, was entirely devoted to social stratification topics. Projected sample size in both years was 600, although the number of persons actually reached in the 1970 survey fell about 10 percent short of that. In the 1971 survey, the full projected sample size was attained, but there was about a 5 percent non-response rate on the magnitude estimation items.

Question 1 in the magnitude estimation section of the 1971 survey was a brief introduction to the technique using a simple physical stimulus:

> Now we're going to do something a little different. It is something like a game in which I'll want you to answer using numbers to tell me how big or little different things are. Here's a page with three circles. Let's say the first circle is equal to 100. (*Show page 1 of booklet.*) Now, if another circle looks twice as big it would be equal to 200; half as big would be equal to 50. Or if a circle looks twenty times as big, it's equal to 2000, or if only one-tenth as big, then it's equal to 10.
>
> a. Now considering the first circle to be equal to 100, write in the space above number 2 what you would give to the second circle.
> b. And what number would you give the third circle? (*Write answer on page 1 of booklet.*)

The three circles (diameter of 2.3 cm., 6.7 cm., and 1.0 cm.) appeared on the cover of a response booklet given to the respondent. When the respondent had completed the preliminary task, the interviewer went on to introduce the subject of status as follows.

> In any community people have different amounts of prestige, respect or status.
>
> The amount of prestige, respect or status a person has can come from many things—for example his income, the way he dresses, his education, his job, his neighborhood, home, looks, car, and so on.
>
> In several questions in this interview we'll ask you to tell us about a person's *general standing*.
>
> By *general standing* we mean the amount of prestige or respect or status *most people would say a person has* because of some characteristic we'll tell you about.
>
> O.K., now let's look at Page 2 in your booklet.
>
> We're interested in the general standing of different occupations, educational levels, and levels of living, like the ones on this list. Just as with

the circles, we'll set up a benchmark at 100 and rate each item compared to that.

Let's imagine a Mr. A. A. Mim; that's short for Mr. Absolutely Average Man-in-the-Middle. We'll consider Mr. Mim's general standing to be 100. Now, for each of the items on the list, would you decide first whether most people would see its general standing as less than Mr. Mim's or more than Mr. Mim's? Then, would you give each item a number to show how much more or less its general standing is than Mr. Mim's 100. There aren't any right or wrong answers. . . .

The interviewees' responses to the magnitude estimation questions took the form of marks in a response booklet with the following format.

	Less than Mr. Mim (0–99)	More than Mr. Mim (101 or more)
Mr. Mim is 100, How Much Is a . . .		
a. salesclerk in a hardware store		
b. eighth-grade education		
c. $13,500-a-year level of living		

There were several format differences between the 1970 and the 1971 items. The changes in the second year's questionnaire were designed to eliminate some of the problems occasioned by the form of the first. In the 1970 version the occupation *carpenter* had been designated as the standard with magnitude 100. (Both Hamblin and Shinn had designated the educational level of *college graduate* as a standard for magnitude estimations. Our choice of the carpenter standard was an effort to find a standard closer to the median of the status range, so that scores below 100 could be easily interpreted as below the median in status, while scores above 100 could be considered above median status. In the Hodge-Siegel-Rossi [Siegel, 1971] prestige scores, the occupation of carpenter was at the midpoint of the status range.)

The problem that arose in connection with the use of the carpenter standard was one of correlation between the respondent's own status characteristics and the status the respondent assigned to the various stimulus items. An analysis of these correlations showed a highly significant departure from randomness in the relationship between the respondent's own family income, education level, and head-of-the-household's occupational level and the status estimates for stimulus items. The clearest relationship was between the individual's estimation of own general standing and the judgment made as to the status of the three single variables. The median correlation across items between the individual's self-assessed general standing and the status assigned to the stimulus items turned out to be 0.50. These high correlations between estimated own status and the other items indicated that the higher the respondents put themselves in relation to the carpenter, the higher they tended to rate every other item; and the lower they put themselves in relation to the carpenter, the lower they tended to rate every other item.

Our designation of the fictitious Mr. A. A. Mim as standard for estimations in the 1971 survey was an effort to avoid these social-distance interactions between the respondent's own status and the standard of reference, by providing a standard whose empirical referent was highly abstract. The effort was apparently successful, since the patterns of correlations between status estimates for items and the respondent's own status characteristics were non-significant.

The other major difference between the 1970 and 1971 question-naires was in the recording of the responses. In the 1971 questionnaire, as we saw above, respondents were asked to record their own responses in booklets that were provided for the purpose. The previous year, re-spondents were asked to give responses verbally as interviewers read the stimulus items and recorded their answers. Since the paper-and-pencil technique used in the 1971 study was less time-consuming for most respondents, it allowed us to ask each respondent to make estimates on a larger number of items in the time alloted to that part of the interview. Because of time limitations, in the 1970 survey we could get estimates from each respondent on only a dozen of the single-value items (status of occupations, levels of income, levels of education). In the 1970 survey, since we wanted information on some 120 items, including 80 occupations, 22 income levels, and 18 education levels, this necessitated breaking the sample into at least 10 groups with different interview forms.

By electing to get information from several groups about a few of the items, we constructed twelve sets of twelve items to be administered to groups with a projected size of fifty each. While forty-five to fifty is larger than the group size needed to get stable pooled results for magni-tude estimations in a laboratory situation, the greater error margins apparently inherent in the survey procedure made our 1970 results seem somewhat unstable. We particularly noticed this instability when we tried to combine results on different items from different interview groups. Some groups seemed consistently to estimate low with respect to the curve described by the results from the rest of the sample, while other groups tended to estimate high. Interactions between the carpenter standard and the social makeup of the various interview groups may also have had something to do with this effect.

The 1971 questionnaire asked for magnitude estimates of the status of 26 single value items—15 occupations, 7 incomes, and 4 levels of education—presented interspersed in a random order. With three interview groups of 200, we were able to get pooled estimates for the status of 45 occupations, 21 levels of income, and 12 education levels. The 1971 estimates appear to be somewhat more stable, probably because of the larger size of the interview groups (average size 190). However, some data inconsistencies remain.

The magnitude estimations presented here are averages rather than the responses of single individuals. Since systematic differences in the ways that different groups view stratification do not seem to be present (or at least are not strong), we have made the assumption that the forces producing errors in individuals' responses are more or less random, and that the pooled or averaged responses give an accurate picture of the basic relationships between objective characteristics and subjective responses conferring status on persons with those characteristics.

The measurement of central tendency that we will report here is the geometric mean (geomean). Since the geomean is not commonly used by sociologists, use of it here demands some rationale. Our rationale is best understood in terms of the typical distribution of status estimates for a single item. The first thing that one notes in looking at frequency distributions of the magnitude estimation responses is that people tend to choose round numbers. The values 50, 90, 100, 110, 125, 150, 200, and 500 appear frequently as estimates. Numbers like 87 or 144 almost never appear. This means that the frequency distributions of estimates do not form smooth, continuous curves. A second obvious property of these distributions is that they are skewed to the right. Wild estimates of status (wild with respect to the general consensus) are nearly always on the high side. (Only one of the seventy-eight distributions for single value items in the 1971 data was skewed left.) In seventy-five out of seventy-eight cases the skew to the right is statistically significant at the 0.001 level. Statistical tests also show marked leptokurtosis for these distributions. Leptokurtic distributions have exaggerated peaks in comparison to normal distributions. Again, seventy-six out of seventy-eight distributions show leptokurtosis at the 0.001 level of significance.

The ordinary arithmetic mean is not a good indicator of the central tendency of these distributions. Wild scores on the high end of the distribution have an excessive influence on the computation of the mean and tend to pull it above whatever central clustering may exist. A statistician's usual response to such problems is to adopt the median instead of the mean, but because of the tendency to choose round numbers, the median of these distributions, more often than not, ends up on a round number. Thus the median estimates for adjacent stimuli will tend to cluster around prominent round numbers, even when the rest of their distributions are distinct.

Psychophysicists, encountering similar distributions of magnitude estimates, opted for use of the geometric mean, which is, in effect, an ordinary mean computed on a variable that has been transformed to its logarithm. The effect of computing the mean of logarithms rather than of natural numbers is to greatly decrease the influence of any wild scores in the high direction, since the high end of the continuum is compressed (while at the same time increasing the influence of any outliers in the low direction). Another reason that Stevens and his associates chose to adopt the geometric mean was that the log transformation it entailed meshed nicely with their theory of a full logarithmic (power) relationship between stimulus and sensation.

Although our distributions of magnitude estimates did not prove to be log-normal (that is, statistically normal under the log transformation), sixty-four of the seventy-eight distributions had lower skewness and kurtosis. The exceptions were items that were estimated to be very low in status, where wild scores were almost as likely to be low as high. Log transformations also reduced, but did not entirely eliminate, the amount of heteroscedasticity, that is, the differences in standard deviation of response from item to item. Standard deviations of the unlogged distributions tended to increase drastically as the mean of the estimates increased. In other words, the errors of estimation appear to be much larger for high-status items than for low-status ones. This result was expected from the psychophysical experiments.

To the extent that the magnitude estimates of status that we gathered are analogous to magnitude estimates of sensation, Weber's law should hold—perceptual error, hence dispersion of the estimates, increases in proportion to the intensity of the stimulus. The relationship between standard deviations and stimulus levels was more complicated for our data, however. The different groups of subjects had standard deviations of different sizes. Some groups tended toward a wider dispersion of estimates than other groups. The standard deviations of the log-transformed data revealed some heteroscedasticity, but in a different pattern. The smallest standard deviations for the log-transformed data were found in the middle of the stimulus range. Log standard deviations are somewhat larger toward the bottom of the stimulus range and larger still for very high status items. This pattern duplicates that reported by Stevens (1971) for log-transformed psychophysical data.

APPENDIX C

Tables

TABLE C-1

Job Resource Characteristics

Job Resources	Mean	Standard Deviation	Correlation with Income	Regression Coefficients Standardized	Regression Coefficients Unstandardized	Contribution to Coefficient of Determination
Occupational income ratio (log)	101.09	*1.279	0.612	0.518	1.092	0.317
Industry income advantage (log)	103.04	*1.146	0.240	0.106	0.405	0.025
Probability corporation owner 68-72	5.4%	0.188	0.336	0.155	1.534	0.052
Probability non-union wage worker 70-72	24.2%	0.371	−0.282	−0.154	0.806	0.043
			Constant = $51.64		R = 0.662	R² = 0.438

*The asterisk indicates that the number in the table is the antilog of the standard deviation of the logged variable.

TABLE C-2
Employment Resource Characteristics

Employment Resources	Mean	Standard Deviation	Corre-lation with Income	Regression Coefficients		Contribu-tion to Coefficient of Determi-nation
				Stan-dardized	Unstan-dardized	
A. *Non-union wage-workers*						
Weeks not unemployed per year (log)	51.29	*1.042	.454	.247	3.16	.112
Mean hours per week (log)	46.56	*1.167	.202	.203	.699	.041
Percentage of well weeks of weeks employed (log)	96.4%	*1.072	.342	.218	1.66	.075
Always employed 68-72	75.5%	.431	.385	.197	1.274	.076
			Constant = $0.00006		R = .551	R² = .304
B. *Other workers*						
Weeks not unemployed per year (log)	50.80	*1.062	.337	.174	1.42	.059
Mean hours per week (log)	48.64	*1.197	.242	.220	.609	.053
Percentage of well weeks of weeks employed (log)	96.2%	*1.072	.257	.198	1.432	.051
C. Always employed 68-72	65.3%	.476	.322	.154	1.174	.050
			Constant $1.94		R = .461	R² = .213
			Both Groups		R = .470	R² = .221

*The asterisk indicates that the number in the table is the antilog of the standard deviation of the logged variable.

TABLE C-3
Area Resource Characteristics

Area Resources	Mean	Standard Deviation	Corre-lation with Income	Regression Coefficients		Contribu-tion to Coefficient of Determi-nation
				Stan-dardized	Unstan-dardized	
Budget index (log)	99.8	*1.057	0.282	0.123	1.18	0.035
Unskilled wage rate (log)	$2.11	*1.159	0.232	0.096	0.336	0.022
Lives 50 miles from S.M.S.A.	15.1%	0.358	−0.274	−0.116	0.845	0.032
Lived in one of the 12 largest S.M.S.A.s in 1968	35.4%	0.479	0.228	0.079	1.089	0.018
Mean city size 68-72 (log)	97,499	*16.07	0.282	(0.071)†	(0.013)†	0.020
Constant = $86.50 R = 0.356 R² = 0.127						

*The asterisk indicates that the number in the table is the antilog of the standard deviation of the logged variable.

†Coefficients in parentheses have T ratios less than two.

TABLE C-4

Intercorrelations (above the diagonal) of Logged Composite Variables and Standardized Path Coefficients (below the diagonal)

	Area	Job	Employment	Unmeasured	Income
Mean (log)	1.00	1.00	1.00	1.00	$51,168
Standard Deviation (log)	*1.202	*1.409	*1.276	*1.403	*1.683
Correlations:					
Area resources (AR)	−	.158	−.011	0	.356
Job resources (JR)	.158	−	.351	0	.662
Employment resources (ER)	(−.068)†	.362	−	0	.470
Unmeasured resources (and error) (UR)	0	0	0	−	.650
Income	.277	.516	.292	.650	−

*The asterisk indicates that the number in the table is the antilog of the standard deviation of the logged variable.

†Coefficient in parentheses not significant at 5 percent level.

TABLE C-5

Relation of Head's and Wife's Schooling to Socio-Economic Position

	Head's Schooling	Wife's Schooling	Multiple Correlation
Mean years of schooling	12.02	11.82	
Standard Deviation of schooling	3.58	2.40	
Correlations with:			
Wife's schooling	.605	−	
Area resources	.206	.188	.221
Job resources	.603	.448	.612
Employment resources	.335	.260	.343
Unmeasured resources	.208	.169	.214
Income	.602	.474	.618
Standardized regression coefficients for:			
Area resources	.146	.100	
Job resources	.524	.131	
Employment resources	.280	.090	
Unmeasured resources	.167	.068	
Income	.497	.173	
Unstandardized regression coefficients for:			
Area resources	0.8%	0.8%	
Job resources	5.1%	1.9%	
Employment resources	1.9%	0.9%	
Unmeasured resources	1.6%	1.0%	
Income	7.5%	3.8%	

TABLE C-6

*Dummy Variable Regression Coefficients of
Status for Each of Three Family
Socio-economic Background Variables*

	Coefficient
Father's Schooling	
Less than six years	48
Six to eight years	80
Nine to eleven years	97
Twelve years	107
Twelve years plus other training	125
Some college	143
College graduate	163
Advanced degree	202
No information	58
Father's Occupation	
Professional, technical, and kindred	150
Managers	116
Self-employed businessmen	107
Clerical and sales	107
Craftsmen and foremen	86
Operatives	77
Laborers	59
Farmers	76
Other	96
No information	94
Family Financial Circumstance	
Poor	70
Average	101
Well-off	133
No information	65

TABLE C-7

*Sample Characteristics and Regression Coefficients for Adult Socio-economic
Characteristics as Affected by Family Background Characteristics
(Insignificant Coefficients Omitted)*

Univariate Statistics	Majority	Area Born: Rural	City	Parental Class (log)	Number of Siblings	Siblings Mobility (log)	Coefficient of Determination
Mean	89.6%	27.0%	31.7%	85.9	3.88	1.00	
Standard deviation	30.6%	44.4%	46.6%	*1.211	2.34	*1.432	
Standardized Coefficients:							
Head's schooling	.167	—	.125	.471	−.146	.196	.369
Wife's schooling	.143	—	.072	.304	−.217	.105	.229
Area resources (log)	—	−.264	.212	—	—	—	.168
Job resources (log)	.182	—	.123	.368	−.098	.131	.258
Employment resources (log)	.115	—	—	.213	—	.084	.065
Unmeasured resources (log)	.122	—	.092	.098	—	—	.044
Income (log)	.212	−.084	.176	.320	−.067	.093	.280
Unstandardized coefficients:							
Head's schooling	1.995	—	.961	20.391	−.223	4.498	
Wife's schooling	1.128	—	.370	8.840	−.223	1.128	
Area resources	—	.896	1.087	—	—	—	
Job resources	1.228	—	1.095	.666	−1.015	.126	
Employment resources	1.096	—	—	.273	—	.056	
Unmeasured resources	1.144	—	1.069	.175	—	—	
Income	1.434	.906	1.218	.875	−1.115	.135	

NOTES

Chapter 2

1. Two forms of this self-identification question were used. In one we asked, "Which class do you think you and the people you know best are in? Give me your reasons for saying that." In the other, the wording was, "In which social class would you say you are right now? Why do you place yourself in that class? Explain as much as possible why you think that is where you or other people would classify you."

Chapter 3

1. Braverman (1974), pp. 417–419. In this discussion Braverman is attempting to show how the membership of the Marxist categories of "productive" and "unproductive" labor have changed, and in particular how clerical and retail sales workers have come to have the same relation to capital that manual workers have had since the inception of industrial capitalism.

2. Where the median education figure given in the census report is seventeen-plus, we have imputed the appropriate median years of schooling (nineteen for the lawyer, twenty for the college professor). In two cases where the median incomes for the overall category are far from reality we have imputed an income figure—$50,000 in the case of both the factory owner and the senior partner in a Wall Street law firm.

3. Braverman, (1974), pp. 424–447.

Chapter 4

1. We tested two types of relationships between schooling and status. In one, status increases as a constant percentage for each additional year of schooling. This is the exponential form that Jones and Shorter argue is the best fitting. The regression equation for this solution (without the dummy coefficients to equate the other data sets to our 1971 sets with a standard of 100 for Mr. Mim) is:

Log 10 status = 1.164 − 0.658 (log 10 school leaving age).

The other form was the power relation that we expect to fit best, and that is also in line with our approach to the other components of status. The regression equation is:

Log 10 status = 2.674 (log 10 school leaving age) − 1.388.

2. Because these cross-modality matchings cannot extend very far into the income levels at which income status increases as a square root function of income (since there is a ceiling on income status), we cannot test to see if respondents are taking the decreasing marginal status utility of income above $14,000 into account. We are operating, therefore, mostly in the range in which income status is a simple linear function.

3. These estimates must be very rough, given both the educational status estimates we are working with and the grouped data on educational levels. Ideally, one would like to work with much more reliable status estimates based on larger samples and with educational distributions given in single years of educational attainment. Then it might be possible to unravel the discontinuities in the regression relation that seems to occur around high school completion. With this much more precise data it would be interesting to explore the extent to which educational status is a combined function of the proportion of an age cohort that has less education than an individual, the proportion that has more, and the proportion that has the same amount.

Chapter 9

1. The findings from our three-factor social arithmetic test (see Chapter 11) suggest that the public may attribute higher status to high-income working-class families than to low-income middle-class families. Profiles of the former usually emerged from the test with geomeans above 100 while profiles of the latter fell below. We can treat this finding as no more than cautionary evidence of the public view, however, since the relevant variables in class analysis were not included in those profiles.

Chapter 11

1. In the 1970 format, "the Carpenters" were named as an average family with a general standing score of 100—Mr. Carpenter's job was carpentering, but no other information was given about the family. In the 1971 version, the standard was more anonymously spoken of as "the Mims," meaning Mr. Absolutely Average Man-in-the-Middle, his wife, and children. No particular occupation was associated with the Mims; likewise, no income or educational level.

2. Because of the small number of profiles in each subgroup, the standard errors of these regression coefficients are large enough that we cannot put much weight on precise comparisons of adjacent coefficients. Overall, the standard errors run about 10% of the magnitude of the coefficient (but are, of course, larger for sub-classes with very few profiles).

3. Here is how we constructed the profiles to satisfy these somewhat contradictory objectives. We started with eighty occupations, the same eighty for which we were soliciting magnitude estimates of status as a single variable. Then, around these eighty occupations, we built a hypothetical universe of 720 profile possibilities—combinations of occupation with income and education. Building this universe, we first developed three possible combinations with income for each of the occupations. One was the median level of income for that occupation, a second was the income enjoyed by men at the ninetieth percentile of the income distribution for that occupation, and the third was the income enjoyed by men at the tenth percentile for the occupation. We projected these income levels from 1960 Census data because 1970 data were not yet available. Next, we developed similar possible combinations of

occupation with education. One possibility was the educational level that was median for the occupation, another the ninetieth percentile, and a third the tenth percentile. Finally, we mixed each of these three education possibilities with the previously generated three income levels to get nine combinations of the two for the occupation. Nine such treatments per occupation times eighty occupations gave us the 720 hypothetical profiles. Eighty-four of these profiles were then chosen by a random-number procedure for use in the 1970 survey and divided into twelve sets. The luck of the draw meant that some occupations wound up in the survey with two or three treatments tested and others none—but no respondent ever judged more than one treatment.

Some of the profiles used in the 1970 survey struck respondents as quite improbable, even "weird." To avoid this reaction in 1971 we moved away from completely random selection of profiles and eliminated some of the extremes from our universe of possibilities. In doing so, though, we maintained our goal of keeping intercorrelations between the profile dimensions fairly low—lower, really, than in social reality.

4. Rossi and others (1974) and Sampson and Rossi (1975) present an alternative method of estimating family social status. They use, instead of magnitude estimation, a category scaling technique. For discussion of the differences between magnitude estimation and category scales, see Shinn (1974).

5. This combination introduces some error since the standards of comparison were different—the Carpenters in 1970 and the Mims in 1971.

6. Dummy variable coefficients for the 1970 data and form variations increase the coefficient of determination to 0.96. The combined regression equation is: Log General Status $= 0.057 + 0.574$ (Log Income Status) $+ 0.290$ (Job Status) $+ 0.096$ (Educational Status). The standardized coefficients are 0.761, 0.199, and 0.224 respectively.

7. Furthermore, the constant in the regression equation is not significantly different from one, which means that general standing is simply the product of the three components weighted by their coefficients. We recalculated the regression and constrained the constant to be exactly one. Note that the coefficients sum to 1.0. The respective standardized coefficients are 0.706, 0.199, and 0.224.

Chapter 13

1. Methodological issues of estimating status attainment models are explored in detail in a major investigation of the determinants of economic success that compares results of regression analyses of Panel Study of Income Dynamics data with comparable analyses of several other data sets (Jencks et al., 1978).

2. The original sample for the survey involved two components; the first was an area probability sample of United States households that aimed at collecting 3,000 completed interviews. The second component of slightly fewer than 2,000 households represented a selection of families who had been interviewed in an earlier survey carried out by the Census Bureau, the Survey of Economic Opportunity. The families selected for the Panel Study of Income Dynamics were those with incomes equal to or below twice the federal poverty level at that time (and in which the head was not over 60).

3. Because there are two different segments of the sample with very different probabilities of a household being selected for the sample, and because there were important and systematic differences in initial response rates and in response rates over the subsequent five years, the Institute for Social Research has developed a complicated weighting system compensating for these various biases in the sample. The calculations reported below all make use of this weighting factor. If weights are not used the estimates are biased by the heavy over-representation of low-income families in the total sample.

4. Because we carried out this analysis using a computer tape in which families were the units it was not convenient to include in the sample the small percentage of

men in this age range who were not household heads all five of these years. Also, our sample excludes men who were in institutions during any of those years.

5. It seems to us that any model that purports to be causal should include some examination of how and why the associations observed in the model exist. Two kinds of research would seem to be relevant, one from the perspective of individuals and the other from the perspective of social structure. Research on the process by which individuals define their situations and make decisions, each following upon the other, during the course of their socio-economic careers could go a long way toward telling us the how and why behind the path models that have been developed for describing that career. One approach to the study of socio-economic careers from such a perspective is Anselm Strauss's analysis of the process of social mobility (Strauss, 1971).

Similarly, research on the why and how of the structure of positions that are available to individuals—particularly in connection with jobs or occupations—is crucial if one is to have a truly causal model of the socio-economic career. In such research the units of observations would not be individuals but jobs, the firms and organizations in which these jobs are embedded, and the general political economy that operates on both organizations and particular positions within organizations. Harrison White's research on vacancy chains provides one example of such an approach to studying the structure of positions (White, 1970). Lester Thurow's analysis of the dynamics of income distribution shows another to this issue (Thurow, 1976). From our point of view the descriptive model offered here has utility not so much in explaining the social position of individuals, as in suggesting to the researcher fruitful areas for causal or explanatory research into, on the one hand, the processes by which individuals pursue their careers and, on the other, the structures of positions that constain that pursuit.

6. Because the log distribution is very close to normal, the geometric mean $51,168 is very close to the median of the distribution. The antilog of the log standard deviation requires some explanation. We are used to thinking of distributions in terms of the range of plus or minus one or two standard deviations from the mean of a distribution. In the case of the arithmetic mean, the ± 1 standard deviation range is plus or minus $35,594. If we were working with the logs of income, the same would be true of the standard deviation of the log distribution; ± one standard deviation woud involve adding or subtracting one standard deviation from the mean of the log values. If we want to represent that standard deviation as a number in relation to the geometric mean, however, we take the antilog of the standard deviation and discover it to be—not an amount that is to be added or subtracted from the mean—but rather, an amount by which the mean is multiplied or divided. The antilog of the standard deviation of the log income is 1.68. Thus, the range of one standard deviation above and below the geometric mean involves multiplying $51,168 by 1.68 and dividing it by 1.68. (And, if one wanted to know the dollar amount represented by two standard deviation above the log mean one would multiply $51,168 × 1.68 × 1.68.)

7. The table we have conjured up as an ideal starting place for a description of income in relation to socio-economic resources would be even better if, in addition to calculating the expected income for each particular combination of area, occupation, and industry, it also took into account age variations. The income profile in relation to age may differ quite a bit from one occupation to another. It may be that for the same occupation it even differs from one industry to another, with some industries having more "dead-end" jobs than others.

8. We experimented with a number of different ways of using this information to describe the relationship between the individual's job characteristics and income and finally settled on a simplified set of four variables that seemed to capture as much of the variance of income as more elaborate schemes using these variables did.

9. For example, a professional or managerial worker in durable-goods manufacturing earned a mean of $16,382 in 1972, and all professional and managerial workers a mean of $15,248. Therefore, the industry advantage for professional and managerial workers in durable-goods manufacturing was 107 percent. On the other hand, professional and managerial workers in an industry where income was lower than $15,248 would have an industry advantage ratio of less than 100 percent.

10. Most respondents, of course, had never had such an ownership interest. Of those who had, most had such an ownership in all five years, so it is possible to think of this variable as basically a dummy variable with a value of one for corporation owners and zero for non-owners.

11. A simple representation of this general area of resources is the total number of hours worked by the individual over the five-year period. We chose not to use that because of the belief that to define income as a simple product of wage rate and hours worked is to miss a great deal in the way of the economic resources which particular work situations represent. A salaried worker generally does not forego income by taking a vacation. He has a "paid vacation." Many wage workers do forego income when they take a vacation. Therefore, a variable involving weeks worked is not an equally good indicator of employment resources for each of them. Similarly, there are many jobs in which the number of hours per week an individual works does not have a simple or direct relationship to compensation. In many salaried positions, hours worked may be as much or more a function of morale or the degree to which the work is enjoyed as it is of the necessity to work that much time to earn a particular income.

12. The bivariate understandardized regression coefficient for city size alone is 0.054 and is highly significant. It is interesting that this coefficient describing the relation between the city size and the actual income of the men in our sample is the same as the coefficient for city size as a prediction of how much people need in order to get along in the local community (Rainwater [1974], p. 57).

Chapter 14

1. In using the wife's education variable available on the P.S.I.D. tape, we have assumed that the education of the individual's wife at the time he was interviewed will provide essentially the same correlations as using the education of the wives married in the early career period would. That is, we have ignored the problem of second marriages and of first marriages that took place a number of years after the individual was launched into his working career.

2. These controls involved place of birth, race, father's occupation, and education, the respondent's judgment of whether the family was poor or not, and present place of residence.

3. It might be noted that the same selectivity variable is available for wife's education and that there, too, the differences in predicted husband's income as a function of selectivity of college attended are considerable. Husbands of women who graduated from highly or very selective colleges are predicted to have incomes two-thirds higher than if their wives graduated from colleges that were not so selective.

4. In addition, Coleman tried to take into account in his class placements what it would have meant for an individual growing up in the 1930s (a fifty-year-old, for example) to have called the parents poor compared to an individual growing up in the 1950s (thirty-five years old and under). As it turned out, Coleman's social class placement of the cells in the cross-tabulation were not much affected by the age of the respondent; therefore, we have not paid much attention to the age variable in our further analysis.

5. The scores were as follows: Lower Class: The Lower Level, 35; High, 55; Working Class: Low, 70; Middle, 90; High, 100; Lower Middle Class: Low, 105; Middle, 115; High, 130; Upper Middle Class: Low, 145; Middle, 185; High, 240. Coleman did not classify any of the cells as Upper Class.

6. The t-ratios for schooling, occupation, and family finances discrepancy scores are 0.53, 0.56, and 0.32, respectively.

7. We experimented with several more elaborate codings designed to capture the individual's racial, ethnic, religious, and regional background, but none of them produced correlations with later socio-economic characteristics sufficiently high to justify the complexity and the instability of regression coefficients occasioned by the small number of cases for several types of ethnic background. With larger samples the

regression coefficients from much more elaborate characterizations would be quite interesting (even though the more elaborate scale did not correlate more highly with income), but for our purposes a simple dichotomy seemed the best choice. Blacks and Spanish-speaking men were grouped together as "not of the majority" because their regression coefficients, both in simple relationships and with controls, tended to be quite similar and equally distant from that of the rest of the sample—characterized as "majority." Therefore, it did not seem worthwhile to keep separate dummy variables for blacks and Spanish-speaking men.

8. Coleman's social classing of parental background had yielded an average parental class score of around 85. (The skimpiness of the data meant that the extremes of status were much under-represented and this seemed to be particularly a problem at the higher end of the scale. In addition there is a net upward social mobility from one generation to the next.) In the case of the siblings the mean social class magnitude for those in the sample was around 100, suggesting an average mobility of about fifteen points. Individuals who had no siblings were given an average mobility score on the sibling mobility scale. The scale was then readjusted so that it has a mean of 1.0.

9. The path coefficients developed from an analysis here will produce somewhat different effects than would be produced if we dealt with each variable individually, since each of the five family background variables can have a different pattern of relationship with different dependent variables (examine the standardized coefficients in Table C-6 again). However, for purposes of schematizing the interconnections between childhood, launch, and adult position the distortions introduced by this simplification are quite minor.

Chapter 15

1. In combining the two models we have done away with one source of error—the error having to do with the translation of a given level of resources into the status associated with those resources. On the basis of the analysis reported in Part I and in Chapter 11, we feel entitled to assume a "true" correlation of 1.0 between income and income status, job characteristics and job status, schooling and schooling status, and similarly a multiple correlation of 1.0 between those three kinds of status and general social standing judged exclusively on those three pieces of information. Obviously, the more individuals know about a person when making judgments of general social standing, the less completely our three status variables may be expected to predict their placements, but the dominant thrust of the data we have been able to work with suggests that, even with a much broader range of information, these three factors would continue to come very close to accounting for all the variance in general social standing.

Appendix B

1. This makes a total of three kinds of nonlinear mathematical functions introduced into the discussion to this point. The differences and similarities between them can be expressed as follows, if we look at each of the three in logarithmic (base 10) form where Y is the dependent variable, X is the independent variable, b and m are constraints:

Exponential function: $\log Y = mX + b$
Logarithmic function: $Y = m \log X + b$
Power function: $\log Y = m \log X + b$

In linear coordinates, the exponential function is concave upward, the logarithmic function concave downward, and the power function concave either upward or downward depending on whether the exponent is greater than or less than 1.0. (If the exponent $m = 1$, the power function reduces to a simple linear function.)

REFERENCES

Alwin, Duane F., and Robert M. Hauser. "The Decomposition of Effects in Path Analysis." *American Sociological Review*, February 1975, pp. 37–47.

Amory, Cleveland. *The Proper Bostonians*. New York: Dutton, 1947.

Atkinson, A. B. "On the Measurement of Inequality." *Journal of Economic Theory* 2 (1970): 244–263.

Bell, Daniel. *The Cultural Contradictions of Capitalism*. New York: Basic Books, 1976.

Birmingham, Stephen. *The Right People*. Boston: Little, Brown, 1958.

Blau, Peter, and Otis Dudley Duncan. *The American Occupational Structure*. New York: John Wiley, 1967.

Boudon, Raymond. *Education, Opportunity and Social Equality*. New York: John Wiley, 1973.

Boudon, Raymond, Philippe Cibois, and Janina Lagneau. "Enseignement superieur court et pieges de l'action collective." *Revue francaise de Sociologie* 16 (1975): 159–188.

Braverman, Harry. *Labor and Monopoly Capital*. New York: Monthly Review Press, 1974.

Carter, Lewis F. "Inadvertent Sociological Theory." *Social Forces* 40 (September 1971): 12–25.

Chapin, F. Stuart. *The Measurement of Social Status by the Use of a Social Status Scale*. Minneapolis: University of Minnesota Press, 1933.

Coleman, Richard, and Bernice L. Neugarten. *Social Status in the City*. San Francisco: Jossey-Bass, 1971.

Conte, Samuel D. *Elementary Numerical Analysis*. New York: McGraw-Hill, 1972.

Counts, George S. "The Social Status of Occupations: A Problem in Vocational Guidance." *The School Review* 33 (January 1925): 16–27.

Davies, A. F. "Prestige of Occupations." *British Journal of Sociology* 3 (June 1952): 134–147.

Davies, James A. "Status Symbols and the Measurement of Status Perception." *Sociometry*, September 1956, pp. 154–175.

Davis, Allison, Gardner, Burleigh B., and Gardner, Mary R. *Deep South*. Chicago: University of Chicago Press, 1941.

Davis, Kingsley, and Wilbert Moore. "Some Principles of Stratification." *American Sociological Review* 10 (April 1945): 242–249.

Duncan, Greg. "Non-Pecuniary Work Rewards." In *Five Thousand American Families: Patterns of Economic Progress*, vol. 2, edited by James N. Morgan. Ann Arbor: Institute of Social Research, University of Michigan, 1974.

Duncan, Otis Dudley. "A Socioeconomic Index for All Occupations, Properties and Characteristics of the Socioeconomic Index." In *Occupations and Social Status*, edited by J. A. Reiss. New York: Free Press, 1961.

Duncan, Otis Dudley, David L. Featherman, and Beverly Duncan. *Socioeconomic Background and Achievement*. New York: Seminar Press, 1972.

Dunlop, John. *The Theory of Wage Determination*. New York: Macmillan, 1957.

Edwards, Alba M. *A Social-Economic Grouping of the Gainful Workers of the United States*. Washington, D.C.: Government Printing Office, 1938.

Executive Office of the President, Office of Management and Budget. *Special Analysis of the Budget 1979*. Washington, D.C.: Government Printing Office, 1978.

Feldman, J., and J. C. Baird. "Magnitude Estimates of Multidimensional Stimuli." *Perception and Psychophysics* 10 (1971): 418–421.

Friedman, Milton. *A Theory of the Consumption Function*. Princeton: Princeton University Press, 1957.

Garbin, A. P., and Frederick L. Bates. "Occupational Prestige and Its Correlates: A Re-Examination." *Social Forces* 44 (March 1966): 295–302.

Goldthorpe, J. H. "Class, Status, and Party in Modern Britain." *European Archives of Sociology* 12, no. 2 (1972).

Goldthorpe, J. H., and K. Hope. *The Social Grading of Occupations: A New Approach and Scale*. Oxford: Oxford University Press, Clarendon Press, 1974.

Gusfield, Joseph, and Michael Schwartz. "The Meanings of Occupational Prestige: Reconsideration of the NORC Scale." *American Sociological Review* 28 (April 1963): 265–271.

Gutman, Louis. "A Revision of Chapin's Social Status Scale." *American Sociological Review* 7 (1942): 362–369.

Haer, John L. "Predictive Utility of Five Indices of Social Stratification." *American Sociological Review* 22 (October 1959): 541–545.

Hamblin, Robert L. "Mathematical Experimentation and Sociological Analysis." *Sociometry* 34 (1971a): 423–452.

Hamblin, Robert L. "Ratio Measurement for the Social Sciences." *Social Forces* 50 (1971b): 191–206.

Hamblin, Robert L. "Social Attitudes: Magnitude Measurement and Theory." In *Measurement in the Social Sciences*, edited by H. M. Blaylock, Jr. Chicago: Aldine Publishing, 1974, pp. 61–120.

Hatt, Paul K. "Occupation and Social Stratification." *American Journal of Sociology* 55 (May 1950): 533–543.

Haug, Marie R., and Marvin B. Sussman. "The Indiscriminate State of Social Class Measurement." *Social Forces* 49 (June 1971): 549–563.

Hauser, Robert M. "Disaggregating a Social Psychological Model of Educational Attainment." In *Structural Equation Models in the Social Sciences*, edited by Arthur S. Goldberger and Otis Dudley Duncan. New York: Seminar Press, 1973.

Himmelfarb, Samuel, and David J. Seun. "Forming Impressions of Social Class." *Journal of Personality and Social Psychology* 12 (1969): 38–51.

Hines, Fred, Luther Tweeten, and Martin Redfern. "Social and Private Rates of Return to Investment in Schooling by Race-Sex Groups and Regions." *Journal of Human Resources* 5 (1970): 316–340.

Hodge, Robert W., and Paul M. Siegel. "The Classification of Occupations: Some Problems of Sociological Interpretation." *Proceedings of American Statistical Association, Social Statistics Section*, 1966, pp. 178–192.

Hodge, Robert W., Paul N. Siegel, and Peter H. Rossi. "Occupational Prestige in the United States, 1925–1963." In *Class, Status, and Power*, edited by Reinhard Bendix and S. M. Lipset. New York: Free Press, 1966, pp. 322–334.

Hodge, Robert W., Donald Treiman, and Peter Rossi. "A Comparative Study of Occupational Prestige." In *Class, Status, and Power*, edited by Reinhard Bendix and S. M. Lipset. New York: Free Press, 1966.

Hollingshead, August B. *Elmstown's Youth*. New York: Wiley, 1949.

Hollingshead, A. B., and F. C. Redlich. *Social Class and Mental Illness: A Community Study.* New York: Wiley, 1950.

Hughes, Everett C. "Prestige." *Annals of the American Academy of Political and Social Science* 325 (September 1959): 45–49.

Inkeles, Alex, and Peter Rossi. "National Comparisons of Occupational Prestige." *American Journal of Sociology* 61 (January 1956): 329–339.

Jencks, Christopher. *Inequality: A Reassessment of the Effect of Family and Schooling in America.* New York: Basic Books, 1972.

Jencks, Christopher. *Who Gets Ahead.* New York: Basic Books, forthcoming.

Jones, Bryan D., and Richard Shorter. "Ratio Measurement of Social Status: Some Cross Cultural Comparisons." *Social Forces* 50 (1972): 499–511.

Kahl, Joseph A., and James A. Davis. "A Comparison of Indexes of Socio-Economic Status." *American Sociological Review* (June 1955): 317–335.

Karplos, Bernard D. "The Mental Test Qualification of American Youth for Military Service and Its Relationship to Educational Attainment." *Proceedings of American Statistical Association, Social Statistics Section,* 1966.

Kavaler, Lucy. *The Private World of High Society.* New York: McKay, 1960.

Kreisberg, Louis. "The Bases of Occupational Prestige: The Case of Dentists." *American Sociological Review* 27 (April 1962): 238–244.

Landecker, Werner S. "Class Boundaries." *American Sociological Review* 25 (December 1960): 877.

Laumann, Edward O., and David R. Segal. "Status Inconsistency and Ethnoreligious Membership as Determinants of Social Participation and Political Attitudes." *American Journal of Sociology* 77 (July 1971): 36–61.

Lenski, Gerhard E. "American Social Classes: Statistical Strata or Social Groups?" *American Journal of Sociology* 50 (September 1952): 139–144.

Lenski, Gerhard E. "Status Crystallization: A Nonvertical Dimension of Social Status." *American Sociological Review* 19 (1954): 405–413.

Light, Ivan H. *Ethnic Enterprises in America.* Berkeley: University of California Press, 1972.

Marcus, Steven. *Engels, Manchester, and the Working Class.* New York: Random House, 1974.

Modligliana, F., and R. Brumbert. "Utility Analysis in the Consumption Function and Interpretation of Cross Section Data." In *Post-Keynesian Economics,* edited by K. K. Kurihari. New Brunswick: Rutgers University Press, 1954.

Morgan, James N., Ismail A. Sirageldin, and Nancy Baerwaldt. *Productive Americans.* Ann Arbor: Institute for Social Research, University of Michigan, 1966.

Nam, Charles B. "Methodology and Scores of Socioeconomic Status." U. S. Bureau of the Census, Working Paper no. 15, 1963.

National Opinion Research Center. "Jobs and Occupations: A Popular Evaluation." *Opinion News* 9 (September 1947): 3–13.

Nee, Victor, and Nee, Brett. *Long Time Californ': A Documentary Study of Chinatown.* New York: Pantheon Books, 1973.

Nelson, Edward E. "Status Inconsistency: Its Objective and Subjective Components." *The Sociological Quarterly* 14 (Winter 1973): 2–18.

Nelson, Harold A., and Thomas E. Lasswell. "Status Indices, Social Stratification, and Social Class." *Sociology and Social Research* 44 (1960): 410–413.

Nisbet, Robert A. *The Sociological Tradition.* New York: Basic Books, 1966.

Osgood, C. E., and Ross Stagner. "Analysis of a Prestige Frame of Reference by a Gradient Technique." *Journal of Applied Psychology* 25 (June 1941): 275–290.

Rainwater, Lee. *What Money Buys: Inequality and the Social Meanings of Income.* New York: Basic Books, 1974.

Rao, Potluri, and Roger Leroy Miller. *Applied Econometrics.* Belmont, California: Wadsworth, 1971.

Reissman, Leonard. *Class in American Society.* New York: Free Press, 1959.

Rossi, Peter H., William A. Sampson, Christine E. Bose, Guillermina Jasso, and Jeff Passe. "Measuring Household Social Standing." *Social Science Research* 3 (September 1974): 169–190.

Sampson, William A., and Peter H. Rossi. "Race and Family Social Standing." *American Sociological Review* 40 (April 1975): 201–214.

Schmitt, David R. "Magnitude Measures of Economic and Educational Status." *Sociological Quarterly* 6 (1965): 387–391.

Schwartz, Joseph. "Taking a Look at Income." Unpublished paper, Harvard University Department of Sociology, September 1974.

Sewell, Allen M., Jr., and Vimal P. Shah. "Socioeconomic Status, Intelligence, and the Attainment of Higher Education." *Sociology of Education* 40 (Winter 1967): 1–23.

Shile, Edward. "Charisma, Order, and Status." *American Sociological Review* 30 (April 1965): 199–213.

Shinn, Allen M., Jr. "The Application of Psychophysical Scaling Techniques to Measurement for Political Variables." *Working Papers in Methodology* no. 3. Institute for Research in Social Science. Chapel Hill: University of North Carolina, 1969.

Shinn, Allen M., Jr. "Relations Between Scales." *Measurement in the Social Sciences: Theories and Strategies*, edited by H. M. Blalock, Jr. Chicago: Aldine, 1974, pp. 121–158.

Siegel, Paul. "Prestige in the American Occupational Structure." Ph.D. dissertation, University of Chicago, 1971.

Simpson, Richard L., and Ida Harper Simpson. "Correlates and Estimation of Occupational Prestige." *American Journal of Sociology* 66 (September 1960): 135–140.

Smith, Maphaeus. "An Empirical Scale of Prestige Status of Occupations." *American Sociological Review* 8 (April 1943): 185–192.

Stevens, S. S. "On Theory of Measurement." *Science* 103 (1946): 677–680.

Stevens, S. S. "On the Psychophysical Law." *Psychological Review* 64 (1957): 153–181.

Stevens, S. S. "Issues in Psychophysical Measurement." *Psychological Review* 78 (1971): 426–450.

Stevens, S. S., and E. H. Galanter. "Ratio Scales and Category Scales for a Dozen Perceptual Continua." *Journal of Experimental Psychology* 54 (1957): 377–411.

Strauss, Anselm L. *The Contexts of Social Mobility: Ideology and Theory.* Chicago: Aldine, 1971.

Suttles, Gerald D. *The Social Order of the Slum.* Chicago: University of Chicago Press, 1968.

Tinbergen, Jan. *Income Distribution: Analyses and Policies.* New York: North Holland/American Elsevier, 1975.

Tocqueville, Alexis de. *Democracy in America.* Translated by George Lawrence. Garden City, New York: Doubleday Anchor, 1969.

U.S. Bureau of the Census. *Census of Population: 1970. Subject Reports. Final Report PC (2)-53. Educational Attainment.* Washington, D.C.: Government Printing Office, 1973*a*.

U.S. Bureau of the Census. *Census of Population: 1970. Subject Reports. Final Report PC (2)-7A. Occupational Characteristics.* Washington, D.C.: Government Printing Office, 1973*b*.

U.S. Bureau of the Census. "Annual Mean Income: Lifetime Income and Educational Attainment for Selected Years, 1956–1966." *Current Population Reports.* Series, P-60, no. 56.

Veblen, Thorstein. *The Theory of the Leisure Class.* New York: Modern Library, 1934.

Warner, W. Lloyd, Marchia Meeker, and Kenneth Eells. *Social Class in America.* New York: Science Research Associates, 1949.

White, Harrison C. *Chains of Opportunity.* Cambridge: Harvard University Press, 1970.

INDEX

Adult attainment: schooling and family background in, 260–76, 340–41
Age: in judging status, 78
Alcohol: as cause of downward mobility, 234–35
Ambition, 66, 67; of Lower Americans, 200; in upward mobility, 238–40
Appearance: personal, 66, 79, 89–91
Area resources: as cause of economic and social wealth, 308–9; interpreting advantages from area of birth, 266; for men, 249–51, 256–59; in status scales, 321, 322; *see also* Housing
Automobiles: for Middle Americans, 170–71; of middle and working classes, 182
Autonomy: money and, 50

Barthel, Diane, 92*n*
Bell, Daniel, 312
Birth: class fixed by, 294; fertility differential, 233; interpreting advantages from area of, 266
Birth rate, 233; by class (1910s, 1920s, 1930s), 232
Blacks: class of, 129; discrimination against, 109; ethnicity and, 92–96, 98, 115; as Lower Americans, 206, 208–9; as Lower Americans at the bottom, 195; melting pot ideology of, 100
Blue-collar workers: identity and style for, 79; magnitude estimate of jobs of, 57, 61; as Middle Americans, 128 (*see also* Middle Americans); white-collar employment and, 54; white-collar workers and, 54, 295–96
Boston survey, 18–24; interview sample, 315–18
Bottom class: occupation of, 190; *see also* Lower Americans
Braverman, Harry, 48
Breeding, 79

Calculation: magnitude estimation, of social standing, 210–21
Capitalism: white-collar workers under, 48
Catholics, 92, 96; ethnicity and, 105; melting pot ideology among, 98, 101; Upper Americans and, 152, 153
Celebrity standing: of top rich, 134–35
Change: class, as less important factor, 294–98; in distribution of income, 295–96, 301–2; in distribution of occupations, 232; elements in, 22–24; how social system should, 299–304; living standard and class, 296; opportunity, social mobility and class, 293–304
Chapin, F. Stuart, 320
Character and behavior defects: as factors in downward mobility, 235–37
Chicanos, 94, 96, 109, 129; ethnic revival and, 115
Childhood resources: family social class as, 266–75; *see also* Families
Children: and downward mobility, 235–36
Class: definitions of, 7–8; popular conceptions of what is and what is not social, 24–27; social standing as, 17–18; *see also specific social classes*
Class consciousness: decline in, 298
Class standing: popular conceptions of, 17–28
Classlessness, 299–301
Cliques, 80–83, 144–49
Clothing, 87–91; of Lower Americans, 193; as measure of difference, 32–33; of Middle Americans just getting along, 166
Clubs, 144–49
College, *see* Education
Commodities: envy of available, money and, 31–33
Community: participation in, by middle and working classes, 182–83; prestige